THE PANDEMIC & THE HOLY SPIRIT

From Lament to Hope and Healing

E21 GNSES Series

The E21 GNSES Series titles are based on annual Scholars Consultations organized by Empowered21's Global Network of Spirit-Empowered Scholars (GNSES). The Consultation brings Spirit-empowered scholars and practitioners from various parts of the world around a pertinent issue which faces global Spirit-empowered Christianity. In support of the movement's vision for "EveryONE by 2033," each Consultation theme explores the role of Spirit-empowered communities in presenting Christ's good news and nurturing the new generation.

Explore These Other E21 GNSES Titles

Global Renewal Christianity: Spirit-Empowered Movements Past, Present, and Future. Vinson Synan, Amos Yong, general editors.

    Volume 1: Asia and Oceania.
        ISBN:978–1–62998–688–3
    Volume 2: Latin America with Miguel Álvarez, editor
        ISBN: 978–1–62998–767–5
    Volume 3: Africa, with J. Kwabena Asamoah-Gyadu, editor
        ISBN: 978–1–62998–768–2
    Volume 4: Europe and North America.
        ISBN: 978–1–62998–943–3

The Truth About Grace: Spirit-Empowered Perspectives. Vinson Synan, editor.
    ISBN: 978–1–62999–504–5, softcover; ISBN: 978–62999–505–2, ebook

Human Sexuality & The Holy Spirit: Spirit-Empowered Perspectives. Wonsuk Ma, Kathaleen Reid-Martinez, Annamarie Hamilton, editors.
    ISBN: 978–1–950971–00–8, softcover; ISBN: 918–1–95071–01–5, ebook

Proclaiming Christ in the Power of the Holy Spirit: Opportunities & Challenges. Wonsuk Ma, Emmanuel Anim, Rebekah Bled, editors.
    ISBN: 978–1–950971–03–9, softcover; ISBN: 978–950971–05–3, ebook

Good News to the Poor: Spirit-Empowered Responses to Poverty. Wonsuk Ma, Opoku Onyinah, Rebekah Bled, editors.
    ISBN: 978-1-950971-11-4, softcover; ISBN: 978-1-950971-12-1, ebook

The Remaining Task of the Great Commission & the Spirit Empowered Movement. Wonsuk Ma, Opoku Onyinah, Rebekah Bled, editors.
    ISBN: 978-1-950971-20-6, softcover; ISBN: 978-1-950971-21-3, ebook

THE PANDEMIC & THE HOLY SPIRIT

From Lament to Hope and Healing

Edited by
Wonsuk Ma, Opoku Onyinah,
and **Rebekah Bled**

ORU
PRESS
Tulsa, Oklahoma USA

The Pandemic and the Holy Spirit From Lament to Hope and Healing
Copyright © 2024 Oral Roberts University

Published by ORU Press
7777 S. Lewis Ave., Tulsa, OK 74171 USA

ORU.edu/ORUPress

ORU Press is the book-and-journal-publishing division of Oral Roberts University.

All rights reserved. No part of this publication may be reproduced, stored in a retrieval system, or transmitted in any form or by any means without the prior permission of the publisher. Brief quotation in book reviews and in scholarly publications is excepted

Published in the United States of America with permission from Empowered21, Tulsa, Oklahoma

Empowered21 aims to help shape the future of the global Spirit-empowered movement throughout the world. This kingdom initiative is served by Oral Roberts University, www.oru.edu.

Cover Designer, Jiwon Kim
Design & Production Editor: Mark E. Roberts
Interior Designer & Compositor, Sandra Kimbell

ISBN: 978-1-950971-22-0 (softcover)
ISBN: 978-1-950971-23-7 (ebook)

Printed in the United States of America

Contents

Foreword	ix
Acknowledgements	xiii
Introduction *Opoku Onyinah and Wonsuk Ma*	1

Part I: Foundational

1. The Bible, Pandemics, and COVID-19   9
   Opoku Onyinah

2. The Message of Lukan Pneumatology   27
   to a Post-Pandemic World
   Glenn Balfour

3. The Ethics of St. Cyprian: Exploring Repentance, Forgiveness,   43
   and Reconciliation for Contemporary Spirit-Empowered Communities
   Cory J. May

4. Pentecostals Among the Plagues: Early Chinese   67
   Pentecostal Theologies of Sickness, Healing, and Pandemics
   Alex Mayfield

5. Pentecostals and Pandemics: A Historical Perspective   83
   Daniel D. Isgrigg

6. The Holy Spirit, Human Suffering, and Healing: 103
   An Initial Pentecostal Reflection
   Wonsuk Ma

7. A Theological Approach to the Origin of Coronavirus   117
   Through the Lens of Pain and Disease
   Jun Kim

Part II: Contextual

8. Pandemic, Depression, and the Church: 139
   A New Norm for the New Normal
   Robert McBain

9. The "Flourishing of Life" in the Spirit on Earth after the   155
   Pandemic?: A Trinitarian Approach to the Eschatological Future
   Sanna Urvas

10. Redeeming the Darkness: A Reflection on How the 173
    Pandemic is Bringing Light and Dignity to a Community
    in a Redlight District of India
    Mathew Daniel and Suhasini Daniel

11. The Shape of Christian Justice in a Global Pandemic: 191
    The Church's Call to a Merciful Advocacy for Roma
    Communities and Asylum Seekers in Eastern Europe
    Melody Wachsmuth

12. The Inequitable Silencing of Many Tongues: A Critical 209
    and Pastoral Response to the Economic, Political, and
    Racialized Dimensions of the Pandemic in American
    Pentecostal-Charismaticism
    Amos Yong and Aizaiah G. Yong

13. COVID-19, Science, and Race: 231
    A Black Pentecostal Engagement
    David Douglas Daniels III

14. Pentecostalism and Coronavirus: Reframing the Message 247
    of Health and Wealth in a Pandemic Era
    J. Kwabena Asamoah-Gyadu

15. Pentecostal Hope in the Age of COVID-19 265
    Peter Althouse and Audrey McCormick

16. Triumphalist Theologies and Pentecostal Responses 281
    to COVID-19
    Hanna Larracas

17. Pentecostal Power and Pandemics: The Impact of the 301
    COVID-19 Pandemic on the Practice of Baptism in
    the Holy Spirit in Ghana
    S. Ofotsu Ofoe

18. COVID-19, the Church, and the Pneumatological Challenge 317
    Jean-Daniel Plüss

19. State-Church Partnerships: Opportunities and Challenges 337
    in Spirit-Filled Responses to the Global Pandemic
    Ulrik Josefsson and Niclas Lindgren

20. Holy Spirit Empowered Teaching: 359
    Stories of Teacher Survival During the Pandemic
    Kim E. Boyd and Philida Rosalind Ignacio

"A Shared Story of Future Hope": Postscript 375
Rebekah Bled and Polly Tjihenuna

Contributors 387
Select Bibliography 393
Name and Subject Index 397

Foreword

This book is important in the light of our current global context. It addresses the question of health and illness in relation to human flourishing through the lens of the recent pandemic. In proclaiming the presence of the kingdom of God, Jesus demonstrated a power that is greater than sickness, whether chronic, infectious, or caused by the demonic. Jesus put sickness, healing, and health at the heart of his ministry, and they are therefore gospel issues for his followers. The healing of the crippled beggar in Acts 3, follows on from the outpouring of the Spirit on the day of Pentecost and the powerful proclamation of the Lordship of the risen Christ. The position of the healing of the lame man early in the story of the church is a reminder that the Spirit of Pentecost is the same Spirit of Jesus (Acts 16:7) who will empower the disciples to do "even greater things" than their master (John 14:12). Pentecostal and charismatic movements have emphasized that the kingdom has come in Christ and is now present among us in the face of suffering and illness. It is, therefore, important to hear Pentecostal perspectives on the pandemic. The essays gathered in this book provide wide-ranging reflection on biblical, theological, and contextual responses and are a timely contribution.

So how do we try to make sense of the pandemic? Was it simply a sign of the brokenness of our world; an act of God; a sociological phenomenon resulting from human behavior that is both fallen and yet retains the image of God? Or maybe it is all of the above? How we view the pandemic reveals our assumptions and beliefs about the world we live in, human nature, our theological convictions, and, most importantly, our personal experience of the pandemic. The essays in this book offer an opportunity to reflect on the pandemic from each of these viewpoints.

From a medical perspective, an epidemic is an outbreak of infectious disease that affects a large segment of a population in one location. When an epidemic spreads over many locations regionally or globally it becomes a pandemic. Major outbreaks of infectious disease are nothing new, but a number of factors have led scientists to conclude that the frequency of pandemics, like that caused by the novel Coronavirus—COVID-19, will likely rise in the coming years.

Most new diseases, like SARS, MERS, Influenza H5N1, Swine flu, Ebola, and Zika, are zoonotic, that is, they occur due to infectious transmission from an animal source to humans. A World Health Organisation report in 2013 states, "Over 30 new human pathogens have been detected in the last three decades, 75 percent of which have originated in animals."[1] Numerous factors have been identified as causal in the increasing frequency of zoonotic infections.[2] Population increase, deforestation and encroachment by humans on animal habits has reduced the boundaries between humans and animals and increased the possibilities for diseases to jump from one to another. Globalization and the mass movement of people, goods, and animals facilitates the rapid spread of disease from one continent to another. An epidemic can quickly become a pandemic. We should not imagine, therefore, that the COVID-19 pandemic was a once-in-a-century occurrence, a rare event that we can now put behind us. Pandemics are here to stay, and it is, therefore, important that we reflect on what the church can learn from the recent experience in relation to its life and faithful witness to God and God's kingdom.

I suggest there is another reason why it is imperative that we learn to think biblically, theologically, and contextually through the experiences of the pandemic. The COVID-19 pandemic elicited governmental responses largely framed by a scientific explanation of problem and solution. However, the world is crumbling in which human reason, embodied in scientific knowledge, is the controlling worldview, with its illusion of control. We, especially, in those of us shaped by the consequences of the European Enlightenment, may resist such a statement. Didn't we come through the pandemic, and hasn't life largely returned to what it was before? The assumption that reason and science are king is so deeply embedded in our worldview that it is almost impossible to imagine otherwise. Dougald Hine, in his recent book, *At Work in the Ruins: Finding our Place in the Time of Science, climate change, Pandemics & All the Other Emergencies*, notes that we face a number of global challenges that cannot be addressed simply through the scientific approach of problem-solution.[3] Mass migration, inequality, racism, and, perhaps the biggest of all, climate change, are not issues capable of being reduced to scientific solution. The scientific method identifies a problem and then works 'downstream' to find solutions. During the pandemic we saw this in action as governments forced lockdowns on their populations in the name of science while we put our hope in a vaccine that would allow us to return to life as before.

The consequences of this approach are still being analyzed but it is clear that, for many populations, especially those dependent on daily wage earning, the lockdown approach proved to be a cure worse than the disease. In his book, Hine calls us to move beyond the scientific approach of problem-solution and instead to pay attention to what is happening 'upstream' to the presenting issue. This is far more difficult, requiring us to examine our assumptions and be open to reframing the way we see this world. As followers of the Lord Jesus Christ reflecting on the pandemic, it is essential that we move beyond what we can learn in problem solving to look upstream at why pandemics are occurring and how God's intentions for his world need to illumine our responses. Such reflection will likely lead us to a much more radical reappraisal of the gospel of progress than we have so far been willing to admit.

This is in fact exactly what the gospel of the kingdom requires of us. The good news of the in-breaking of God's upside-down kingdom is only good news if we are willing to abandon our assumptions about power, control, rights, and much more. The COVID-19 pandemic was a gift to the global church in so far as it reminded us that we are not in control of our lives, work, and ministries. It reminded us of the fragility of human existence, of our complete dependence on God, and of what is truly important in the light of eternity. It reminded us that our God is present in the midst of suffering and that sickness and death hold no fear for those who are empowered by the Spirit who raised Jesus from the dead. The pandemic is an urgent call to reimagine life framed by the Lordship of Christ and to find our story not in modernity's illusion of progress and control but in the kingdom that is here and not yet.

Dr. Paul Bendor-Samuel, MD,
Executive Director of the Oxford Centre
for Mission Studies, UK.

Notes

1 Kate Jones, Nikkita Patel, Marc Levy, et al., "Global Trends in Emerging Infectious Diseases," *Nature* (2008) 451, 990-994, cited by https://www.emro.who.int/fr/about-who/rc61/zoonotic-diseases.html, accessed August 3, 2023
2 S. Lakshmi Priyadarsini, M. Suresh, Donald Huisingh, "What can we Learn from Previous Pandemics to Reduce the Frequency of Emerging Infectious Diseases like COVID-19?" https://www.sciencedirect.com/science/article/pii/S2589791820300190#sec2, accessed August 3, 2023
3 Dougald Hine, *At Work in the Ruins: Finding our Place in the Time of Science, Climate Change, Pandemics & all the Other Emergencies* (London: Chelsea Green, 2023).

Acknowledgements

As usual, this book builds upon the presentations to the 2021 Scholars Consultation of Empowered21 in Dubai. Excited to be able to physically travel and gather for the Consultation, we gladly endured the stringent health checks and requirements. The theme of "pandemic" was real as signs of COVID-19 were all around us, including the hybrid mode we adopted by combining in-person and virtual presentations. Dubai, the host city, was ultra-modern with its warm generosity. However, we were mindful of its multicultural population and religious context. Our attempts to connect with local (but all "international") Christian communities were marginally successful.

The editors want to thank the book contributors. We work closely with the authors to bring their unique experiences and writing styles, while trying to maintain a degree of consistency. This book also contains several chapters previously published elsewhere with some updates and revisions. The original publications are identified in the notes of the relevant chapters.

This title is the first to appear under the GNSES Series. The Global Network of Spirit-Empowered Scholars (GNSES) was formally launched in 2023 as the Empowered21 entity organizing and publishing the Scholars Consultation material. For this, and continuing support, we want to thank the leadership of Empowered21. The editors are also grateful to ORU Press, as this is the fifth Consultation title published by this Sprit-empowered publisher.

Editors
Christmas, 2023

Introduction

Opoku Onyinah and Wonsuk Ma

Throughout history, there have been struggles between human beings and nature. Prominent among such struggles are pandemics, which often become game changers by altering the course of history with regards to the accompanying economic hardships, collapse of empires, ideological persecution, wars, or break-down of religious, and socio-political structures. Usually, after every major outbreak of a pandemic, the world systems experience massive paradigm shifts. At the end of 2019, the world experienced one such pandemic, COVID-19, that was to change the course of history forever. The disease was discovered in China, specifically in Wuhan in the Hubei Province in December 2019. The World Health Organization (WHO) declared it a global pandemic on March 11, 2020. WHO defines it as an infectious disease caused by the SARS-CoV-2 virus,"[1] which is characterized by fever, shortness of breath, and coughing.

WHO statistics showed that the virus had infested 696,120,461 people globally, 6,922,780 of whom died.[2] The death toll included people of all calibers including the rich and poor, educated and illiterate, and politicians and businesspeople. Unfortunately, some of the survivors have to live with various damaged internal organs.

As usual, the suffering associated with the pandemic generated various conspiracy theories. Mark Lynas, a British author and journalist, drew attention to ten such theories:[3]

1) The virus was spreading through the 5G mobile networks, using the electromagnetic spectrum. Based upon this, some people destroyed some cell phone towers in some countries.
2) The perception that Bill Gates, the North American businessman, advocated: to use the COVID-19 vaccination program to implant digital microchips in people so that their movements could be tracked and controlled.
3) The coronavirus escaped from a Chinese laboratory.

4) The virus was an intentionally created biological weapon by China.
5) The notion that the United States military deliberately imported the virus into China.
6) The introduction and consumption of genetically modified crops were responsible for the virus.
7) The belief that the COVID-19 virus did not actually exist, and that it was just like the normal flu. Therefore, the perceived pandemic was just a subtle way a few people were using to take away the freedom of the masses.
8) The that the "perceived pandemic" was a subtle way the pharmaceutical companies were using to sell their products.
9) The COVID-19 cases and death rates had been inflated by state authorities to impose lockdown measures on the people.
10) The argument that it was the fulfilment of biblical prophecies concerning end times, especially the 666 mark, which is the biblical symbol of the antichrist (Rev 13:15–18).

As of now, these conspiracy theories have been unsubstantiated and baseless. In most cases, WHO had to come in to demystify the theory such as in the case of the 5G conspiracy, which the WHO clarified that the virus could not travel on mobile networks.

Besides the fear that the virus instilled in people, the protocols associated with it, such as the use of alcohol-based sanitizer, no personal contact with others, and the use of nose and mouth masks, made life very uncomfortable. The application of these protocols was further complicated among Christians. In addition to the above, during church services, the microphones and the podium had to be constantly sanitized. In some countries, community buildings such as offices, shops, schools, churches, mosques, and markets had to be fumigated.

Working at the office was also a challenge. In most cases, workers had to spray alcohol-based sanitizers on files and letters before passing them on to one another. The challenge of paying salaries caused companies to lay off some of their staff. Others divided their workers into two or more groups with each group working for one week or month while the other groups stayed at home. Still others also introduced virtual or remote working arrangements where staff worked from remote locations such as from their homes. These arrangements became necessary so that in case of an infection, the organization would not have to be closed down.

Health workers suffered a lot as many of them were infected and others died. A majority of the non-life-threatening surgeries were put on hold. In many countries, the medical facilities were overstretched, as they could not contain the number of cases they had to handle.

Visitation to family members, friends, and church members had to be minimized, because they could spread the virus in case someone was a carrier. Travelling by air, sea, or land had to be controlled, since every country controlled its borders. Some businesspeople who had to deal with cross-border businesses suffered financial losses, since their travels were controlled.

The church suffered seriously during the pandemic. Churches were among the institutions that were closed. Even when the ban was lifted for church services to be held, in many countries the elderly and children were admonished to remain at home. The reasoning was that the elderly who had underlying health conditions were vulnerable to infection, and children were difficult to control. Many people, including Christians lost their jobs during the pandemic, especially those in the hospitality services. Some churches were unable to pay the salaries of their pastors and staff because there were no church services for some time.

In the midst of all these, some Christians including pastors and church leaders spiritualized the virus. Some claimed it was a punishment from God, while others thought it was from the devil and could be resisted through prayer and fasting. From this perspective, many Christians fasted and prayed for God's intervention. The majority of the Christians, however, prayed for the Lord to provide a solution. When vaccines were developed, because of the conspiracy theories, some Christians as well as others who strongly held on to such theories were hesitant to take the vaccine. Meanwhile, as expected, the nations that developed the vaccines had to vaccinate their citizens before selling or donating to the developing nations. The more the vaccines delayed the more people died.

People who died through the infection did not have the normal befitting funerals organized for them by their families. More worrying were the bereaved who could not be comforted as visitation to such people was discouraged because of the possibility of being infected. Unfortunately, in some countries, survivors were stigmatized, and others feared to get closer to them.

2021 Dubai Consultation

All this provides the backdrop of the E21 Global Network of Spirit-Empowered Scholars Consultation held from October 13–14, 2021, in Dubai, United Arab Emirates, from which this book is the outcome. This gathering took place in the COVID-19 environment: the restrictions were felt in the flights, at the airport, and in the hotel lobby and restaurants. As usual, all participants had to secure negative test results before returning home. Despite these reminders of the pandemic, the Dubai meeting was a huge improvement from the 2020 global conference, which was originally planned for Jerusalem, but pivoted to a completely online mode at the last moment.

The Dubai consultation sought to reflect on how the global Spirit-empowered church responded to the COVID-19 pandemic. Consequently, the consultation surveyed various studies of global, regional, area, and local value, exploring the theological, ecclesiological, and missiological aspects of the church's interaction with the pandemic. The co-chairs prepared the Theme Description to facilitate the presenters:

> This year's Consultation seeks to address how the global Spirit-empowered movement (SEM) has addressed the global COVID-19 pandemic. This theme envisions various studies of global, regional (e.g., a continental), areal (e.g., West African), national, or local value exploring the theological, ecclesiological or missiological aspects of the church's interaction with the pandemic. The Consultation plans to give its priority attention to the regional and area studies, while the book and the author's presentation would provide a helpful global picture of the movement. Possible topics could include the following:
>
> - Divine Healing and Medical Healing: The Implications of Faith on Scientific Research on COVID -19
> - Christians Response to Plagues and Pandemics: How have Christians responded to pandemics and plagues in the centuries?
> - Historical Christian Perspectives on Plagues and Pandemics
> - The Bible, Plagues/Pandemics, and COVID-19
> - Theological Reflections on Plagues and Pandemics

- Evangelism and Missions in Post COVID-19 era
- COVID-19 and Its Implication for Christian Community
- The Face of the Church in Post-COVID-19 Era
- The "Flourishing of Life" in the Spirit on Earth in Delicate Tension with Eschatology.
- Socio-Cultural Life in a Post-COVID-19 Era
- Political and Economic Lives in a Post-COVID-19 Era
- Educational Systems in a Post-COVID-19 Era
- Family Life in a Post-COVID-19 Era
- COVID-19 Pandemic and Its Implications for Church Administration
- Psychological Implications on the COVID-19 Pandemic
- The State-Church relation in the Context of the Pandemic

This intellectual exercise is rooted in the reality and state of the Spirit-empowered movement of the area. The crux of each study will be the unique role that the Spirit-empowered Movement can play germinated out of its own distinct theological, spiritual, and missional identity. The study may provide an opportunity to identify unique (spiritual as well as contextual) gifts. Hence, there may be "foundational" studies covering biblical, theological, missiological, and philosophical layers of the SEM's identity. As in all the Consultations, this gathering and the ensuring book project are also intended to be a space for mutual learning. There may be "friends" of the SEM offering their ecclesial or geographical reflection on the fellow SE communities. The Consultation, therefore, desires to be a space and process through which the participants learn how various SE communities are working towards world evangelization, and even non-SE participants could provide helpful insights to the movement to fulfill its evangelistic call.

Nine regionally based studies on the pandemic and the church's response were presented. Four studies were presented physically and five were conducted via Zoom. One third of the presenters were new to the Scholars Consultation, the rest were quite familiar with Empowered21. The studies focused on biblical, theological, and seven on contextual/experiential aspects. The presentations cut across various regions; four from Europe, two from Africa, two from North America, and one from Asia. The consultation gave a picture of what was happening at the global level concerning the COVID-19 pandemic. The discussions gave the particpants a deeper understanding of the situation to enable them fine tune their studies for this book.

6 The Pandemic and the Holy Spirit

The Book Project

The co-chairs of the Consultation recognized the time-sensitive nature of the theme; thus, deciding to fast-track the book process. As usual, the insight gained from the consultation caused the editors to commission more people to help bring various aspects of COVID-19 to make the book more comprehensive. The editors also agreed to re-print several previously published studies with necessary updates. The final outcome of the consultation and the commissioned chapters is the publication of this book. The book has all-inclusive representation across the globe with diverse experiences, and a good number of both male and female authors.

The book is organized thematically, beginning with two chapters examining a biblical perspective of pandemics, and offering an applied Lukan Pneumatology to post-pandemic life. The book then gives three historical studies before moving to themes of pain, suffering, and depression in Pentecostal perspective, justice and oppression, Pentecostal messaging during the pandemic, and Pentecostal institutional responses respectively. Among other examples, these chapters share specific case studies of the racialized dimension of the pandemic, as well as how Spirit-empowered communities ministered hope during the pandemic through praying, giving of testimonies, and telling stories of healing, and community outreach. In some cases, the Spirit-empowered churches had to repackage their practices in order to suit the protocols of the day. The pandemic brought about a new state-church partnership, which offers both opportunities and challenges, which the Spirit-empowered church must explore to sharpen our ministry for world evangelization.

Notes

1   World Health Organization, "Coronavirus Disease (COVID-19)," https://www.who.int/health-topics/coronavirus#tab=tab_1, accessed February 6, 2023.
2   Worldometer, "2019 Coronavirus Pandemic," https://www.worldometers.info/coronavirus/, last updated October 4, 2023.
3   Mark Lynas, "COVID-19, Top 10 Current Conspiracy Theories," April 20, 2020, https://allianceforscience.cornell.edu/blog/2020/04/covid-top-10-current-conspiracy-theories/.

I
Foundational

1 The Bible, Pandemics, and COVID-19[1]

Opoku Onyinah

Abstract

This study makes a survey of the Bible to find out the origins of pandemics, plagues, and disasters. It assumes that the fall of humanity might have been the remote cause of all natural disasters. The various systems of government, the abuse of the planet, and the breakdown of human rights are all evidence of the repercussions of the Fall. COVID-19 could be the natural outcome of the mismanagement of the resources God has given to humankind. Despite this, God uses all things to draw people to himself; thus, the church is call upon to rise up and catch up with the move of God.

Introduction

The COVID-19 pandemic has caused many people to find out what the Bible says about pandemics. A pandemic describes a disease that infests many people or whole country or the world. In this sense, COVID-19 is a pandemic. The word pandemic does not appear in the Bible; however, it is associated with the word plague. A plague is a contagious disease which kills many people. The word plague is translated in the *Strong's Exhaustive Concordance* from four Hebrew words (*negha'*, *makkāh*, *maggēphāh*, and *deber*) in the Old Testament (e.g., Exod 11:1; Num 11:33; Deut 28:61; Psalm 106:29), and two Greek words (*mástix* and *plēgḗ*) in the New Testament (e.g., Mark 3:10; Rev 9:20).[2] These words, translated plague, appear 120 times in the Bible and refer to sudden outbreak of diseases and disasters, which are considered the outcome of divine anger. An English word, which is also associated with plague in the Bible, is pestilence. The word is translated from the Hebrew term *deber* and the Greek term *loymos*. It is used forty-seven times in the Old Testament and three times in the New Testament. In both cases, that is in the Old Testament Hebrew *deber* and New Testament Greek *loymos*, the *Strong's Exhaustive Concordance* translates them as plagues. It is used in connection with wasteful diseases, earthquakes, and suffering. Thus, in the Bible, a plague is used in a wider sense with regards to calamities, contagious diseases, natural disasters and suffering in general. The sudden outburst of a novel corona virus in 2019 makes it appears like a plague in the Bible. Against this backdrop, this essay examines what the Bible says about plagues with the view to drawing lessons from the Old Testament (OT) and the New Testament (NT) to connect it with COVID-19, and by that make recommendation of the responses needed by the church.

Plagues in the Old Testament

In the ancient world, various meanings were read into plagues and natural disasters. This mindset was clearly pictured in the Lord's dealing with his people in the OT. This section briefly discusses how plagues were considered in the light of God's dealing with Israel.

Some Plagues in the Book of Genesis

The flood in the time of Noah can be considered a calamity which affected the then known world (Gen 6–7). The account shows that people had become so evil that God decided to send the flood to wipe out humanity and preserve Noah and his family to continue procreation. Thus, this was a disaster which was carried out by the Lord because people continued to increase in sin (Gen 6:5–8).

In Genesis 12:17, the Lord inflicted Pharaoh and his household with plagues. The Lord did this because Pharaoh had taken Abraham's wife, Sarai. Abraham had told a lie that Sarai was only his sister because he feared that if had told Pharaoh that Sarai was his wife, he might have killed him and taken his wife. The fact that Pharaoh inquired about her and took her showed his emotional weakness and the desire in his heart. Although Abraham was also guilty of telling a lie, the Lord infested serious diseases on the Pharaoh's household as a form of intervention to stop Pharaoh from sinning.

The famine in Egypt during the time of Joseph can be considered a plague (Gen 41–42). It was a natural disaster that affected the known world, but the Lord through Joseph made a great intervention for the Egyptians and the other nations. God used the situation to bring about the slavery and subsequence deliverance of the people of Israel, which become a picture of the redemption which was to be provided by Christ. The Lord had already told Abraham over 400 years earlier (Gen 15:12–16) that his offspring would become slaves, but he would also deliver them. This means the Lord was in total control of the affairs.

The Ten Plagues in Egypt

Plagues become popular in the Bible as the Lord used ten plagues to redeem the Israelites from Egypt (Exod 7–12). The plagues were used as judgement against the gods of Egypt (Exod 12:12), as judgment on the Egyptians for the way they mistreated the people of Israel (Exod 9:14), as assurance to the people of Israel of God's overall sovereign power, and then as assurance of his provision and care for those who worship him (Exod 7:3).

The plagues were in forms of disaster such as turning water into blood (Exod 7:14), infesting the Egyptians with diseases such as boils (Exod 9:13), and bringing death on livestock and on firstborns (Exod 9:1; 12:29). In all these, God proved his sovereignty over the Egyptian king and their gods to bring about his plan of redemption. The sovereignty of God to overrule human weaknesses and efforts to accomplish his purpose was established in the presentation of the plagues. The following show how these were demonstrated:

First, the Lord, knowing that Pharaoh would harden his heart (Exod 3:19–20) endorsed it for him to harden it more in order for him to demonstrate his power (Exod 4:24). Second, the first nine plagues took place in the land of Egypt, but not in the area the Israelites were living. In these first nine plagues, those people who lived on the side of the Egyptians were infested with the plagues. No matter who the person was, living in the side of Egypt was the landmark to be affected by the plagues. The distinctions were between the places where the Egyptians and Israelites lived. Although both nations were living on the same land, there were distinctions between the dealings of the Lord on those who believed in him and those who did not.

Third, the last plague where all firstborns died took place in the whole land of Egypt including where the Israelites lived. The people of Israel were saved because they were instructed by the Lord to apply on the door post, the blood of a lamb slaughtered by each household, or where necessary two households. Firstborns in a house belonging to an Israelite who did not apply the blood on the door post were also to die. The plausible was that firstborns of foreigners who lived among the Israelites who applied the blood would also be saved. The distinction between people here was faith in the Lord and obedience to him.

Fourth, the lessons gathered here go beyond the people of Israel and the Egyptians. It is evident from the story that sometimes the Lord deals differently with the people who believe in him, just like Moses and the Israelites, and those who failed to accept him, represented by Pharaoh and his people (Exod 8:23; 9:4). In addition, the stories show that the Lord can preserve his own while judging those who fail to accept him, yet his people must stay in faith and obedience. Finally, it is also evident that during the course of the plagues, taking instructions from the leaders was absolutely essential since disobedience could lead to destruction, regardless of who is involved.

The Plague of the Fiery Serpent

On their way to the land of Canaan, the people of Israel were bitten by poisonous snakes which cost the lives of many. The cause of this great death was assigned to the Israelites speaking against God and Moses; thus, they sinned against the Lord (Num 20:4–9). The pandemic which broke out here was clearly assigned to sinning against the Lord.

The Plague on Israel as Judgment on David's Sin

There was a great pestilence during the reign of King David for counting the people of Israel. The scripture clearly says that it was the Lord who sent a pestilence upon Israel which cost the lives of 70,000 men (2 Sam 24:15). The reason was that David had sinned against the Lord for counting the people. Normally, a census should not cause a plague. Therefore, the reason for the plague could either be that David might have done this out of pride because of the victories he had won in battles, or that he had failed to satisfy the provision in the law regarding counting the people (1 Chron 18–20; Exod 20:11–16). Both pride and disobedience are possible reasons for the Lord to inflict plagues on his people.

The Exile of the People of Israel

The Northern Kingdom of Israel was taken captive by the Assyrians and deported to Assyria. The writer of 2 Kings shows that this happened because the Israelites had sinned against the Lord (2 Kings 17:7¬–13).

Similarly, the Southern Kingdom, Judah, was captured and exiled to Babylon because they despised God's word and scoffed at God's messengers (2 Chron 36:15–20). Thus, disobedience to the Lord leads to calamities, including exile, and not excluding plagues.

Other Causes of Plagues in the Old Testament

In Exodus 15, soon after the Israelites had crossed the Red Sea, the Lord told them that if they would pay attention to his word, he would not bring on them the diseases he brought on the Egyptians. The implication is that if they did not obey him, he could bring on them the plagues he brought on the Egyptians (Exod 15:26). Thus, making the Lord the remote cause of plagues on his people.

In Exodus 30, the Lord instituted the tabernacle tax. Its payment guaranteed protection from plagues since it was to remind them of their delivery from slavery in Egypt and how the Lord had taken all firstborns of the Israelites as his own (Exod 30:11–16). Whenever a census was taken (e.g., Num 1), each Israelite, twenty years old or more, was to pay a tax of half a shekel to help maintain the tabernacle and services. The payment of ransom money reminded them that they were sinners who had been redeemed; they were owned by the Lord. This means if the Israelites failed to pay this money, there could be plagues. Thus, the reason for the outburst of a plague during the census ordered by David when Israel failed to pay for the ransom.

There was a clear indication in the Law that disobedience to the Lord would result in curses, including the outburst of pandemics. Failure to follow the contents of the law would result in plagues and disasters, such as fire outbreak, crop failure, enemy attacks, captivity, destruction of plants by insects, and drought (Lev 26:24–35, 40–44; Deut 28:15–24).

One of the serious consequences of Israel's disobedience to the law was embodied in the principle of jubilee. The law required that the jubilee year was to be treated like a sabbatical year, with the land lying fallow. It also required the compulsory return of all property to its original owners or their heirs. Failure to obey the law amounted to the abuse of the land and mistreatment of the poor and the vulnerable. The outcome was enormous curses on the people, eventually leading to captivity which would in turn give rest to the land

From this perspective, then, for the Old Testament, plagues and calamities were all assigned to disobedience to the Lord. In this regard, the prophets requested repentance from the people of Israel (Joel 2:13–15; Isa 3:9–15; Amos 5:12–15).

The New Testament

The New Testament does not directly deal with plagues and pandemics. Plagues, however, are placed in a slightly new perspective. Examination of this becomes our focus now.

Our Lord Jesus Christ

When some people told Jesus about the death of some Galileans who went to offer sacrifices, Jesus' answer threw more light on divine concept of calamities (Luke 13:1–6). The Jews might have been concerned about the death of these religious people who might have protested against the collection of temple tax by the Governor Pilate. Jesus' response shows that the death of the Galileans was one aspect of the many disasters that could occur. Accordingly, he pointed to the fallen tower of Siloam which killed eighteen people in Jerusalem. He refused to relate the calamity directly to people's sins, as thought by the Jews (cf. John 9), but rather affirmed the sinful nature of humanity. However, he showed that the person who lives in disobedience could not escape sudden perish, while all fail to repent, including those who escape calamities, would face spiritual death.[3] The most important thing to learn from a disaster is to allow it to lead you to repentance.

Jesus did not end his teaching there. He continued with the parable of the barren fig tree (Luke 13:6–9), which depicts Israel as a fruitless fig tree which has been given time to repent, otherwise it would come under God's judgment. In a broad sense, Jesus teaches that God treat all people with his kindness which demands repentance. Once the opportunity to repent passed away, God would pronounce his judgment. As stated earlier, the most important thing to learn from a disaster is to allow it to lead you to repentance.

Jesus again touches on calamities such as earthquakes, famines, and pestilences when he was responding to questions on the signs of the end times by his disciples in that which is referred to as the Olivet Discourse

(Luke 21:5–28; Matt 24–25; Mark 13). He taught that difficult times lay ahead which could affect all people including his disciples. These included natural calamities, such as earthquakes, famines, and pestilences as well as persecution. His disciples were not to give up but to testify about him in these situations. By this, Jesus has shown that although calamities may appear as the judgment of God towards sinners, they can also befall all people. In John 9:1–3, he affirmed that suffering may be the result of God wanting to reveal his glory.

We can, therefore, summarize from Jesus' teaching that plagues and suffering in general do not necessarily depict God's judgement only. They can be outcome of natural calamities that can affect all people including God's people. The response of those who witness plagues is to examine themselves and make their ways right with their Creator.

The Apostles

We do not have a direct reference of plagues by the apostles. There is, however, a reference to famine during the reign of Claudius (Acts 11:27–30). The famine had been predicted by Prophet Agabus as that which would spread over the known Roman world. Consequently, the apostles saw it a fulfilment of prophecy and provided voluntary support, according to their individual abilities to those who were living in Judea. The dimension that this adds to our study is that when there is a natural calamity, the people of God need to support the victims according to their abilities.

Besides this, there are several passages, such as Romans 5:3; 2 Corinthians 1:6; 1 Thessalonians 5:6; and 1 Peter 4:12–16, which speak about sufferings as resulting from persecution against Christians. This generally comes from the enemies of the gospel.

Other passages also teach us that the Fall of humanity has made suffering part of life (Gen 3:1–24; Rom 5:12–14; Rom 8:18–25). The whole creation has been "subjected to futility" (Rom 8:20) as a result of the disobedience of Adam which caused the fall of humanity. Through the death and resurrection of Christ, creation has a hope of being "set free from its bondage to decay" (Rom 8:21), the believers now "live between the times" of "the already" but "not yet" (Eph 4:30; cf. Rom 5:9; Gal 5:5).

The Christian's complete redemption is in the future. The implication of this tension is that Christians are also exposed to natural calamities, including sickness and sufferings.[4] Thus, the apostles did teach that calamities of all kinds do affect people including Christians. Therefore, should Christians experience calamities or see others going through them, there is the need for Christians to support each other according to their abilities.

Summary of Plagues in the Bible

From the ongoing discussions, we see that plagues are not good, and, in fact, represent the fallen nature of humanity, God's judgement, discipline, or curses. From the OT perspectives, it was the disobedience of God's creation, specifically humanity or God's people that often led to the outburst of plagues. Once there was an outbreak of a plague, God expected repentance and dependence upon him for its cessation. In the NT, it was a sign of the fallen nature of humanity which could affect all people. Although God has a way of protecting his own, all creation groan for the final redemption of the people of God. No matter the cause of a plague, God uses it to demand repentance from people.

Linking Biblical Plagues with COVID-19

In view of the biblical perspective of plagues, the following can be assumed for the COVID-19 pandemic, which is like a plague in the Bible. It can be said that COVID-19 is one of the outcomes of the original sin and the fall of humanity which took place in the Garden of Eden (Gen 3). As the ground and the snake were cursed, natural calamities and suffering have become part of humanity. Human beings have abused the earth since the Fall until today. This abuse expresses itself in many ways. For example, it expresses itself in mishandling the planet. There is the destruction of nature, including trees, mountains, and oceans. There is extraction and overconsumption of all available resources including oil and minerals, which are followed by pollution and waste. Scientists speak of the total abuse of the planet, which is the extraction of hydrocarbons from the earth and deposit of such gasses and particles in the atmosphere, bodies of animals, soils, and oceans.[5]

Furthermore, abuse is evident in authoritarian governments, bad governance, and dictatorships, with its resultant effects of corruption, greed, crime, and human right breakdowns. These bring about economic hardship, poverty, instability, and violence. Linked to these is the desire for wealth which sometimes leads to cheating, human trafficking, exploitation, and even killings. Some people with the aim of amassing wealth and power even go to the extent of ritual murder; that is, killing people to sacrifice to the gods for power or wealth. There is an imbalance in the world's trade system, which leads to luxury, consumerism, and excessive accumulation of wealth by the rich. The strong, whether individuals or nations, lord themselves over the vulnerable.

Another abuse of humanity which resulted from the Fall is depicted in weapons of mass destruction, which include nuclear, chemical, biological, and radiological. These can kill or bring substantial damage to human beings, physical structures, and nature's structural and animate objects, such as mountains, tress, and animals.

A further type of abuse on humanity is the abuse of the human body. There is the attempt to change the human body, which includes homosexuality, lesbianism, transgenderism, exhibitionism, among other practices. Men, for example, have attempted to experiment conception and delivery through sciences.

Related to this is the abuse of body painting, which involves artwork painted directly on naked human skin. Unlike body painting, which is temporary, there is tattoo, which is a type of piercing that breaks the skin with the view to modify the body by inserting a lasting ink or dye into the layer of the skin. There is also body piercing, which is the pricking of the body to make an opening for jewelry to be worn or an implant to be inserted in the desired parts of the individual's body including the genitals. Human beings are abusing the body in forms of exploration, experiments, and pleasure.[6]

The effects of these abuses can be catastrophic for humanity. These can bring about diseases, wars, climate changes, defect in humanity, pandemics, and plagues, which are not necessarily from God; they can be humanity's own made calamities. Thus, COVID-19 can be because of such abuses from human beings themselves. Second, COVID-19 can be said to be a judgment from the Lord.[7] The discussions from the biblical perspective of plagues show that when there is disobedience or sin, the Lord allows or sends a plague in a form of judgment. From this standpoint, the abuse of the earth, humanity, governance, and the human body can all lead to God's judgement. The Lord, who does not change, condemned these practices in the Bible (Jer 34:8–22; Zeph 1:10–11; Mic 2:1–3; Isa 3:18–24; 5:8–10, Mal 3:6). If he brought judgment on the people of old because of their disobedience to him, why can he not do the same in the contemporary generation?

In a nuanced way, could COVID-19 be an intervention from God? Why so? A lot was being said about climate change, ecology, and the abuse of the planets before COVID-19. However, the outbreak of the novel corona virus led to lockdowns of nations and businesses. Our roads and air spaces were all quiet as there were less vehicles running and airplanes flying. There were less ships on the sea and trains on the land. The land has had its freedom for some time. Is this not a form of jubilee?

Work had become so important that before COVID-19, some people worked seven days a week. People were all preoccupied with their survival and worked helplessly. The principles of Sabbath were downplayed by many, including Christians. Some Christians even held business meetings on Sundays. COVID-19 gave people mandatory rest, as various governments locked down nations. Social distancing reduced the rushed culture. People were forced to remain home with their families unless there was an emergency. Could this not be God's intervention?

Until the outburst of COVID-19, there was little talk about God in the world systems, especially in the West. COVID-19 has caused some people to search for the reasons for our existence on earth. Some even thought that was the end of the world. COVID-19 has caused people to ask questions such as: What is the meaning of life? Why is our existence on earth? What is my purpose in life? Is death the end of life? Is there God? Are we responsible to him?[8] At least some people have begun to seek God or even to speak about his presence. Significant is the alleged statement from the Italian Prime Minister, Giuseppe Conte, that "We have lost control, we have killed the epidemic physically and mentally. Can't understand what more we can do; all solutions are exhausted on ground. Our only hope remains up in the sky, God rescue your people."[9] This "made up" statement is nevertheless significant in the sense that it gives us a clue about what is going on in the mind of some people. People are trying to find meaning in God and ask him for help.

Before COVID-19, churches were so consumed with programs that, in some cases, they had forgotten the Lord of the programs. In many cases, inside and outside activities had occupied Christians to an extent that there was no time for the individuals to wait upon their Master for his instructions. Some pastors were proud of their possessions and boasted in them instead of boasting in the Lord. Some Christian denominations were subtly competing with one another. Factions continued to grow within denominations. COVID-19 has caused the denominations to come together than before, factions have reduced, and are not fighting against one another but fighting against COVID-19 together. Home churches have been strengthened, pastoral care has been renewed, and Christian families have been strengthened. Husbands and wives have been more united.[10] Now how should the church respond?

The Church's Response

COVID-19 was the unexpected visitor. The church had not prepared for this. In this condition, some churches did not know how to handle it. On the other hand, many churches were able to read the times and showed the love of God to the larger society. This sections takes an overview of how some churches responded to the challenge.

The Presence of God in All Situations

COVID-19 should not take the church by surprise. The church should remind itself that the Lord is in all situations and conditions. COVID-19 was not a surprise to God. Therefore, Christians should not be in a state of agitation. Being in a state of agitation causes people to be panicky, confused, terrified, lose self-control and not know what to do. People who are agitated sometimes act wrongfully and overreact in many ways. A Christian in a state of agitation will be demanding God to act immediately as he acted in the old time, saying that otherwise he is not real or not with us as he was with the people in the Bible. Agitation causes some people to overindulge in vices with the aim of getting out of the situation. It is not healthy for a Christian to be in a state of agitation. Agitation shows a lack of trust in the Lord. It shows that we do not know the one we have come to believe. It shows that we do not know that the Lord owns and controls the world. It shows that we have lost confidence in the Lord and lament as if we were unbelievers. The church should know and believe that the Lord is in full control and will work it out for the good of his people.[11]

Know the Will of God and Communicate the same to the World

Jesus expected the Pharisees and the Sadducees of his time to be able to interpret the times (Matt 16:1–3). Similarly, he expected his disciples to be able to instruct people in times of crises (Matt 13:51–52; 28:18–20; John 16:13). Christians must ask God for his will in all situations. Knowing his will may come through direct revelations, such as through visions, dreams, prophetic messages, word of knowledge or word of wisdom. However, as Jesus expected his disciples who were indwelled with the Holy Spirit to do, Christians should be able to interpret the new through the old. In other words, Christians should be able to use the scriptures to interpret the COVID-19 pandemic through the Holy Spirit who lives in them. This is the duty of the disciples of Christ, especially Christian leaders, apostles, prophets, bishops, evangelists, pastors and teachers.

The Church must Cooperate with God

Knowing the will of God must lead to cooperation with the Lord. The church needs to find out and follow the lessons the Lord is teaching his people. For example, one of the lessons that comes out clearly from COVID-19 is the need for the church to rest in the Lord. The Lord would like the church to relax, reflect, and wait on him. There have been many activities of the church without the Master's presence. Although the church needs money to run its programs, it appears to have relied too much on manipulations and gimmicks to extract money from people. The Lord wants the church to meditate, wait, and call upon him.

Although the church survives on prayer, the majority of its prayer meetings have been that of playing, showing off, and the making of empty noises. Instead of praying to strengthen or deepen oneself in the Lord, the church has settled in the safe haven of the prosperity gospel and deliverance. Instead of proclaiming the word to snatch people from the hands of the evil one and cast demons from those who are possessed, the church keeps on raising "church goers" who have not been discipled to know their identity in Christ. There is little or no real communication with the Lord. The Lord wants his people to meditate, relax, and rest in him, for it is in resting in him that will give strength to the church and help its members know him and execute his will.

Another lesson is the need for total dependence upon the Lord. What God's people need is "our daily bread." Sometimes God's people want many things that are not necessary. We break down buildings and put-up new ones. We crave exquisite clothes and jewelry. We want new models of vehicles, and we do unworthy comparisons that kill the joy of our neighbors. The desire for these may pull the church to run programs that are dried out and result in weariness. The Lord wants his people to trust him to supply our daily bread.

Pruning of the church is another lesson that can be learned. Merely gathering people for singing, preaching, taking offering and tithing do not make the church. While this may be some activities of the church, the real church is the assembly of individuals who have acknowledged God's reign in their hearts and relationships. The church consists of the citizens of the kingdom. When we talk of the kingdom, we do not refer to the buildings, sanctuaries, denominations, nor programs organized by some people. The church is the visible community of those who live by the kingdom values. There are many charlatans within the church communities that people are unable to distinguish. Although people would want the governments to sanitize church denominations, democracy does not permit it and neither does Jesus. This is buttressed by the Parable of the Weeds (Matt 13:36–43). When the servants told the master to pull down the waste, he said they should wait until the harvest time. With COVID-19, it is the Lord, who is himself, pulling up like harvest time, sifting the bad seeds within the system. He knows what he is doing. The church must know the will of their God and cooperate with him.

Reconsider the Way We Do Church

COVID-19 must compel Christian leaders to examine how we do church in our generation.[12] While it is comfortable to attend services of large gathering and meetings, it appears that the church was losing sight of the importance of home meetings and wallowing in outward celebration. Public gathering, and its accompanying display in preaching, singing, and praying has been the order of the day. There has been the need to support praying with instrument to make noise to show that people are praying; preaching has to be supported by soft music to cool down the heart. Hard messages of repentance, judgment, and hell would have to be mellowed down. We would have to be politically correct in order not to offend people. The negative aspect of human rights was being used to tame the message of God. The lockdown of public gathering brought down the display aspect of doing a church. There was no gathering to show off. The Lord would like his people see how we can connect the biblical way of doing church with modern technology without losing the biblical worth.

When God called Abraham, he wanted him to train and build his household with God's commands and instructions (Gen 18:19). Passover was celebrated in households (Exod 12). The New Testament churches were held in houses. The family system has crumbled. The Lord wants us to rebuild it. The Lord wants us to strengthen families and by that strengthen the church at homes. Now we have access to modern technology. How can we do home church with modern technology? There is the need for the church to explore this.

There is the need for the church to change its message. The church needs to revisit the basic message of the gospel, which demands repentance of sin, and the acknowledgement of the Lordship of Christ Jesus, to be saved. The church needs to offer its services free of charge instead of commercializing various aspects of the messages as evidenced in the so-called prosperity gospel. Thus, there is the real need to disciple those who go to church to be truly committed to the message of Christ. COVID-19 draws attention to the fact that people can die at any moment, regardless of race, position, wealth, or age. There is, therefore, an urgent need for the church to revisit the message of the end times. People may need to reconsider whether there is life after death or not. The church has the answer to this and needs to package it in the modern way to present it.

Opportunity to Support the Poor and Vulnerable

The church must take the opportunity to support the poor and needy. The Lord is concerned for people in both their material needs and social context. In the Old Testament, the Jubilee mandate was to free the people from being overburdened and to assist the poor up in wealth equalization (Lev 25:8–13; Deut 15:7–11). Furthermore, it meant that no person would be permanently trapped in poverty. In addition to the Jubilee, God included in the law for Israel that they were not to oppress the poor, take advantage of the widow or lend money and charge interest (Exod 22:21–27). The object behind God's command to his people is rooted in his compassion for those in difficult socio-economic conditions. The prophets declared that God's people must meet the physical needs of the people, which include sustenance, justice, and strength as well as their spiritual needs (Isa 11:4; 41:17; 61:1–3). Furthermore, our Lord Jesus considers any act of good deed to the poor or needy as done for him (Matt 25:40–45). Thus, Jesus equated serving or neglecting the poor with serving or neglecting God. He deals with poverty from all fronts—physical, emotional, and spiritual (Luke 4:18–19; 11:2–26).

The apostles' readiness to support the poor is seen in their instructions to church leaders of their time, including the collections for and ministry to the poor, care for widows and orphans, and the sharing of possessions (e. g. Acts 11:27–29; Gal 2:11; 2 Cor 8–9; 1 Tim 5:3–16; James 1:27). The church must take a cue from these and increase its services to the poor and the needy within and without the body of believers. The services of the church should not just be to do something in the public eyes for recognition or favor but to provide services to the vulnerable.

Opportunity for the Vulnerable to Rise Up

The church must take the opportunity to speak about God's ability to supply the needs of people. COVID-19 led to the closure of natural borders, leaving the rich and the poor to themselves. Many developing countries have been depending upon the West. Meanwhile there are enough natural and human resources in such nations. Top on the issues which have brought about the woes of these dependent countries are bad governance, bribery, corruption, and mismanagement. This is the period that the church must hammer the demand for justice and to be self-supporting. Many countries started manufacturing their own personal protection equipment because the rich as well as the poor needed them. It is an opportunity for the church to speak about fair economic market and also opportunity to bring home God's ability to all nations to support themselves.

Opportunity to Catch up with the Knowledge Revolution

COVID-19 gives the church the opportunity to catch up with the knowledge revolution. The church is always expected to shine within a dark world, even using the tools of the world. The Old Testament was written in the Hebrew language. The New Testament was written in Aramaic. In the

New Testament era, the Aramaic had replaced Hebrew as local language of the Jews. Both Hebrews and Aramaic came from the same family. However, the apostles and other authors of the NT used the lingua franca of the period, thus Greek. By this, they were able to communicate their message to the people.

In the sixteenth century, Martin Luther used printing to spread the knowledge of the Bible which eventually sparked Protestant Reformation. It was the then newly mechanized movable type of press that helped to spread biblical, religious, and theological ideas in Europe in the era.[13] The printing press helped the missionaries to translate the Bible into various vernacular languages for the indigenous recipients.

Ron Luce, the CEO of Generation Next, describes the knowledge revolution that has shaken the world in our time as exponential, by which he means the speed keeps intensifying.[14] He shows that now the rule of the game is whoever learns fastest wins. He laments how some companies which could not change have collapsed.[15] Central to contemporary knowledge revolution is Artificial Intelligence (AI) where computers think faster and interact with humans, in such a way that people may not even realize it is a computer. Robots now perform many tasks for humans. We have self-driven vehicles, trains, and auto piloting. The technology of hologram, where a person's image appears as the real person, is used to offer interpretation. How is the church responding to these modern technologies?

COVID-19 has shown the nakedness of the church and our unpreparedness. It is always humans who provide information into a database so that the data can be accessed. The computer does not feed itself. The church needs to sponsor and train more people as engineers and technologists who will be able to provide Christian languages, values, and principles to the data. With this new wave, the church's failure to cope with the speed will be a serious catastrophe for the church's future. Thus, God, using all means to communicate to his people, through COVID-19, has spoken to the church to catch up to speed.

Conclusion

Making a survey through the Bible, this essay has shown that COVID-19 could be one of the outcomes of the original sin and the Fall. The

Fall expresses itself in inflicting abuse on the planet. It is evident in authoritarian governments, bad governance, dictatorships, corruption, greed, crime, weapons of mass destruction, injustice, disrespect for the human body, and the breakdown of human rights. The effects of these abuses could be catastrophic for humanity, including pandemics. Thus, COVID-19 could be the natural outcome of the mismanagement of the resources God has given to humankind.

On the other hand, it has been shown that COVID-19 could be a judgment from the Lord, since the unchanging God judged the people in the biblical era with plagues for disobedience to his command. COVID-19 was also presented as a possibility of an intervention from God for people to reconsider the way the world was governed. No matter the cause of the pandemic, the Lord would want his creation to turn to him in repentance and depend upon him.

The church was encouraged not to panic, but to know the Lord who owns and controls the world. Then, take advantage to reconsider the way church is done, support the needy, encourage the weak to rise up, and catch up with the knowledge revolution.

Notes

1 An earlier version has been published with slight changes in *Responding to the Uninvited Visitor: COVID-19 Pandemic and the Lessons it has Taught Us*, eds. Opoku Onyinah and Alfred Koduah (Benenda: Langaa Research & Publishing CIG, 2024), 37-54.

2 For example, see the term "plague" in James Strong, *Strong Exhaustive Concordance* (Nashville: Crusade Bible Publishers, 1960), 79.

3 Walter L. Liefeld, "Luke," *The Expositors Bible Commentary with New International Version: Genesis, Exodus, Leviticus, Numbers*, Frank E. Gaebelein, ed. (Grand Rapids: Zondervan, 1989), 968–970.

4 Keith Warrington, *Healing and Suffering Biblical and Pastoral Reflections* (Carlisle: Paternoster, 2005).

5 J. T. Trevors, "Total Abuse of the Earth: Human Overpopulation and Climate Change," *Water, Air, Soils Pollution: An International Journal of Environmental Pollution* 205 (2010), 113–114.

6 For more about the abuse of the human body see, Nancy R. Pearcey, *Love thy Body: Answering Hard Questions about Life and Sexuality* (Grand Rapids: Baker Books, 2018).

7 John Piper, *Coronavirus and Christ* (Wheaton: Crossway, 2020), 61–72.

8 Moulay Driss El Maarouf, Taieb Belghazi and Farouk El Maarouf, "COVID-19: A Critical Ontology of the Present," *Educational Philosophy and Theory* 53:1 (2021).

9 "This 'quote' from the Italian Prime Minister About Coronavirus is Made Up," March 24, 2020, https://fullfact.org/online/conte-bolsonaro-covid-coronavirus/.

10 As the president of the Bible Society of Ghana, in my personal interaction with Christians from various denominations, many wives said that COVID-19 caused their husbands to remain at home. This circumstance helped them to rekindle their family devotions and that renewed their marriages.

11 Jason Mandryk, *Global Transmission, Global Mission: The Impact and Implications of the COVID-19 Pandemic* Kindle Edition (Downers Grove, IL: Operation World, 2020), 74–80.

12 See Israel O. Olofinjana, "Faith Perspectives: Six Theological Responses to Coronavirus," March 23, 2020, Centre for Missionaries from the Majority World, https://cmmw.org.uk/2020/03/23/faith-perspectives-six-theological-responses-to-coronavirus.

13 Richelle McDaniel, "The Spread of Knowledge via Print" in *History of the Book: Disrupting Society from Tablet to Tablet* (Monmouth, OR: Western Oregon University Digital Commons, 2015), 29–41.

14 Ron Luce, *Faith at the Speed of Light: Experiencing Exponential Growth while Surfing the Wave of Change* (Tustin, CA: Trilogy Christian Publishing, 2019), 24.

15 Luce, *Faith at the Speed of Light*, 26.

2 The Message of Lukan Pneumatology to a Post-Pandemic World

Glenn Balfour

Abstract

Pentecostal theology finds its biblical epicentre in the Lukan corpus. That is to say, in both Luke's Gospel and the Acts of the Apostles there is a clear emphasis on the empowering work of the Holy Spirit. In the earlier volume this is most evident in the growth and development of Jesus Christ. In the later volume it is evident in the growth and impact of the earliest Christian communities. This empowering is necessary for mission and ministry, and its purpose is for healing, salvation, and transformation. This offers a message of genuine hope to our post-pandemic world.

Introduction

In this chapter we explore the empowering qualities of the Holy Spirit conveyed in the Lukan corpus.[1] First, however, let me set a few parameters. We will occasionally use the masculine pronoun for the Holy Spirit. This, however, is not intended to suggest the Spirit is male. Indeed, the predominant use in the New Testament of a neuter noun to refer to the Holy Spirit, πνεῦμα (*pneuma*), helps demonstrate that grammatical gender should not be confused with biological gender.[2] We will also read the Lukan text through a specifically Christian lens. In particular, we will read it in light of subsequent Christian Trinitarian formulations. This is to acknowledge that our treatment of biblical texts will be, I trust, critically aware, but also hermeneutically confessional.

Second, let me say something about our methodology. We will focus on explicit references to the Holy Spirit in the Lukan corpus, in order to highlight the activity of the Holy Spirit. We are conscious that in doing so we will not generally take into account implicit references. We are also conscious that this still requires a judgement call on the times the explicit terminology (*pneuma*) is indeed a reference to the Holy Spirit. These limitations, however, are less significant for the Lukan corpus that they are for other biblical corpora.

Third, let me defend our insistence on "getting theology" from the Lukan corpus. For sure, Pentecostal theology uses the Lukan corpus especially as the biblical source and mandate for its distinctive pneumatological emphases.³ Our very name comes from the Jewish festival named in Acts 2:1 that marks the inauguration of the new era in which the Spirit is poured out "on all flesh" – Pentecost.⁴ Indeed, scholars have noted an intentional connection between the commencement of the Gentile mission here and this Jewish harvest festival. And in the book of Acts especially, of course, the Holy Spirit may be broadly understood as empowering the church for mission. This is epitomized in Jesus' final instruction before he is taken up to heaven: "But you will receive power when the Holy Spirit has come upon you; and you will be my witnesses in Jerusalem, in all Judea and Samaria, and to the end of the earth" (Acts 1:8).⁵

A traditional riposte to Pentecostal theology has been effectively to dismiss the Gospels and Acts as sources for Christian theology since their primary concern is history. This riposte can be dealt with in one fell swoop with recourse to Redaction Criticism. Redaction Criticism amply demonstrates that, while the Gospels and Acts certainly use a narrative framework, their primary concern is theology!⁶

Empowerment in Luke's Gospel

Of course, it is in the Lukan corpus that we see the most sustained treatment of what we might describe as the "empowerment reception" of the Holy Spirit. We do not have to wait until we get to Acts, moreover, before we see it. It is very present in Luke's Gospel. This helps us appreciate the lines of continuity between the two biblical Testaments regarding Spirit empowerment.

The writer derives some pneumatological features from (or at least shares them with) wider Synoptic tradition. Let us list some of these, since they demonstrate how, in wider Christian tradition generally, the empowering work of the Holy Spirit is a clear element of early Christian thought. Jesus baptizes the truly repentant in the Holy Spirit (Luke 3:16 // Mark 1:8; Matthew 3:18; John 1:33), and the unrepentant in fire (Luke 3:7–9, 17 // Mathew 3:7–10, 12).⁷ The Holy Spirit descends into Jesus like a dove at his baptism (Luke 3:22 // Mark 1:10; Matthew 3:16; John 1:32). Notice here the typically Lukan "visible empowerment" redactional comment – "in bodily form like a dove." Notice too another typically Lukan redactional comment in the very next line of narrative: "Jesus, full of the Holy Spirit. . ." (4:1).[8] Jesus is now led by the Spirit into the desert where he is tempted (Luke 4:1 // Mark 1:12; Matthew 4:1).

There is also the sharing of the virgin birth narrative with Matthew's Gospel (Luke 1:35 // Matthew 1:18, 20), in which Mary conceives Jesus by the Holy Spirit. Here again we see a typically Lukan empowerment redactional comment – "The Holy Spirit will come upon you, and the power of the Most High will overshadow you." There are two further typically Lukan pneumatological redactional comments in material the Gospel shares with Matthew's Gospel. In Luke 10:21 Jesus "rejoices in the Holy Spirit" (cf. Matthew 11:25, where Jesus simply speaks); and in Luke 11:13 Jesus says that the Father will give specifically "[the] Holy Spirit" to those who ask him (cf. Matthew 7:11, where Jesus says that the Father will give "good gifts").[9]

Perhaps even more significantly, there are also a number of uniquely Lukan references to the Holy Spirit, all of which are hallmarked by an empowerment theme. That is to say, people are filled with the Holy Spirit, and thereby supernaturally empowered to do something (immediately). It is noticeable, moreover, how all this material occurs before Jesus begins his ministry. In short, it forms part of the Lukan motif of, first empowerment, then ministry. (Cf. Luke 24:49; Acts 1:4–5.)

John the Baptist "will be filled with the Holy Spirit" (1:15; cf. v. 17) from his mother's womb! Indeed, it is possible to discern the moment this happens. In 1:41–44 his mother, Elizabeth, greets her relative, the newly pregnant Mary, and is also "filled with the Holy Spirit;" and at the same time "the baby leaped in her womb" (v. 41). Elizabeth is clear about what has just happened – "As soon as the sound of your greeting reached my ears, the baby in my womb leaped for joy" (v. 44). So, the prenatal John the Baptist is filled with the Holy Spirit and does something supernatural! Notice too how his growth is described later – the child "grew and became strong in [the] Spirit" (1:80).[10]

As we have noted, Elizabeth is "filled with the Holy Spirit" (1:41), and again does something supernatural. She immediately exclaims that her younger relative is carrying her Lord (1:42–43)![11] This supernatural boldness in proclaiming divine truth is a hallmark of being filled with the

Holy Spirit throughout the Lukan corpus (e.g., See Acts 4:31). Mary too is empowered by the Spirit. The angel Gabriel tells her, "The Holy Spirit will come on you, and the power of the Most High will overshadow you. . ." (1:35). Notice here the typically Lukan juxtaposition of "Spirit" and "power." This is a repeated motif in the Lukan corpus, especially in Acts, and the result is supernatural – ". . .So the holy one to be born will be called the Son of God." Subsequently, Mary too proclaims divine truth (1:46–55); and she is explicitly named among the 120 believers who meet together to pray. By implication, then, she is filled with the Holy Spirit and speaks in other tongues on the Day of Pentecost (Acts 1:14; 2:1-4).

Zechariah is "filled with the Holy Spirit" (1:67; and he too immediately does something supernatural; he prophesies (1:67). Simeon is empowered by the Holy Spirit (2:25–27): "The Holy Spirit was on him;" it had been revealed to him "by the Holy Spirit" that he would not die until he had seen the Lord's anointed one; and he comes "by the Spirit" into the temple. Again, the result is that he proclaims divine truth (2:28–35).[12]

Now we come to the preparation of the principal character – Jesus, the anointed one! It is important to note that, unlike John the Baptist, Jesus is not filled with the Holy Spirit before he is baptized in water. (John the Baptist, by contrast, we have already seen is filled with the Holy Spirit as an unborn baby.) This is not to undermine the divinity of Jesus – Luke's Gospel is one of only two Gospels explicitly to include the virgin birth tradition, which declares Jesus to be "the Son of God" and "the Lord" (1:35, 43). Rather, it is to make empowerment by the Holy Spirit a specific, discrete, and necessary event for ministry. This applies even to the Lord Jesus Christ himself! And so, it most definitely applies to us!

Let me unpack this more. It is noticeable how Jesus is explicitly empowered by the Holy Spirit before he begins his ministry. And it is this that makes Luke's Gospel too Pentecostal for most Pentecostals! The implication is clear: it is not just that Jesus didn't begin his ministry until he was "filled with the Spirit" – he couldn't begin his ministry until then. Of course, the corollary point is clear for us: if it's good enough for Jesus, it's good enough for us! To see this, we need to turn to Luke 3–4. We have already noted that, despite the many remarkable things associated with Jesus' birth and early years, he does not do anything supernatural or commence his ministry during these years. This is true in all four New

Testament Gospels; but in Luke's Gospel the reality of this, and the lack of mention of Jesus being "filled with the Holy Spirit" during these years is all the more noticeable. So, we now come to Jesus' baptism, recorded in all three Synoptic Gospels, and the immediately ensuing descent of the Holy Spirit into him, recorded in all four canonical Gospels.

In Luke 3:22a, after Jesus is baptized, "the Holy Spirit descended on him in bodily form like a dove." Then we read some uniquely Lukan words, which can appear to be unconnected to this – "Now Jesus himself was about thirty years old when he began his ministry" (v. 23a). Indeed, most English Bibles make this the start of a new paragraph, introducing the genealogy of Jesus. Without denying a connection with the following genealogy, it is possible, however, to see a further significance in these words. Namely, Jesus himself – like everyone else in the "preparation chapters" of Luke's Gospel – begins his ministry (and notice, *begins*) only once he has been empowered by the Holy Spirit. His role as the anointed one can only begin once he is anointed! The recording of Jesus' genealogy (3:23–38) takes some "time out" from the narrative. So, the narrative itself jumps straight from 3:22 to 4:1. Some uniquely Lukan material here now takes on a new significance. First, 4:1 begins with the line, "Jesus, full of the Holy Spirit. . ." This is, surely then, not a description of Jesus as he has always been over the last thirty years. It is a description of Jesus in light of what has just happened – the Holy Spirit has descended on him in bodily form like a dove! This is something new about Jesus. Jesus, then, is the final named person in Luke's Gospel to be empowered by the Holy Spirit; and so, he can begin his ministry.

Jesus is now "led by the Spirit" (4:1b) into the desert, where he confronts the devil on the devil's own "territory."[13] Following this, Jesus returns to Galilee "in the power of the Spirit" (4:14). The typically Lukan juxtaposition of Jesus being "filled" with the Spirit and now being in the "power" of the Spirit is all too apparent. His "Spirit empowered" ministry is about to begin! (Cf. Acts 10:38.) In light of this, the uniquely Lukan moment that happens next (4:16-21) now has even greater poignancy. Jesus goes back home to Nazareth. He goes into his home synagogue on the Sabbath day – just as he usually would. Yet this time something is different. The Spirit has descended on to him (3:22); he is full of the Spirit (4:1); he is in the power of the Spirit (4:14). And, of all passages, which *haftarah* does he read? Isaiah 61:1–2 (cf. Isaiah 58:6):

> The Spirit of the Lord is on me,
>> because he has anointed me to proclaim good news to the poor.
>
> He has sent me to proclaim freedom for the prisoners
>> and recovery of sight for the blind,
>
> to set the oppressed free,
>> to proclaim the year of the Lord's favor (Luke 4:18–19).[14]

With everyone's eyes fastened on him, his first (Lukan) words to the public are these: *"Today* this scripture is fulfilled in your hearing." The ministry of Jesus begins *now*! Indeed, in the second volume of the Lukan corpus, Peter sums up the ministry of Jesus with these words:

> . . .God anointed Jesus of Nazareth with the Holy Spirit and power, ... he went around doing good and healing all who were under the dominion of the devil, because God was with him (Acts 10:38).

This verse serves as an excellent summary of Lukan Christology – Jesus did what he did by the power of the Spirit. The point is clear. The Holy Spirit empowers for ministry. This is true for everyone, even Jesus. Indeed, Jesus is the ultimate paradigm of Spirit empowerment.

It is significant that, now the empowered ministry of Jesus has begun, there is very little mention of the Holy Spirit in the rest of Luke's Gospel.[15] The point has been established. And notice the newness of Jesus' empowered ministry: he teaches about the kingdom of God as being here and now; he operates new healings (cf. Isaiah 35:5–6a); and he delivers from evil spirits.[16] This set the theological scene for the next instalment of God's empowered people. Indeed, we cannot but notice Jesus' final words at the end of Luke's Gospel (24:47–49):

> . . . repentance for the forgiveness of sins will be proclaimed in [Christ's] name to all nations, beginning at Jerusalem. You are witnesses of these things. I am sending what my Father has promised you; but stay in the city until you have been clothed with power from on high.

Empowerment in Acts

As noted above, this sets us up for what comes next in the Lukan schema. In Acts 1:5, the risen Jesus repeats his command to the disciples: "Do not leave Jerusalem, but wait for the gift my Father promised. . . For John baptized with water but in a few days, you will be baptized with [the] Holy Spirit."[17] A few verses later he tells them, ". . .you will receive power when the Holy Spirit comes on you; and you will be my witnesses. . ." (1:8). This promise of the Father is fulfilled in Acts 2:1–4. Indeed, the intertextuality between the events described in Acts 2:1–4 and the dedication of Solomon's Temple (2 Chronicles 5:11–14; 7:1–3) – 120 priests sounding the trumpet, and fire from heaven filling the whole "house" – is clear. The writer hereby offers a message of hope in the midst of contemporary traumatic events. With the Second Temple destroyed in 70 CE, God's Spirit-indwelt and empowered people provide an alternative temple![18]

Peter is clear what the events of that day of Pentecost signify (2:16–17): ". . .this is what was spoken by the prophet Joel: 'In the last days, God says, I will pour out my Spirit on all people. . .'" He subsequently clarifies this further (2:33): "Exalted to the right hand of God, [Jesus] has received from the Father the promised Holy Spirit and has poured out what you now see and hear." He assures the crowd that this, along with forgiveness, is the birth-right of all who repent and are baptized (2:38b–39): ". . .and you will receive[19] the gift of the Holy Spirit. The promise is for you and your children and for all who are far off – for all whom the Lord our God will call." And so, Acts is replete with believers being empowered by the Holy Spirit in order both to commence and to enter even new phases of ministry and mission. We can continue with Peter. A little later he is (again) "filled with the Holy Spirit" and addresses the Sanhedrin (4:8–12). A little later still, while the disciples are praying, the place is shaken, they are all (again) filled with the Holy Spirit (4:31) and speak the word of God boldly. One can only assume "all" here includes Peter.[20]

We can move on to Stephen. The twelve tell all the disciples to choose seven men who are "full of the Spirit and wisdom" (6:3), who will oversee the care of the widows. The first named man, Stephen, is singled out for some further description – he is "full of faith and of the Holy Spirit" (6:5).[21] Stephen's opponents, moreover, cannot stand against "the wisdom and the Spirit" (6:10) with which he speaks (cf. Luke 12:12). And finally, "being full of [the] Holy Spirit" (7:55),[22] he gazes intently into heaven and sees the glory of God, and Jesus standing at the right hand of God. The Holy Spirit empowers Stephen for martyrdom; and the Son of Man stands in honor as he welcomes him home (7:56–60).[23]

The Holy Spirit is integral to the inclusion of Samaritans in the new covenant. In Acts 8:14–19, people in Samaria have accepted the word of God, but the Holy Spirit has not yet "fallen on" (*epipiptō*; ἐπιπίπτω) them.

They have only been baptised in the name of the Lord Jesus. So, Peter and John are sent to them from Jerusalem, and pray for them "so that they receive [the] Holy Spirit" (v. 15). When Peter and John lay their hands on them, "they received [the] Holy Spirit (v. 17).[24] Indeed, Simon the sorcerer can see the people receiving the Holy Spirit with his own eyes.

Notice the laying on of hands here. In fact, there are only three times in Acts when people receive the Holy Spirit without this (2:2–4; 4:31; 10:44). This is similar to the healing ministry of Jesus in the Synoptic Gospels – there is laying on of hands, unless circumstances prevent it. What should we "hear" in this? Perhaps that observable, visible, tangible, transformative empowerment is such a vital work of the Holy Spirit that it is imparted physically (cf. Romans 1:11). Certainly, the Holy Spirit is not limited by physics (cf. John 4:21–24; 2 Timothy 2:9)! But the point is made: the empowering work of the Holy Spirit is a real, objectively observable, imparted, event.

The Holy Spirit is equally integral to the inclusion of Gentiles in the new covenant. In Acts 8:29, the Spirit tells Philip to go over to the Ethiopian's chariot. (Note that in 8:26 an angel of the Lord had spoken to Philip, telling him to go on the journey.)[25] And when everything is done, "[the] Spirit of the Lord snatches Philip away" (8:39). In Acts 10:19–20 Peter is still thinking about the vision he has just had, when the Spirit speaks to him and tells him He has sent the three men that have just arrived (cf. 11:12).[26] Peter goes to Cornelius's house in Joppa[27] and tells Cornelius and his gathered (Gentile) family and friends about Jesus of Nazareth (10:34–43). While he is still speaking, "the Holy Spirit 'fell on' (*epipiptō*; ἐπιπίπτω)[28] all who heard the message" (v. 44). The Jewish believers were astonished that "the gift of the Holy Spirit has been poured out even on Gentiles. For they heard them speaking in tongues and praising God" (vv. 45–46). Peter is clear. No one can prevent these Gentiles being baptized in water (*qua* Gentiles), since "they received the Holy Spirit just as we did" (v. 47). And so, another new, quantum leap in missional terms is validated – more than that, demanded – by Spirit empowerment (cf. 11:15–17; 15:8)! This is certainly a "gateway moment" (cf. the Samaritans in Acts 8:17). That does not, however, make it non-paradigmatic. Indeed, a further empowering reception of the Holy Spirit by Gentiles is recounted in Acts 19:6. The missional agenda of the Holy Spirit in all this is clear. Related to this, the church in Jerusalem notes how the Holy Spirit is one of the decision-makers in them asking Paul's Gentile converts to abstain from just three things (15:28).[29]

Finally in Acts, we must turn to Paul. The epochal ministry of Paul is hallmarked by the empowering qualities of the Holy Spirit. This is evident occasionally in the uncontested Pauline letters (e.g., Romans 15:18–19); but of course, it is most evident in the Lukan presentation of Paul's ministry. In the days immediately following his Damascus Road experience, Ananias tells Saul that the Lord Jesus had sent him to Saul, so that Saul would see again "and be filled with the Holy Spirit" (9:17). Barnabas first takes Saul "under his wing" (9:27; 11:25–26) – and Barnabas is identified as "a good man... full of the Holy Spirit and faith" (11:24).[30]

While the prophets and teachers at Antioch are worshipping the Lord and fasting, the Holy Spirit says, "Set apart for me Barnabas and Saul for the work to which I have called them" (13:2). And so, the two go, "sent on their way by the Holy Spirit" (13:4). In the very first account of an event recounted on their first missionary journey, Saul is filled with the Holy Spirit (13:9), confronts Elymas, and the Lord blinds Elymas for a time (cf. Acts 9:8). Notice how the word order of "Barnabas and Saul" (12:25; 13:2, 9) now changes to "Paul and Barnabas" (13:13, 43, 46, 50). It is as if this new level of Spirit empowering now makes Paul rather than Barnabas the appropriate person to "head up the team."

Early on in the second missionary journey, Paul and his new team are intending to make their way back through all the churches in Asia Minor that Paul's earlier team had planted. God, however, has other ideas (16:6–7). They change direction "having been forbidden by the Holy Spirit to speak the word in Asia" (v. 6). They attempt to go again, but "the Spirit of Jesus" does not allow them (v. 7). And finally in a vision they are directed towards Troas (vv. 8–10).[31] The Holy Spirit brings divine strategy for a new day. The good news is about to come to Europe!

In 19:2–6 Paul asks some disciples of John the Baptist in Ephesus, "Did you receive the Holy Spirit when you believed?" (v. 2). They reply that they haven't even heard there is a Holy Spirit. Paul first baptizes them in the name of the Lord Jesus. He then lays his hands on them, "and the Holy Spirit came upon them, and they spoke in other tongues and prophesied" (v. 6). Notice again the laying on of hands, and overt supernatural activity – this is physical impartation of empowerment by the Holy Spirit.

There is something further to note here. This is the final account of Spirit reception in the Lukan corpus. So, the reference to specifically twelve male disciples, as well as the juxtaposition of the baptism in water by John with "baptism in the Spirit" by Jesus, may suggest that this is being presented by the writer as paradigmatic for the ministry of Jesus being continued by his followers (cf. Luke 9:1; Acts 1:5; 11:16).[32]

There is only one more set of references to the Holy Spirit in Acts. These are all related to Paul's plans to go to Rome (19:21; 20:22–23; 21:4–11). They occur at or near the end of his third missionary. They offer a final dramatic element to the empowering work of the Holy Spirit, especially related to the prophetic. On this occasion the prophetic is not just "forth-telling;" it is also "foretelling."[33] At the end of his third missionary journey, Paul resolves "in the Spirit" (19:21) to make his way back to Jerusalem, and ultimately from there to Rome.[34] This theme is picked up again shortly (20:22–23). As Paul says goodbye to the Ephesian leaders, he tells them: "Compelled by the Spirit, I am going to Jerusalem. . . the Holy Spirit testifies to me that prison and persecutions are waiting for me in each city." Having nearly arrived at Jerusalem, Paul and his team spend a week with the disciples in Tyre; but the disciples there keep warning Paul "through the Spirit" not to go any further (21:4).

It is evident what is happening here. The disciples have the same prophetic awareness that Paul has about there being danger ahead for him; yet their own human care for Paul makes them interpret this as a warning for him not to go any further! (See also 1 Thess 5:20–21a.) A further prophetic voice in this is that of the prophet Agabus (21:10–11). We in fact have already met Agabus in Acts once before. Some ten years earlier, before Paul began his ministry, he "signified through the Spirit" that there would be a great famine throughout the [Greco-Roman] world (11:28). The writer is clear: this occurred during the reign of Claudius (41 – 54 CE). Here Agabus appears again, and dramatically tells everyone what "the Holy Spirit says" – the Jewish leaders in Jerusalem will hand Paul over to the Gentiles. On hearing this, all the disciples again urge Paul to go no further (21:12). Paul refuses – he is ready even to die in Jerusalem for the name of the Lord Jesus (v. 13). Everyone's final line is the perfect way to end moments like this – "The Lord's will be done" (v. 14).

There is one further explicit reference to the Holy Spirit in Acts. In 20:28, Paul instructs the Ephesian leaders to keep watch over themselves and the whole flock, "of which the Holy Spirit has made you overseers (*episkopous*; ἐπισκόπους), to keep shepherding the church of God, which he acquired through his own blood." The Holy Spirit appoints leaders of the visible, localised church of God![35]

Conclusion

This typically Lukan "empowering" reception of the Holy Spirit, which brings about healing, salvation, and transformation, through a "Spirit-filled" people, offers a message of genuine hope to our post-pandemic world. There is a divine source of "empowered speech," which proclaims the good things of heaven here on earth (Rom 14:17).[36] The power of physical presence and impartation offers a brake on recent trends towards an overly digital, fractured, remote-working, and even "remote church" lifestyle. And the Holy Spirit associates himself with new, innovative, situations, which require leadership, wisdom, and prophetic utterance. He even gives insight into the future. The Spirit's penchant for unchartered mission settings is ideally suited for this brave, new, post-pandemic, world!

There are also lessons to learn. The account of the Holy Spirit's steering of Paul and his team to Europe shows us that we need to allow time to consider. Sometimes a full stop is not the full stop! The account of Paul's increased focus on Rome shows us that we need to be careful not to confuse the "voice of the Spirit" with our own voices – especially when it comes to the prophetic. Indeed, sometimes the wisest prophets are the ones that know when to say nothing (Acts 21:9). We need to be careful not to confuse our own spirits – our own emotions, vested interests, and preferences – with what the Spirit is saying (1 Thess 5:19–21.)

The Holy Spirit does not work independently of us – he works in co-operation with us. Or rather, we work in co-operation with him. Our understanding of spiritual gifts alone makes this much clear (1 Corin 14:28, 32). But we see this too in Acts – the only sustained biblical account of the earliest Christian communities.[37] The first generation of believers had to learn how to adapt and apply their faith in new and unimaginable situations. Whether it was the phenomenon of the Holy Spirit being "poured out" on excluded, unclean Gentiles, not yet even baptized in the name of Jesus Christ (Acts 10:44); or whether it was the healing and releasing power of the Spirit being made accessible to those physically absent (Acts 19:12; 15:5) – so much is clear.

And now it is *our* turn to create pathways for open access and participation in the redemptive, transformative, healing, saving power and presence of the Holy Spirit! This is not new for new's sake, or shock for its own sake; this is creativity for people's sake! The innovation and creativity that necessity drew out of us during COVID-19 was not just for the moment. This creativity, driven by the imperative of mission, is to be welcomed and sought after constantly. It has clear Lukan precedent. It is something we need to both welcome and harness as a vehicle for the presence and power of the Holy Spirit.

It would be naïve to think that this post-pandemic world marks a return to normality, tranquility, and certainty. That world is more the illusory construct of modernity than it is the reality for most people most of the time. The post-pandemic world will continue to see seismic change, war, hardship, and uncertainty. All the more reason to hear the message repeated throughout the Lukan corpus. We must be empowered by the Holy Spirit to bring about real healing, real salvation, and real hope. Let the mission statement of Jesus near the start of the Lukan corpus remain our mission statement too:

> "The Spirit of the Lord is on me,
>   because he has anointed me to proclaim good news to the poor.
> He has sent me to proclaim freedom for the prisoners
>   and recovery of sight for the blind,
> to set the oppressed free,
>   to proclaim the year of the Lord's favor" (Luke 4:18–19; Isaiah 61:1–2).

Notes

1 In a previous publication we explored the qualities of the Holy Spirit conveyed in the rest of the Bible. See, Glenn Balfour, "The Value of Biblical Pneumatology to a Post-COVID-19 World," in *The Remaining Task of the Great Commission & The Spirit-Empowered Movement*, eds., Wonsuk Ma, Opoku Onyinah, and Rebekah Bled (Tulsa, OK: ORU Press, 2023), 11–26.

2 In the Hebrew Bible, the Noun for 'spirit' / 'wind' is רוּחַ (*ruach*). It is Feminine. Specifically in John's Gospel, a new term for the Holy Spirit is παράκλητος (*paraklētos*). It is Masculine.

3 The Lukan corpus comprises Luke's Gospel and the Acts of the Apostles.

4 The Greek term πεντηκοστή (*pentēkostē*) literally means, "fiftieth." The Jewish festival of *Shavuot* was given this name since it occurs fifty days after Passover. The Greek term is first used this way in the 2nd BCE Septuagint (*Tobit* 2:1; 2 *Maccabees* 12:32).

5 We use the *New Revised Standard Version (NRSV)* or *New International Version (NIV)* for most biblical texts.

6 E.g., See Hans Conzelmann, *The Theology of St Luke* (New York: Harper and Row, 1961).
We might note here that the Lukan corpus makes up just over a quarter (28 percent) of the New Testament canon. To ignore its theological contribution, then, is to ignore the largest single corpus in the New Testament.

7 Pentecostals in particular can make an exegetically flawed connection between the baptism of fire mentioned in Matthew and Luke ("Q"), and the tongues of fire in Acts 2:1–4. (Cf. 2 Chronicles 5:11–14; 7:1–3.)

8 It is equally possible to see redactional pneumatological comment in the Johannine presentation of this narrative – the Spirit descends and "remains" (*menō*; μένω) on Jesus (John 1:32–33).

9 There are three references in Acts to the role of the Holy Spirit speaking through the (Jewish) scriptures: 1:16; 4:25; 28:5. This theme is also shared with the other two Synoptic Gospels (Matthew 22:43; Mark 12:36).

10 The contrast between this and the descriptions of Jesus' growth (2:40, covering his first twelve years; 2:52, covering his years from aged twelve to about thirty) is clear. There is no mention of Spirit in the developmental growth of Jesus. He is not "filled with the Spirit" until he is around 30 (3:22–23a). More on this shortly.

11 The Greek noun *kurios* (κύριος) can have a very "low" sense (almost, "sir"), and a very "high" sense. In the Septuagint (LXX) it is the most frequent Greek rendering of the Divine Name, YHWH (יהוה).

12 Anna is another uniquely Lukan character associated with the birth narratives of Jesus. She also proclaims divine truth about Jesus (2:38). No mention is made of her being filled with the Holy Spirit. It is clearly stated, however, that she a prophet – and, by implication, that she has been one for a long time (2:36–37). In other words, she had been empowered by the Spirit long before the Lukan narrative starts!

13 Notice how the language is softer in both later Synoptic Gospels (cf. Matthew 4:1) than it is in Mark's Gospel (1:12). In Mark's Gospel, the Spirit "casts out" (*ekballō*; ἐκβάλλω) Jesus into the desert.

14 For a helpful treatment of the Greek text, see, Alan J. Thompson, *Luke* (EGGNT; Nashville: B&H Academic, 2016), 73–74.

15 There are just the two redactional comments we have noticed elsewhere (Luke 10:21; 11:13).

16 These three activities are central to the public ministry of Jesus in all three Synoptic Gospels.

17 This is one of only two uses of the words "baptized in the Holy Spirit" in Acts. (Cf. Acts 11:16.)

18 For a treatment of various links between Acts 2:1–4 and contemporary Greco-Roman texts, see John R. Levinson, *Filled with the Spirit* (Grand Rapids, MI: Eerdmans, 2009), 329–331.

19 The same Greek verb is used by every New Testament writer for someone "receiving" the Holy Spirit – *lambanō* (λαμβάνω). (In other settings, the Verb is more usually translated as, "I take.")

20 This means there are *three* cited instances of Peter being filled with the Holy Spirit (Acts 2:4; 4:8, 31).

21 A little later (6:8) he is singled out again, as being "full of grace and power", who does "great signs and wonders among the people." In light of the other "tandem references" here (6:3, 5, 10), it seems that "power" (*dunamis*; δύναμις) is tantamount to "Spirit" (*pneuma*; πνεῦμα).

22 The participle emphasises the continuity of the action – he is full of the Holy Spirit as he gazes into heaven.

23 Stephen's prayer echoes Jesus' own uniquely Lukan prayer of forgiveness. (Cf. Acts 7:60; Luke 23:34.)

24 The use of the Imperfect (rather than Aorist) Tense emphasizes the *continuity* of the action. The implication is that Peter and John lay their hands on the people one by one, and they receive the Holy Spirit one by one.

25 It is intriguing that the Lukan corpus emphasizes the role of the Holy Spirit in the life of the early believers, and yet also – and often in close proximity – the role of angels. See, for example, Luke 1:11–20, 26z-38; 2:9–14; 16:22; [21:43]; Acts 10:3–6; 12:7–11.

26 In the earlier incident (vv. 3–8), it is in fact an angel of the Lord who comes to Cornelius in a vision and tells him to send the three men. We should not limit the recourses at God's disposal! (See Hebrews 1:14.)

27 The link with an earlier prophet who went to Joppa in order *not* to preach to the Gentiles is clear (Jonah 1:3).

28 The same verb is used here that is used in 8:16. The Holy Spirit leaves no-one in doubt on both occasions!

29 It is clear from the context that these three things are all perceived to have associations with pagan worship.

30 Again, notice the "twining" of being full of the Holy Spirit with another attribute, implying a causal relationship between them (6:3, 5, 8; 10:38; 13:52). In a similar vein, in Acts 9:31, the Holy Spirit causes the church the experience of "comfort." This reinforces the empowering facet of the Holy Spirit.

31 Notice here how the activity of the Holy Spirit is in close proximity to visions. This is another trait in Acts.

32 Compare Levinson, *Filled*, 337.

33 On the Holy Spirit as primarily the "Spirit of Prophecy" in Acts, see Max Turner, *The Holy Spirit and Spiritual Gifts* (London: Paternoster, 1999.), 37–56. Compare David G. Peterson, "The Pneumatology of Luke-Acts: The Spirit of Prophecy Unleashed," in Sean A. Adams and Michael Pahl, eds., *Issues in Luke-Acts: Selected Essays* (Piscataway, NJ: Gorgias Press, 2012), 195–216.

34 The reference here could be to Paul's spirit or to the (Holy) Spirit. In light of what comes next (Acts 20:22–25, 37–38; 21:4–14) we prefer to read this as a reference to the Holy Spirit.

35 See, Daniel McGinnis, *Missional Acts: Rhetorical Narrative in the Acts of the Apostles* (Eugene, OR: Pickwick, 2022), 28ff.

36 See, Max Turner, *Power from on High: The Spirit in Israel's Restoration and Witness in Acts* (JPTSup 9; Sheffield: Sheffield Academic, 1996), 168.

37 For more on the uniqueness of Acts within the New Testament corpus, see Craig L. Blomberg and Darlene M. Seal, *From Pentecost to Patmos* (Nashville: B&H Academic, 2021), 9–11.

3 The Ethics of St. Cyprian: Exploring Repentance, Forgiveness, and Reconciliation for Contemporary Spirit-Empowered Communities.

Cory J. May

Abstract

The Ethics of St. Cyprian explores the life and ministry of the influential 3rd-century North African bishop. The aim, in part, is to examine Cyprian's heart for Christ, and practice of Christian ethics, to obtain further clarity on the issues that plague our contemporary Western Evangelical Church. Additionally, Cyprian's struggles and sacrifices can aid in excavating potential solutions for Western Spirit-Empowered Christians, who diligently minister to the wounded, inside and outside the body of Christ, spiritually lacerated by ideological confusion, and identity dysphoria from our current sociopolitical crisis.

Introduction

Western Spirit-empowered communities, principally within the United States, are experiencing specific and continual conflicts inside and outside their spiritual unions. To an extent, this has always been the case. However, arguably, the primary problems, at least currently for some Christians, appears to be intensified from inside the Western church. Various Christians, those who at one point self-identified as Evangelical and Fundamentalist, are progressively leaving Western Spirit-Empowered communities or are on the verge of doing so. Those Christians emancipated from the deceptive oppositional-binary reasoning and who do not view controversial issues as deriving solely from outside of Christendom, are asking themselves what factors are causing this trend or movement.

Some former Christians and current jaded believers claim there is a lack of biblically centered leadership within the church. Other individuals state the Western church exists in contradiction and hypocrisy: it is incredibly political but has no biblical conceptualizing and application of scriptural social justice.[1] Elements of these views are legitimate.

For example, some Western Spirit-empowered communities struggle with the allure and skewed exploitation of particular identity politics. The pronounced variants of identity politics have manifested through gender confusion, hyper-sexuality, and secular and Christian racialized nationalism.[2] Matters are further complicated when these ideological dispositions and discourses employ concealed principles of relativism vis-à-vis distorted Western democratic principles of equality. I refer to this as the Hermeneutic of Equality.[3] These are serious issues, along with other complex crises that require empathetic, humanizing, and sensitive approaches to possible solutions.

One consideration that Spirit-empowered communities within the Western world need to assess is cultivating their knowledge of our spiritual lineage with the Church Fathers. From this suggestion, we now turn to an influential and arguably relatively unappreciated Church father named Saint Cyprian of Carthage.[4] Exploring Cyprian's leadership and ethics, which developed amid perpetual crisis, provides vital lessons for our contemporary Spirit-empowered communities. His biblical advocacy of repentance, forgiveness, and reconciliation are essential to a distraught Western Christianity and the leadership of the non-Westernized global Church, which maintains its biblical faith in Christ.

The Humility of St. Cyprian of Carthage

Thaschus Caecillius Cyprianus (c200–258 A.D.), also known as St. Cyprian of Carthage, was born of wealthy parentage of Berber descent in Northern Africa. Historians have difficulty uncovering documents that reveal the finer details of Cyprian's life as a child to adulthood. However, scholars maintain he received a prestigious classical education that allowed him to establish a lucrative career as a Roman lawyer and rhetorician. As a lawyer, it is assumed Cyprian comprehended the basic standards of effective argumentation. His training would also involve lessons in eloquent delivery. Cyprian exceeded the standards of mediocrity and established himself as an influential orator before his conversion to Christianity.[5] The lack of detail regarding Cyprian's worldly life is frustrating but is not uncommon when we assess him with other Church Fathers. Yet, we will explore some of the information we know of Cyprian concerning our contemporary period.

To a large extent, contemporary Western culture endorses counterintuitive and counterproductive systems of emotionalism and sensationalism. These elements have in various ways affected Western Christianity, its ministries, and theologies whereby Christ Jesus is not glorified, but the agents who claim to serve him. How often have we listened to a Christian's testimony, who seemingly boasted and gloated over their former sinful life, as if there was an absence of shame? Has there ever been a moment of eerie concern upon hearing a Christian recount their past life, and your spirit grew disturbed, because you felt the individual was concealing their enjoyment of worldly pleasures?

A shroud of mystery exists that conceals the details of Cyprian's secular character and life before he embraced Christ Jesus as his Lord and Savior. The perception of mystery appears very intentional, a well-developed decision possibly from embarrassment, shame, and disgust of his former life in the world. Through this speculation, Cyprian's resolution could also derive from his humility and theological foci to glorify Christ, from whom Christ has made him into, which was a loving and loyal servant. Cyprian alludes to this in brief descriptions of his former life. These descriptions are always associated with the freedom, joy, peace, and blessings he received upon being grafted into the body of Christ. For example, we can understand aspects of Cyprian's views in his letter to a close friend, Donatus. In one section of the letter, Cyprian states, "While I was still lying in darkness and gloomy night, wavering hither and there, tossed about on the foam of this boastful age, and uncertain of my wandering steps, knowing nothing of my real life, and remote from truth and light. . . ."[6] Cyprian's statement is situated within his discourse on the skewed nature of Roman culture and his sinful life as an educated and wealthy citizen. Like many other people, Cyprian enjoyed all the debauchery that Roman culture provided. In describing this aspect of his former life, he exhibits self-awareness and humility rarely seen among Christians throughout history.

A life apart from Christ is a life ignorant of its human destiny. Cyprian alludes to this belief in his description of wandering in life without any meaningful goal or purpose. He was driven primarily by satisfying the self-interest of his ego. Cyprian's description also leads the reader to his inability to conceive of receiving salvation in his dark state of existence, and how awareness of salvation stemmed solely from divine revelation via divine mercy. Cyprian's words elicit strong imagery as he explains:

> These were my frequent thoughts. For as I myself was held in bonds by the innumerable errors of my previous life, from which I did not believe that I could by possibility be delivered, so I was disposed to acquiesce in my clinging vices; and because I despaired of better things, I used to indulge my sins as if they were actually parts of me, and indigenous to me. But after that, by the help of the water of new birth, the stain of former years had been washed away, and a light from above, serene and pure, had been infused into my reconciled heart –after that, by the agency of the Spirit breathed from heaven, a second birth had restored me to a new man –then, in a wonderous manner, doubtful things at once began to assure themselves to me, hidden things to be revealed, dark things to be enlightened, what before had seemed difficult began to suggest a means of accomplishment, what had been thought impossible, to be capable of being achieved; so that I was enabled to acknowledge that what previously, being born of the flesh, had been living in the practice of sins, was of the earth earthly, but had now begun to be of God, and was animated by the Spirit of holiness.[7]

Cyprian's theo-psychology of sin and submission to the reasoning and action morally defined as such, provides startling imagery for anyone who attempts to understand him on a significant level. Cyprian articulates a form of realism, from his desire to understand reality as reality is through Christ, which cultivates his empathy for the human-Other from shared experiences. We witness summarized fragments of Cyprian's conceptualization of repentance, forgiveness, and reconciliation from this statement. I argue that humility is inferred from the fundamental self-awareness of Cyprian's genuine conviction of his sin and desire to be with God.

Cyprian's reference to bonds alludes to the Apostle Paul's words in Romans 6:20: "For when you were slaves of sin, you were free in relation to righteousness" (see also, Matthew 11:26, and 2 Timothy 3:6). Cyprian's view of sin, error, what we may view as forms of trauma, and those things alike, collectively construct a system of psychological distortions that perverts our reasoning and behavior in the world. The haunting aspect of Cyprian's statement also expresses the unavoidable thoughts of questioning his existence and reflections from his intrinsic ethical conscience.

Cyprian describes the self-contradictory nature of his sinful life as an existence of degenerated awareness, the inability to acknowledge his sins, because he engaged in modes of avoidance, and denial, which created concealment. Cyprian believed he reached a state of suspicion or partial awareness of his then-current state of emptiness and unhappiness, which thrust him into uncertainty regarding whether he could change the way he lived. Cyprian's words allude to despair from the initial ethical questioning of his sinful lifestyle and inability to conceptualize what freedom from that life entailed. Despair stemmed from the normalization and comfortability of practicing sin, bringing about the illusion of stability.

Another interesting aspect of Cyprian's statement is the representation of sin. Sin was the extension of Cyprian's core human self. Sin was an intrinsic identity, a way of reasoning, and a complementary set of behaviors attached to him as if they were inseparable. Sin was the fundamental means of understanding his existence. Sin represented Cyprian's pseudo-human destiny. In part, Paul summarizes this in Titus 3:3, "For we too were once foolish, disobedient, deceived, enslaved to various lusts and pleasures, spending our life in malice and envy, hateful, hating one another." Cyprian creates a shroud of mystery regarding the process of his salvific awakening. He articulates aspects of his sinful life as relevant only concerning his life in Christ. Cyprian references "the water of new birth," which could be interpreted as the word of God or physical water baptism. Either way, Cyprian provides the reader with solid imagery as if his sinful state represented an existence in darkness and gloom, peacefully pushed away by the emergence of the Spirit's invigorating and transformative presence. Repentance, forgiveness, and reconciliation were processes and states of existence that Cyprian eventually became aware of as a possibility, and ultimately represented his authentic existence within reality. These elements become substantial aspects of his ministry and theology. Repentance, forgiveness, and reconciliation were central to how Cyprian constructed his ecclesiology and conceptualized Christian leadership.

Cyprian's pneumatology is expressed in his salvific experience.[8] "The agency of the Spirit breathed from heaven" becomes a fusion of specific biblical verses and theological foci.[9] The statement could represent Cyprian's assertion of the Spirit's sovereignty, divinity, and ministry within the salvific plan of humanity. Within this thought, Cyprian's statement is expressed in John 14:26, "But the Helper, the Holy Spirit whom the Father will send in my name, He will teach you all things, and remind you of all that I said to you." Cyprian reinforced the role of the Spirit as teacher, guide, and healer. According to Cyprian, the Spirit assisted in removing his doubt, ignorance, and lack of self-awareness. The Spirit instilled hope within Cyprian's mind and spirit. The Spirit aided Cyprian in arriving at a progressive, fuller illumination of the degradation that once defined his existence. Cyprian's new life was in God, and his existence received an energetic resuscitation directed towards Christ as it occurred within Christ. The Spirit of holiness is the person who brings divine energy to Cyprian's new life in the world. This view also alludes to the creation account of Genesis 2:7 regarding the "breath of life."

I want to suggest there are two baptisms that Cyprian alludes to and a third unacknowledged baptism that he endured which revealed itself during his episcopate: the baptisms of water, Spirit, and suffering. Through the empowerment and guidance of the Holy Spirit, Cyprian would undergo intense suffering through persecution, church schisms, and a destructive plague and develop the heroic leadership he exhibited during his service as the Bishop of Carthage. The turmoil Cyprian endured functioned as a way to reveal and refine his ethics and character *vis-à-vis* repentance, forgiveness, and reconciliation through sacrificial service.

Testimonies of Cyprian's Character

In examining Cyprian's character from a different perspective, we must discuss a significant influence on his conversion. The individual who ministered to him functions as a potential example of Christian ethics and leadership for Cyprian. Interestingly enough, we are provided insight into this mystery by Pontius of Carthage.[10] Pontius was a close friend of Cyprian. He was also a loyal colleague as a presbyter within Cyprian's episcopate in Carthage. In some ways, the relationship between Cyprian and Pontius resembled that of Paul and Luke. Pontius wrote, *The Life and Passion of Cyprian*, in which he sought to provide a genuine testimony of Cyprian's ministry and dedication to God. Like Cyprian, Pontius avoids detailed discussions of Cyprian's secular life, pointing out that it served very little importance, compared to who he was as a Christian. Pontius explains:

> He may have had pursuits previously, and liberal arts may have imbued his mind while engaged therein; but these things I pass over; for as yet they had nothing to do with anything but his secular advantage. But when he had

learned sacred knowledge, and breaking through the clouds of this world had emerged into the light of spiritual wisdom, If I was with him in any of his doings, if I have discerned any of his illustrious labors, I will speak of them; only asking meanwhile for this indulgence, that whatever I shall say too little (for too little I must needs say) may rather be attributed to my ignorance than subtracted from his glory. While his faith was in its first rudiment, he believed that before God nothing was worthy in comparison of the observance of continency. For he thought that the heart might then become what it ought to be, and the mind attain to the full capacity of truth, if he trod underfoot the lust of the flesh with the robust and healthy vigor of holiness.[11]

Pontius highlights an aspect of Cyprian's maturity within his spiritual infancy. Pontius, to an extent, alludes to the possible initial coalescing of Cyprian's ethics. Holiness, or sanctification within Christ, influences Cyprian's conceptualizing of how we achieve our full potential as Christians and ultimately fulfill our human destiny in union with our Triune God. Yet, scrutinizing this speculation, how can we ascertain the intended state of the human heart? How can the human mind reach its total capacity in truth, and what consists of this truth?

Biblically, the heart could represent our inner-being, the nexus of our emotional, physical, psychological, and spiritual constitution. This belief is alluded to in Romans 10:9: "that if you confess with your mouth Jesus as Lord and believe in your heart that God raised him from the dead, you will be saved." The human mind left unto itself will only make an idol of its existence, and its self-interest becomes a means of worship. However, within Christ, our minds are transformed, and through the Spirit, we obtain access to God's will (Rom 12:20; 1 Corin 2:16). Pontius directs the reader to Caecilius the Presbyter. Pontius viewed Caecilius as an essential individual God primarily used to lead Cyprian unto Himself. Pontius reflects on this by stating:

> He had a close association among us with a just man, and of praiseworthy memory, by the name Caecilius, and in age as well as in honor a presbyter, who had converted him from his worldly errors to the acknowledgment of the truth divinity. This man he loved with entire honor and all observance, regarding him with an obedient veneration, not only as the friend and comrade of his soul, but as the parent of his new life....[12]

Pontius speaks of Caecilius as if he knew him intimately beyond ministerial colleagues. He displays sincerity in describing Caecilius' character and relationship with Cyprian and the entire Carthage church. Caecilius appears to be a mature Christian leader who influenced Cyprian, even when he ascended to the Bishop of Carthage. The relationship between Caecilius and Cyprian elicits images of Paul's relationship with Timothy, or St. Ignatius of Antioch (c50–c117 A.D.), to Bishop Polycarp (69–155 A.D.). Pontius describes the strength of their bond that developed to the extent that Cyprian cared for Caecilius' wife and children after his death. Their bond represented a complex relationship in Christ that strengthened throughout their friendship and ministerial service. Ultimately, it cultivated a genuine spiritual familial bond.[13] Absent is the presence of historical records regarding Caecilius' secular life and ministry in the Lord within Carthage. This applies likewise to Pontius. A striking correlation between these three men. Perhaps this is a testimony of their humility, shame from their former sinful lifestyle, and complete dedication to glorifying God in their then-current sanctified lives. Contemporary Spirit-empowered communities could benefit from reflecting upon this aspect of Cyprian, Pontius, and Caecilius' theological ethic of humility.

Cyprian and the Conception of Shame

To a certain extent, aspects of contemporary Western society have sought to redefine and displace our traditional conception of shame. Sociocultural and religiopolitical ideologies have encouraged people to reject their feelings of shame and urged them to violate social norms, and government laws when they oppose how certain people construct their identities and how they choose to live in the world. These individuals are encouraged to be unapologetic for being proud of who they are. In principle, these declarations have legitimacy within specific contexts. However, these ideologies are destructive when employed to secularize Christianity and ultimately remove its influence within Western society. Consequently, these ideologies allow people to redefine sin as something else and possibly reinterpret sin as a subjective religious concept associated with a fictitious god. Matters are complicated when these secular ideologies influence Christians, attempting to sanctify them and synthesizing these beliefs with Christian principles. Thus, we currently live in a Western society where shame and humility are absent, which elicits the rise of fierce pride and narcissism.

Yet, Cyprian, Pontius, and Caecilius provide our Spirit-empowered communities with powerful testimonies. They are testimonies of humility and healthy expressions of shame that avoid the possibility of glorifying their sinful secular lifestyles. These men primarily focused on praising God, and their former lives were only relevant in demonstrating the repentance, forgiveness, and reconciliation achieved within Christ Jesus. Cyprian was a Spirit-empowered Christian who the Lord used to progress through the religiopolitical structure of the Catholic Church. Cyprian was roughly forty-six years old when he converted to Christianity and was baptized into the faith around 246 A.D. It is essential to interpret him in community with Christians like Caecilius and Pontius, who taught and learned from Cyprian throughout his episcopate. I argue that in Cyprian's life and ministry, we witness the convergence, the synthesis of the baptism of the Holy Spirit, and the baptism of Suffering within the context of persecution.

Persecution: Cyprian's Faith in Context

Cyprian was not ignorant of Christian persecution before his physical and spiritual birth. As a Roman citizen of prominence, it is safe to assume that he was aware of the various Christian persecutions that occurred under Roman emperors. For example, there was Emperor Nero (54–68 A.D.), Domitian (81–96 A.D.), Trajan (98–117 A.D.), Hadrian (117–138 A.D.), and possibly the massacre of Lyons and Vienne during 177 A.D. under Marcus Aurelius (161–180 A.D.), Septimius Severus (193–211 A.D.) and Maximinus Thrax (235–238 A.D.).[14] These were clear demonstrations of the skewed Roman religiopolitical disdain for Christianity. Moreover, there is the likelihood of various historiographies within Christian and non-Christian religiopolitical traditions that provided different interpretations of these persecutions. It is not difficult to surmise the level of reflection received by Cyprian as he utilized his legal mind in discerning the level of rationale that elicited the variant demonstrations of Christian persecution.

Additionally, Caecilius influenced Cyprian, and it is reasonable that he and other Christians provided Cyprian with their experiences of discrimination and opinions of these irrational Roman religiopolitical persecutions. Cyprian admired the writing and theology of Tertullian (155–220 A.D.). Tertullian and other influential Christian martyrs likely informed Cyprian's view of Christian persecution. Nevertheless, we can entertain the possibility that Cyprian's baptism of the Spirit and baptism of suffering was anticipated, desired to a certain extent, and obtained within the community of the saints that transcended geography and time. The ancient union of these faithful believers with their Triune God had reinforced the principles of repentance, forgiveness, and reconciliation in the context of impending death, *vis-à-vis* sacrificial service. I am reasoning from historical *realism* and contemporary religiopolitical criticism, elevating the sacrifices of the ancient church, and reexamining aspects of our current Western American church through its *exaggerated* perceptions of persecution.

I argue that elements of the Western church vicariously project themselves upon the ancient church, to reimagine itself within the context of extreme persecution. Through concealed religious identity politics, this vicarious projection assists aspects of the Western church in establishing itself as the ideal representation and embodiment of Spirit-filled Christians over other Christians worldwide. Our contemporary Spirit-empowered communities could benefit from reflecting upon this view. The taint of this skewed religious vicarious projection contributes to the irrational religious fanaticism observed within the Western church, perpetuating the identity politics that decays aspects of our sanctified faith. Unfortunately, this process pushes people away from Christianity, the church, and biblical interpretations of Christ Jesus. Cyprian's focus on repentance, forgiveness, and reconciliation which formed his ecclesiology and conception of Christian leadership, was refined in the context of persecution. From here, we will briefly discuss elements of the church's schisms, persecution, and plague that further revealed aspects of Cyprian's ethics.

The Turmoil of Cyprian's Episcopate

In 248 A.D., Cyprian was elected Bishop of Carthage.[15] Two years later, in 250 A.D., Emperor Decius pronounced an edict that initiated the persecution of Christians, caused a massive division within the church, and strengthened the power of the Roman religiopolitical world.[16] Decius proclaimed an edict that forced all inhabitants of Rome to offer sacrifices to the Roman State and its ancestral gods. Roman citizens who submitted to the mandate and gave their religiopolitical sacrifice had received a Certificate of Peace (*Libelli Pacis*), also known as a Certificate of Sacrifice. Cyprian was infuriated by these Christians; some were clergy who relinquished their faith upon hearing the edict. Those who submitted were known as the *lapsi* or the lapsed: former Christians turned apostates. Cyprian comments on the initial irrational response of some of these individuals, stating: "Immediately at the first words of the threatening foe, the greatest number of the brethren betrayed their faith, and were cast down, not by the onset of persecution, but cast themselves down by voluntary lapse."[17] Cyprian asserts the fear of the edict and the compulsion of self-preservation compelled former believers to leave the church voluntarily.

The lapsed were typically placed in three categories. First, there is the *sacrificati*. These individuals had sacrificed to an idol via the Roman state and its gods. Second, there were the *thurificati*, individuals who burnt incense at the altar of the Roman gods. Last, the *libellatici* were individuals who bribed Roman officials into providing them with certificates to deceive people into thinking they obeyed the mandate.[18] In a touching display, Cyprian expressed his anguish from a former sister in Christ who turned away from the church, becoming a *sacrificati*. Cyprian writes:

> And, therefore, I ask that you will grant my desire, and that you will grieve with me at the death of my sister, who in this time of devastation has fallen from Christ; for she has sacrificed and provoked the Lord, as seems manifest to us. And for her deeds, I in this day of paschal rejoicing, weeping day and night, have spent the days in tears, in sackcloth, and ashes, and I am still spending them so to this day, until the aid of our Lord Jesus Christ, and affection manifested through you, or through those my Lords who have been crowned, from whom you are about to ask it, shall come to the help of so terrible a shipwreck.[19]

Cyprian's pastoral heart ached at knowing people with whom he developed a deep bond had abandoned their love for Christ Jesus. We can only imagine the level of anxiety, depression, and vulnerability Cyprian felt during these moments of physical and spiritually violent persecution. However, there were loyal Christians who rebelled against Decius' decree. These were the Christian martyrs and confessors. Martyrs received two categories: those killed, and individuals tortured, imprisoned, and thought to die eventually. The confessors were those Christians who proudly proclaimed their faith, rejected the mandate and embraced their torture and imprisonment.

Decius' edict caused Cyprian and other Christians to flee from persecution.[20] Their decision ignited further conflict and division within the church from individuals who previously expressed disdain towards Cyprian. Some of Cyprian's opponents questioned his leadership, accusing him of cowardice during this period. Henk Bakker comments on the then-current questioning of Cyprian's escape, which is justifiably still scrutinized by contemporary readers. Bakker pointedly explains:

> During the vacancy of its pivotal leadership the Church was endangered by intricacies and intrusion as well. Cyprian's well considered 'escape' was, by all means, a hazardous enterprise, though he kept 'in tune' with the Carthaginian congregation by writing pastoral letters on a regular basis. The bishop's motives for the 'retreat' are unclear and remain a mystery to us.[21]

Bakker later references Cyprian and Tertullian's disagreement regarding martyrdom and fleeing from persecution. Tertullian was a strong-minded Christian who is interpreted as endorsing martyrdom over and beyond fleeing from persecution. The implications being Tertullian appeared to interpret cowardice and self-preservation as the motives for running. Cyprian disagreed, and Bakker reinforced a positive view of Cyprian's actions. Bakker indicates a particular passage where Cyprian implies that, although he went into hiding, if the Roman authorities truly wanted to capture him, they would find him.[22]

The Novation Schism was another concern for Cyprian. St. Fabian was the Bishop of Rome from 236 A.D. to his martyrdom in 250 A.D., during the initial Decian persecution. Fabian's death eventually led in 251 A.D. to the election of Cornelius as the new Bishop of Rome. Bishop Cornelius and Cyprian agreed that restoration was possible for the lapsed if they performed various penance. The election of Cornelius and the restoration of the lapsed were opposed by Novatian (200–258 A.D.), a scholar and theologian. Between 251–258 A.D., Novatian was elected the antipope. He argued that only God could forgive the lapsed; therefore, repentance, forgiveness, and reconciliation of the lapsed into the fellowship of the saints was impossible. For Novatian, the lapsed were alienated from the church regardless of their desire to return to the church. Eventually, Novatian was excommunicated from the church, and scholars believe in 258 A.D., he was martyred during the Valerian persecution. In 251 A.D., the Decian persecution ended, and Cyprian returned to the public's eye from hiding, continuing to refute the church's enemies and provide biblical leadership to the saints.

Cyprian was a Christian leader who not only endured persecution through relying on his faith and love for Christ but also from his calling to serve, protect, and edify God's people. Another testimony of Cyprian's strong will and empathetic heart is witnessed throughout one of the most destructive plagues in recorded history: The Plague of Cyprian.[23]

The Plague of Cyprian

A testament of a Christian's faith can be explored in various ways. For some people, it rests within their ability to endure persecution. Others may express the genuineness of their faith in the ability to survive chaotic events and exhibit their Christ-like disposition upon facing death. The Roman Empire experienced a destructive pandemic from roughly 250–270 A.D., known as the Plague of Cyprian. Some scholars advocated that around 252 A.D., the plague decimated Carthage. Pontius and Cyprian provide crucial accounts of its destruction within Carthage. Pontius' account of the plague is informative and intriguing from a psychosocial perspective. He provides a view of the plague's devastation of Carthage, but also the behavior of certain people towards it, most of which represents a complete disregard for human life:

> Afterwards there broke out a dreadful plague, and excessive destruction of a hateful disease invaded every house in succession of the trembling populace, carrying off day by day with abrupt attack numberless people, everyone from his own house. All were shuddering, fleeing, shunning the contagion, impiously exposing their own friends, as if with the exclusion of the person who was sure to die of the plague, one could exclude death itself also.[24]

The destructive plague did not discriminate based upon one's ethnicity, gender, nationality, political views, religion, or social status. Everyone suffered. Although the precise nature of the plague is ambiguous, it attacked its victims in ways some scholars in our contemporary period would view as anthrax, the Bubonic plague, the Ebola virus, influenza, and smallpox.[25] Pontius recounts how the plague created enormous fear from the populace relating to the incessant death toll that increased its casualties daily. Pontius explains that many people attempted to avoid and ignore the plague in ways that demonstrated a surprising form of escapism. Particular attention is upon Pontius' reference to people exposing everyone, including their friends, to the epidemic as if endowed with a special immunity.

Another shocking element in Pontius' account is the absence of the human will to live. Some individuals had seemingly randomly and callously exposed other healthy and innocent people to the plague's destructive effects on the human body. Perhaps they felt their gods would protect them regardless of their ignorance. Here we witness the binary-oppositional conscience and behavior to the Christian principles of self-sacrificial love and service to our neighbor. We also see the confusion, fear, and inability of some people to handle their current pandemic in reasonable ways.

Pontius mentions, "There lay about the meanwhile, over the whole city, no longer bodies, but the carcasses of many, and, by the contemplation of a lot which in their turn would be theirs, demanded the pity of the passer-by for themselves."[26] The implication of Pontius' expression is the absence of personalization for those victims of the plague. They ceased being mothers, daughters, sons, fathers, etc., in the new reality of humanistic despair devoid of eschatological hope. Bodies became impersonal carcasses representing the human mind and body's fragility. Those suffering had laid among the corpses, understanding they too would decay from personalization to depersonalization, a person with concrete identities with decreasing vitality to a lifeless unidentifiable figure. Pontius depicts the cruel selfishness of those seeking to survive this horrific event: "No one did to another what he himself wished to experience."[27] Here we see the binary-oppositional principle of the scriptural Golden Rule, displayed in Luke 6:31, "Treat people the same way you want them to treat you."

Pontius describes the context from which Cyprian felt a deep need to aid everyone. Their pandemic created a context whereby divine revelation and the divine presence emerged. The Holy Spirit sought to demonstrate the love of Christ for humanity through those Christians who submitted to him through their passion for their Triune God.

Cyprian, the Holy Spirit, and COVID-19

There are striking similarities between what Cyprian and countless other people experiences relating to our current situation with the COVID-19 pandemic. Our contemporary period has experienced a global catastrophe claiming millions of lives. COVID-19 has decimated families and relationships and deeply affected people's religious faith in various ways. However, a persisting frustration connected to sheer shock rests in how our contemporary plague has been politicized within the secular and religious worlds. The hyper-politicizing of COVID-19 exacerbates the realistic levels of fear, paranoia, and trauma we have experienced worldwide. Hyper-politicizing creates challenges for those who are strong within their religious faith, and those who embody a genuine secular humanism that establishes the necessary empathy to care for anyone suffering. How often have we witnessed responses to COVID separating Western America through Democrat and Republican party lines? What were your thoughts about seeing people being defiant, refusing to wear protective masks, and practicing a distance of six feet from one another to minimize the spread of disease? How do we process the individuals who refused to believe COVID-19 was a "real" disease, but rather a political "illusion" to manipulate the masses, despite the increasing casualties, including those within their network of friends and family?

Pontius refers to Cyprian as the "Pontiff of Christ" and one who was well-equipped to unite and empower Christians within the plague. Pontius alludes to Cyprian uniting the Carthian Christians, emphasizing their Christian responsibility, faith in Christ, and importance of being empathetic towards the human-Other:

> Then afterwards he subjoined, that there was nothing wonderful in our cherishing our own people only with the needed attention of love, but that he might become perfect who would do something more than the publican or the heathen, who, overcoming evil with good, and preaching a clemency which was like the divine clemency, loved even his enemies, who would pray for the salvation of those that persecuted him, as the Lord admonishes and exhorts.[28]

God rewards his children who sincerely sacrifice themselves for the betterment of those around them. The reward is often a heightened experience of God's presence and love, in conjunction with the individual in union with God, maturing further into the image of Christ. The two

New Testament commandments usher the human conscious and spirit to focus outside themselves and onto God and humanity to fulfill its full potential as God's children in a fallen world. Cyprian, influenced by these and other biblical principles, touches the collective spirits of his Spirit-empowered community and assists in increasing its members. Former and current enemies, former and current persecutors of Christians who inflicted pain and trauma upon them, were forgiven and provided a level of compassion that saturated their context with God's presence. Cyprian's account of events demonstrates a deep spiritual awareness of what was occurring in his present time. He fully understood his responsibility as a Christian leader, and how this related to the divine message he was commissioned to preach to the Carthian Christians, as they physically aided everyone within Carthage.

Cyprian's account of the plague was cataloged in his treatise, *On Mortality*. He is conscious of the strong-willed and Spirit-empowered Christians enduring the trials and temptations of the epidemic. Yet, he expressed a deep concern for those whose faith was weakened and shattered by the catastrophic event, which lasted for roughly twenty years. Verses like Luke 21:11 guide Cyprian: "and there will be massive earthquakes, and in various places plagues and famines; and there will be terrible sights and great signs from heaven." For him, true faith, in part, is strengthened by understanding the prophetic word of Christ, and knowing the Spirit precedes us in preparing our current perseverance and future victory. Cyprian exclaimed: "Behold, the very things occur which were spoken; and since those occur which were foretold before, whatever things were promised will also follow; as the Lord himself promises, saying, 'But when you see all these things come to pass, know that the kingdom of God is at hand'" (Luke 21:31).[29] The Christian's experience, faith, love, and self-sacrifice are conduits of the Holy Spirit, which create the kingdom of God within our hearts, and gradually manifest its presence on earth. Cyprian questions the believer's affection and overall dependence upon their present world, relating to their salvation and security in Christ. Self-worship through preserving one's life at the neglect or expense of the human-Other is an irrational desire. It rejects our eternal eschatological promise for a temporal existence of sinful pleasure.

Cyprian understood the danger of helping those suffering from the plague. He viewed those dangers as justified and necessary in fulfilling the Christian's responsibility on earth. Fragments of the eschatological fulfillment and kingdom of God were partially experienced by those who laid down their life for others in need. Those individuals who could not fend for themselves, those impaired by anxiety, depression, and chronic physical pain, were highly valued in a world that discarded them as deceased when they were still breathing. Yet, never to romanticize scripture or the reality of their current situation, Cyprian was well aware of the issues that disturbed the Carthage Christian community:

> But, nevertheless, it disturbs some that the power of this disease attacks our people equally with the heathens, as if the Christian believed for this purpose, that he might have the enjoyment of the world and this life free from the contact of ills; and not as one who undergoes all adverse things here and is reserved for future joy. It disturbs some that this mortality is common to us with others; and yet what is there in this world, which is not common to use with others, so long as this flesh of ours still remains, according to the law of the first birth, common to us with them? So long as we are here in the world, we are associated with the human race in fleshly equality but are separate in spirit.[30]

For Cyprian, all Christians are called to a baptism of suffering. Scriptural clarity was necessary for the Christian regarding what this baptism entailed and that we do so in community and not in isolation when undergoing it. He emphasized it was through the power of the Holy Spirit, in communion with the saints, which established the evangelistic aim to bring the unbeliever into the experience of our eschatological hope. Collective suffering was not a sign of communal righteousness, but a conduit of empathetic connection between the saved and unsaved. Collective suffering established a set of shared experiences whereby the presence and activity of God were seen as it related to the saved serving the unsaved.

Within the darkness resided a glimmer of light, and within the presence of despair arose transformative spiritual hope. Cyprian testifies to the Holy Spirit moving among Jews, Gentiles, Christians, and non-believers that united everyone through their universal humanity (Imago Dei). He states,

> By the dread of the mortality and of the time the lukewarm are inflamed, the slack are nerved up, the slothful are stimulated, the deserters are compelled to return, the heathens are constrained to believe, the ancient congregation of the faithful is called to rest, the new and abundant army is gathered to the

battle with a braver vigor, to fight without fear of death when the battle shall come, because it comes to the warfare in the time of the mortality.[31]

Cyprian experienced the remarkable transformative power of the Spirit as people turned towards Christ amid uncertainty and death. The tragedy of the plague was a context and conduit for the creation of empathy, love, self-sacrifice, and salvation for those who responded to Yahweh's voice. Within this view, we can interpret and connect the inner spiritual transformation of empowerment with sanctification vis-à-vis conforming to the Image of Christ (Imago Christi). Spirit-empowerment, in this context, is character transformation through genuine love for Christ that overflows upon the human-Other, fulfilling the two New Testament commandments and the Great Commission.

Salvation did not provide a special privilege that liberated the Christian from pain and suffering. Rather, salvation was intricately connected to a series of purposes centered on the will of God. Christians and non-Christians experienced pain, suffering, trauma, and tragedy together. These elements were chosen conduits to create, instill, embody, and display sincere love and self-sacrifice for the human-Other. The Spirit would use the genuine empathy of the unsaved for the saved for his purposes. In Cyprian's view, to be disturbed by the equality we share with non-Christians was to deny or be ignorant of the prophetic word of God, which informs us of why and how we are victorious even when experiencing physical death. The aim, in part, was to help establish physical and spiritual equality within Christ.

Cyprian provides one of the most vivid descriptions of those suffering from the plague. Yet, despite this knowledge, he was not deterred from representing Christ to those inflicted with the various deteriorating effects of the pandemic. The reader is left in relative awe and fear when Cyprian explains:

> This trial, that now the bowels, relaxed into a constant flux, discharge the bodily strength; that a fire originated in the marrow ferments into wounds of the faces; that the intestines are shaken with a continual vomiting; that the eyes are on fire with the injected blood; that in some cases the feet or some parts of the limbs are taken off by the contagion of diseased putrefaction; that from the weakness arising by the maiming and loss of the body, either the gait is enfeebled, or the hearing is obstructed, or the sight darkened—is profitable as a proof of faith.[32]

We must empathetically understand that Cyprian witnessed numerous people experiencing the horrific effects of the plague firsthand. He was surrounded by countless carcasses, smells, and the fear and paranoia of the people; yet this did not deter him from mobilizing the Carthian Christian community to help everyone in need. Everyone needed to be saturated in the love of Christ. How can we relate to Cyprian and the Spirit-empowered Christians of the Carthian church? Does the Western American church represent those Carthian Christians who existed in a distorted form of Christian escapism? Or have we preached and embodied the gospel to those who suffered and died during our contemporary pandemic?

Cyprian exhibited outstanding leadership, compassion, and self-sacrifice in this chaos by helping those who suffered. That same year witnessed the rise of Valerian as emperor of Rome. Four years later, Valerian reignited the Roman religiopolitical disdain for Christianity. Valarian persecution began in 257 A.D., bringing about the death of Cyprian through beheading on September 14th, 258 A.D. Our discussion of Cyprian's Spirit-filled life and commendable leadership does not end at his physical death. It concludes by examining the condition of his heart that governed his life, ministry, and theology.

Empathetic Resonance: Forgiveness, Repentance, Reconciliation

The presence of ambiguity, concealment, and deception within the church had shaped aspects of Cyprian's ecclesiology. Cyprian obtained self-awareness of these issues through biblical testimony and divine discernment. This belief and examples within the church reinforced Cyprian's adherence to his responsibility as a Christian leader to remain conscious of his salvific journey. I am referring to his sinful secular life and the Christians that God brought into his life to lead him to the process of repentance, forgiveness, and reconciliation. This personal experience was the foundation for the empathy and humanizing actions Cyprian expressed towards the human-Other, both saved and unsaved. Cyprian's empathy and humility governed how he ministered to Christians and the apostates of his time, as well as his commitment to reinforcing the spiritual authority of the church. These elements are intertwined.

Cyprian was adamant that there is only one true spiritual Church established by the birth, death, and resurrection of Christ Jesus. Genuine salvation is only achieved through Christ, and his Church on earth is the sole conduit for the process of repentance, forgiveness, and reconciliation. In his thirt-nineth letter, Cyprian states, "There is one God, and Christ is one, and there is one Church, and one chair founded upon the rock by the word of the Lord."[33] In one of his most influential treatises, *On the Unity of the Church*, Cyprian exclaims:

> God is one, and Christ is one, and his Church is one, and the faith is one, and the people are joined into a substantial unity of the body by the cement of concord. Unity cannot be severed; nor can one body be separated by a division of its structure, nor torn into pieces, with its entrails wrenched asunder by laceration. Whatever has proceeded from the womb cannot live and breathe in its detached condition but loses the substance of health.[34]

Individuals could only obtain a Spirit-infused life in Christ through the sole conduit of the Church, and only decay that led to death existed outside of the Church. This demarcation is witnessed in Cyprian's verbal expression of his spirit and heart for the lapsed:

> If we reject the repentance of those who have some confidence in a conscience that may be tolerated; at once with their wife, with their children, whom they had kept safe, they are hurried by the devil's invitation into heresy or schism; and it will be attributed to us in the day of judgment, that we have not cared for the wounded sheep, and that on account of a single wounded one we have lost many sound ones. And whereas the Lord left the ninety and nine that were whole, and sought after the one wandering and weary, and Himself carried it, when found, upon His shoulders, we not only do not seek the lapsed, but even drive them away when they come to us; and while false prophets are not ceasing to lay waste and tear Christ's flock, we give an opportunity to dogs and wolves, so that those whom a hateful persecution has not destroyed, we ruin by our hardness and inhumanity.[35]

Cyprian understood the distorted reasoning that compelled some former Christians to forfeit their faith. He also displayed emotional intelligence in empathizing with those who wanted to be forgiven and reconciled. Some people left or created the illusion of rejecting the church to save their families. Cyprian was convicted, likely from the Spirit, that to reject someone's genuine repentance was a greater sin than those committed by some of the lapsed. Christ Jesus is the apex example of seeking out the lost to forgive and reconcile with God and Jesus' Spirit-empowered family. Cyprian chose to forgive and reconcile individuals who sincerely repented for their sins. He refused to reject family members whom Christ had embraced. "We ruin by our hardness and inhumanity," is a difficult portion of Cyprian's statement that causes self-examination regarding those who refused the repentance, forgiveness, and reconciliation of the former lapsed. Some of these individuals, clergy or not, were not of Christ, and if they were, were not Spirit-empowered and made their decisions from apathy and pride.

Conclusion

My discussion of Cyprian concludes by encouraging the Spirit-empowered global community to engage the writings of St. Cyprian of Carthage. Your engagement with Cyprian's writing will expose you to the complexity of who he was as a Spirit-filled Christian, a bishop with a pastoral heart, and a Christian leader whose love for Christ extended to the human-Other. Unfortunately, I could not articulate the complexity of Cyprian's life, ministry, and theology within this brief discussion. However, the Holy Spirit is our teacher and will instruct anyone who continues to learn about the influential bishop of Carthage. I hope through engaging his work, the Spirit who dwells within us will enrich your life, ministry, and love for the human-Other as they seek repentance, forgiveness, and reconciliation with our Lord and Savior, Jesus Christ.

Notes

1 Kenneth J. Stewart provides a penetrating religiocultural critique of what he views as an increasing identity crisis within Western evangelicalism. Stewart, in part, seeks to excavate and meticulously explore the Protestant Evangelical roots within the ancient church. Contemporary Spirit-empowered communities, and Christians who seek fuller knowledge of their spiritual heritage, would benefit from engaging Stewart's scholarship. See, Kenneth J. Stewart, In *Search of Ancient Roots: The Christian Past and the Evangelical Identity Crisis* (Downers Grove, IL: IVP Academic, 2017).

2 There are different forms of secular and Christian racialized nationalism. Three examples are represented by the Oath Keepers, Proud Boys, and Three Percenters. These groups are classified as Far-Right, Neo-Fascist,

para-military organizations involved in the January 6th, 2021, United States Capital riot. The New Black Panther Party and Not Fooling* Around Coalition are considered extremist Black nationalist organizations.

3 The Hermeneutic of Equality is an elusive concept employed within contemporary secular and religious sociopolitical beliefs. It is an obscure set of contextualized ideas that are often self-contradictory and internally incoherent regarding the harmony of reasoning, actions, and goals. The primary aim of individuals and groups who employ the hermeneutic is to promote a generalized conception of equality. However, the very definition of equality is questionable as the logical qualitative and quantitative differences in life that define reality are disregarded to satisfy the individual or group's self-interest.

4 There are roughly twelve treatises, three books, and eighty-two letters attributed to Cyprian. My aim is not to cover every aspect of his written work or discuss his primary theological focuses. Cyprian was a complex church father, and it is impossible to convey the complexity of his character and ministry within this brief discussion. Instead, I am attempting to initiate specific reflection and contribute to established discourses upon his life and ministry for the global Spirit-empowered community.

5 Pontius and Saint Cyprian, "The Life and Passion of Cyprian by Pontius the Deacon," *The Complete Works of Saint Cyprian of Carthage*, Phillips Campbell, ed. (Merchantville, NJ: Evolution Publishing, 2013), 3–4. John Alfred Faulkner, *Cyprian the Churchman* (Marrickville, Australia: Wentworth Press, 2016), 18–19. Brian J. Arnold, *Cyprian of Carthage: His Life & Impact* (Fearn, UK: Christian Focus, 2017), 33–35. Vincent Hunink, "St. Cyprian, A Christian and Roman Gentleman," *Cyprian of Carthage: Studies in His Life, Language, and Thought*, Henk Bakker, Paul van Geest, and Hans van Loon, eds. (Leuven, Belgium: Peeters Publishers Leuven, 2010), 36. Lactantius, "Divine Institutes, Book V.1.," https://www.newadvent.org/fathers/07015.htm, accessed December 20, 2021.

6 Cyprian, "Letter 1: To Donatus," 284.

7 Cyprian, "Letter 1: To Donatus," 284.

8 Michael Haykin, "The Holy Spirit in Cyprian's to Donatus," *Evangelical Quarterly: An International Review of Bible and Theology in Defense of Historic Christian Faith* 83:4 (October 2011): 321–329.

9 Haykin provides an alternative interpretation from Campbell's reference of the word "breathing" by using the word "drank," 323. Haykin relies upon an interpretation by Allen Bent. See Allen Bent, *On the Church: Select Treatise, St. Cyprian* (Yonkers: SVS Press, 2011), 52.

10 St. Jerome (c342-420) references Cyprian and Pontius in *On Illustrious Men*. Cyprian and Pontius are discussed in chapters 67 and 68.

11 Cyprian, "The Life and Passion of Cyprian," 3–4.

12 Cyprian, "The Life and Passion of Cyprian," 5.

13 Faulkner mentions that Cyprian took the name of Caecilius at his baptism. From this perspective, we can surmise a certain level of intimacy, influence, and love between the two men. However, Campbell posits the possibility that Caecilius was kin of Cyprian. Campbell asserts that the Caecili was a "notable family in Republican Rome who managed to maintain their prestigious position under the empire." Faulkner, *Cyprian the Churchman*, 20; Cyprian, "The Life and Passion of Cyprian,"16–17; Arnold, *Cyprian of Carthage*, 38; Hunink, "St. Cyprian," 36.

14 Henry Bettenson and Chris Maunder *Documents of the Christian Church* (New York: Oxford University Press, 2011), 9–15; William Byron Forbush, *Fox's Book of Martyrs* (Grand Rapids: Zondervan, 1954), 5–22; Euseibus, *The History of the Church from Christ to Constantine*, G. A. Williamson trans. (New York: New York University Press, 1966), 96–98, 103–105, 110, 188, 273–280, 287, 292–298; Justo L. Gonzalez, *The Story of Christianity, Volume 1: The Early Church to the Dawn of the Reformation* (New York: Harper One, 2010), 43–58. Bakker, et al., *Cyprian of Carthage*, 59, 61, 71, 72; Arnold, *Cyprian of Carthage*, 45–46, 49–53.

15 Kyle Harper, *The Fate of Rome: Climate, Disease, and the End of an Empire* (Princeton University Press, 2019), 136.

16 Arnold, *Cyprian of Carthage*, 65. Bakker, et al., *Cyprian of Carthage*, viii, 1, 35, 61, 71, 165, 178; Faulkner, *Cyprian the Churchman*, 66–71.

17 Cyprian, "On the Lapsed," 54.

18 Arnold 2017, 75. Bakker, Geest, and Loon 2010, 12; 13; 48; 53; 56; 71; 150; 205-207; 219; 220; 221; 270.

19 Cyprian, "Letter 20: Celerinus to Lucian," 325–326.

20 Bakker, et al., *Cyprian of Carthage*, 50, 72.

21 Bakker, et al., *Cyprian of Carthage*, 50.

22 Bakker, et al., *Cyprian of Carthage*, 61–62, 72.

23 Unfortunately, in some academic circles, Cyprian's views of the plague may be questionable and unreliable. Harper references the neglect of Cyprian's account of the plague by various contemporary scholars of antiquity. Harper states, "This neglect has many causes, including changing fashions that have tried to question the severity of the third-century crisis. But more

subtly, the neglect originates in a failure to appreciate how exceptional true pandemic events have been." Harper, *The Fate of Rome*, 136.

24 Cyprian, "The Life and Passion of Cyprian," 8.

25 Harper, *The Fate of Rome*, 141-142.

26 Cyprian, "The Life and Passion of Cyprian," 8.

27 Cyprian, "The Life and Passion of Cyprian," 8.

28 Cyprian, "The Life and Passion of Cyprian," 9.

29 Cyprian, "The Life and Passion of Cyprian," 9.

30 Cyprian, "On Mortality," 119.

31 Cyprian, *On Mortality*, 123.

32 Cyprian, "On Mortality," 122.

33 Cyprian, "Letter 39: To the People, Concerning Five Schismatic Presbyters," 362.

34 Cyprian, "On the Unity of The Church," 32.

35 Cyprian, "Letter 51: To Antonianus About Cornelius and Novation," 387–388.

4 Pentecostals Among the Plagues: Early Chinese Pentecostal Theologies of Sickness, Healing, and Pandemics

Alex Mayfield

Abstract

This study will examine early Chinese Pentecostal views on healing and sickness and ascertain how these affected their responses to contagious disease. First, it will investigate the cultural backdrop for Pentecostal healing by exploring the competing conceptions of sickness and health in the medical marketplace of southern China. Second, it will look at how early Chinese Pentecostals interacted with and responded to this mix through their own historical experiences with plague, sickness, and healing. It will conclude with a reflection on how early Chinese Pentecostal views correspond to more recent Pentecostal responses to the COVID-19 pandemic.

Introduction

> *The plague is raging in Hong Kong, but we have the lintel and the two side posts of our doors covered with the Blood of the Lamb . . . As yet none of us have caught the plague, not a single soul, but please look at Deut 7:15. May the Lord have mercy. The total number of cases of the plague here have been near a thousand, and all fatal, except about fifty. Not one of us are a bit afraid.*[1]

"Pentecostal" and "plague" are two words that rarely find themselves in the same sentence. One recalls images of fire, revival, and modern televangelists. The other evokes pictures of rats, death, and medieval peasants. Yet, when Mok Lai Chi sat down to write his letter to *The Apostolic Faith* in the early summer of 1908, the two words could not be more intimately related. Between May and June of that year, over 750 people in Hong Kong died of the plague. By the end of the year, the count would be almost 1,000.[2] Unfortunately, this was not the first and would not be the last time that plague would strike the city. Between 1895 and 1929, successive waves of plague continued to "rage" in Hong Kong, ultimately killed over 20,000 people. All the while, Mok and his Chinese and Western co-workers were getting their Pentecost and taking shelter under the Blood of the Lamb. These early Pentecostals believed in the power of God to save them from plagues, sickness, and death, and they cited scriptural passages like Deuteronomy 7:15 and Psalm 91:10 as their sources. Many went so far as refusing medicine—both Western and Chinese varieties. If anyone doubted this approach, Pentecostal periodicals published articles and testimonies which illustrated that God could heal even the most dangerous diseases.

Yet, those are not all the stories told by Pentecostals in and around Hong Kong. Besides the glowing reports of healing, there were also obituaries. While no reports of plague deaths were reported among Pentecostals in Hong Kong, there were several recorded instances where Pentecostals died from other tropical diseases like malaria, smallpox, cholera, and dysentery.[3] These sorts of diseases had always been prominent in warm climes of southern China, but regional displacement during the nineteenth and early twentieth centuries helped to increase the spread of many contagions. The third plague pandemic, for example, began in Yunnan in 1855, continued for the next 104 years, and killed upwards of 12 million people, mostly in China and India. This human toll, measured both in deaths and emotional strain, provides an important backdrop for understanding the appeal and development of Pentecostal theology in China during the early twentieth century. More than a spiritual high for the believer, the experience of Spirit baptism was part-and-parcel of a belief system that promised access to divine healing and safety from deadly diseases. In the multireligious marketplace of China, this promise held a ready appeal to many would-be converts.

This study, then, will contextualize and analyze the basic views of sickness and healing among early Chinese Pentecostals to gain a better grasp of how global Pentecostalism responded to contagious disease. First, it will investigate the cultural backdrop for Pentecostal healing by exploring the competing conceptions of sickness and health which swirled in the polycentric medical marketplace of Southern China. Second, it will look at how early Chinese Pentecostals interacted with and responded to this mix through their own historical experiences with plague, sickness, and healing. Finally, it will conclude with a brief reflection on how early Chinese Pentecostal views on sickness and healing may or may not be helpful to modern Pentecostal communities.

Sickness and Healing in Late Nineteenth and Early Twentieth Century China

The Chinese healing arts always demonstrated a diverse array of practices and beliefs. Among healing practitioners, there were major philosophical differences about the root cause of disease, the proper way to treat them, and even the nature of the human person. Classically oriented scholars might privilege hierarchical cosmology in crafting their prescriptions, Daoist healers might focus on restoring the balance of yin and yang, traditional healers might seek to appease local spirits, and Buddhist monastics might help a sick person balance the four elements in their body. Of course, this litany assumes a clear distinction among practitioners, and such was not often the case.[4] Chinese medical practice often blended various systems together in an effort to achieve efficacious results.

By the middle of the nineteenth century, these diverse conceptions and practices were faced with two other claimants to the art of healing: Western medicine and Christian faith healing. Both modes of healing spread quickly in China throughout the nineteenth and early twentieth centuries. However, while earlier Chinese healers might have been happy to mix methodologies, both Western medical professionals and Christian faith healers took a far more exclusive approach to healing. Chinese Pentecostal conceptions of sickness and health were forged in this intense meeting of cultures, and Pentecostal approaches to healing often defined themselves against other forms of Chinese healing. Even still, notes of traditional approaches remained embedded within Chinese Pentecostal theology.[5] To better understand this, it is necessary to outline important aspects of traditional Chinese medicine.

Spirits and Relational Cosmology

The Book of Songs, written sometime between the eleventh and seventh centuries B.C.E., contains copious mentions of the spirits meeting out blessing and curses. As one poem warns, "A visit from the Spirits can never be foreseen; the better reason for not disgusting them."[6] Hence, from a very early time, Chinese cultures embraced multi-layered visions of reality where the realm of the spirits, gods, or ancestors could have dramatic impacts on the realm of human affairs. In this relational cosmology, spiritual causes were part of everyday existence. Spirits could be responsible for small inconveniences such as stubbed toes or losing your way, and they could cause the rise and fall of kingdoms, natural disasters, or epidemics.[7]

Early approaches to Chinese medicine incorporated this same worldview. Physical ailments were often treated as the result of spiritual causations. For example, medical texts from the Mawangdui manuscripts, dating to around 200 B.C.E, include numerous prescriptions which are exorcistic in nature.[8] One solution for curing swelling of the groin included the following incantation:

> Spirit of Heaven send down the sickness-shield. Spirit Maids according to sequence hear the spirit pronouncement. A certain fox has seized a place where it does not belong. Desist. If you do not desist, I will hack you with an axe.[9]

The Mawangdui texts also illustrate that this spiritual causation was in the process of being supplemented with more naturalistic explanations. Yet, despite these newer theories, supernatural causation retained a meaningful explanatory power to many Chinese people and practitioners of the healing arts. Incantations, exorcism rituals, and shamanistic healing were on display in the modern era when Christian missionaries arrived.

Personal Responsibility

Following the end of the Warring States period (221 B.C.E.), Chinese medicine began to incorporate more naturalistic theories to account for the causes of sickness and health. Called the "New Medicine" by Unschuld, these newer theories still exhibited the marks of relational cosmology, but they instead emphasized the internal relation of the body's organs to its external environment. Mirroring the ordering of the state under the Qin, these new theories sought to put the body in order through pacification and the creation of harmony. Various theories abounded, including vessel theory, yin-yang theory, and five-phase theory, but all held in common the belief that physical ailments were, by and large, logistical problems to be solved.

The ethos of these new methodologies was encapsulated most succinctly by the shared slogan of Ge Hong (ca. 280-340 C.E.) and Tao Hongjing (456–536 C.E.), "My fate lies in my own hands, not in Heaven!"[10] In other words, sickness was an obstacle to be overcome through dedicated study and personal discipline. People could obtain good health by correctly aligning their bodies—both internally and externally—with the observable nature of reality. Importantly, while this approach places the impetus on individuals to care for their own health, it also places high importance on medical practitioners who had detailed—and often conflicting—interpretative theories for how one should order one's body.

Medical Pragmatism

This, then, leads to a final important aspect of traditional Chinese medicine. Within a relational cosmology, health is the product of a number of interrelated and sometimes arcane connections to the various realms of existence. Discerning the cause and solution for an ailment, thus, is a complex procedure and rife with potential for error. Yet, the belief in a principled and ordered universe also meant that solutions could be found with enough trial and error; the theory may change, but the system does not. As such, Hong Hai observes that "The principle tenets of [traditional Chinese medicine] are not immutable laws of nature but pragmatic heuristic models found from empirical experience."[11] Chinese medicine is, if anything, about finding practical solutions.[12] And while this holds true for practitioners, it was doubly true for the masses of Chinese people who relied upon a medical field littered with religious/medical professionals with differing opinions. As medical professionals sought out the correct solutions, Chinese people sought out medical professionals who could offer more efficacious solutions. If one treatment did not work, they would move on to the next. This pragmatic approach to health explained the relatively quick embrace of Western medicine, but it was also important for Christian groups who practiced faith healing.

The relational cosmology, spiritual causation, emphasis on personal autonomy, and pragmatism of traditional Chinese medicine created an environment in which Pentecostal healing was readily understandable and a viable medical alternative for a great number of Chinese people. As the reasoning goes, if the Pentecostals' God could heal one of smallpox or protect one from the plague, then the Pentecostals must be doing something right.

Early Chinese Pentecostal Healing Among the Plagues

By the late nineteenth century, the health marketplace of China was quickly changing as new Western ideas and people began to compete with traditional Chinese conceptions. This is especially true for southern China, where the yearly spread of tropical diseases and the burgeoning plague pandemic were met in force—and perhaps perpetuated by—an influx of Western medical missionaries.[13] This meeting of medical cultures produced new institutional and public health initiatives which sought to bring the best of Chinese and Western medicine together to meet Chinese health needs. In Western controlled ports like Hong Kong, sanitarian approaches, like the quick disposal of bodies and regular cleaning of public spaces, were adopted to combat the spread of diseases like plague. Likewise, hospitals, like Hong Kong's Tung Wah Hospital, fused Western and Chinese medical practices to care for a Chinese populace wary of the new Western medicine.[14]

The reports and healing testimonies of early Chinese Pentecostals struck a very different tone. Rarely seeking to accommodate Chinese cultural norms, Pentecostal theologies of sickness and healing were often oriented directly against both Chinese and Western medical practices. Nevertheless, in the process of defining themselves against these competitors, early Chinese Pentecostals often retained aspects of both as they reoriented them into a Pentecostal theology of sickness and health.[15]

Pragmatic Conversion

Shortly after arriving in China, Alfred G. Garr pinned a letter to the British periodical *Confidence* as part of a global effort among Pentecostals to clear up the issue of "missionary tongues." Many of the earliest Pentecostal missionaries believed that God had given them the ability to speak foreign languages and that this ability would speed the evangelization of the world.[16] Garr had faced his own share of disappointment in not finding anyone who understood his tongues speech. Nevertheless, he came to believe that tongues were not really Pentecostals' largest asset. Theorizing on his own approach, he wrote:

> If I could speak Chinese perfectly and explain to the Chinese that God had given it to me without studying it, they would not believe, but would think I was deceiving them, and at the least there would be great room for doubt in their minds. But if we can come to them in the faith "once delivered to the saints," and in the name of Jesus heal their sick, lame, and blind, they cannot doubt that the blind were blind, nor the lame lame, but will have to know that this work is supernatural. [17]

Time would vindicate Garr's initial assessment. While theologies of tongues speech became theological hallmarks of classical Pentecostal groups in the West, healing was a preeminent doctrine among Chinese Pentecostals. This is largely because healing was why a great number converted. For those who were healed, the message of the Pentecostals simply "worked," and so they embraced the message that followed.

Virtually every issue of *Pentecostal Truths*, the first Chinese-language Pentecostal periodical, contained testimonies of healing or stories of conversion in which healing played a prominent role. These stories often followed a straightforward pattern: (1) a person was in ill health, (2) the person converted or received Spirit baptism, (3) they were healed and in good health. On one level, this pattern simply stresses the ability of Jesus to heal, but the model was often used as a rhetorical device to stress the effectiveness of the Pentecostal message over and against other forms of medicine. Mok Lai Chi even framed his own conversion using this paradigm in an early issue. Mok recalled that his family was continually in poor health despite frequent trips to the doctor and their embrace of Western medicine. His family was only "healed by Jesus" after he and his wife's Pentecostal baptism, after which the entire family was in good health and no longer "relied on the doctors and medicine of this world."[18]

The testimony of Tang Tong Shen, a Jiangsu native and captain in the Chinese navy, struck similar tones. Tang's fourth son became sick while he and his family were stationed outside Shanghai. Tang tried everything within his power, but even "famous doctors could not cure him," and his son seemed destined for the grave. Then, a relative told him about the Apostolic Faith church in Wusong and the miracles occurring therein. Tang determined that "wholehearted worship" was all that would save his son. He joined the church, and after weeks of prayer, his son recovered.[19] Another testimony of healing from Mrs. Lee Wu Si of Hong Kong recounted multiple instances of healing and conversion taking place in her family. In reflecting on this, she simply recalled, "There is an old Chinese saying: If there is no reaction to treatment, there is no cure."[20] Pentecostals' treatments for sickness—the laying on of hands, anointing with oil, intercessory prayer—produced reactions for many Chinese, and in finding the cure, they found God.

Pentecostals in China wholeheartedly embraced this pragmatic stance held by would-be converts, yet it came with a cost. Pentecostal missionaries and Chinese pastors quickly became known throughout the surrounding community as healing specialists and converts often treated them as if they alone had the power and specialized skillset to heal.[21] Even more problematic were issues caused when prayer was not answered. If a loved one died or ill health returned, people sometimes gave up the faith altogether. Not published as often in periodicals, Ethel Strickland, a missionary to Hong Kong, recalled the story of one Chinese couple whose child had died shortly after their conversion to Christianity. The couple had converted, hoping that the message of healing would prove efficacious. Strickland recalled that "on the day of the funeral the father having lost confidence in the Jesus doctrine turned again to his idols."[22] As one pragmatic option among many, the Pentecostal promise of healing was often set aside when it did not work as intended.

Personal Responsibility and Healing

[Healing, however, was more than a "good" on offer by early Chinese Pentecostals. Rather, believing in healing was an essential part of the Pentecostal gospel and a prerogative for every true believer. Reflecting on the sacrifice of Christ, one anonymous sermon summarized the high view of healing held by many Chinese Pentecostals:

> If we firmly follow God's truth, the Lord Jesus does not only save our souls but also heals our bodies. There are many sick people. Why is that? Because they do not believe in Jesus and rely on people. Jesus' sacrifice on Golgotha has two purposes. If we accept complete salvation, firstly, we will be saved by the Lord Jesus; secondly, we can be healed by him.[23]

Here, the author unites spiritual salvation and physical healing into a singular work of divine atonement. To be healed by Jesus, one must trust in Jesus and demonstrating that trust often entailed a very specific set of requirements laid out by Chinese Pentecostal communities.

This tight connection between healing and salvation among early Chinese Pentecostals was an inheritance from earlier Holiness groups who also practiced faith healing.[24] Groups like A. B. Simpson's Christian and Missionary Alliance placed a heavy emphasis on the power of the "Great Physician" in their missionary work in China. Likewise, the earliest Chinese theologies of Pentecostal healing mirrored hardline Holiness stances, which construed sanctification as freedom from sin and its physical manifestations (i.e., sickness).[25] If one was not freed from sin, as the logic goes, then one could not be free from its effects. This connection helps clarify the above testimonies, which linked healing and conversion and Pentecostal baptism. Individuals' soteriological experiences were mirrored in their physiological experiences.

This hardline stance led to two extremes. First, this approach to sickness has the potential for stigmatizing those who fail to receive healing. Pentecostals would not have agreed with Ge Hong and Tao Hongjing's slogan, "My fate lies in my own hands, not in Heaven!" Yet, they would agree that people were often responsible for their own lack of healing. As one author noted, "Many people do not understand the significance of Jesus' body, so they suffer from diseases and die. Since they rely on doctors, the power of Jesus' atonement is hampered."[26]

The second extreme was one that early Chinese Pentecostals shared with other Pentecostal groups in the West: a disdain for professional medical care and taking medicine. At best, medicine was simply portrayed as less of a less effective product. Testimonies of healing from sickness or disease regularly stressed the inability of doctors—Western and Chinese—to heal ailments that were healed by God. Li Shing Fat, a Pentecostal in Hong Kong, testified that in his old life as an "idol worshipper," he enjoyed burning gospel tracts. When he became sick, his family took him to all the best doctors, but nothing worked. After he listened to his relatives and converted, he received the baptism in the Spirit, and his incurable sickness was healed.[27] On the more extreme side, some Pentecostals vilified the taking of medicine altogether. As one tirade claims, "If physicians ask you to take medicine, do you not know that medicine is actually poison? Hence if you take it, it will kill you and make you not pay any respect to Jesus' atonement."[28] Here, medicine is not just a sign of lack of faith or holiness. Rather, medicine is a deadly toxin that will both kill your body and your soul.

This aversion to medicine caused particularly acute problems when it came to infectious diseases and local governments. Mung San Ling, a prominent Chinese pastor for the Pentecostal Holiness Church, recalled a harrowing story of his son's bout with diphtheria. After a protracted period of fervent but unsuccessful prayer, his son's condition became severe. Eventually, "medical aid was resorted to since the disease was contagious and according to the laws of Hong Kong, if he had died in this condition we would have been prosecuted."[29] Mung's son recovered, but the case emphasizes the problematic ways that Pentecostal healing utilized a personal autonomy that was not always beneficial to the surrounding community. Mung believed that his son's sickness was "a conflict of spirits over his soul as well as his body."[30] Yet, his soul and body were not the only things at risk due to the infectious nature of the disease. Here, it must be emphasized that Chinese Pentecostals and the Pentecostal missionaries they worked with clearly understood the risks posed by infectious diseases, yet they continued to skirt the edge of public mandates.[31]

Relational Sources of Sickness

That said, while early Chinese Pentecostals shared an understanding of the risks of infectious disease with public health officials, they did not share many of the same assumptions about the origin of ailments and disease. In this way, they reflected the relational views of sickness within the Chinese culture of the time. It is true that few Chinese Pentecostals demonstrated some level of knowledge of Western medicine and germ theory, but when most theorized about the origin of an illness, it was usually supernatural in nature.

Echoing the oldest forms of Chinese cosmology, early Pentecostals tended to portray sickness as caused by demonic forces. Mung San Ling's testimony of his own healing bears this out. After being sick for several months, he asked to receive prayer from the Pentecostal mission located in Shaukiwan, Hong Kong. As the saints gathered around, he "knew that [the illness] was the trap of the devil to hinder [him] and keep [him] from preaching."[32] After prayers and supplications, Mung was healed and began his life as a preacher. Another account from "Brother Weirui" claimed that the devil had become envious of his joy after his Pentecostal experience. Beset by beriberi, he languished for a month and refused to take medicine before God healed him.[33] As another Chinese Pentecostal described it, God delivers believers from "the devil of disease by the work of Jesus."[34]

More intriguingly, many testimonies also attribute sickness directly to God. In these accounts, sickness is often portrayed as a sort of trial by fire in which an illness causes the lukewarm faith of a believer to come alive. Woo Kwai Shan's story is prototypical:

> I heard the gospel in my hometown and learned of the true God. I forsook the dumb idols. Though I believed in the Lord, I had not repented. I was arrogant, furious, unruly, smoking. I mistook that my soul would have eternal life by

not worshipping idols. I thank God he has not forsaken me. He disciplined me with various ailments. I was greatly worried and in pain. For three years, I had heart, lung, brain, stomach, and eye diseases. My parents loved me very much and took me to many local and foreign famous doctors. I took many medicines, and there was no improvement to my predicament.[35]

After encountering an elder sister who had been healed following a Pentecostal experience, Woo visited a church in Yuanfeng where he saw Mok Lai Chi preaching. Realizing he was "deep in sin" and this was the cause of his disease, Woo repented, was baptized in the Spirit, and thereafter healed. Interestingly, this same pattern could hold true for Pentecostals who were supposedly already on fire for God. In this vein, Zeng Kam's story is particularly interesting. After his baptism in the Spirit, he felt prompted to leave his job and devote himself to ministry. After a few years of resisting the call, he was "whipped by the Lord" until he obeyed. After enduring a painful skin ulcer on his thumb for months, he quit his job and was healed.

While some Western Pentecostals might balk at the idea of attributing illness to God, this second point of supernatural origin reveals the relational cosmology which lies behind early Chinese views on healing. Caught up in the world of the divine and demonic, Chinese Pentecostals often saw illness as a manifestation of the cosmological battle between the forces of good and evil. In that battle, unbelievers were exposed to diseases caused by the forces of Satan. Believers, on the other hand, could be free from disease so long as they remained in a good relationship with the Lord by living obediently free from sin.

End-time Plagues

As such, early Chinese Pentecostal testimonies were very good at describing where an individual's sickness and healing came from, but they seldom remarked upon the larger contexts of illness within a community. Plagues and pandemics appear in Pentecostal testimonies, but they are always a backdrop for a story of individual healing or conversion. In the few cases where space is given to understanding contagious diseases in general, Chinese Pentecostals fell back on Latter Rain theology to describe the origin of mass infections. In so doing, they retained the relational cosmology of sickness by giving it an eschatological context.

In one of the few articles to even mention plague in *Pentecostal Truths*, the unnamed author warned his readers:

> Natural and human disasters are pressing on us. Unexpected chaos and unusual tragedies are striking. Plagues, earthquakes, flooding, fire, and war are coming unceasingly . . .Attention! Attention! Are these not the signs of Jesus' coming? . . . If God did not have mercy on the people in ancient times, would he forgive the people of this age? Dear readers, haven't you noticed that warnings are heard all the time? If plagues, earthquakes, wars, flooding, and fires are not God's righteous warnings to the world, they are the signs of Jesus' second coming.[36]

For this author, the prevalence of various plagues in recent years was not primarily due to China being caught in the grip of the third plague pandemic. Rather, it was a divine sign that Christ was coming soon. While this can be seen as just another example of premillennialist pessimism about the state of the world, there is a more hopeful Latter Rain corollary.

Chinese Pentecostals believed that the world was becoming worse prior to Christ's arrival, but they also believed that God's grace had been poured out to combat the forces of darkness. Just as an increase of plagues is a sign of the second coming, so was the renewed gift of healing in the church. As another unnamed author from *Pentecostal Truths* proclaimed, "Therefore, God restores divine healing in the church. Many people are healed by God and have testified of Him in many churches . . .Thousands of people have been healed by Jesus. The number is uncountable."[37] Early Chinese Pentecostals, then, saw plagues as both a sign of the world's sinful state and as a stage on which God's grace could be displayed.

The Importance of Pentecostal Views on Disease, Healing, and Plagues for Today

Early Chinese Pentecostals' theologies of sickness took shape within the competitive and pluralistic market for the healing arts. In that marketplace of ideas, traditional views of multi-layered cosmologies and relationality mixed with scientific worldviews and solution-oriented practices. Chinese Pentecostals defined themselves in this world and against it. They were willing to compete with other approaches to healing, yet they also required the sick to embrace new ways of life and new visions of the cosmos. In that new world, sickness and sin were closely bound together, and the believer was caught up in a new narrative about the need for holy living and the imminent end of the world.

More than an interesting case study about the nature of contextual Pentecostal theology, however, early Chinese Pentecostal theologies of disease and healing also provided a helpful foil—or perhaps mirror—to the approaches of many Pentecostals in our own time. They do this in two ways. First, the cultural environment in which Chinese Pentecostals developed their theologies serves as a potent reminder that pluralistic conceptions of sickness and health continue to impact Pentecostal theologies of healing today. Divine healing was, by all accounts, a major driver of Pentecostal growth in China, yet the willingness to "compete" on the market of healing arts also made room for Pentecostal ministers and missionaries to be seen as little more than ritual healers and Christianity a sort of pay-per-heal system. Their pluralist context also should give modern Pentecostals—and especially those in the West—cause for examining the conflicting views of health and wellbeing on offer in modern society. If early Chinese Pentecostals theologized their pre-existing cultural frameworks of healing, they are not alone.

Second, their theology sheds light on the potential harm that can be caused by an overly dogmatic theology of sickness and healing. Early Chinese Pentecostals' admirable faith in divine healing often came with an ominous dark side. The use of strict Holiness approaches to healing and healing's close theological linkage to salvation made any illness a loaded existential encounter in which temporal and eternal life hung in the balance. Any failure or lack of faith could have dire consequences on both the individual and the church community. This is particularly important when infectious diseases are considered. Early Chinese Pentecostals tended to treat illnesses as singular crises. They were trials of faith, potential miracles, or opportunities for conversion for individuals. In so treating sickness, however, early Chinese Pentecostals rarely reflected on the larger contexts and impacts that their practices could have. For example, rather than bring healing, Pentecostals' refusals to take medicine and their willingness to skirt public health policies may have perpetuated the spread of contagions in the surrounding community. In such circumstances, the Latter Rain gift of healing might have become a stumbling block that not only hindered the advance of the gospel but endangered those to whom the gospel was meant to be preached.

Unfortunately, similar shortcomings were observable in many Pentecostal responses to the recent coronavirus pandemic. Unexamined positions on health and hyper-individualist framings of infectious disease were just as common in 2020 and 2021 as they were in 1908. While unfortunate, there is yet hope. As this volume illustrates, a Pentecostal belief in the power of God to heal does not necessitate either of these short-sighted approaches. Pentecostals can—and should continue to—recover a more responsible and holistic theology of the miraculous, healing power of God.

Notes

1. Mok Lai Chi, "A Chinese Brother Writes of the Plague," *The Apostolic Faith*, July and August 1908, 4.
2. Hong Kong Report on the Blue Book for 1908, Appendix K. Medical and Sanitary Reports, K11.
3. For example, see Blanche Appleby, "Heroism on the Mission Field," The Latter Rain Evangel, June 1918, 20; William H. Turner, "A Plague of Cholera, *The Pentecostal Holiness Advocate*, November 18, 1937, 6; Aimee Semple McPherson, "The Story of My Life," *The Bridal Call Foursquare*, January 1925, 12–13.
4. Paul U. Unschuld, *Traditional Chinese Medicine: Heritage and Adaptation*, Bridie J. Andrews trans. (New York: Columbia University Press, 2019), 53.
5. This is largely due to the way in which Chinese Pentecostals defined themselves against traditional religions. In so doing, they share much in common with other converts from traditional folk religions. See, Birgit Meyer, "'Make a Complete Break with the Past.' Memory and Post-Colonial Modernity in Ghanaian Pentecostalist Discourse," *Journal of Religion in Africa* 28:3 (1998), 316–349.
6. "Grave," *The Book of Songs*, Arthur Waley, trans. (New York: Grove Press, 1996), 264.
7. For example, the oracle bone inscriptions from the Shang are divinations which often point towards certain spirits causing havoc on political events. See, *Sources of Chinese Tradition*, compiled by William Theodore de Bary and Irene Bloom, vol. 1 (New York: Columbia University Press, 1999), 8–12.

8 *Early Chinese Medical Literature: The Mawangdui Manucripts*, translated and commentary by Donald J. Harper (London: Kegan Paul International, 1997), 4, 69–76.

9 The person is then beaten seven times with a cloth. "MSE.I.124," Early Chinese Medical Literature, 262.

10 As found in Unschuld, "Quotations from Medical Classics," *Traditional Chinese Medicine*, 22–23.

11 Hong Hai, *Principles of Chinese Medicine*, 2nd Ed. (London: Imperial College Press, 2016), 91.

12 Unschuld sums up this pragmatism with the phrase, "whatever works is right." Unschuld, *Traditional Chinese Medicine*, 15.

13 Catanach draws attention to the way human technology, especially in relation to trade and travel, were a major reason for the transnational spread of the third plague pandemic. See, I. J. Catanach, "The 'Globalization' of Disease? India and the Plague," *Journal of World History* 12:1 (2001), 131–153.

14 Angela Ki Che Leung, "Glocalizing Medicine in the Canton–Hong Kong–Macau Region in Late Qing China," *Modern Asian Studies* 54:4 (2020), 1345–1366.

15 Meyer, "Make a Complete Break with the Past."

16 For more on this, see Gary B. McGee, "Shortcut to Language Preparation? Radical Evangelicals, Missions, and the Gift of Tongues," *International Bulletin of Missionary Research* 25:3 (July 2001), 118–122.

17 A.G. Garr, "A letter from Bro. Garr," *Special Supplemental to Confidence*, May 1908, 2.

18 Mok Lai Chi, "Divine Healing," *Pentecostal Truths* 五旬節真理, March 1909, 4. I am eternally grateful for the work of Connie Au in translating the extant copies of *Pentecostal Truths* into English. Without her work, this study would not be possible.

19 Tang Tong Shen, "Letter from Tang Tong Shen of Bao Shan County, Jiangsu," *Pentecostal Truths* 五旬節真理, November 1914, 3.

20 Mrs. Lee Wu Si, "How Wonderful! The Saviour is Our Great Physician," *Pentecostal Truths* 五旬節真理, April 1917, 2.

21 For more, see Alex R. Mayfield, "Pentecostal Hong Kong: Mapping Mission in Global Pentecostal Discourse," (Ph.D. diss., Boston University, 2021), 336–353.

22 Ethel Strickland, "A Funeral," *The Pentecostal Holiness Advocate*, October 5, 1933, 4.

23 "The Healing Power in the Atonement," *Pentecostal Truths* 五旬節真理, May 1909, 3.

24 James Robinson, "Conclusion," in *Divine Healing: The Holiness-Pentecostal Transition Years, 1890–1906: Theological Transpositions in the Transatlantic World* (Eugene, OR: Pickwick, 2013), 183–208.

25 Jonathan R. Baer, "Perfectly Empowered Bodies: Divine Healing in Modernizing America," (Ph.D. diss., Yale University, 2002), 185.

26 "The Healing Power in the Atonement," 3.

27 Li Shing Fat, "No Medicine, Simply Healed by the Lord," *Pentecostal Truths* 五旬節真理, March 1915, 1.

28 "The Healing Power in the Atonement," 3.

29 Mung San Ling, "Mung San Ling & His Family," *The Pentecostal Holiness Advocate*, May 23, 1923, 13–14.

30 Mung, "Mung San Ling & His Family," 13.

31 Mung, "Mung San Ling & His Family," 13.

32 Mung, "Mung San Ling & His Family," 13.

33 Brother Weirui, "God Heals Beriberi," *Pentecostal Truths* 五旬節真理, January 1909, 1.

34 Unknown, "Divine Healing," *Pentecostal Truths* 五旬節真理, March 1909, 4.

35 Woo Kwai Shan, "Sin is the Cause of Diseases," *Pentecostal Truths* 五旬節真理, April 1917, 2.

36 Unknown, "The Signs of Jesus' Return," *Pentecostal Truths* 五旬節真理, November 1909, 2.

37 Unknown, "Close to the Door," *Pentecostal Truths* 五旬節真理, May 1909, 3.

5 Pentecostals and Pandemics: A Historical Perspective

Daniel D. Isgrigg

Abstract

This article seeks to compare the variety of responses to the cultural dynamics that took place during the 2020 COVID-19 global pandemic as compared to the 1918 Spanish Influenza pandemic. It explores issues related to theologies of healing, sickness, and death. It also explores the tensions that existed in both relations to the government and in local church sentiments about public health and safety. It concludes by pointing out the cultural perplexities today that have conditioned Pentecostals today to respond in different ways, especially as the COVID-19 virus.

Introduction

When the COVID-19 global pandemic began in the early months of 2020, no one anticipated the duration or the effects it would have on the world. Within months of it first making headlines in the United States, virtually the whole world was shut down. Across the nation, schools, businesses, and churches closed their doors in order to stop the spread of the novel Corona virus. At first, churches seemed to comply with recommendations, believing it to be a short-term situation. But the health guidelines from the CDC, such as limiting gatherings of more than fifteen people and mask wearing, were met with glowing levels of resistance in the church world. Some in the Christian community urged conformity to these measure in order to promote the public health. Others resisted these restrictions due to questions of its severity, suspicions about government overreach, and issues of religious freedom. It wasn't long before the pandemic became politicized, and people were taking sides. As hospitals ICU beds filled up and the death toll continued to rise, the debate became even more polarizing in Christian circles. By the time a vaccine became available in March 2021, the death toll had reached over 600,000 in the United States and 4 million deaths world-wide.

A global pandemic of this scale has only happened once in the past century coinciding with the global Spirit-empowered movement. In 1918, the world experienced the outbreak of the H1N1 virus that became known as the "Spanish Influenza." During 1918–1919, an estimated 500 million people contracted the virus and 50 million died as a result. The pandemic hit the United States in several waves in the Fall 1918 and again in Spring 1919. In cities around America, schools were canceled, public events were forbidden, and churches were directed by Health Departments not to meet. The closing of churches highly affected nearly every Pentecost body in the fledgling movement. Soon after, reports of outbreaks across the globe signaled that the "Spanish" influenza was a becoming a global pandemic that would eventually take the lives of 50 million world-wide.

Despite taking place in the formative years of the Pentecostal movement, the only scholar to take note of this event was Kimberly Alexander in her 2006 book, *Pentecostal Healing*.[1] Alexander discovered the data about the Spanish Flu in her research on models of healing in the various streams of Pentecostalism. Alexander could not, of course, anticipate that Pentecostals would be plunged into a similar situation nearly a century later. Because of this, it is necessary to explore the story once again to analyze how Pentecostals issues of closure of churches, ministered to the sick, and responded to the public authorities during the 1918 global pandemic and how this compares to Pentecostal responses today.

1918–1919 Influenza Pandemic

Beginning in October 1918, tales of influenza began to filter into many of the early Pentecostal papers. In the *Pentecostal Evangel*, a headline declared, "All Assemblies Closed" in Springfield, Missouri, where the AG and headquarters had recently re-located. The editors reported to the readers that the Health Department had closed down all activates including churches, but assured readers that Pentecostals could easily adapt to the situation. Rather than gathering together, they admonished, "Let the saints devote the time they would spend at meeting to the Word and prayer."[2] By November, health departments around the U. S. were urging churches to be closed to slow the pandemic. C. H. Wooley of Portland reported, "Our meetings were closed a week ago by Federal order, on account of the Spanish Influenza, but God is working. Several have been healed, and one saved since we discontinued the meetings."[3] Ministers saw this as an opportunity to take minister on a one-on-one basis, particularly praying for the sick. Alice Luce commented:

> Our meetings were filling up once more, when the order to close was issued by the Health Department on account of the Spanish Influenza. So, we have held no meetings for the past month, but our time has been taken up more than ever in visiting the Christians and those seeking salvation, as well as praying with the sick.[4]

Similarly, in the Church of God, W. J. Parsons notes, "We can't have any services at the church on account of the Influenza, but God will bless, sanctify and baptize with the Holy Ghost at home."[5]

The onset of the pandemic not only effected local churches, but also impacted the regional and national denominational meetings as well. In anticipation of the November 1918 General Assembly of the Church of God, A. J. Tomlinson made the decision to cancel the annual meeting because of the influenza outbreak. He said, "On account of the Influenza epidemic, we are left in somewhat of an awkward position, but we are going to brace up and make the best of it, and I want all of our people to do the same."[6] A similar situation took place in Memphis when the outbreak of influenza caused governmental officials to close schools and churches in September 1918. Bishop C. H. Mason had just moved to Memphis where the nearly 500 deaths convinced him to forgo any plans for their first Holy Convocation in Memphis.[7]

Pentecostal papers also documented the impact of the virus across the globe. One of the hardest hit areas was India, where missionaries gave tragic accounts of the loss of life. Missionary Will Norton reported, "We have just heard of a village where every male person in the entire village has died of it and of another village where there was practically nobody left, either male nor female. These stories are being duplicated in many places."[8] C. H. Schoonmaker even describes the progression of the sickness: "The throat is the first attacked by a germ and then it strikes direct for the lungs. Pneumonia appears in many cases within twenty-four hours from the time of the attack. In two or three days, the patient dies." He concludes, "It is worse than any attack of the plague India has ever had."[9] While the majority of reports came from India, the effects of the virus were felt world-wide. In East Africa, Fran Moll reported, "I cannot describe the sights I have seen. People wail for their dead for days. . . Nearly all of our Christians had it, but only one died."[10] In Central America, Missionary Mrs. Schoenich reported "the healing of one while desperately ill was the means of conviction upon the ungodly. A native for whom they had long prayed has since put away her idols."[11] In West Africa, the city of Philadelphia was particularly hit hard by the influenza. Yet the Faith Tabernacle stood strong in faith and reported over fifty were healed of the virus and no deaths were reported.[12] And in England, Sunderland leader, A. A. Boddy, contracted the virus and was "laid up for some weeks," but managed to survive the illness and eventually recovered.[13]

Missionaries were on the front line of combatting the virus and caring for the victims. But in their compassion, many became victims themselves. One of those was Nellie Andrews Norton, who died because of her ministry to people with the influenza virus. The tribute records, "When the influenza came into our midst last month, she did not spare herself, but worked night and day caring for the sick until she herself came down with the disease."[14] In Fiji, a missionary couple volunteered to help the suffering in the makeshift hospital but the wife contracted the disease and died, leaving the husband alone to carry the mission work.[15] In the midst of these losses, accounts celebrate the sacrifice of these missionaries and reminded readers that death was a "promotion" to heaven for sacrificing their life here on earth.

Theologizing Healing and Death

The influenza pandemic certainly tested these believer's understanding and faith in the Pentecostal theology of healing. For most Pentecostals, sickness and disease is considered part of the fallen world and that healing is available by the power of God. So when the influenza pandemic started, requests for prayer for afflicted believers of all ages filled the Pentecostal papers. Though churches were closed, the disease did not deter pastors and evangelists from visiting the sick in their homes and praying for healing. A. J. Tomlinson reports, "Our ministers have been almost worn out at times praying for the sick. I, myself, have prayed for as high as thirty in one day."[16] Harold Hunter notes from Tomilinson's diary that he admitted he prayed for the sick even while sick and suffering himself, but never told anyone.[17] Praying with people came at great risk to their own health. Some had miraculous protection for themselves. G. F. Taylor notes that he prayed "with more than one hundred cases, and I did not take it."[18] Similarly, the Tomlinson's home had become a "veritable hospital except for the use of medicine" as Mary Jane Tomlinson welcomed people suffering with the virus into their own home.[19]

Prayer for healing went beyond just prominent ministers. One account described a mother's prayer for her twelve-year-old girl:

> The power of God filled the room until the beds shook. . . . The Lord just used my hands to go over her body, and laid them first on her head, then on her lungs, abdomen and right down to the end of her toes. Oh, it was so precious, how after ministered so often to these afflicted parts, Jesus came right in our midst and showed us he was enough.[20]

C. Youngblood had the influenza only a few hours before "a few of the Church of God folk got around my bed and prayed for me and anointed me with oil and the power of God took hold of me and I got up shouting and giving God the praise for the healing of my body."[21] W. J. Parsons testified that while his wife who was suffering from the influenza his daughter was praying for her, she fell under the power and was baptized in the Holy Ghost. When she came up from the ground, "she laid her hands on her head still speaking in other tongues and her mother was completely healed and they both danced under the power for a long time."[22]

Medicine

Early Pentecostals had a distrust of medicine. Though some recognized that medicine had value, they believed that there was a "better way" through faith in the Great Physician as their healer.[23] Joseph Williams notes that for Pentecostals, disease was spiritual and therefore required spiritual remedies. He says, "For many Pentecostals, reliance on human aid seemed antithetical to their understanding of the spiritual nature of disease; sickness's origin in spiritual realities necessitated otherworldly solutions far removed from physicians prescriptions."[24] One Pentecostal noted that medicine was "all right for the children of the world, but not for God's children."[25] In response to the pandemic, A. F. Browder argues, "Should we use medicines after we take our case to God? No. . . . If you take medicine, it hinders God from working the case."[26]

It wasn't that all Pentecostals believed medicine was sinful. Instead, Pentecostal believed that "trusting in Jesus" for health was a better way and a "shorter way" to healing than the unpredictable days of early medicine. W. C. Samples comments that when he contracted the virus, "Did we send for a doctor? No. We went down on our knees and prayed till victory came, got up and began preaching."[27] Pastor John B. Huffman of the Pentecostal Church of God in Blytheville, Arkansas, claimed that over 100 people "trusted the Lord for their healer" during this disease and were healed "all without one drop of medicine."[28] Similarly, Mollie Milligan testified that "He healed my little daughter and I of the Spanish Influenza without one drop of medicine."[29] The mandate to trust the Great Physician over doctors was the highest form of faith. Robert F. Dunn notes that when his family was all down with influenza, he chose to trust God over health professionals. "You know the law of our country is so they want us to use medical aid; but when we took his word, and laid it down at his feet, as it were, and told him that I was his word and his promise, God came to our refuge [sic] and brought us through."[30] Yet, this rejection of doctors and medicines in favor of divine health had risk. One man lost his wife who had "trusted the Lord completely for her body about twenty-three years, refusing doctors and medicines" yet she died from the pandemic when "the dear Lord saw fit to call her."[31]

Some held up the theology that God would not only heal the sick, but that faith in the Great Physician would give special protection to Pentecostal believers.[32] J. H. King testified that though it was not due to his own merit, "I prayed earnestly that I might escape and God assured me that I should not have it."[33] Somehow, the baptism in the Spirit added a layer of protection or power. G. F. Taylor noted that in a city where the virus was rampant, "[i]t is remarkable, however, how few of our people have died with it."[34] Similarly, the notable early leader, Robert Craig of San Francisco, shared that though over 2,000 had died in the city, not one in their mission died from the influenza.[35] The power of the Holy Spirit also mitigated the fear of contracting the virus. One saint declared, "I have been in this city during the terrible epidemic of influence but praise the Lord I have felt good and I knew my path was clean if I should be summoned."[36] Some, like Smith Wigglesworth, focused on the role faith plays in protection against the virus. He proclaimed, "Some would have passed away with influenza God had not intervened, but God stepped in with a new revelation, showing us we are born from above, born by a new power."³⁷ Blanch Appleby declared, "This influenza is like a might epidemic is sweeping over the land, but if the blood is on the doorposts and the lentils of our hearts there is protection here."³⁸

Though many Pentecostals testified to healing, there were some who also had to deal with the lingering aftereffects of the virus. Lula Ferguson described the effects the disease had on her body. "I don't know what it is to have a minute of ease since I had the fever. It left me in an awful fix. I can't eat anything or drink water, but what it nearly kills. It has made my heart weak too, and since I have had this flu, I can't hardly get a long breath and am so nervous I can't sleep at night."³⁹ G. F. Taylor had lingering intense psychological effects.⁴⁰ "My brain seems to be as a block of ice at times. I do not suffer so much in body as I do in mind."⁴¹ Taylor struggled with this condition for a considerable time afterwards.

Death

Although faith and divine healing were strong, death was certainly not a topic they avoided addressing. Pentecostal papers gave regular space for obituaries where families could honor the victims, even more so during the pandemic. This was especially true in the *Pentecostal Holiness Advocate* where for several months the paper was filled with testimonies of those who were "Asleep in Jesus" or "At Rest." Taylor commented in November of 1918:

> The Advocate takes special pride in giving space to obituaries. We are glad to do this, even for the most humble. Loved ones are glad to see tributes of respect given to their dead, and it is our pleasure to give space to these.⁴²

The stories of loss in these obituaries are certainly tragic. From mothers and fathers leaving behind children to the death of small babies, no one was spared from loss. For example, the obituary of Mollie Shackleford of Fork Ridge, Tennessee, declared she died after a ten-day bout with the influenza, leaving six children to mourn her death.⁴³ Another told of Hannah Runion, who had been healed of typhoid fever and filled with the Holy Ghost at a meeting in Tennessee. But tragically, only a month later, she contracted the influenza and died, leaving a husband and five children grieving until the coming of Jesus.⁴⁴

Grief was not a sign of weakness or lack of faith but was fully on display in the papers for all to read. One mother who lost a seven-month-old boy commented, "Oh how sad our home is now. His voice is hushed, his little bed is vacant, and there is a vacant place in our hearts."[45] Another family recalls that at the death of their daughter, "She called us to pray with her before she died, and we could hear her praising God as long as she had breath. She said, all was well."[46] For early Pentecostals, death was a part of life as medicine was still unproven, and vaccines were yet to be invented. Yet, those who shared the grief of death publicly also acknowledged the dignity of hope for Jesus' return and the comfort that their loved ones were with the Lord.

The Pandemic in Tulsa and Aimee Semple McPherson

As a case study in the way Pentecostals navigated the pandemic, I turn to the story how Aimee Semple McPherson ministered in Tulsa, Oklahoma in the middle of the 1918 pandemic. Invited by S. A. Jamieson, pastor of 5th and Peoria Assembly of God, McPherson was scheduled to conduct a meeting beginning November 3, 1918.[47] However, the sudden onset of the influenza in Tulsa prompted Jamieson to contact McPherson in New York about postponing the meeting since Tulsa city officials closed all public meetings. McPherson considered the matter seriously, but she felt the Holy Spirit urge her, "You go in faith and the ban will be lifted and the churches will be open the day you get there."[48] She was willing to come to Tulsa, not to defy the ban or officials, but in faith that God would be true to his word and the ban would be lifted.

Making her way across the Midwest, she arrived in Tulsa on Sunday November 10, 1918. Just as prophesied, the day she arrived local officials lifted the ban on church gatherings, and she immediately started holding services.[49] Throughout the next twenty-two days, desperate people filled the several hundred-seat sanctuary of 5th and Peoria/Full Gospel Tabernacle seeking salvation and healing. In light of the World War and global pandemic, McPherson delivered a fiery sermon on the coming Bridegroom.[50] Many came to the Lord and were healed. One attendee testified, "After coming home, the power was still on me all night and it seemed as if I were lowering and drawing up buckets of blessings all night."[51] Her meetings were so wildly successful that the church doubled in size. There were powerful manifestations of the Spirit including singing in tongues, or what early Pentecostals called "the heavenly anthem." Jamieson said of her ministry:

> From the first meeting until she left, the Spirit's presence and power were felt, sinners were saved, seekers after the baptism received the precious gift of the Holy Ghost and many were healed. . . . On one night the power of God was very manifest, so much so that her hands burned like fire, and as she touched the saints, they felt the power, and many were slain under the power.[52]

Because of the influenza pandemic, McPherson took her ministry also to the streets of Tulsa, touring in her "Gospel Car" equipped with a large fold out chart illustrating the road to heaven and the road to hell. She remarks, "We found in the street work an undreamed-of wealth of opportunity for personal contact with the sinner and the down-cast."[53] Men and women came to Christ right on the sidewalk, as many as twenty at a time. One account tells of two ladies who knelt on the sidewalk and "tears splashed on the running-board." But she also saw first-hand the effects the Spanish Influenza was still having on the city as there were "ceaseless calls for visiting among epidemic victims day and night."[54] On the streets she spent hours praying for the sick. She says, "The epidemic still raging, and many having been weakened and afflicted, we stood hours at a time praying for the sick, and Jesus helped those who came to him."[55] While there no specific testimonies of healing were given, one report notes, "We were called into homes where poor people were lying so low their eyes seemed glassy, and the rattle in their throats, but the Lord marvelously raised them up!"[56] Unfortunately, Tulsa had several more waves of the influenza until April of 1919, and a total of 7,350 people there died of the virus.[57]

While the city was recovering from the months of devastation by the virus, McPherson returned to Tulsa in May 1919. This visit led to one of the most significant revivals in Tulsa's history. Anticipating a huge crowd, Jamieson secured the three thousand-seat Tulsa Convention Center. The crowds were enormous and as many as 250 people were at the altar every night.[58] These two meetings in Tulsa not only helped Tulsa's Pentecostal community grow exponentially but also helped Sister McPherson become a household name, as one of the reporters dubbed her "Lady Billy Sunday."[59] Attendees to McPherson's meetings heard the full gospel message and were exposed to the healing gospel. Mrs. Tyred Berwald of Tulsa testified:

> The Lord worked in a mighty way, and the power fell, saving sinners, baptizing saints with the Holy Spirit. I heard the true gospel preached and, oh, how I praise the Dear Lord! The Holy Ghost convicted me of sin and Jesus washed me with his precious blood and baptized me with the Holy Ghost. I spoke in tongues as they did on the day of Pentecost.[60]

So, while the effects of the pandemic were tragic in human suffering and death, the Pentecostal church responded in compassion. McPherson's revival ignited the city and legitimized the Pentecostal community in Tulsa. From this event, the next generation of new Pentecostal churches were founded, most of which are still thriving today.[61]

Pentecostal Responses: Then and Now

One cannot look back and the Spanish Influenza epidemic without noticing a number of parallels from the 1918–1919 pandemic to how Pentecostals are navigating the complex situation of COVID-19 today. What we have seen so far is that early Pentecostals who faced the global pandemic exhibited two essential characteristics that allowed them to navigate the challenge: compassion for the sick and compliance with governmental mandates. However, particularly in North America, there are some cultural perplexities today that have conditioned Pentecostals today to respond in different ways, especially as the COVID-19 virus has endured much longer than the Spanish Influenza pandemic. While the situation continues to unfold in today's churches, I conclude by analyzing some of the tensions that condition Pentecostal responses today.

Compassion & Healing

Early Pentecostals endured the worst pandemic to that point in history. Although they believed in healing, they didn't promise that their faith in God would protect them from the disease. Many people caught it; many people died. Yet, they also testified that God was a healer, and many were preserved through it or were healed from it. the 1918–1919 pandemic reveals nuances to our understanding of Pentecostal healing theology. Most Pentecostals looked to Jesus for both healing from the virus and for divine health. Ministers went out to pray for the sick with great risk to their own health. But they did so in faith, believing that compassion for the suffering was worth the risk and that faith in the

Great Physician would be there to provide healing if they were also infected. In either case, it was their faith in God and prayer that got them through. But more than that, people believed that through their personal prayers and the prayers of others, God could heal the sick and be protected from the virus.

What is interesting today is that it is harder to find healing testimonies from COVID-19 in Pentecostal publications and other mediums. Of course, one reason is that few Pentecostal denominations still publish a paper or magazine that would give voice to such testimonies. It is easy to find calls for prayer for friends and loved ones on social media outlets, yet there are not as many testimonials of individuals being healed from COVID-19. However, in Pentecostal circles, a few significant examples exist. Missouri Representative, Cori Bush, is reported to have recovered "in thirty minutes" after her pastor, Charles Ndifon the Nigerian pastor of Kingdom Embassy International Church, prayed for her healing from COVID-19.[62] Another high-profile recovery was that of Greg Mundis, the executive director of Assemblies of God World Missions. Mundis contracted the virus and his health worsened until he was placed in a medically induced coma. But he eventually recovered and praised God for the prayers of the AG family that helped him have a miraculous recovery.[63]

But a larger issue is the politicization of the pandemic that has tempered a vocal response in the public square from those who are sick asking for prayer and testimonies from those who have recovered. People in general are reluctant to share their experiences in fear of the backlash that can come. This has particularly been the case now that vaccines are available. To ask for prayer puts a person in a place for questions about vaccination status, issues over controversial treatments and other stigmas. Calls in Spirit-empowered circles of "faith over fear" are strong and are putting pressure on believers to not be stigmatized by personal medical choices.

While early Pentecostals were operating from a place of rejection of medicine and doctors in favor of trusting in God's healing, Pentecostals are more likely to reject medical advice out of suspicion of the government, rather than rejection of science. It is significant that an NBC poll found that 88 percent of Democrats were vaccinated verses only 55 percent of Republican, a demographic that includes the large majority of white Pentecostals.[64] This shows that, at minimum, views on public health are influenced by political beliefs in addition to medical concerns. Regardless of the validity of these political and medical factors, it has certainly complicated the responses of Pentecostals believers in a way not present in the 1918 pandemic.

Compliance & Cooperation

When the 1918 pandemic started, state and local officials issued orders for churches to be closed and revival meetings to be postponed. In almost all cases, Health Department and local guidelines were followed by Pentecostal ministers and leaders. There was little in the way of defiance of public health officials. It is true that some saw the epidemic as a hinderance to the work of the gospel, but these sentiments were not directed at the government. It was clear the Pentecostals took a posture of compliance when it came to health department requests for shutdowns and quarantine rules.

The contemporary Pentecostal responses to the situation with COVID-19 are not quite as clear cut. During the initial days of the outbreak, Pentecostal denominations responded in similar way as early Pentecostals. Virtually every Pentecostal denomination issued guidelines encouraging compliance for mandatory closures and guidelines for masks and distancing when churches opened. For example, following the deaths of twelve prominent bishops in the Church of God in Christ, Bishop Charles Blake instructed their ministers:

> We implore you, our pastors, to adhere to the recommendations of the CDC and NIAID. Negative consequences, including possibly more deaths could occur as a result of unadvised and premature resumption of church services and other religious gatherings that defy the current public health recommendations.[65]

Officials in the COGIC church were perhaps the most vocal about following guidelines and the churches were often the most cautious in re-opening.[66] Similar responses by the United Pentecostal Church, where Superintendent, Dr. David Bernard, comments:

> In the short term, we can take all reasonable precautions and follow the directions of our government without harming the mission of the church. If everyone follows the best medical advice, we hope to get through this crisis in a relatively short time. We don't want to be responsible for prolonging the crisis or thwarting the strategy for defeating it. By following this advice, we are not compromising the word of God but doing what is best for both the church and the community.[67]

General Overseer of the Church of God (Cleveland, TN), Timothy Hill, recognized the suspicion among his members of government overreach. But he also countered the idea that freedom does not include personal responsibility for the sake of the community:

> Keep in mind that while you may have a right to assemble and practice your religious beliefs, we also have a right and a responsibility to be good neighbors to those in our community. Under no circumstances would we want an outbreak of the coronavirus or any other illness to be spread within our congregation, or to others.[68]

For many pastors of denominational churches, the external pressure of higher ecclesial authorities tempered the tendencies of Pentecostal pastors to decide for themselves how to respond. While Pentecostal ecclesiology often shuns hierarchy, the majority of churches followed CDC guidelines out of a general sense of responsibility to public health both during the stay-at-home and re-opening phases. Many pastors appreciate having authoritative denominational guidance to appeal to as they navigate the challenges of instituting such restrictions. In their case, appealing to authority in the decision-making process proved much less controversial. This approach seems to be similar to early Pentecostals, who while lamenting the loss of worship and ministry opportunities, appealed to the scriptural sense of compliance to obey mandates.

Where pushback against compliance is seen most is among independent charismatic churches, primarily identified with the New Apostolic Reformation. These churches often do not operate under authoritative structures. Like the Spirit-empowered movement in general, these churches value autonomy and recognize the individual's ability to hear from God for themselves. Spirit-filled ministers felt empowered to make their own judgments about what is best for their congregations or what they believe the Spirit would "lead" them to do. But issues of non-compliance go much deeper than just the right to do whatever they want. Animated by conservative political proclivities, resistance to mandates have become a battle ground for issues of religious freedom and individual rights.[69] This is quite different from what we see in 1918, where there was little in the way of protest to the mandates, nor were there any feelings of singling out of churches. There wasn't the same sense of governmental suspicion, despite being people well acquainted with persecution by both religious and non-religious segments of society.

One possible explanation for the difference in responses is the nature of Pentecostal constituencies themselves. Early Pentecostals were often the "dis-inherited" of American culture. While not true of all Pentecostals, most churches were among the poor and marginalized. This is quite different than Spirit-empowered churches today. Some of the most vocal critics of COVID-19 restrictions and regulations are among the largest and most affluent segments of the movement, namely those among the independent, prosperity-leaning, charismatic ministers.[70] Ministers in these networks are often part of mega-ministries that enjoy a level of privilege and autonomy. As was mentioned before, Spirit-filled ministers cherish the ability to self-determine God's will internally and tend to reject to authoritative structures around them. It should be no surprise that these groups who rejected denominational control would be hesitant to accept governmental control as well. It is also not coincidental that this segment of ministers are also among the supporters of the anti-establishment President, Donald Trump, whose controversial style mirrored the leadership aesthetics of independent Charismatic ministers who, celebrate their ability to "break away from constraints imposed by traditionally organized groups."[71] This anti-government sentiment naturally fed into what Erica Ramirez notes as "Pentecostal disrespectability politics" inherited from nineteenth-century Evangelicalism.[72] Distrust for the government, doctors, autonomy and anti-clericalism as agents of liberalism (or worse, Satan himself) runs deep in the tradition. But when coupled with power and privilege, these tendencies animate the resistance to a whole different level.

In addition, there is an embedded set of theological beliefs within Pentecostals and Charismatics equally at play here. As was pointed out by J. Kwabena Asamoah-Gyadu, health and wealth Pentecostalism in the United States and in places like Africa have a high view of the believer's authority both to heal and to have power over sickness and disease. He says, "In contemporary Pentecostal/Charismatic Christianity, spiritual and material prosperity follows the cursing of evil and so the coronavirus was problematized as an 'agent of Satan' inflicted on the world not just to upset our lives, but also to trouble seriously the people of God."[73] Therefore, the exercising of that spiritual authority to curse disease, rebuke demonic forces, and declare health and overcoming power is strong in these independent Charismatic ministries. This is very similar to approaches taken by Charismatic/NAR ministers like Kenneth

Copeland and others who tried to nullify the effects of the virus in the world through declarations of faith, speaking curses on the disease and rebuking the demonic forces. The non-compliance tendency seen in the United States and Africa seems to unite along two power dynamics: suspicions of authority structures that justifies resistance and spiritual power that privileges the Spirit-filled believer.

Even with these current high-profile exhibitions of non-compliance, it is important to recognize that this group is by no means homogeneous. The 67 million Spirit-empowered believers in North America include Pentecostals and mainline Protestant and Catholic Charismatics, not just independent charismatic ministries and churches that are often the majority of voices on Christian media.[74] World-wide, those numbers are even more diverse across the 644 million Spirit-empowered believers, half of which are Charismatic Catholic. This diversity has led some scholars to acknowledge a range of "pentecostalisms" rather than singular Pentecostal identity, recognizing that each have a great diversity of cultural identity, spiritual ethos, theology, and liturgies. It may be accurate to say that alongside a vocal segment of resistance, there is plenty of silent compliance for the same reasons as early Pentecostals, although admittedly there is little data to go on.

Conclusion

Looking back on the pandemic of 1918 is beneficial for Pentecostal believers today. Not only does it remind us that we have faced this peril before, but also that the same ingredients that got them through in the past is needed today. Pentecostals were people of prayer who believed that God was alive and active even in a pandemic. They prayed with the sick and cared for those who were suffering. Spirit-empowered believers today should do nothing less. But beyond that, Pentecostals were willing to take reasonable measures to keep people in their communities safe. In many cases, Spirit-empowered congregations have done so as well through heeding the recommendations and governmental regulations that sought to protect public health. As the pandemic has continued to linger, much longer than 1918 believers had to face, these things have become harder to sustain. Yet, as much as it is possible, Spirit-empowered church must continue to draw from the wells of compassion and responsibility to continue to be love our neighbors and protect our witness for Jesus Christ.

Notes

1. Kimberley Ervin Alexander, *Pentecostal Healing: Models in Theology and Practice* (Blandford Forum, UK: Deo, 2006), 215–224.
2. *Christian Evangel*, October 19, 1918, 4.
3. "Portland, Ore.," *The Christian Evangel*, November 16, 1918, 1.
4. Alice Luce, "Mexican Work in California," *Christian Evangel*, December 14, 1918, 14.
5. W. J. Parsons, "Rome, GA," *Church of God Evangel*, November 2, 1918, 3.
6. "Overseers," *Church of God Evangel*, November 9, 1918, 2.
7. Calvin McBride, *Walking into a New Spirituality* (New York: iUniverse, 2007), 77.
8. "Among our Letters," *Latter Rain Evangel*, February 1919, 12.
9. "Bombay India," *Christian Evangel*, January 11, 1919, 10.
10. "Missionary Notes," *The Christian Evangel*, March 8, 1919, 10.
11. "Among our Letters," *Latter Rain Evangel*, February 1919, 13.
12. Adam Mohr, "Faith Tabernacle Congregation, the 1918–19 Influenza Pandemic and Classical Pentecostalism in Colonial West Africa," *Studies in World Christianity* 26:3 (2020): 226.
13. "Pentecostal Items," *Confidence*, January-March 1919, 6–7.
14. A. N. The Homegoing of Mrs. Nellie Andrews Norton of Dhond, India," *Christian Evangel*, February 8, 1918, 8.
15. "Missionary Notes," *The Christian Evangel*, March 8, 1919, 10.
16. A. J. Tomlinson, "Editorial," *Church of God Evangel*, November 9, 1918, 2.
17. Harold D. Hunter, "Pentecostal Responses to the 1918–1919 Influenza Pandemic," International Pentecostal Holiness Church News, April 4, 2020, https://iphc.org/gso/2020/04/04/pentecostal-response-to-1918-1919-influenza-pandemic/, accessed 29 August 2021.
18. G. F. Taylor, "Editorial," *Pentecostal Holiness Advocate*, December 12, 1918, 1.
19. Kimberly Alexander, "Perilous Times: 1918 Flu Pandemic," IPHC Experiences, December 2003, 23.
20. Ida G. Buchwalter, "Healed by the Power of God," *The Christian Evangel*, March 8, 1919, 9.
21. J. C. Youngblood, "Trenton, Ark," *Church of God Evangel*, December 14, 2018, 3.

22 W. J. Parsons, "Rome, GA," *Church of God Evangel*, November 2, 1918, 3.

23 See a full account of early tensions with Pentecostals and medicine in Daniel D. Isgrigg, "The Concept of Disease in the Pentecostal Tradition," in *All Creation Groans: Toward a Theology of Disease and Global Health*, Daniel W. O'Neill and Beth Snodderly, eds. (Eugene, OR: Pickwick Publishing, 2021), 102–122.

24 Joseph W. Williams, *Spirit Cure: A History of Pentecostal Healing* (New York: Oxford, 2013), 31.

25 Florence Burpee, "Hints Regarding Divine Healing." *The Weekly Evangel*, January 1, 1916, 6.

26 A. F. Browder, "Power in Jesus Blood to Heal the Sick," *The Pentecostal Holiness Advocate*, April 3, 1919, 5.

27 W. C. Samples, "Bushnell, Fla.," *Church of God Evangel*, March 1, 1919, 4.

28 John B. Huffman, "Many Healed of Influenza," *Pentecostal Herald*, January 1919, 2.

29 Mollie Milligan, "Laurel Hill, FLA.," *Pentecostal Herald*, January 1919, 4.

30 Robert F. Dunn, "Reelsboro, N. C.," *The Pentecostal Holiness Advocate*, April 17, 1919, 15.

31 J. G. W. McNeely, "Piedmont, S. C.," *The Pentecostal Holiness Advocate*, April 3, 1919, 13–14.

32 Alice Luce, "Mexican Work in California," *Christian Evangel*, December 14, 1918, 14.

33 J. H. King, "Monthly Letter," Pentecostal Holiness Advocate, December 19, 1918, 6.

34 "Editorial Thoughts," *Pentecostal Holiness Advocate*, November 7, 1918, 1

35 R. J. Craig, "San Francisco, Calif.," *Christian Evangel*, December 28, 1918, 1.

36 Ida May Lopez, "Key West, Florida," *Church of God Evangel*, November 23, 1918, 4.

37 Smith Wigglesworth, "Faith Based upon Knowledge," *Confidence*, October-December 1919, 60.

38 Blanche Appleby, "But Prayer: Scouting 'mid Perils of Plague and Robbers," *Latter Rain Evangel*, November 1918, 6.

39 Lula Ferguson, "Autun, SC," *Pentecostal Holiness Advocate*, December 12, 1918, 5.

40 Karen Lucas, "Remember 1918: This is Not our First Pandemic," *Encourage* 7:5 (May 2020), 4–5.

41 G. F. Taylor, "Editorial," *Pentecostal Holiness Advocate*, December 12, 1918, 1.

42 G. F. Taylor, "Editorial," *Pentecostal Holiness Advocate*, November 7–14, 1918, 1.

43 E. W. Anderson, "At Rest," *Church of God Evangel*, November 9, 1918, 3.

44 Mrs. B. L. Shepherd, "Asleep in Jesus," *Church of God Evangel*, November 9, 1918, 2.

45 Ellis J. Boswell, "Middleton, Ga.," *Pentecostal Holiness Advocate*, December 19, 1918, 9.

46 Sallie Mull, "Gone Home," *Church of God Evangel*, November 2, 1918, 3.

47 "Announcement of Meetings," *The Bridal Call*, October 1918, 16–18; "Tulsa, Oklahoma," *Bridal Call*, November 1918, 11.

48 "Gospel Auto News," *Bridal Call*, December 1918, 11.

49 "Notes from the Log Kept on the Transcontinental Auto Trip Thus Far," *Bridal Call*, December 1918, 16.

50 "Reign, Silence, Reign," *The Bridal Call*, December 1918, 1–2.

51 "Testimonies from Tulsa," *The Bridal Call*, January 1919, 8–9.

52 "A Testimony and Report from Pastor S. A. Jamieson, of Assembly of God Tabernacle, Tulsa, Okla.," *The Bridal Call*, December 1918, 9–10.

53 "Gospel Auto News," *Bridal Call*, January 1919, 10–11.

54 "Gospel Auto News," *Bridal Call,* January 1919, 10–11.

55 "Revival Meetings," *Bridal Call*, January 1919, 14–15.

56 "Revival Meetings," *Bridal Call*, January 1919, 14–15.

57 Debbie Jackson, "Throwback Tulsa: 1918 Flu Outbreak Brought Quarantine to Tulsa," *Tulsa World*, March 19, 2020, https://tulsaworld.com/news/local/history/throwback-tulsa-1918-flu-outbreak-brought-quarantine-to-tulsa/article_9be88df8-6f23-51e5-9920-2a5f10c79eb6.html.

58 "Tulsa Evangelistic Meeting," *The Christian Evangel*, June 14, 1919, 9; "Report of the Tulsa Evangelistic Meetings Conducted by Evangelist Aimee Semple McPherson, at Convention All," *Bridegroom's Messenger*, June 1919, 4.

59 "How God Captured the Press," *The Latter Rain Evangel*, July 1919, 12. "Woman Initiates Revival Tonight," *Tulsa Morning Times*, May 17, 1919, 3.

60 "Healed of Appendicitis," *Bridal Call*, February 1920, 19.

61 See, Daniel D. Isgrigg, Pentecost in Tulsa: *The Revivals and Race Massacre that Shaped the Pentecostal Movement in Tulsa* (Lanham, MD: Seymour Press, 2021).

62 https://www.msn.com/en-us/news/us/cori-bush-healed-of-covid-in-30-mins-through-telephone-faith-healing/ar-BB1gQx0m, accessed August 28, 2021.

63 Kristel Ringer Ortiz, "AGWM Personnel Making Miraculous Recoveries," AG News, April 24, 2020, https://news.ag.org/en/News/AGWM-Personnel-Making-Miraculous-Recoveries.

64 Chuck Todd, Mark Murray, and Ben Kamisar, "NBC News Poll Shows Demographic Breakdown of the Vaccinated in the U.S.," August 24, 2021, ttps://www.nbcnews.com/politics/meet-the-press/nbc-news-poll-shows-demographic-breakdown-vaccinated-u-s-n1277514.

65 "Statement from Presiding Bishop, General Board, and COVID-19 Advisory Commission," Church of God in Christ, May 23, 2020, https://www.cogic.org/covid19/presiding-bishops-updates/statement-from-presiding-bishop-general-board-and-covid-19-advisory-commission/.

66 David Daniels, "COVID-19, Science, and Race: A Black Pentecostal Engagement," *Spiritus: ORU Journal of Theology* 6:1 (2021):141–155.

67 https://www.ladistupc.com/covid-19-update, accessed August 28, 2021.

68 Timothy M. Hill, "Should we have Church?", Church of God Communications, March 17, 2020, https://www.churchofgodcommunications.com/covid/should-we-have-church-services%3F.

69 Andrea S. Johnson, Lloyd Barba, Daniel Ramírez, and Roy A. Fisher, "The Theology that has Motivated One Pastor to Keep Holding in-Person Services," *The Washington Post*, March 24, 2020, US Dailies, https://www.proquest.com/docview/2382320429, point out that Oneness groups are part of "a longer history of sectarian groups guarding the church and the restored faith against intrusion by either government or more mainstream forms of Protestantism."

70 See the example of Guillermo Maldonado who has rejected vaccines out of eschatological fears. Karol Kuruvilla, "Florida Megachurch Pastor Tells Evangelical Congregants Not To Take COVID-19 Vaccine," Huffington Post Online, December 9, 2020, https://www.huffpost.com/entry/guillermo-maldonado-covid-19-vaccine-evangelicals_n_5fcfef83c5b6787f2a9b8cc3. It is also interesting that the charismatic television network, Daystar, hosts a regular television program that opposes vaccination featuring Robert F. Kennedy, Jr. and other anti-vaccine doctors. https://vaccines.daystar.com

71 Brad Christerson and Richard Flory, *The Rise of Network Christianity: How Independent Leaders are Changing the Religious Landscape* (Oxford, UK: Oxford University Press, 2017), 125-26.

72 Erica Ramirez, "Who's Laughing Now? Pentecostal Disrespectability Politics," Political Theology Network, July 8, 2021, https://politicaltheology.com/whos-laughing-now-pentecostal-diss-respectability-politics/.

73 J. Kwabena Asamoah-Gyadu, Pentecostalism and Coronavirus: Reframing the Message of Health-and-Wealth in a Pandemic Era," *Spiritus: ORU Journal of Theology* 6:1 (2021): 157–174; 160.

74 Todd M. Johnson and Gina A. Zuro, eds., "Pentecostals/Charismatics, 1900–2050" *World Christian Encyclopedia Online*, http://dx.doi.org/10.1163/2666-6855_WCEO_COM_0102, accessed June 27, 2021.

6 The Holy Spirit, Human Suffering, and Healing: An Initial Pentecostal Reflection[1]

Wonsuk Ma

Abstract

Pentecostals have emphasized the charisma of healing in their over-a-century history. Their theology has been formulated from the unique reading of the scriptures and experiences. The current COVID 19 pandemic provides an opportunity to take an in-depth look into its belief in and claims of supernatural healing. This study identifies four areas where this belief finds new opportunities and challenges, both theological and practical.

Introduction

In less than half a year, the COVID 19 pandemic has affected almost every area of our personal and corporate life. The pandemic has reached nearly all the countries of the world. By the end of 2020, more than 80 million have been infected by the virus, and close to two million have lost their lives. And it will get worse before the turning point. The way we live, work, and worship has changed drastically. The truth is this is going to be a new normal. Even if vaccines are now rolled out in some countries, the virus may be here to stay, at least for a while. In this age of uncertainty and anxiety, the church's role as a healing community has become more crucial than ever before. I want to share several key lessons I have learned as a Pentecostal Christian who believes in God's healing. These lessons are: the validity of healing in Christian life and mission, the extent of illness and healing, the "not-yet" reality of healing, and the community dimension of disease.

I am a member of Oral Roberts University, founded by and named after Oral Roberts (1918–2009), the famous healing evangelist of the twentieth century. Thus, I have a vested interest in the subject. "Pentecostal" or "Pentecostalism" is used as a generic term encompassing the full spectrum of the Christian family, which believes in and practices the immediate and supernatural work of the Holy Spirit in our day.

The Validity of Healing in the Christian Life and Mission

Healing through the power of the Holy Spirit was a significant part of Jesus' ministry. Peter summarized it: "God anointed Jesus of Nazareth with the power of Holy Spirit, and . . . he went around doing good and healed all who were under the power of the devil, because God was with him" (Acts 10:38).[2] Thus, healing is an integral part and sign of the kingdom of God ushered in by Christ. When he commissions his disciples, healing is also prominent. As he sends the seventy, for example, he commands them, "Heal the sick who are there and tell them, 'The kingdom of God has come near to you'" (Luke 10:9). The early church experienced a strong emphasis on healing as we read in the book of Acts (e.g., Acts 3:1–10). Unfortunately, throughout church history, including today, this blessed gift of God has often been marginalized at the fringe of the Christian life. This shift is often attributed to the prevailing rationalistic approach to the Bible and the Christian faith, especially in the West. The so-called "demythologization" of the Bible treats anything beyond human reasoning as a myth. The effect of the rationalization of the Christian faith does not limit its impact on the West. This "sanitized" version of Christianity has spread throughout the world by its missionaries who established the theological institutions patterned after Western practices and its resources. When this Western worldview collides with those in the global South, which take the supernatural world seriously, the missionary version of Christianity prevails. Unfortunately, the version of the gospel presented by the West is less than the "full gospel." The assumption that the unseen world is non-existent has led to a defective Christian worldview with an "excluded middle."[3] Healing in Christian life and theology is one of the casualties in this rational treatment of the Bible, and this flawed system has won the culture war. For example, Louis Berkhof's massive (833 pages) *Systematic Theology* has five occurrences of "healing," and four of them appear in a half-page discussion on "The charismatic gift of healing." He affirmatively dismisses the validity of healing today: "There is no scriptural ground for the idea that the charism of healing was intended to be continued in the Church of all ages."[4]

This is not to say that historic churches have completely eradicated healing in their church life.[5] The Catholic Church maintains the sacrament of healing in its liturgy and ritual, and so does the Anglican Church.

To a Pentecostal, however, these traditions lack the active faith in God's healing, let alone the empowering presence of the Holy Spirit for believers to minister healing. In "The Order for the Visitation of the Sick" of The *Book of Common Prayer of the Anglican Church* (1928), there is only one mention of the Holy Spirit: "And forasmuch as *he* putteth *his* full trust only in thy mercy, impute not unto him *his* former sins, but strengthen *him* with thy blessed Spirit."[6] In contrast, the emergence of the modern Pentecostal movement has restored the expectancy of divine healing as part of its spirituality and theology. In the United States, at the turn of the twentieth century, healing houses mushroomed, reclaiming the potency of God's healing.[7] The healing movement was part of the Holiness movement, and its leaders were charismatic and sometimes controversial in their exaggerated claims and moral failures. In the twentieth century, the burgeoning Pentecostal movement inherited and formalized the belief into doctrines. For example, the twelfth "truth" of the U. S. Assemblies of God reads:

> DIVINE HEALING: Divine healing is an integral part of the gospel. Deliverance from sickness is provided for in the atonement and is the privilege of all believers. (Isaiah 53:4,5; Matthew 8:16,17; James 5:14–16).[8]

In an elaboration of this belief, the denomination developed a position paper. Its four headings reveal the critical parts of the belief: 1) Divine healing is an integral part of the gospel; 2) Divine healing is provided in the atonement; 3) Divine healing is a gift of God's grace for all; and 4) Divine healing will be fully realized when Jesus returns.[9] The position paper is squarely in line with the consensus that the baptism of the Holy Spirit (with speaking in tongues) and divine healing are the most common Pentecostal experiences with the Holy Spirit.

How then have Pentecostals understood the COVID pandemic in light of their strong belief in divine healing? Responses range from a complete denial of the pandemic reality to a sober reflection on the very nature of Christianity birthed in the context of persecution and suffering. Surprisingly, among the Pentecostals, the main message has not been healing but something else entirely. Frequently heard is the claim of God's victory over the virus, sometimes extended to civil disobedience against government measures such as a mask-mandate. Triumphalism with a naïve hint of denial is one such response. Examples abound especially in the initial stage of the pandemic.

There is at least another element (as discussed below) that has affected Pentecostal response (or lack thereof) to the pandemic. This does not deny that Pentecostal churches and believers continue their prayers for the victims of illness, including the pandemic, with a continuing faith in God's (yes, physical) healing. Whether hesitation, ambivalence, or radical claims of victory, the pandemic has revealed several areas of Pentecostal healing theology yet to explore. For example, prevention should be included as part of healing or wellness. Despite this ambivalence, Pentecostals are called to proclaim God's healing as a rare and timely gift to the whole church and the world.

The Extent of Illness and Healing

The Pentecostal accomplishment in the restoration of divine healing is, more specifically, the recovery of the physical dimension of healing in Christianity. One can observe that all passages where healing is mentioned refer to physical healing. Even the cases of demon-possession are always presented with the immediate physical infirmity. For example, people brought to Jesus a demon-possessed man who could not talk (Matt 9:32). Jesus never ignored the physical part of the illness and healing.[10] When healing attains other extended meanings, such as moral, spiritual, national, etc., restoration of the physical and material levels is the starting point and foundation for all the levels of healing and restoration. The often-quoted promise of God's healing of the land to Solomon is an example:

> When I shut up the heavens so that there is no rain, or command locusts to devour the land or send a plague among my people, if my people, who are called by my name, will humble themselves and pray and seek my face and turn from their wicked ways, then I will hear from heaven, and I will forgive their sin and will heal their land (2 Chron 7:13–14).

The "healing of the land" is a comprehensive restoration, but it starts with God's healing and restoration from the drought, natural disaster, and plague. Without meeting the basic physical needs, the Christian message on spiritual welfare would fall on deaf ears.

Today, even if the church believes in divine healing, many Christians are quite unsure of how it will happen. This trend is particularly noted in the more developed countries, where healing is consistently relegated to the medical sector. Even in a discussion about God's healing, only a brief time or space is allocated to physical healing. More time is spent on expanding healing to social, ethical, and spiritual aspects. Some examples are healing in family, social groups, racial relations, and creation. Although these are all essential parts of God's healing, this "expansion" is an outgrowth of the foundational level of healing: physical. *Together Toward Life* is the latest statement on mission adopted by the World Council of Churches. Under the heading of "Mission as Healing and Wholeness," one can find five statements. The opening paragraph introduces the section:

> #50 The Spirit empowers the church for a life-nurturing mission, which includes prayer, pastoral care, and professional health care on the one hand and prophetic denunciation of the root causes of suffering, transformation of structures that dispense injustice, and pursuit of scientific research on the other.

The closest to our discussion is in #53, after a statement on various health care programs that the church can be involved in:

> Healing processes could include praying with and for the sick, confession and forgiveness, the laying on of hands, anointing with oil, and the use of charismatic spiritual gifts (1 Cor 12). But it must also be noted that inappropriate forms of Christian worship, including triumphalistic healing services in which the healer is glorified at the expense of God and false expectations are raised, can deeply harm people. This is not to deny God's miraculous intervention of healing in some cases.

While the West has gradually lost the belief and practice of divine healing due to its rational thinking rooted in the Enlightenment,[11] believers in the non-western world (or "global South"), regardless of denominational belonging, commonly believe and expect that God would heal their sick bodies today just as Jesus did 2,000 years ago. Notably, the Pentecostal recovery of the healing gift and ministry has impacted the Christian witness. For example, the message and ministry of healing was the genesis of Paul Yonggi Cho's ministry. In the outskirts of the war-torn capital of South Korea, among the desperate slum dwellers, his first act of the church plant was God's healing. Cho and his ministry partner, Jashil Choil, visited a paralyzed woman in the neighborhood every day, and they fasted and prayed for her healing. The seven-year bedridden woman was miraculously healed. The testimony of her miraculous healing electrified the whole crowd, and the good news of a good and powerful God spread quickly.[12] Thus, healing has been the bedrock of Yoido Full Gospel Church's birth and growth to become the world's largest single congregation.[13] Therefore, the growth of Pentecostal-charismatic Christianity owes significantly to the countless "healing crusades," such as those by Reinhard Bonnke, and the grassroots believers empowered by the Holy Spirit to bring the message of God's healing. The explosive growth of the indigenous-type Christianity in Africa, particularly in the second half of the twentieth century, is frequently attributed to the Christian adoption of African worldviews and felt-needs. One of these is the expectation of divine healing, which the indigenous religions regularly feature.[14] The physicality of divine healing creates an awe effect that would crack open the hard shell of the indigenous worldviews and beliefs.[15]

However, there is more to God's complete plan for life: the wholistic vision of healing and restoration. The physical level of healing is only the starting point. But only a small number of people experience true healing verified by medical professionals, despite glowing claims of miraculous healing. The picture of God's comprehensive healing and restoration is found in Isaiah 32:

> ...till the Spirit is poured on us from on high, and the desert becomes a fertile field, and the fertile field seems like a forest. The LORD's justice will dwell in the desert, his righteousness live in the fertile field. The fruit of that righteousness will be peace; its effect will be quietness and confidence forever. My people will live in peaceful dwelling places, in secure homes, in undisturbed places of rest (Isa 32:15–18).

God's full restoration starts with the material level (that is, the transformation of the land), expanding to the moral (justice and righteousness), achieving security and tranquility, and culminating in ultimate and perfect peace (or shalom). The community context of this prophecy is also evident. Many historic churches have captured this wholistic vision of healing and restoration, but sometimes they bypass the foundational layer of physical healing. The Pentecostal recovery of physical healing and the historic churches' commitment to the spiritual and ethical dimensions of restoration appear to be vital parts of the Christian message. There has been an encouraging sign that Pentecostal theology has steadily explored the expanded vision of healing.[16]

The "Not-Yet" Reality of Healing

In reality, as alluded to above, the healing movement has long been caught between the provision of divine healing and the reality of "unhealing." The New Testament shows that "healing for all diseases" is a feature of the inaugurated kingdom of God, and this applies both to Jesus (e.g., Mark 6:56) and his disciples (e.g., Luke 10:9). Granted that the healing power of Jesus and his disciples cannot be identical,[17] Jesus, nonetheless, commands his disciples explicitly to "heal the sick." The modern Pentecostal movement has taken this promise and command seriously and continued it. Many are well aware that there are many who are not healed, even if healing testimonies abound. The genius of the movement is its relentless belief in divine healing despite many unfulfilled cases. One example of the surety of this promise is the belief in "healing in the atonement," as observed above. The U. S. Assemblies of God, like other classical Pentecostal denominations, rightly brings the eschatological framework to serve as a disclaimer:

> We are living at present between the first and second appearances of Jesus Christ. At his first coming, he provided, through his life, death, and resurrection, atonement for sin and its consequences. In this era, divine healing, a gift of God's grace, is seen as a proleptic expression of the complete redemption of the human body. At his second coming, what was begun will be brought to completion—salvation from sin and all its effects will be realized. In this period of the "already and not yet" some are healed instantly, some gradually, and others are not healed.[18]

Oral Roberts, the mid-twentieth-century healing evangelist, was well aware of this dilemma. A former student of his "City of Faith" Medical School reflects:

> [At the City of Faith] there were some who got gloriously healed, both medically and supernaturally. But there were some people whom we walked with through their diseases. And, of course, some people died in the "City of Faith." The tension of that reality was not lost on us. . . . Roberts would tell us, "All people who believe in God and trust him get healed. Some get healed immediately, some get healed eventually. But all get healed ultimately."[19]

He also offered another cause of unhealing: the lack of faith. According to Roberts, God desires a healthy and abundant life for his people, and Jesus is the receptacle full of healing power. It is then human responsibility to release their faith to receive the power of healing. In his words, "The knob on the door is on our side. We have to open the door; then God will reveal his treasures to us."[20] This element of faith is a consistent theme among healing preachers,[21] and only at the eschaton will the full measure of faith be realized.

Then, what is the value of insisting on healing, which may result in more disappointments than celebration? A strong justification is found in healing as a sign of God's kingdom already ushered in by the coming of the Messiah:

> When John, who was in prison, heard about the deeds of the Messiah, he sent his disciples to ask him, "Are you the one who is to come, or should we expect someone else?" Jesus replied, "The blind receive sight, the lame walk, those who have leprosy are cleansed, the deaf hear, the dead are raised, and the good news is proclaimed to the poor" (Matt 11:2–5).

And Jesus often links his healing with the coming of God's kingdom:

> Jesus went throughout Galilee, teaching in their synagogues, proclaiming the good news of the kingdom, and healing every disease and sickness among the people. . . and people brought to him all who were ill with various diseases, those suffering severe pain, the demon-possessed, those having seizures, and the paralyzed; and he healed them (Mat 4:23–24).

Pentecostals have also recognized that the crucial role of healing serves as a sign of God's kingdom already present among God's people, foreshadowing complete redemption with a glorified body. The above-mentioned position paper calls the latter function as "a proleptic expression of the complete redemption of the human body."[22] This "sign" function is experienced in daily life in two specific ways. The first is the role of healing in evangelism. A historical study correlates the ministry of Rev. Ik-du Kim, a Korean Presbyterian healing evangelist in the 1920s, with the spike of the growth in Christianity in the Japanese-ruled nation.[23] For four years beginning in 1919, the number of members grew 35 percent, achieving an annual increase of 8.75 percent! Similarly, scholars attributed the resurgence of Chinese Christianity in the 1980s to adopting "Pentecostal" beliefs in and practices of miracles such as healing.[24] The exponential growth of Pentecostal Christianity worldwide is indeed credited to the unique message of healing.[25] The second is that the eschatological anticipation for the full restoration motivates the believers to live daily life victoriously despite the disappointing not-yet-healed suffering. At the same time, Christians are called to be the bearers of the kingdom sign and believe and pray for God's healing. This is where a particular meaning is found in Pentecostal belief and practice of divine healing.

The Community Dimension of Disease

Pentecostal spirituality is best expressed and experienced in a community context. Its worship is characterized by lively body movements such as clapping, raising hands, dancing, laying on of hands for prayer, and dynamic vocal expressions such as "amens" and "hallelujahs" in the middle of preaching, jubilant singing, and passionate prayers, including an erupted unison prayer by the entire congregation. Also, its participatory worship involves elated speeches such as prophecy, speaking in tongues, etc. The congregation often shouts with "Oh yeah," "Amen," "Hallelujah," "Praise the Lord," "C'mon," or "Preach brother!" in their response to preaching. Accordingly, its koinonic life is equally dynamic. Food, laughter, hugging, and shouting are regular features among Pentecostals. This behavioral pattern led Hollenweger to argue that Pentecostal spirituality has the "Black Oral Root."[26] This celebration amid suffering is where the initial reflections on the pandemic are placed among Pentecostals.

Therefore, it is expected that the biggest challenge of the COVID pandemic is the communal aspect of Pentecostal life and mission. As the pandemic has radically impacted social life, including churches, in many places, face-to-face activities are pivoted to virtual platforms. In spite of the celebrated technology, there are elements such as sharing meals and people touching one another through hugging, handshakes, and the laying of hands in prayer that the virtual church version cannot produce. When the pandemic triggered various restrictions, the initial resistances came from Pentecostal-charismatic congregations. This resistance was then combined with triumphalistic theology and muddled with political debates on the freedom of religion. For example, a Florida megachurch pastor was arrested for defying the local government's restrictions by holding in-person worship services.[27]

The pandemic has also challenged the individualized theology of illness and healing as the Pentecostal notion of illness has been understood as a personal affair. Other than praying for healing for those who suffer from

COVID, the Pentecostal theology of healing appears to be unprepared for this widespread (thus, community) reality of the pandemic. This may be similar to the Christian (and, particularly, Pentecostal) response to the HIV/AIDS or Ebola epidemic. As seen in the "truth" above, the Pentecostal doctrine of healing is Christologically rooted. The pneumatological link is with the "power" (e.g., Acts 1:8) and spiritual gifts (e.g., 1 Cor 12:9). It has not yet fully explored the life-giving, sustaining, and renewing work of the Spirit. The pandemic provides Pentecostals an opportunity to reassess their theology and practice of healing. It further challenges them to expand and revisit their theology to embrace the ethical and social level of healing, as we witness inequality in medical service and vaccine availability.

Conclusion

The global pandemic has afforded both an opportunity and challenges to the Pentecostal belief and practice of healing. Healing, traditionally marginalized in historic Christianity, has found its prominence in our days, in part through the unprecedented growth of Pentecostalism. The pandemic's extent and gravity may have overwhelmed Pentecostals, causing an initial hesitation in their healing practice. However, this dark situation is the precise circumstance to which they should bring the good news of God's healing. Healing, both in the ministry of Jesus and his followers, is the prime expression of his compassion and sign of the presence of God's kingdom, inaugurated by Christ and is present in its full force. And the wholeness of life takes the physical dimension as foundational and crucial for other layers of healing. Pentecostal communities are positioned to communicate the good news to the sick, both individuals and communities, to turn to the Creator and Redeemer of life. At the same time, the eschatological nature of the present age causes us to groan with anticipation, hope, and pain in solidarity with the whole creation (Rom 8:22). There are two points for Pentecostals to move forward.

The pandemic has challenged Pentecostal theology and the practice of healing. The study identified at least two areas, which Pentecostals are encouraged to expand their healing theology. The first is the scope of Pentecostal "healing": to add prevention as part of God's healing. This widening vision of healing would also lead toward partnership with science and medicine, and God and humans. However, this broadening view of healing should come with a warning lest divine healing succumbs into medical service as seen in Christian history.

The second area is the communal nature of the pandemic, which directly challenges the community-orientation of Pentecostal life and worship in several critical areas. Pentecostal healing theology will have to embrace this communally infected disease. The infection of the virus knows no religious, ethnic, gender, or national boundaries. It impacts both those who are in and outside of the body of Christ. While maintaining its exclusive claims, Pentecostals will have to embrace a local and global community as a whole. Treating the pandemic as a disaster may provide a helpful way to reimagine Pentecostal healing.

J. Kwabena Asamoa-Gyadu, an African scholar, calls us to return to the persecuted and marginalized context of Christian origin. It is not the claim of entitlement that all the believers are to be healed and blessed, for example, by the preachers of the "health and wealth gospel." At the same time, any evil cannot withstand the might of God.[28] Similarly, N. T. Wright takes us to the roots of human suffering as revealed in the Bible and Christian history and explores responses appropriate to God's people in the world.[29] Therefore, Pentecostals are encouraged to embody the sign of God's kingdom, already inaugurated but not yet consummated, through believing in and praying for healing. In the face of the pandemic, Pentecostals are called to expand their theology of healing to embrace the communal dimension. This would entail the revision of its understanding of the community. Positive signs are already appearing.

As Pentecostals continue their theological journey to expand and refine the theology and practice of healing, they will rise beyond the struggle: becoming healers through the presence and empowerment of the Holy Spirit to live victoriously and witness boldly on earth. This in-between nature of our present life also allows us to see medical science as part of God's healing gift. At the same time, they are also called to be the theological gatekeeper to remind the church that God's healing takes the physical and material levels as foundational.

Notes

1 An earlier version of the study appeared under the same title in in *Christianity and Covid-19: Pathway for Faith*, Chammah J. Kaunda, Atola Longkumer, Kenneth R. Ross, and Esther Mombo, eds., (London: Routledge, 2021). Used by the permission of the publisher.
2 Scripture quotations are from the New International Version.
3 Paul G. Hiebert, "The Flaw of the Excluded Middle," *Missiology: An International Review* 10 (1982), 35–47.
4 Louis Berkhof, *Systematic Theology* (1932 original, Grand Rapids: Eerdmans, 1966), 667.
5 See Amanda Porterfield, *Healing in the History of Christianity* (Oxford: Oxford University Press, 2005).
6 For example, "The Order for the Visitation of the Sick" in *The Book of Common Prayer* (1928), http://justus.anglican.org/resources/bcp/1928/Visitation_Sick.htm, accessed on November 19, 2020.
7 Vinson Synan, "A Healer in the House? A Historical Perspective on Healing in the Pentecostal/Charismatic Tradition," *Asian Journal of Pentecostal Studies* 3:2 (2000), 190–197.
8 "Assemblies of God 16 Fundamental Truths," https://ag.org/Beliefs/Statement-of-Fundamental-Truths#12, accessed November 19, 2020.
9 (US) Assemblies of God, "Divine Healing" (2010), https://ag.org/Beliefs/Position-Papers/Divine-Healing, accessed November 19, 2020.
10 This emphasis on the physical dimension of healing may find a similar argument in "the materiality of salvation" passionately argued by Miroslav Volf, "Materiality of Salvation: An Investigation in the Soteriologies of Liberation and Pentecostal Theologies," *Journal of Ecumenical Studies* 26: 3 (1989): 447–467.
11 For example, Yung Hwa, *Mangoes or Bananas?: The Quest for an Authentic Asian Christian Theology*, 2nd ed. (Oxford: Regnum Books, 2014), esp. 3–6.
12 David Yonggi Cho, *Dr. David Yonggi Cho, Ministering Hope for 50 Years* (Alachua, FL: Bridge-Logos, 2008), 33–40.
13 Younghoon Lee, *The Holy Spirit Movement in Korea: Its Historical and Theological Development* (Oxford: Regnum Books, 2009), 95.
14 For the case of the Church of Pentecost in Ghana, see Amos Jimmy Markin, *Transmitting the Spirit in Mission: The History and Growth of the Church of Pentecost* (Eugene, OR: Wipf & Stock, 2019), chs. 4 (historical study) and 6 (theological analysis).

15 Julie C. Ma and Wonsuk Ma, *Mission in the Spirit: Towards a Pentecostal/Charismatic Missiology* (Oxford: Regnum Books, 2010), 59–71.

16 Daniel Isgrigg, "Healing for All Races: Oral Roberts' Legacy of Racial Reconciliation in a Divided City," *Spiritus: ORU Journal of Theology* 4:2 (2019): 227–256.

17 Keith Warrington, *Jesus the Healer: Paradigm or Unique Phenomenon?* (Carlisle, UK: Paternoster Press, 2000), esp. 141–163.

18 (US) Assemblies of God, "Divine Healing" (2010).

19 Clay Powell, "Becoming a Whole Person Medical Professional: Reflections from an ORU Medical Student," *Spiritus: ORU Journal of Theology* 4:2 (Fall 2019), 207–208.

20 Oral Roberts, *Expect a Miracle: My Life and Ministry* (Tulsa, OK: Oral Roberts, 1984), 43.

21 For a detailed discussion, see R. Samuel Thorpe, "An Overview of the Theology of Oral Roberts," *Spiritus: ORU Journal of Theology* 3:2 (Fall 2018), 267–271.

22 (US) Assemblies of God, "Divine Healing" (2010).

23 Jun Kim, "A Historical and Theological Investigation of the Healing Movement in Korea: With Special Reference to Ik-du Kim, Seong-bong Lee, and Yong-gi Cho" (Ph.D. dissertation, Oxford Centre for Mission Studies/Middlesex University, 2020), 76–78.

24 E.g., Selena Y. Z. Su and Allan H. Anderson, "'Christianity Fever' and Unregistered Churches in China," in *Global Chinese Pentecostal and Charismatic Christianity*, Fenggang Yang, Joy K. C. Tong, and Allan H. Anderson, eds., (Leiden, Netherlands: E. J. Brill, 2017), 226–227.

25 Elizabeth Salazar Sanzana, "'Silver and Gold Have I None': Healing and Restoration in Pentecostalism," in *Pentecostal Mission and Global Christianity*, Wonsuk Ma, Veli-Matti Kärkkäinen, and J. Kwabena Asamoah Gyadu, eds., (Oxford: Regnum Books, 2014), 131–133.

26 Walter J. Hollenweger, *Pentecostalism: Origins and Developments Worldwide* (Peabody, MA: Hendrickson, 1997), 18–141.

27 Patricia Mazzei, "Florida Pastor Arrested After Defying Virus Orders," *New York Times*, March 30, 2020, https://www.nytimes.com/2020/03/30/us/coronavirus-pastor-arrested-tampa-florida.html.

28 Kwabena Asamoah-Gyadu, "The Christian Calendar and COVID-19: Reflections on the Problem of Evil and the Might of God," *Lausanne Global*

Analysis 9:5 (Sept 2020), https://www.lausanne.org/content/lga/2020-09/the-christian-calendar-and-covid-19, accessed December 8, 2020.

29 N. T. Wright, *God and the Pandemic: A Christian Reflection on the Coronavirus and Its Aftermath* (London: SPCK, 2020).

7   A Theological Approach to the Origin of Coronavirus through the Lens of Pain and Disease

Jun Kim

Abstract

This article discusses one of the most frequently asked questions among today's Christians. Where did the coronavirus originate? I examine the belief that the coronavirus is a spiritually motivated punishment/curse for sins. The focal point is not to offer a complete analysis of the cause of the coronavirus pandemic but to argue that the perennial association of pain/disease with divine punishment is unnecessary by elucidating the creation narrative and the Edenic curse in Genesis 1–3 from biblical and theological perspectives.

Introduction

While the coronavirus pandemic has caused multidimensional crises such as mortality risk,[1] physical and mental illness,[2] economic recession,[3] political conflicts between nations,[4] and marginalization of the weak and the poor through the exacerbation of health, economic, and educational gaps,[5] the Christian world has been inundated with theological disputes and confusions as to the origin of the coronavirus. Regarding this, N.T. Wright points out Christians' "knee-jerk reactions"[6] that their focal point tends to quickly become a "sign of the End," "a moment of opportunity [for massive turning to God]," and divine punishment.[7] While these views have circulated worldwide, perhaps, the most contentious interpretation is that the coronavirus is a spiritually motivated curse. Since "Both woman [Eve] and man [Adam] are punished in the most vital areas of their existence, and thenceforward the resulting pain and travail have affected all humanity,"[8] the connection between pain/diseases and curse appears plausible. As this theological perception is prevalent in the Pentecostal/charismatic circles,[9] pain together with disease, death, childbearing, and the labor of tilling the ground becomes an element of a whole package as the repercussion of sin and God's punishment. Consequently, pain and diseases readily become objects for removal. However, a loose definition of pain and disease often leads to theological ambiguity through oversimplification and sweeping generalizations as it collectively treats multifaceted issues of suffering. In fact, the perennial association of pain/disease with sin and God's punishment must be called into question if one considers biblical and theological aspects of the origin and the nature of pain and diseases. Therefore, central to the Christian understanding of the origin of the coronavirus pandemic is the discussion of what constitutes punishment and what was significantly affected by the punishment for Adam and Eve. This research discusses the intrinsic connection between pain/diseases and spiritual punishment and the corresponding obligation of today's Christians by exploring three major themes: 1) the creation and pain, 2) the fall and disease, and 3) the coronavirus pandemic and our tasks.

The Creation and Pain

This section seeks to answer two pivotal questions: Did the fall trigger all sorts of pain? Is it tenable to always/often consider pain a negative consequence of the divine curse? The answers are to be drawn from the following biblical and theological discussions of the origin of pain based on the story of the fall and divine punishment in Genesis 3.

The Origin of Pain

The term "pain" first appears in Genesis 3, and it is used three times in two different forms but in the same root: *istsabown* (v. 16) and *etseb* (vv. 16 and 17). For the first usage in אַרְבֶּה עִצְּבוֹנֵךְ וְהֵרֹנֵךְ הַרְבָּה the main verb *rabah* (which originally means to be many or great in the basic *Qal* Stem) is used in the *Hiphil* Stem with a causative nuance and repeatedly modified by the same verb *rabah* in the infinitive absolute form to "intensify a finite verb."[10] With these two verbal accents, two translations are possible: "I will intensify your pain"[11] and "I shall greatly multiply your pains."[12] Synthesizing the two grammatical aspects of the main verb, one should recognize that the unusual "emphatic construction . . . underscores the intensity of the punishment."[13] The focal point of God's punishment is not the incursion of the pain but the increased degree of the pain. The Greek rendering for the main verb in LXX is πληθύνω which also echoes the same idea of multiplication and increase.[14] These grammatical aspects draw one's attention to a special connotation of the multiplication process, which highlights intensifying what is initially provided.[15]

The fall did not introduce new elements of what Adam and Eve would undergo but partially changed and distorted what was inherent in God's plan for creation, except death. Procreation appears not as a curse but as the central point of God's blessings for humanity in the pre-fall era (Gen 1:28). In addition, cultivating the ground was already part of God's will for Adam before the fall (Gen 2:5). Thus, the physical labor of tilling was Adam's vocation which had been divinely "ordained."[16] Although many have assumed that a curse was placed on the woman and the man, "no curse is uttered against humans,"[17] but only for the serpent (Gen 3:14) and the ground (Gen 3:17). When the fall instigated a series of divinely ordained punitive measures as a consequence of Adam and Eve's sin, the term curse might not be the most fitting descriptor for God's multifaceted disciplinary actions for them, given its overwhelmingly negative undertones for humanity in its entirety. Moreover, the major usage of the term pain in Genesis 3 was applied primarily to two areas (childbearing and tilling the ground),[18] not to every aspect of human life. This nuanced interpretation calls into question the prevalent, formulaic belief that the original sin unleashed a universal maelstrom of pain as a categorical curse upon all of humanity. This discussion affirms that in most essential aspects of life from the outset, the intrinsic nature of pain was not always associated with sin or God's punishment. In this regard, what seems to better allude to Genesis 3 is that sin intensifies pain in some aspects of human life, not that sin causes all pains through God's punishment.

Pain and The Goodness of God's Creation

Pain/suffering has been the controversial topic of theological debates on theodicy since the time of the early church fathers. One of the central questions is if pain/suffering was inherent in the pre-fall era. According to John Hick, the issue has been broadly discussed under the major theme of good and evil by two traditions: Irenaean and Augustinian.[19] In the Irenaean perspective, God's creation, including humanity, was not made in the sense of perfection since only God can be perfect.[20] Humanity was considered as an "infant"[21] to "receive growth"[22] and grow "perfect through suffering."[23] That is why the main focus of the Irenaean view of evil is described as "God's process of soul making."[24] In this regard, pain/suffering was not attributed to the fall of Adam and Eve since it is believed to inherently exist in God's creation from the beginning. In the Irenaean view, pain/suffering is not purely evil but "divinely created."[25]

Although the Irenaean perspective helps one to recognize the natural presence of pain and suffering prior to the fall and their positive functions, admittedly, some critical counterarguments are possible. It impairs the image of the good and merciful God to the degree that "all arguments in justification of suffering promote bitter resentment against the author." "It justifies animal pain only from the perspective of human good."[26] Perhaps, the most pungent criticism is that if there were not "some tremendous transformations . . . in the realm of nature at the time of the Edenic curse,"[27] the need for salvation would have been limited only to the spiritual dimension in conflict with Romans 8:19–22: "The whole creation has been groaning in travail together until now" and "the creation waits with eager longing for the revealing of the sons of God." Regarding this, it seems more tenable to argue that there was a dramatic change wrought by the fall with the emphasis that the Edenic curse intensified the degree of pain, not necessarily in the sense that it caused all pain.[28]

On the contrary, the Augustinian tradition, which has been dominant in the church history, has attributed the origin of evil to "either sin or punishment for sin"[29] while denying "God's authorship of evil."[30] Thus, evil elements were believed not to exist in the so-called "place of bliss, Paradise,"[31] until the fall. Augustine contended that "our first parents in paradise, before they sinned, were free from all perturbation,"[32] and there was "no taste of labor, pain, or death."[33] This view certainly helps our discussion by recognizing the Edenic curse as the beginning of the significant transformation in the realm of the natural kingdom and does not directly tarnish the good image of the merciful and omnipotent God. Despite its valuable contributions, it does not provide a flawless explanation as to the practical and empirical presence of evil, as criticized by Hick: "a totally evil entity could not possibly exist; so far as anything has being it is good, and if it had no goodness it could not be at all."[34] Moreover, it is problematic that the Augustinian theological premise that "all nature, that is, every spirit and everybody, is naturally good"[35] appears incompatible with the existence of what is described as not good in Genesis 2:18 since the loneliness of Adam had occurred before he sinned and it had nothing to do with the concept of sin.

The belief that there was no pain before the fall is generally supported with "direct and valid inference from the biblical affirmation that God viewed the world which he had made and 'behold, it was very good.'"[36]

This idea temptingly leads to a presupposition that God's world must be good without pain. However, it is essential to note that God's evaluation of the creation with the term "good" does not imply the absence of evil or anything which is not good. The biblical usage of the Hebrew term טוֹב (*tob*) is not heavily related to the concept of the absence of pain, whereas it has very a "fluid"[37] and "broad range of meaning."[38] Furthermore, in all the Semitic languages, *tob* often carries a utilitarian connotation of "the practical utility of an object, an action, or a situation, with reference to its being 'useful' or 'advantageous.'"[39] In this regard, *tob* in Genesis 1 is believed to describe "an object's quality and fitness for its purpose."[40] The creation narrative on the goodness of God's creation in Genesis 1 does not refer to what we may call the perfect world where we presume there is no pain. The key element by which we discern the goodness of God's created world is not human-centered belief but God's mysterious and sovereign will that finite human beings cannot fully grasp. God's usage of good is not supposed to be biased or measured in the way "we are inclined to identify good with whatever is pleasant to us at the present and evil with what is personally unpleasant, uncomfortable, or disturbing."[41] In this regard, Erickson is right when he contends that "good is to be defined in relationship to the will and being of God. Good is what glorifies him, fulfills his will, conforms to his nature."[42] Pain, therefore, does not need to be regarded as evil because it always hurts. Although important to God, the way we feel about the created world, especially its goodness, is not the basis of the good world. Instead, "whatever he wills or decrees to be good is therefore good, simply because he declares it to be so."[43] In fact, Augustine did not fully deny the positive value of pain as he said:

> But pain which some suppose to be in an especial manner an evil, whether it be in mind or in body, cannot exist except in good natures. For the very fact of resistance in any being leading to pain, involves a refusal not to be what it was, because it was something good; but when a being is compelled to something better, the pain is useful, when to something worse, it is useless.[44]

For Augustine, the presence of pain itself is not an absolute condition of evil. Instead seemed to focus on what the pain promotes. This idea was echoed in Augustine's view on patience as he argued that "When it [suffering] is a good cause, then is it true patience. . . . They which rightly use the suffering, these in verity of patience are praised, these with the prize of patience are crowned."[45] In other words, pain can also be considered instrumental and neutral, not necessarily always in the sense of evil.

Universal Nature of Pain

What is the difference between the nature of human beings before and after the fall? Obviously, we cannot treat Adam and Eve in the Garden the same as we are today since the nature of humans was affected by the fall to a certain degree. However, this does not provide an absolute justification for the idea that they were totally different beings from twenty-first-century humanity. They were made as intellectual beings to name every living creature (Gen 2:19), recognize what is good for food (Gen 3:6), and justify their faults by reasoning (Gen 3:12–13). They were also emotional beings. Adam expressed "an exclamatory outburst"[46] at first sight of Eve (Gen 2:23). Genesis 3:6 also affirms their ability to feel the tree's good, delightful, and desirable aspects.

There must be some essential characteristics of humanity that underlie what constitutes women and men from the creation to the present despite the difficulty to fully grasp to what degree they are different and similar before and after the fall. When Adam and Eve were created materially out of dust (Gen 2:7) and ribs (Gen 2:21), they lived in the material world where they made physical contact with animals, plants, rocks, water, wind, and so on. They built up their perceptions of the material world through basic human senses of touch, sight, hearing, smell, and taste. These basic senses are deeply associated with the human ability to feel pain as the feeling of touching – even in other senses – can be acknowledged as pain when it exceeds a certain level of pressure. It seems to be true that many times the negative notion of pain or suffering, influenced by our experiential knowledge developed in our contexts, results in the following: "The Garden of Eden is held up to faith as a place in which there was no sort of suffering."[47] The questions now become, what is the point of commanding Adam and Eve not to eat the tree of knowledge if there was no sense of fear which can be regarded as a sort of pain and normally carries a negative emotional connotation (Gen 2:17)? Why did God need to cause "a deep sleep to fall upon the man" to take one of his ribs and close up its place with flesh (Gen 2:21)? If our negative perception of pain leads to an intuitive idea that pain is always evil and thus the created world before the fall did not have any form of pain, what Williams argues below is worth thinking about:

> Suffering is due, in part, to the kind of world God made. . . . in a world of finite entities – whether animate or inanimate – the occurrence of pain may be a beneficent sign of limit of capabilities, a kind of boundary marker to go so far and no farther. Something as small as the aching of a muscle is a positive warning against overdoing in labor and thus is a pointer to proper and balanced action. The pain felt is by no means a punishment of God for wrong activity but a positive signal of human limitations.[48]

Williams' point is enlightening in the sense that pain is not always evil and that "some forms of suffering are parts of the creation."[49] This idea is further supported by Douglas Hall, as he believes that there were at least four basic elements of suffering in the pre-fall era, such as loneliness, limitation, temptation, and anxiety.[50] This perspective helps us to begin to see pain not merely as a divine curse but as part of God's will in the creation. In a sense, some sort of pain by nature can be considered neutral and natural. In this regard, Erickson believes in the presence of natural evil "as being present from the beginning, but neutral in character."[51] Moreover, pain can hardly be considered entirely evil, particularly when it is embodied in good form of God's creation. The intensified pain of childbearing and tilling the ground reminds us not only of the serious consequences of sin but also of "an impending joy,"[52] and God's blessings as "the blessing of Gen 1:28 would be fulfilled in a context of suffering."[53] Although this study does not nullify the occasional connection between pain and God's punishment, it points to the main argument that the inseparable association of pain with curse has no rigorous biblical and theological foundation in the Genesis story of the fall.

The Fall and Diseases

The connection between sin and diseases as a divine curse is further discussed in this section to expand its theological implication to the coronavirus pandemic.

Origin of Diseases

Understanding the origin of diseases is not straightforward since there is no biblical reference that adopts the term disease to explain its origin, whereas death evidently originated from sin (Rom 12:12¬–15 and Gen 3:19). Consequently, most discussion relies on theological implications of the effects of the death wrought by the punishment.[54] In discussing the origin of diseases, what seems crucial is its existence as epistemological reality, not as an ontological possibility. That is to say when diseases could have existed as probability before the fall, there would not have been the consciousness of diseases as a threat of fatality since the mortality certainly appeared after the fall. In this regard, the issues of diseases should concern more of the post-fall era. For Erickson, "after the fall there were diseases for them to contract."[55]

As this idea is also found in classical Pentecostal doctrine,[56] Jean-Claude Larchet's research can help us understand how the early church fathers considered the original sin as "the initial cause of illness."[57] The common rationale is that "The curse, involving the coming of death to humankind, also included a whole host of ills that would lead to death."[58] Since the immortal woman and man became liable to death, it is believed to naturally develop the process of impairing the wholeness of human bodies through physical disintegration from birth. Interestingly, some of the normal parts of aging have recently been adopted as pathological disorders, such as osteoporosis and a fall in testosterone levels in men.[59] Much about this idea is appealing, particularly since some of the biblical understanding of the human body fits this scheme quite well: Every creature suffers its deterioration since they are born to "be liberated from its bondage to decay" (Rom 8:21).[60] As human cells contain the DNA to age, human life is a battle against what causes our bodies to return to dust (Gen 3:19). Therefore, diseases seemed to be actualized when Adam and Eve became mortal. Therefore, it can be argued that diseases inherently have a negative spiritual orientation as they started having destructive power through God's punishment of death. However, this does not justify the inseparable tie between sin and sickness for today's Christians,[61] mainly because illness has characterized the new nature of the creation after the fall. This idea will be further explored in the following section.

Neutral Aspect of Diseases

One aspect that is often ignored in the study of disease is its neutral characteristic embodied in the natural law. Human disease is not an independent entity that exists on its own since "human diseases only exist in relation to people."[62] It is instead "an abnormal condition"[63] that "impairs normal functioning [of the body]."[64] Understanding disease, therefore, focuses more on the way our body responds to the disease-trigger factors – both internal and external. This ultimately allows one to see that pathogens like the coronavirus are external mediums that cause diseases inside the human body.[65] Concerning internal factors, genetic elements could increase the risk for disease, which is seldom associated with the spiritual life of the sick since sicknesses are potentially present even before birth. Regarding this, the theological bias of Jesus' disciples to attribute the blindness of a man from birth to the sin of the man or his parents was corrected when Jesus answered, "It was not that this man sinned, or his parents" (John 9:1–3).

To discuss the instrumental nature of the internal and external factors, one should recognize that many can suffer from diseases as they are simply exposed to much higher possibilities of being sick than others, genetically or environmentally.[66] In this regard, we need to give special attention to the suffering of godly people as Macchia cautions Pentecostals, saying that "Those who suffer innocently and unavoidably can leave the meetings of such evangelists [healing practitioners] empty-handed and filled with self-condemnation."[67] The disease does not always/often need to be a spiritual punishment/warning/lesson. In this regard, Wright is correct to warn today's Christians of what he calls "easy-going vending-machine theology (one sin in, one punishment out)."[68] The Bible often adopts disease and death naturally without attributing them to sins: Mephibosheth's limp caused by accident (2 Sam 4) and the deaths of Eli (1 Sam 4) and Lazarus (John 11) for example. In Pauline literature, the sickness of Paul's co-workers was presented "in a somewhat neutral fashion" (Phil 2:25–30; 1 Tim 5:23; 2 Tim 4:20),[69] and "God chose to use a form of suffering to extend his kingdom in Galatia and to achieve his will."[70] In addition, the healing ministry of Jesus was not "always connected with the forgiveness of sin."[71] These biblical examples show that the divine punishment of diseases that had spiritually originated as a penalty characterized the new natural norms of the changed creation due to the fall. Thus, the human vulnerability to diseases needs to be recognized primarily in the sense of "a universal context of suffering"[72] in the post-fall era, even though individual sin can occasionally lead to sickness,[73] not necessarily in the sense of always/often.

Coronavirus Pandemic and Our Tasks

Coming back to the specific issue of the coronavirus pandemic, one may still want to ask whether the pandemic is from God,[74] the devil,[75] or something else. As this research, however, questions the commonly believed spiritual interpretations of the coronavirus pandemic, perhaps, the right question that we need to ask is not exactly where the coronavirus is from? The more we focus on the origin of the pandemic, the greater confusion we will have. In this regard, this research encourages today's Christians to focus on a more constructive question of what can we do for the coronavirus context? Although there can be various approaches, two points are to be presented.

Stop the Acceleration of the Suffering

If the coronavirus pandemic helps us to see the reality of the suffering world, it forces us to think about ourselves[76] and our surroundings, such as family, neighbors, society, other countries, and the natural environment. Surprisingly, Pentecostal ministers and scholars previously felt the need for holistic salvation for the whole creation even before the pandemic broke out in 2019. David Yonggi Cho admitted in 2005 his pastoral blindsight three years before his retirement:

> I recently began to realize some shortcomings of my 47-year ministries. The Bible clearly says that for God so loved the world that he gave his one and only Son. It does not say that God gave his Son for God so loved the man. . . My evangelistic ministries have been man-centered without including the world.[77]

Admittedly, the concept of Pentecostal holistic salvation tends to be individual and human centered. As scholars[78] have written on Pentecostal eco-theology, Kimberly Alexander's view encapsulates the central point as follows:

> For Pentecostals to minister healing effectively in the twenty-first century, they must embrace a ministry of healing that addresses all areas affected by sin and the fall: the healing of the earth, the healing of the divisions of race and gender, the oppression of the weak by the strong, the exploitation of the poor by the rich. Empowered by the Spirit, Pentecostals must bring healing to every area made sick by structural sin.[79]

We should have listened to the messages attentively since it was a timely self-introspection among Pentecostals before the coronavirus outbreak. The recipient of divine healing is indeed not only humankind but also every creature because "the creation was subjected to futility" and "the whole creation has been groaning in travail together until now" (Rom 8:20–22). According to Wright's interpretation of the passage, "We are painfully aware of a big gap between the people we are right now (weak, frail, muddled, corruptible) and the people we shall be (risen from the dead into a glorious, new, and immortal physicality). At the moment, this means that we share the groaning of creation."[80] It is theologically sure that "Because of man's sin and God's curse, the earth itself has likewise been in travail."[81] It is, therefore, of paramount importance to regard every creature as the recipient of divine healing since the fall affected the relationships between God and humanity and the natural environment. A holistic restoration should be made in every aspect of the creation.

Despite the difficulty of etiology to elucidate the origin and the transmission pathway of the outbreak, scientists and specialists at the United Nations Environment Programme present the "six important points." This report explains what underlies the outbreak. "Human-induced environmental changes modify wildlife population structure and reduce biodiversity, resulting in new environmental conditions that favor particular hosts, vectors, and/or pathogens."[82] It seems an expected result that as the human race abused the natural environment by occupying the territories of wildlife and impairing the biochemistry of the earth through industrial crusade, the higher possibility of exposure to pathogens was inevitable. As every creature was subjected to futility, humankind has intensified the level of suffering.[83] Perhaps, it is not an untenable idea that the earth is fighting against humanity to survive by sending natural calamities and pandemics.[84] What makes the pandemic crisis worse is the ramification of individualism that often marginalizes the poor and the weak of the Global South, although universal unity is the key to stamping out the virus.[85] Sadly, the global response to the pandemic is not equal as "Only 6.2 percent of people in low-income countries have received at least one dose" at the time of this writing, while "55 percent of the world population has received at least one dose."[86] And socio-politico-economic evil structures continually exacerbate the medical and educational gaps for the oppressed in many Global South countries. In a sense, the accelerator of suffering must be neither God nor devils, but myopia and egoistic humankind. It is, therefore, an urgent call for Pentecostals to "relate pneumatology beyond the confines of the individual Christian life and the fellowship of the church to the renewal of the entire creation and the transformation of culture and society."[87] Before it is too late, we need to realize our responsibility to pray for divine healing for the whole world, whether animate or inanimate. Healing must not be only for people but for the entire universe, as the concept of healing (*rapha*) in the Old Testament is broad enough to include the process of making materials whole such as a broken altar (1 Kings.= 18:30), infertile land (2 Chron 7:14) and undrinkable water (2 Kings 2:19–22). If we cannot stop the acceleration[88] of the ongoing suffering for the universal "We," it will eventually destroy the individual "I." Therefore, it should be heard again by today's Christians that in God's creation, every life matters.

Save Lives from the Coronavirus

There are various Christian groups that defy government orders intended to prevent the spread of COVID-19. Most of the core issues seem to be categorized as political, religious, or mixed matters. As political issue concerns much broader dynamics, this section focuses more on the religious aspect, particularly as some fundamentalists have fought their self-declared holy fight for their faith against the COVID-19 regulations to ban mass gatherings for Sunday worship services. When this group of people does not comply with the mass gathering ban, it is often observed that the government restrictions are taken as satanic or antichrist maneuvers to weaken churches[89] or religious persecution.[90] What appears to underlie the issue is our Christian value on the law of the sabbath as another pastor believes that "Our Lord has taught us to gather for worship at least one day in seven. . . . Christ is worth it."[91] Although their personal religious piety should be respected, its theological justification is still questionable and even dangerous when imposed as a normative Christian belief in the specific context of COVID-19. The problem appears complicated since it concerns another Christian value of loving our neighbors. Then the question is, when these two religious elements conflict with each other, what should be weighed more? Despite its complexity, the answer is straightforward since this issue directly concerns the salvific works of the divine healer in John 5:5–18 and Luke 6:6–11. Did Jesus break the sabbatical law when he healed the sick people on the sabbath? Obviously, he violated the law of the sabbath in the eyes of the teachers of the law and the Pharisees (Luke 6:7). However, the touchstone to discern "what is not lawful to do on the sabbath" (Matt 12:2) must be the Lord of the sabbath who affirms that "I desire mercy and not sacrifice" (Matt 12:7) and "So it is lawful to do good on the sabbath" (Matt 12:12).

In considering the lesson of these stories, one should remember that the most critical violation of God's commandment is not missing the Sunday services but not loving God by not loving our neighbor (Matt 22:36–40)[92] intentionally or unintentionally. As this issue may continue, we need to consider if Jesus would be pleased with our sacrifice that has sacrificed someone's life, not ours. There is a great danger of turning our worship practice into a blind commitment to legalism[93] if one does not ask about the true meaning of worshiping God. In this regard, this coronavirus pandemic must be the right time to ask ourselves Jesus' question, "I ask you, is it lawful on the sabbath to do good or to do harm, to save life or to destroy it?" (Luke 6:9). When we are desperately waiting for divine healing, the healing process must not begin with our egoistic blind faith that deceives Christians to care only for the churches and personalizes the divine mercies that God universally willed for communal *all*, including non-believers and every creature (Psalm 145:9).

Conclusion

This research has sought to question and challenge Christian responses that often attribute the coronavirus pandemic to punishment and curse, viewed as spiritually oriented. While noting that the spiritual interpretation of the coronavirus pandemic is not always necessary, there is a remaining uncertainty about the origin of the coronavirus. However, it is important not to inundate our emotions with bitterness and despair that hinder us from recognizing what we can learn from the context of suffering and moving forward to what we can do. When the pain makes us feel that it hurts, it also helps us be alarmed to protect ourselves from other potential pains that might come and be even more severe in the future. In this regard, whether the coronavirus pandemic was caused by God, the devil, sin, or nature, it has partially served as a pedagogical tool to teach the urgent need for healing not only from the coronavirus but also from the virus of individualism resulting in making the poor and the weak suffer more, human-centered growth that sacrifices the earth, and our shortsighted focus on the "already" and less on the "not yet" of the kingdom. Therefore, the coronavirus is an urgent call to restore the notion of the communal and eschatological "we" as we desperately wait for divine healing today. One should remember that it is a valuable lesson in pain that we need to lament and pray together for the healing of the true "we" God created in his image.

Notes

1 Cara Murez, "COVID Has Killed More Americans Than the Spanish Flu did in 1918," U. S. News, September 21, 2021, https://www.usnews.com/news/health-news/articles/2021-09-21/covid-has-killed-more-americans-than-the-spanish-flu-did-in-1918. See also, "WHO Coronavirus (COVID-19) Dashboard," World Health Organization, https://covid19.who.int/, accessed September 18, 2021.

2 Nirmita Panchal, Rabah Kamal, Cynthia Cox and Rachel Garfield, "The Implications of COVID-19 for Mental Health and Substance Use," KFF, February 10, 2021, https://www.kff.org/coronavirus-covid-19/issue-brief/the-implications-of-covid-19-for-mental-health-and-substance-use/.

3 M. Szmigiera, "Impact of the Coronavirus Pandemic on the Global Economy - Statistics & Facts," Statista, September 15, 2021, https://www.statista.com/topics/6139/covid-19-impact-on-the-global-economy/.

4 Eric Taylor Woods, Robert Schertzer, Liah Greenfeld, Chris Hughes, Cynthia Miller-Idriss, "Covid-19, Nationalism, and the Politics of Crisis: A Scholarly Exchange," *Nations and Nationalism* 26 (October 2020), 807–825.

5 "Everyone Included: Social Impact of COVID-19," United Nations Department of Economic and Social Affairs, accessed September 18, 2021, https://www.un.org/development/desa/dspd/everyone-included-covid-19.html. See also, "COVID-19 Impacts on Child Poverty," UNICEF, https://www.unicef.org/social-policy/child-poverty/covid-19-socioeconomic-impacts, accessed September 17, 2021.

6 N. T. Wright, *God and the Pandemic: A Christian Reflection on the Coronavirus and Its Aftermath* (Grand Rapids, MI: Zondervan, 2020), xi.

7 Wright, *God and the Pandemic*, 6.

8 J. Rodman Williams, *Systematic Theology from a Charismatic Perspective* (Grand Rapid, MI: Zondervan, 1996), 130.

9 Pavel Hejzlar, *Two Paradigms for Divine Healing: Fred F. Bosworth, Kenneth E. Hagin, Agnes Sanford, and Francis MacNutt in Dialogue* (Leiden, Netherlands: Brill, 2010), 159.

10 Bruce K. Waltke and M. O'Connor, *An Introduction to Biblical Hebrew Syntax* (Winona Lake, IN: Eisenbrauns, 1990), 581.

11 Victor P. Hamilton, *The Book of Genesis Chapter 1–17* (Grand Rapid, MI: Eerdmans, 1990), 195.

12 Gordon J. Wenham, *Genesis 1–15* (Nashville: Thomas Nelson, 1987), 81.

13 Kenneth A. Mathews, *Genesis 1–11:26* (Nashville: Broadman and Holman, 1996), 249.

14 Johan Lust, Erik Eynikel, and Katrin Hauspie, *A Greek-English Lexicon of the Septuagint* (Stuttgart: Deutsche Bibelgesellschaft, 2003).

15 The identical expression of הַרְבָּה אַרְבֶּה is found two more times only for the multiplication of Abraham's descendants through Ishmael (Gen 16:10–11) and Isaac (Gen 22:16–17). Cf. The term *nathan* seems more proper to be used for the initial process of providing what Adam did not have. The word is used to describe the childless situation of Abram as it says, "O Lord GOD, what wilt thou give me, for I continue childless, and the heir of my house is Eliezer of Damascus. . .Behold, thou hast *given* me no offspring" (Gen 15:2–3, emphasis added).

16 Gerhard Von Rad, *Genesis*, rev. ed. trans., John H. Marks (Philadelphia, PA: Westminster John Knox, 1972), 94.

17 Donald E. Gowan, *Genesis 1–11: From Eden to Babel* (Grand Rapids, MI: Eerdmans, 1988), 59.

18 The relational struggle between Adam and Eve could be deduced from Genesis 3:16b, but not necessarily in the sense of pain.

19 John Hick, *Evil and the God of Love*, rev. ed. (New York: Harper and Row, 1978).

20 Irenaeus, "Against Heresies" in *Ante-Nicene Fathers: The Apostolic Fathers, Justin Martyr, Irenaeus*, vol. 1, eds. Alexander Roberts, James Donaldson, and A. Cleveland Coxe (Grand Rapids, MI: Eerdmans, 1950), 521.

21 Irenaeus, "Against Heresies," 521.

22 Irenaeus, "Against Heresies," 522.

23 C. S. Lewis, *The Problem of Pain* (London: The Centenary Press, 1940), 93.

24 Millard J. Erickson, *Christian Theology*, 3rd ed. (Grand Rapids, MI: Baker Academic, 2013), 393.

25 Hick, *Evil and the God of Love*, 333–336.

26 Keith Miller, "And God Saw That It Was Good: Death and Pain in the Created Order," BioLogos, November 21, 2012, https://biologos.org/articles/and-god-saw-that-it-was-good-death-and-pain-in-the-created-order-2.

27 John C. Whitcomb, Jr. and Henry M. Morris, *The Genesis Flood: The Biblical Record and its Scientific Implications* (Philadelphia, PA: The Presbyterian and Reformed, 1961), 459.

28 Death was obviously introduced as a new element after the fall. This topic is to be further discussed in the next section on the fall and diseases.

29 Hick, *Evil and the God of Love*, 172–173.

30 David Hionides, "Against 'Irenaean' Theodicy: A Refutation of John Hick's use of Irenaeus" (PhD diss., Dallas Theological Seminary, 2018), 165.

31 Augustine, "City of God," in *Nicene and Post-Nicene Fathers: St. Augustine's City of God and Christian Doctrine* vol. 2, ed. Philip Schaff (Grand Rapids, MI: Eerdmans, 1956), 271.

32 Augustine, "City of God," 271.

33 Augustine, "City of God," 271.

34 Hick, *Evil and the God of Love*, 55.

35 Hick, *Evil and the God of Love*, 351.

36 Hick, *Evil and the God of Love*, 170.

37 Mathews, *Genesis 1–11:26*, 146.

38 Wenham, *Genesis 1-15*, 18.

39 Bonn Höver-Johag, "טוב," in *Theological Dictionary of the Old Testament* vol. 5, eds. G. Johannes Botterweck and Helmer Ringgren, trans. David E. Green (Grand Rapids, MI: Eerdmans, 1986), 299–304.

40 See Wenham, *Genesis 1-15*, 18 and Mathews, *Genesis 1–11:26*, 146.

41 Erickson, *Christian Theology*, 396.

42 Erickson, *Christian Theology*, 396.

43 Erickson, *Christian Theology*, 386.

44 Augustine, "Against the Manichaeans," in *Nicene and Post-Nicene Fathers: St. Augustine's City of God and Christian Doctrine*, vol. 4, ed. Philip Schaff (Grand Rapids, MI: Eerdmans, 1956), 355.

45 Augustine, "On the Holy Trinity, Doctrinal Treatises, Moral Treatises," in *Nicene and Post-Nicene Fathers: St. Augustine's City of God and Christian Doctrine* vol. 3, ed. Philip Schaff (Grand Rapids, MI: Eerdmans, 1956), 528.

46 Hamilton, *The Book of Genesis Chapter 1–17*, 179.

47 Douglas John Hall, *God and Human Suffering* (Minneapolis, MN: Augsburg, 1986), 55.

48 Williams, *Systematic Theology*, 127–128.

49 S. Boonyakiat, "Suffering," in *Global Dictionary of Theology*, eds. William A. Dyrness and Veli-Matti Karkkainen (Downers Grove, IL: IVP, 2008), 859.

50 Hall, *God and Human Suffering*, 56–59.

51 Erickson, *Christian Theology*, 398.

52 See Mathews, Genesis 1:11:26, 249–250, and John H. Sailhamer, "Genesis," in *The Expositor's Bible Commentary* vol. 1, eds. Tremper Longman III and David E. Garland (Grand Rapids, MI: Zondervan, 2008), 92.

53 Mitchell M. Kim, "The Blessings of the Curse: Fulfilling Genesis 1:28 in a Context of Suffering," (PhD Diss., Wheaton College, 2010), 73.

54 This theological perception is not only Christian but also universally religious since "illness was seen primarily as punishment by the gods." See Stephen Pattison, *Alive and Kicking: Towards a Practical Theology of Illness and Healing* (London: SCM Press, 1989), 38; Wright, *God and the Pandemic*, 2.

55 Erickson, *Christian Theology*, 559.

56 "Divine Healing," Assemblies of God, https://ag.org/Beliefs/Position-Papers/divine-healing, accessed September 1, 2021.

57 Jean-Claude Larchet, *The Theology of Illness*, trans. John Breck and Michael Breck (Crestwood, NY: St. Vladimir's Seminary, 2002), 26–33.

58 Erickson, *Christian Theology*, 559.

59 Misha Ketchell, "What Exactly is a Disease?" *The Conversation*, July 24, 2019, https://theconversation.com/what-exactly-is-a-disease-120622.

60 The Greek word for decay refers to "a process of disintegration/deterioration," and "subjection to decay" "as it affects nature corruptibility." See Frederick William Danker, "φθορά," in *Greek-English Lexicon of the New Testament and Other Early Christian Literature*, 3rd ed. (Chicago, IL: University of Chicago, 2001), 1054–1055.

61 Although the notion that sin leads to sickness is not a normative formula, there are many cases that diseases resulted from sins in the Bible. God also used infirmity and death as punishment in the New Testament as well. See Erickson, *Christian Theology*, 554–559; John Christopher Thomas, *The Devil, Disease and Deliverance: Origins of Illness in New Testament Thought* (Sheffield, England: Sheffield Academic, 1998), 299.

62 Jackie Leach Scully, "What is a Disease," *European Molecular Biology Organization Reports* 5:7 (July 2004), 650.

63 *The American Heritage Medical Dictionary Online*, s.v. "Disease," accessed on September 25, 2021, https://www.ahdictionary.com/word/search.html?q=Disease.

64 *Merriam-Webster's Medical Dictionary Online*, s.v. "Disease," accessed on September 25, 2021, https://www.merriam-webster.com/dictionary/disease.

65 "A pathogen is defined as an organism causing disease to its host." See Francois Balloux and Lucy van Dorp, "Q&A: What are Pathogens, and What Have They Done to and For us?" National Center for Biotechnology Information, https://www.ncbi.nlm.nih.gov/pmc/articles/PMC5648414/, accessed September 16, 2021.

66 Unhygienic condition of poor countries can be an example for the higher risk of sickness in an environmental sense without having a spiritual association with curse.

67 Frank D. Macchia, "Theology, Pentecostal," in *The New International Dictionary of Pentecostal Charismatic Movements*, ed., Stanley M. Burgess (Grand Rapid, MI: Zondervan, 2002), 1136.

68 Wright, *God and the Pandemic*, 17.

69 Thomas, *The Devil, Disease and Deliverance*, 304.

70 Keith Warrington, *Healing and Suffering: Biblical and Pastoral Reflections* (Waynesboro, GA: Paternoster, 2005), 138.

71 Erickson, *Christian Theology*, 765.

72 Williams, *Systematic Theology*, 131.

73 Warrington acknowledges from James' perspective that when "suffering might be related to personal sin.... James does not assume that sin always causes suffering." See Warrington, *Healing and Suffering*, 172.

74 According to Alexander, the Wesleyan Pentecostals also believe that sickness can be caused by God as a pedagogical tool and divine punishment. See Kimberly. E. Alexander, *Pentecostal Healing: Models in Theology and Practice* (Dorset, U.K.: Deo Publishing, 2006), 202.

75 Understanding the reality of devil's power to cause sickness, scholars cautions that there is always a great danger or temptation to emphasize the spiritual warfare in a dualistic venture and to "too quickly attribute aberrant physical and psychical phenomena to demon possession." See Frank D. Macchia, "Theology, Pentecostal," 1137; Kimberly E. Alexander, *Pentecostal Healing*, 202; Millard J. Erickson, Christian Theology, 419.

76 The pandemic reminds us of the most unrecognized value of suffering as a part of our Pentecostal identity together with spiritual empowerment. In

a sense, Pentecostals are the recipients of suffering since "they had been counted worthy of suffering disgrace of the Name [of Jesus] (Acts 5:41)." In this regard, Martin W. Mittelstadt's insight on suffering deserves our attention, especially since in our Pentecostal studies, there is "a noticeable lack concerning implications of the Spirit-filled life when juxtaposed with suffering." See Martin W. Mittelstadt, *The Spirit and Suffering in Luke-Acts: Implications for a Pentecostal Pneumatology* (New York: T&T Clark International, 2004), 136.

77 Hyeong-geun Lim, ed., *Cho Yong-gi Moksa Ildaegi: Yeouidoui Moghoeja* [Biography of Rev. Yong-gi Cho: The Minister of Yoido] (Seoul: Seoul Book, 2008), 563.

78 For further bibliographic information on Pentecostal ecotheology see Harold D. Hunter, "Pentecostal Ecotheology from the Margins," *Cyberjournal for Pentecostal-Charismatic Research* 27 (July 2020), http://www.pctii.org/cyberj/cyberj27/hunter.html.

79 Kimberly E. Alexander, "the Pentecostal Healing Community," in *Toward a Pentecostal Ecclesiology: The Church and the Fivefold Gospel*, John Christopher Thomas, ed. (Cleveland, TN: CPT, 2010), 204.

80 Wright, *God and the Pandemic*, 43.

81 Williams, *Systematic Theology*, 130.

82 Maarten Kappelle, "Six Nature Facts Related to Coronaviruses," April 08, 2022, the United Nations Environment Programme, https://www.unep.org/news-and-stories/story/six-nature-facts-related-coronaviruses.

83 Natural disasters such as earthquakes and storms are believed to be natural as well as man-made. See Emmanuela Douyon and Alyssa Sepinwall, "Hurricanes in Haiti have Historically been 'Man-Made Disasters' as Much as Natural Ones," The Washington Post, August 20, 2021, https://www.washingtonpost.com/outlook/2021/08/20/earthquakes-storms-are-natural-haitis-disasters-are-man-made-too/.

84 The Washington Post released data based on the analysis of federal disaster declarations that "Climate change has turbocharged severe storms, fires, hurricanes, coastal storms and floods – threatening millions" and about one-third of North Americans have experienced a weather disaster since June. See Sarah Kaplan and Andrew Ba Tran, "Nearly 1 in 3 Americans Experienced a Weather Disaster this Summer," The Washington Post, September 4, 2021, https://www.washingtonpost.com/climate-environment/2021/09/04/climate-disaster-hurricane-ida/.

85 It is repeatedly reported that "Health experts have long argued that the coronavirus will continue to thrive as long as parts of the world lack

vaccines." See Silvia Amaro, "WTO chief 'very concerned' about the unequal distribution of Covid vaccines," CNBC, December 2, 2021, https://www.cnbc.com/2021/12/02/covid-vaccines-wto-chief-very-concerned-about-unequal-distribution-.html.

86 "Coronavirus (COVID-19) Vaccinations," Our World in Data, https://ourworldindata.org/covid-vaccinations?country=OWID_WRL, accessed December 7, 2021.

87 Macchia, "Theology, Pentecostal," 1136.

88 It is notable that "Since 1980 alone, the number of outbreaks per year has more than tripled. The number of new infectious diseases like Sars, HIV and Covid-19 has increased by nearly fourfold over the past century." See Bryan Walsh, "Throughout history, nothing has killed more human beings than infectious disease. Covid-19 shows how vulnerable we remain – and how we can avoid similar pandemics in the future," BBC, March 26, 2020, https://www.bbc.com/future/article/20200325-covid-19-the-history-of-pandemics.

89 See Mya Jaradat, "Will Religious Leaders Fight for – or against – COVID-19 Vaccinations?" Deseret News, December 19, 2020, https://www.deseret.com/indepth/2020/12/19/22176429/religious-leaders-covid-19-vaccination-pew-research-evangelical-protestant-jewish-catholic-muslim; and David Oyedepo, "Can you Imagine Anyone Bringing Coronavirus Patients to me and I Won't Lay Hands on Him?" Facebook, August 29, 2020, https://www.facebook.com/davidoyedepoministries/videos/653990758566643; Daniel Silliman, "Pentecostal Pastor Won't Stop Church for COVID-19," Christianity Today, March 19, 2020, https://www.christianitytoday.com/news/2020/march/pentecostal-la-pastor-defies-covid19-coronavirus-order.html.

90 Tony Spell, "Baton Rouge Area Pastor Defies Governor, Welcomes Large Gathering into Church Service," interviewed by Lester Duhe, Central City News, March 19, 2020, https://www.wafb.com/2020/03/18/baton-rouge-area-pastor-defies-governor-welcomes-large-gathering-into-church-service/.

91 Andre J. Ellington, "Trinity Bible Chapel, Which Broke COVID Rules, Fined for Contempt of Court, Locked Down," Newsweek, July 30, 2021, https://www.newsweek.com/trinity-bible-chapel-which-broke-covid-rules-fined-contempt-court-locked-down-1614870.

92 The two commandments of loving God and our neighbor are inseparable since it is impossible to love God without loving our neighbor (1 John 4:20).

93 Legalistic judgment tends to be based on external acts called an "ethical system," which is "governed primarily by obedience to prescribed laws or rules." See D. K. McKim, *Westminster Dictionary of Theological Terms* (Louisville, KY: Westminster John Knox Press, 1996), 159.

II
Contextual

8 Pandemic, Depression, and the Church: A New Norm for the New Normal

Robert D. McBain

Abstract

The COVID-19 pandemic caused a global increase in symptoms of anxiety and depression and disrupted the delivery of mental health services in many countries. This study explores a Spirit-empowered response to the challenges caused by the pandemic. It does so by reimagining the pandemic's impact in reflection on the disciples' dismay at Jesus' passion and then the joy at the new life they received due to Jesus' resurrection. In this reimagining process, Jürgen Moltmann's theology of hope is used to show that Christ stands in solidarity with those who suffer because he too experienced what they experience. Beyond this, the resurrected Christ gifts new life to believers, grounding them in his life where the Spirit sustains them even during the most profound suffering. The study reimagines the pandemic's impact in light of the disciples' experience of Jesus' resurrection. It shows how the church can stand in solidarity and help people whose mental health has been compounded by the pandemic. This requires the church to act as peace-bearers, displaying solidarity, transparency, and empowerment in a way that develops wholesome Christian friendships.

Introduction

The world changed very quickly. One day everything was normal, then the next day, there was a toilet roll shortage. As the instruction to stay home for two weeks to flatten the curve turned into months, the place where my family and I lived returned to more idyllic times. Children played in the street and fished by the stream with their friends. Families went for walks and bike rides and neighborhoods enjoyed a renewed community emphasis. The pandemic seemed to bring out the good in people. Neighbors asked after each other, and churches and other social institutions distributed food and other necessities. Things seemed relatively peaceful, but the fact was that beneath the surface, the pandemic was causing a lot of damage. People wondered if the pandemic was real or if it was fabricated to push a nefarious agenda that sought to take away human freedoms.[1] Being an election year in the United States, the pandemic seemed to magnify the distrust already evident in the country between supporters of the two political parties.² It also acted as a backdrop to social movements that appeared to bring out the worst in people.³

The Pandemic's Impact on Mental Well-being

At an individual level, the pandemic separated families, whether by death from COVID-19 (or "underlying health conditions") or social distancing. Others found themselves trapped at home in volatile environments. For example, reports of intimate partner violence (IPV) were expected to increase during the pandemic as victims were forced to stay home with their abusers. Instead, rates dropped because victims could not connect safely with agencies.⁴ There was also a similar drop in child abuse cases where calls to child abuse hotlines fell by 62 percent, and referrals from schools dropped by 92 percent. One source wrote, "Pediatricians across the country are sounding the alarm: The stress of unemployment and financial insecurity has strained relationships between children and those who care for them. The closures of schools and day cares have forced children closer to adults who may not be safe."⁵

Reports carried out by many organizations all showed the pandemic had negatively affected people's mental health.⁶ Complaints included an increased number of people having difficulty sleeping or eating, increased alcohol intake and substance use, and worsening chronic health conditions.⁷ More people reported anxiety disorder symptoms, depressive disorder, and trauma-and-stressor-related disorders. Younger adults, racial/ethnic minorities, essential workers, and unpaid adult caregivers reported worse mental health outcomes, increased substance use, and elevated suicidal thoughts.⁸ The data from these and other surveys suggest that the rise was representative worldwide.⁹ The World Health Organization (WHO) surveyed 130 countries, and 93 percent reported "disrupted or halted critical mental health services" because of the pandemic.¹⁰

Reimagining the Pandemic's Impact

This study explores a Spirit-empowered response to the challenges imposed by the pandemic upon peoples' mental health. The study does so by reimagining the pandemic's events in reflection of the disciples' experience of Jesus' passion and resurrection.[11] At the beginning of Passion Week, Jesus and his disciples triumphantly entered Jerusalem. The disciples were overjoyed because their hopes over the last three years had culminated to this point where their Messianic expectations were about to be met. However, all their hopes and dreams crumbled when Jesus was captured, underwent corporal punishment, and was put to death. As David Turner put it, "The triumphal entry is shown in reality to be a very tragic entry."[12] The disciples' response was one of fear, hopelessness, denial, and grief. One of their members even committed suicide (Matt 27:3–5).[13] However, although the disciples' old way of life lay shattered, the resurrected Jesus miraculously appeared to them as they isolated themselves at home (John 20:19–23). In the interaction that followed, Jesus breathed on them and said, "Receive the Holy Spirit" (v. 22). In doing so, he inaugurated a new life, new relationship, new connectivity with God, and empowerment to function as a missional community to bring the gospel to a suffering world.

In reimagining the disciples' experiences together with our own, we see how, like the disciples before Jesus' Passion, people before the pandemic had their own hopes, dreams, and expectations. Like the Passion, the pandemic shattered these. Among many things, people experienced financial instability, strained relationships, and disruption of their regular everyday schedule—life was not as it was once. Isolated in their homes, people felt vulnerable as they realized that their old way of living was not as stable as they thought. Yet, in the same way that the disciples experienced the resurrected Christ amid their uncertainty and vulnerability, those affected by the pandemic can likewise experience the resurrected Christ's divine breath and enter into a new normal filled with resurrection life, hope, and purpose.

Two questions emerge when we reimagine the impact of the pandemic in reflection on the disciples' experience of Jesus' passion and resurrection. The first question relates to the individual believer. It concerns the theological implications for believers whose mental well-being has been negatively affected by the pandemic and whose experiences parallel the pre-resurrection experiences of the disciples. The second question is community oriented. It looks at the post-resurrection experiences of the disciples and asks how the Spirit-empowered church can help depression sufferers affected by the pandemic.

A Definition of Depression

Before answering the first question, let me first provide a brief summary of depression. *The Diagnostic and Statistical Manual of Mental Disorders* (DSM-5), published by the American Psychiatric Association (APA), lists seven different depressive disorders. Common symptoms of all of these are "the presence of sad, empty, or irritable mood, accompanied by somatic cognitive changes that significantly affect the individual's capacity to function. What differs among them are issues of duration, timing, or presumed etiology."[14] The experience of depression itself is a whole-person experience that affects one's mind, behavior, body, and relationships. Dorothy Rowe describes the experience as like being in prison:

> Intellectually you know that you are sharing space with other people, that you are talking to them, and they are hearing you. But their words come to you as if across a bottomless chasm, and even if you can reach out and touch that other person, or that other person touches you, nothing is transmitted to you in that touch. No human contact crosses the barrier.[15]

Rowe uses imagery that reveals the complexity of depression and reveals a dichotomy between knowing and the sense-experience. It isolates sufferers from everything real[16] and forces them into a position where they feel abandoned and experience deep identity and existential issues.[17] Depression does this by eroding the foundational aspects through which people construct and interpret their reality. This causes problems for all sufferers, but it may arguably cause a double burden for Pentecostals because Pentecostals strongly emphasize the role of experience in their lives.

Wolfgang Vondey explains that Pentecostals interpret their life experiences through a Spirit-led reading of the Scripture and community interaction. These contribute to their everyday encounters with Christ facilitating their Christian formation and growth.[18] Basically, through daily interactions with the Spirit in their lives, Pentecostals expect to experience God. By experiencing him, they interpret their reality and find their identity.[19] Herein lies the problem, however. Because depression attacks the nexus of human experience where the Christian meets God through the Spirit, sufferers can no longer experience God, or any relationship for that matter, in the way in which they are accustomed. The inability to experience relationships causes sufferers to feel abandoned and have deep, existential issues.[20] This leaves them at an impasse because if sufferers "can no longer relate to God, and if their self-image and interpretation of the world depends on their experience of God, then to experience such abandonment is, in a very real sense, to lose part of themselves."[21] This results in a loss of identity, which further blocks their ability to engage with and interpret formational God experiences. They are left at a standstill, isolated from themselves, their community, and their God.

Using Moltmann to Get Beyond Depression's Impasse

One way to get beyond this impasse is to recognize that feeling abandoned by God is not unique to believers experiencing depression. Moltmann argues that it is also true of Christ, whose experience of God during his passion was a struggle with "forsakenness." Moltmann explains that Jesus's cry— "My God, My God, why have you forsaken me?" (Matt 27:46)— was an expression of profound abandonment by the God upon whom Jesus set all of his hope. It is the "cry of the God-forsaken Christ for God." Therefore, because Christ endured God abandoning him, he can intervene and stand in solidarity with those who experience the same.[22] As Moltmann put it, "the suffering Son of man is so much one of us that the unnumbered and unnamed, tortured, and forsaken human beings are his brothers and sisters."[23]

Going beyond standing in solidarity with humanity through his passion and crucifixion, the resurrected Jesus comes to humanity with the gift of new life through the Spirit. In the disciples' case, Jesus miraculously appeared to them when they felt the most hopeless and abandoned after witnessing his torture and death (John 20:19–23). Moltmann sees the resurrected Christ breathing on the disciples at this point as the act that rebirthed their faith (John 20:22).[24] In this, the God who endowed humanity with life (Gen 2:7) now endows believers with new life through the gift of the Spirit. The disciples' reception of this life is their birth from above (John 3:3–8), which Jesus promised to his followers (John 14:19).

Moltmann says that the new life the disciples received is a life filled with living hope. This living hope has two elements to it. The first is that it is a present-day reality with present-day implications. The second is that the living hope also carries an eschatological element linking the here and now with Christ's second coming.[25] The present-day and eschatological reality of the new life means that God is present even amidst the most intense feelings of suffering and abandonment.[26] "Man," Moltmann says, "is taken up without limitations and conditions, into the life and suffering, the death and resurrection of God."[27] By being "taken up without limitations," all the positive and negative factors of being human are taken up in the suffering, rejection, and death of God.[28] The point is that the theology of a God who was crucified enables humans to live to the fullest even when experiencing profound misery.

Reimagining the pandemic's impact in light of this discussion shows that experiences of depression are not alien to believers. Whether isolation, abandonment, meaninglessness, psychological torture, etc., these were also experienced by Christ. Moreover, the resurrection power that rebirths believers changes them and unites them to the eternal reality of the eschatological hope and its present-day implications. This means that a believer's experiences of depression do not overrule the fact that they are eternally changed through their total rebirth. The believer is changed into a new creation with their life grounded in Christ's life (Col 3:3) in whom they live and move and have their being (Acts 17:28).

How the Church Can Help People Impacted by the Pandemic

The previous section sought to show how Christ stands in solidarity with depression sufferers. It also showed that the new life believers have in Christ means that they are grounded in Christ's life where the Spirit sustains them despite their feelings and thoughts. This section continues to reimagine the pandemic's impact in light of the disciples' experience of the resurrection to show how the church can stand in solidarity and help people whose mental health and experiences of depression are compounded because of the pandemic.

At first glance, it appears the church has quite a challenge on its hands because the church struggled even before the pandemic to help those suffering from mental health issues like depression. For instance, back in 2014, Lifeway's research revealed local churches were failing their congregations regarding mental health. Many in the run-up to the pandemic criticized the church for handling mental health in ways that did not reflect God's love.[29] Since there is doubt about the church's effectiveness in exhibiting Christ's love before the pandemic, one questions how effectively the church can help people post-pandemic.

Moltmann's understanding might be helpful at this point. He sees the church as a place in human history where the messianic vision of the future is balanced with the present-day revelation of the kingdom of God. Within this balance, God affirms that he is present even in the most challenging situations. The church's task, then, is to reveal Christ's resurrection light in the present age and inspire hope and provide people with life's meaning.[30] To paraphrase Swinton, the church is called to demonstrate the first fruits of the resurrection so that people are resurrected in the here-and-now and experience the fullness of life within God's kingdom.[31] Moltmann describes the Spirit's role in this endeavor as one in which he reaches out beyond the church for the world's transformation and redemption. The church functions as both a gathering and sending community that comes together in worship and mutual trust while going out into the world seeking to practically help society's marginalized, vulnerable, hurting, and those impacted by the pandemic.[32]

Christians as Peace-Bearers

Moltmann's and Swinton's understanding of the church's role is apparent in the disciples' encounter with the resurrected Christ in John 20:19–23 in the way that the new life the disciples received was a life typified by peace (vv. 19; 21). Peace in the New Testament expresses the "wholeness" and "harmony" of restored relationships.[33] When Jesus appeared to the disciples with the greeting "Peace be unto you" (v. 19), he was bestowing peace on an occasion when the disciples needed it.[34] It showed the disciples that he did not hold their failures against them; instead, he wanted their relationship restored.[35] Through his greeting, Jesus acted as an envoy communicating to the disciples what his passion and crucifixion accomplished for them—it achieved the peace that originates from restored relationships (Col 1:20–23).[36] This is an integral point for reimagining the church's response to those suffering due to the pandemic because it provides the church with confidence that regardless of its pre-pandemic inefficiency in helping those with mental health issues, it now has a clean, "post-pandemic" slate.

Moreover, in keeping with what Moltmann said about the church being a sending community that helps society's marginalized, vulnerable, and hurting, Jesus' bestowal of peace upon the disciples shows that the church is also commissioned to bear peace to others (v. 21).[37] Forgiveness of sins was to play an essential role in this activity (v. 23).[38] As the disciples, accompanied by the Spirit, preached the gospel and pressed home its implications, they pronounced forgiveness for those who received their witness.[39] The commission to the disciples and its focus on forgiveness coincide with what Swinton calls the "pastoral task," which aims "to help people hold on to Jesus in these difficult times without unnecessary guilt or blame."[40] This means that depression sufferers ought to receive the peace that comes from being accepted by the church just as they are, so they in no way feel guilty for having the condition. The church should never make people think their condition was caused or compounded because they never prayed enough, confessed the word enough, or pled Jesus' blood enough. The church should not view them or make them feel "less Christian."

Practical Application: Developing Friendships

Like the disciples, the church is called to maintain and restore peace. The type of peace Jesus pronounced upon and commissioned his disciples into has individual, communal, and societal implications. Yet, Jesus did not just pronounce peace or proclaim the forgiveness of sins. He also employed some type of gesture that proved to the disciples that reconciliation had taken place. That he stood in the midst of them showed solidarity (v. 18). That he showed his scars to the disciples revealed transparency and openness (v. 20). By breathing on them and sending them, he showed he wanted to empower them (v. 22). In some ways, Jesus' actions reveal a paradigm for the church as it negotiates the pandemic to help those suffering. The church should stand in solidarity with those suffering, be transparent and vulnerable to its own problems, and empower people with mental health issues and not disempower them. These are activities that the church has had difficulty with in the past. Yet, they are activities innate to the church. A simple application of which is through the development of genuine friendships.

Moltmann emphasizes that the type of friendship Jesus modeled is not built upon the principle that like attracts like. He argues that friendship in the New Testament takes place among people who are different.⁴¹ Swinton agrees with Moltmann and notes how Jesus built his friendships on grace and love.⁴² To quote Swinton, "The church's task is to provide a physical and spiritual space where people perceived by society as 'different' can find a home, where there is neither Jew nor Greek, male nor female, mentally ill nor mentally healthy, but only travelers struggling together to sustain faith in God and trust in one another."⁴³ Practically, this involves making spaces in the church where people with depression and those negatively experiencing the pressure of post-pandemic life can be affirmed. We should note that there is a close association between healing and space with the interaction that goes on within human relationships, forming spaces and places into what they become. From this perspective, incarnational and eschatological concepts help develop a theology of space and place. The Holy Spirit plays a vital role in this because he indwells Christians with God's presence. Therefore, Christians act as the incarnational body of Christ in the spaces and places they occupy.⁴⁴

The concept of making space in the church goes beyond creating self-help groups. Self-help groups can be helpful, but they also tend to isolate those who attend them from others in the church by enforcing the differences between those who attend and those who do not. This imposes the distinction that those in the group are different or unable to cope in comparison to those outside the group. Instead, I am proposing a practical outworking of friendship that comes naturally as people live within the community in and outside the church building. It is about being kind, available, and present in a way that provides a mutually supportive atmosphere. In this atmosphere, people journey together through life, striving to know themselves, each other, and Christ better. As Moltmann put it, "In every true friendship, we can experience God. It is the presence of his friendly Spirit which makes those who are friends so alive and their friendship so inexhaustible. They continually describe new things about one another."⁴⁵ The church can practice this type of friendship to help those suffering from mental health issues caused by the pandemic, for such friendships produce peace.

Conclusion: The Isenheim Altarpiece

In bringing this chapter to a close, I want to reference the Isenheim Altarpiece painted by Matthias Grunewald circa 1512, for St Anthony's

Monastery in North-Eastern France. This monastery cared for people suffering from St Anthony's Fire (i.e., ergotism). When it is in its open state, the altarpiece depicts Christ's crucifixion in horrific splendor. He is nailed to the cross. His corpse is grotesquely contorted and carries a greenish decomposed hew. His body is perforated with whipping pustules showing the effects of St Anthony's Fire. To the ill onlooker being cared for in the monastery, the message is clear that Jesus associates with their suffering and social ostracization, which he takes upon himself. The altarpieces' message to us is the same—Jesus stands in solidarity with those who suffer because he experienced what they are experiencing. Moreover, the altarpiece's place at the center of the monastery also serves to remind us that the local church has a central role in the community and a responsibility to help people affected by the pandemic in the same way St Anthony's Monastery helped people in its community. This requires the church to act as peace-bearers, displaying solidarity, transparency, and empowerment in a way that develops wholesome Christian friendships.

Notes

1 For example, a video shared on Facebook on July 26, 2020, argued that the pandemic was a hoax and a conspiracy to control the general public: https://www.facebook.com/Lucas7.johnson.52035/videos/vb.100012769188873/1023119518123678/?type=2&theater. The Facebook fact checkers refuted this, and Reuter's later wrote their own response to conspiracy theorists. See "Fact Check: The Coronavirus Pandemic is not a Hoax or a Conspiracy to Control the General Public," *Reuters*, August 20, 2020, https://www.reuters.com/article/uk-factcheck-hoax/fact-check-the-coronavirus-pandemic-is-not-a-hoax-or-a-conspiracy-to-control-the-general-public-idUSKBN25G2KM, accessed September 20, 2022. David Robson published an article using social history to explain why people downplayed COVID and choose to listen to COVID myths and conspiracy theories. See Robson, "Why Smart People Believe Coronavirus Myths," *BBC: Future*, April 6, 2020, https://www.unic.ac.cy/da/2020/05/07/why-smart-people-believe-coronavirus-myths-bbc-future/.

2   USA Today ran an article describing how the 2020 American elections deepened the nation's divide which further negatively impacted people socially, emotionally, and physically. See Alia E. Dastagir, "A Close Presidential Election Deepens the Nation's Divide. How do We Live Together Now?" November 6, 2020, https://www.usatoday.com/story/news/nation/2020/11/06/2020-election-american-divided-polarized-and-unsure-how-cope/6179404002/.

3   I am referencing the protests and riots that occurred during the pandemic following the death of George Floyd. Many Americans seemed to have a polarized view of these events. See Hakeem Jefferson, et al., "Black Americans Support the Floyd Protests. Whites are Divided. Here's Why," The Washington Post, June 10, 2020, https://www.washingtonpost.com/politics/2020/06/10/black-americans-support-floyd-protests-whites-are-divided-heres-why/.

4   See Megan L. Evans, et al., "A Pandemic within a Pandemic — Intimate Partner Violence during Covid-19," *New England Medical Journal* 383 (December 10, 2020): 2302.

5   See Samantha Schmidt and Hannah Natanson, "With Kids Stuck at Home, ER Doctors See More Severe Cases of Child Abuse," *The Washington Post*, April 30, 2020, https://www.washingtonpost.com/education/2020/04/30/child-abuse-reports-coronavirus/.

6   For instance, a report by the Kaiser Foundation showed that the percentage of US adults that reported that the pandemic had negatively affected their mental health increased from 32 percent in March 2020 to 53 percent in July 2020. See Nirmita Panchal, et al., "The Implications of COVID-19 for Mental Health and Substance Use," *Kaiser Family Foundation*, February 10, 2021, https://www.kff.org/coronavirus-covid-19/issue-brief/the-implications-of-covid-19-for-mental-health-and-substance-use/. The Kaiser Family Foundation (KFF) is a nonprofit organization that focuses on national health issues and analysis. A survey by the Center for Disease Control (CDC) revealed a significant increase in the number of people experiencing mental health challenges from April to June 2020 compared with the same period in 2019. See Mark Czeisler, "Mental Health, Substance Use, and Suicidal Ideation During the COVID-19 Pandemic—United States, June 24–30, 2020," *Center*

for Disease Control and Prevention: Morbidity and Mortality Weekly Report 69:32 (Aug 2020): 1049, 1057. According to a study in December 2020 by the US Census Bureau, more than 42 percent of survey respondents reported symptoms of anxiety or depression. This is an increase from 11 percent in December 2019. See Allison Abbot, "COVID's Mental-health Toll: How Scientists are Tracking a Surge in Depression," Nature, February 3, 2021, https://www.nature.com/articles/d41586-021-00175-z.

7   Panchal, et al., "The Implications of COVID-19."

8   Czeisler, "Mental Health," 1049, 1057.

9   Abbot, "COVID's mental-health toll."

10 Alison Brunier and Carla Drysdale, "COVID-19 disrupting mental health services in most countries, WHO survey," World Health Organization, October 5, 2020, https://www.who.int/news/item/05-10-2020-covid-19-disrupting-mental-health-services-in-most-countries-who-survey.

11 I am indebted for John Swinton's blog "The New Norm is Not the Old Norm with a Different Hat On," *Sanctuary*, last modified June 10, 2020, https://sanctuarymentalhealth.org/2020/06/10/john-swinton-covid-19-new-norm/. Swinton writes about reimagining the new norm in light of the disciples' experience of the resurrection. Being a blog, Swinton only writes briefly on this idea, which this study expands upon.

12 David Turner, *Matthew*, (Grand Rapids, MI: Baker Academic, 2008), 497.

13 "Godly sorrow brings repentance that leads to salvation and leaves no regret, but worldly sorrow brings death" (2 Cor 7:10). Mark Altschule discusses how later commentators interpreted this verse to refer to two different kinds of despair (i.e., depression): a despair that led to life, and a despair that led to death. In Judas' case, his betrayal of Jesus was not too great a sin for forgiveness, but his despair was of a worldly kind that allowed Satan to work in his life and destroy him. Therefore, Judas' despair corresponded with a desire to "un-be." See Altschule, "The Two Kinds of Depression According to St. Paul," *The British Journal of Psychiatry* 113 (1967): 779–780.

14 American Psychiatric Association, *Diagnostic and Statistical Manual of Mental Disorders*, 5th ed [DSM-5] (Washington, DC: American Psychiatric Association, 2013), 155.

15 Dorothy Rowe, *Depression: The Way Out of Your Prison* (London: Routledge, 1996), 1–2.

16 Archibald D. Hart and Catherine Hart Weber, *Unveiling Depression in Women* (Grand Rapids, MI: Fleming H. Revell, 2002), 19.

17 John Swinton, *Spirituality and Mental Health Care: Rediscovering a "Forgotten" Dimension* (London: Jessica Kingsley Publishers, 2001), 114–116.

18 Wolfgang Vondey, *Pentecostal Theology: Living the Full Gospel* (London: T & T Clark, 2017), 15. Stephen Land concurs with Vondey. Land cites B. L. Campos, who describes the Pentecostal experience as the community's mode of living within which understanding moves from experience to testimony to doctrine to theology and back again in an ongoing dynamic. According to Land, the biblical story sits behind this interaction giving it shape. See Stephen Land, *Pentecostal Spirituality: A Passion for the Kingdom* (Cleveland TN: CPT Press, 2010), 36.

19 Robert D. McBain, *Depression, Where is Your Sting?* (Eugene, OR: Resource Publications, 2021), 82.

20 Swinton, *Spirituality and Mental Health Care*, 114–116.

21 Swinton, *Spirituality and Mental Health Care*, 115.

22 Jürgan Moltmann, *Jesus Christ for Today's World* (Minneapolis, MN: Fortress Press, 1995), 34–36. Within Moltmann's theology of the suffering, Christ also incorporates the notion of a suffering God. Using 2 Cor 5:19, Moltmann says that when Christ died on the cross, experiencing God's forsakenness, God also experienced forsakenness by the Son. So, both suffer but in different ways. He writes: "God goes with us, God suffers with us. So, where Christ, God's Son, goes, the Father goes too. In the self-giving of the Son, we discern the self-giving of God," 37–38.

23 Moltmann, *Jesus Christ for Today's World*, 39.

24 Moltmann, *Jesus Christ for Today's World*, 81. Moltmann delineates the Christian new birth from reincarnation and the idea of renewing something that is old. He states quite firmly that the Christian new birth has none of those connotations. He argues that the Christian new birth is a one-time unrepeatable event in which the believer is born again by the Holy Spirit to eternal life. "It is the once-and-for all and final new birth of a human life for the new, eternal creation of heaven and earth, and the beginning of the fulfilled promise of God." Thus, Christians are born again into a living eschatological hope that offers assurance in the here and now. Moltmann, *The Source of Life*, 27–29).

25 Moltmann, *Jesus Christ for Today's World*, 81. By Moltmann's reckoning, faith that is true can never be lost because the believer's new life comes from the Holy Spirit. The new life comes from above and is eternal, therefore it cannot be overcome. Therefore, salvation comes from God's faithfulness to the believer and not from the believer's faithfulness to God.

26 Moltmann writes, "Even if I am lost to myself, I am never lost to the faithful God. Even if I give myself up, God never gives me up," *The Source of Life* (London: SCM Press, 1997), 323.

27 Moltmann, *The Crucified God* (London: SCM Press, 1994), 277. He refers to this as a "Theology after Auschwitz," and comments that there would have been no theology *after* Auschwitz had there not be theology *in* Auschwitz.

28 Moltmann, *The Crucified God*, 278.

29 LifeWay Research, "New Study of Acute Mental illness and Christian Faith," https://lifewayresearch.com/mentalillnessstudy/, accessed June 23, 2020.; Ed Stetzer, "The Church and Mental Health: What Do the Numbers Tell Us?" April 20, 2018, https://www.christianitytoday.com/edstetzer/2018/april/church-and-mental-health.html. I discuss the church's attitude towards depression and the reasons behind this attitude in *Depression, Where is Your Sting?*, 4–6, 89.

30 Richard Baukham, *The Theology of Jurgen Moltmann* (Edinburgh, UK: T&T Clark, 1996), 36, quoted in John Swinton, *Resurrecting the Person: Friendship and the Care of People with Mental Health Problems* (Nashville, TN: Abingdon, 2000), 130.

31 Swinton, *Resurrecting the Person*, 130. Swinton describes Jesus' resurrection as a threefold event with each event having its own meaning and implications for the church: it was a historical event; an eschatological event; and it is a way of being.

32 Moltmann, *The Source of Life*, 95–96.

33 John Wilkinson, *The Bible and Healing: A Medical and Theological Commentary* (Grand Rapids: Eerdmans, 2000), 11–13; 17; 18.

34 See Craig Keener, *John* (Grand Rapids, MI: Baker Academic, 2010), 1201–1202.

35 Colin G. Kruse, *John: An Introduction and Commentary* (Downers Grove, IL: IVP Academic, 2017), 446.

36 Lincoln explains that this peace comes from knowing Jesus will free his followers to fulfil their commission, because it removes any need to fear others' opinions, hostile attitudes or persecuting actions. See Andrew T. Lincoln, *Gospel According to St John* (London: Continuum, 2006), 498–499.

37 In this commission, Jesus sends his disciples into the world in the same way that the Father sent him: to do his will (6:38–39; 8:29), speak his words (3:34; 8:28; 12:49; 14:24; 17:8), perform his works (4:34; 5:36; 9:4), and win salvation for all who believe (3:16–17). See Lincoln, *Gospel According to St John*, 498–499.

38 In John's Gospel, sin is primarily failing to acknowledge God's revelation in Jesus (cf. 8:24; 9:39–41; 15:22, 24). Throughout John's Gospel, Jesus' words and works are depicted as bringing about a judgment that the recipients make on themselves by either responding to the Gospel message in belief or exposing their sin through their unbelief. See Lincoln, *Gospel According to St John*, 499.

39 Lincoln, *Gospel According to St John*, 499. Keener is clear that only God has the power to forgive sins, but he recognizes that believers can play a role in other believers' forgiveness in the following ways: prayer (1 John 5:16–17), ministry to nonbelievers, and mediating God's forgiveness through the word they bring (20:21; 16:8–11). See Keener, *John*, 1207.

40 John Swinton, *Finding Jesus in the Storm: The Spiritual Lives of Christians with Mental Health Challenges* (Grand Rapids: Eerdmans, 2020), 206.

41 Moltmann, *The Spirit of Life*, 257–258.

42 Swinton, *Resurrecting the Person*, 72–74.

43 Swinton, *Resurrecting the Person*, 74–75.

44 D. J. Louw refers to this as a "theology of affirmation," which interacts with the ontological issues that affect social status and identity. A theology of affirmation understands being human in eschatological terms and sees it as an ontological category that uses the events of Jesus' death and resurrection to define humanity. See D. J. Louw, "Space and Place in the Healing of Life: Towards a Theology of Affirmation in Pastoral Care and Counselling," *Verbum Et Ecclesia* 29:2 (May 2008): 434–438.

45 Moltmann, *The Spirit of Life*, 259.

9 The "Flourishing of Life" in the Spirit on Earth after the Pandemic?: A Trinitarian Approach to the Eschatological Future

Sanna Urvas

Abstract

The COVID-19 pandemic has forced us to experience hardship in our communities, but it has also directed our eyes and thoughts toward the future; what will it look like? The coming kingdom of God is foretold in certainty but not yet fully here. However, Apostle Paul reveals some aspects of it in Romans 14:17–19; that kingdom of God is not about eating or drinking but about peace and mutual edification. This essay will explore what could be the fullness of life that is promised, according to Psalms 92:13, as "they will flourish in the courts of our Lord." The Holy Spirit brings the presence of our Lord to the earth, but to understand the kingdom of God, we need a trinitarian approach to the topic. The inspiration for the construction is taken, among others, from Amos Yong, John Zizioulas, William Atkinson, and Daniela Augustine, and several Church fathers. This theological construction will lead to an investigation of how the global body of believers could support and encourage those who have suffered the most during this pandemic: women and children in the poorest communities. I will offer my constructive proposal to encourage, especially women in the body of Christ. I utilize the biblical image of Mary, following the tradition from the East and West, to present a role model for Charismatic, Spirit-filled women to become active and empowered in their communities. There is also a practical example. This pragmatic approach follows the paradigm of Charismatic Christianity, which strives to increase the knowledge of Christ but even more so to share the fullness of life in the Spirit with all humankind.

Introduction

The COVID-19 pandemic has forced us to experience unprecedented hardship in our communities, but it has also directed our eyes and thoughts towards the future, far and near. Our hope for the future can be expressed in Christian theology as waiting for something promised but not yet visible. Jürgen Moltmann wrote how hope is central to our faith and that Christ is our hope (Col. 1:27). "Christianity is eschatology, is hope, forward-looking and forward moving, and therefore also revolutionizing and transforming the present."[1] Sin was interpreted as despair by Moltmann,[2] and that is surely something God has not desired for his people. Instead, we can trust the words of the Psalmist that the righteous, those who are planted in the house of the Lord, "they will flourish" (Psalm 92:13).

Simon Chan brings forth concern for this Moltmannian model as too occupied with only the need to transform the present and neglecting the eternal hope. He wrote: "The present historical process is in a very real sense continuous with the future kingdom of God. Commitment to the world is based on attachment to the kingdom of God present in the world rather than on detachment from the snares of the world."[3] Therefore, to balance the perspective of hope for the future, it is necessary to focus on the question, how should we understand the kingdom of God at present, which is linked to the eternal, and should we do something about it? Veli-Matti Kärkkäinen points out how "church is a preceding sign pointing to the coming righteous rule of God in the eschaton."[4] He is reflecting the idea of Wolfhart Pannenberg, who in turn underlines the role of the church as a "signifier of the kingdom of God not through self-equating, but through the resolute differentiation of her own presence from the future of the coming kingdom."[5] Thus, the church as a signifier ought to be reflected through the concept of a kingdom.

However, this cannot be understood without a trinitarian vision of a community. Daniela Augustine writes about human existence:

> as an unceasing liturgical askesis expressed in communal striving toward tangible depicting the protocommunal trinitarian life in and through the daily life of the community. In and through the Spirit, humanity is to become what it beholds: the visible, living iconography of the invisible God in the cathedral of the cosmos.[6]

This is a central orientation for this essay, to find a way to flourish in life in the Spirit. This vision springs from the insights of the Trinity, which glorify God and his kingdom. The aim is to concentrate on spiritual, affective, and sufficient material well-being.

We read from the apostle Paul that the kingdom of God is not about eating or drinking but peace and mutual edification, and righteousness, peace, and joy in the Holy Spirit (Rom. 14:17–19). Additionally, we can learn from the book of Revelation that this kingdom, which is already but not yet present, requires us to focus on Christ and to work in order to remain in waiting for the soon coming king. Theodore Stylianopoulos has demonstrated how the repeated words of Christ in the book of Revelation, "I know your works," point in their writing context to the works or deeds as labor (*kopos*), patience (*hypomene*), love (*agape*), faith (*pistis*), and service (*diakonia*).[7] Believers are either praised for having these attributes in their lives or condemned according to the lack of them. This can be heard as an encouragement to the church to maintain the good practice of Christian life and love. The permanent division of condemnation between the light and darkness has not yet happened. Thus, we need to pay attention to our works and deeds until the coming of Christ. According to Stylianopoulos, the apostle John calls for Christians to have a counter27cultural way of life amidst a non-Christian society.[8] We are empowered by the Spirit to succeed in this challenge.

I have two perspectives on my topic. One approach is practical, but the other is ontological. Flourishing means well-being, which can be understood as affective and material. All we have is a gift from God (Psalm 16). To understand the flourishing of life in the Spirit, it is vital to understand the causality of human dependence on God and our intentions towards our neighbors. This essay explores the trinitarian approach to the well-being of humans and the community of believers, starting from the Holy Spirit, a gift and love flowing from the Father while remaining as a sanctifying Spirit while dwelling in the mystery of the Trinity. Steven Studebaker argues that the experience of a Spirit baptism should inform Pentecostal trinitarian theology.[9] However, my goal is to let trinitarian theology inform ecclesiology, especially from the ontological perspective, because the experiential dimension of the Spirit baptism would tie the commencing of the discussion too much to the anthropological side. The human experience is employed, after all, but then narrowed to the experience of women. Thus, the text proceeds to elaborate this trinitarian vision in the context of a church as a community and especially in the context of Pentecostal Mariology, drawing inspiration from the mother of Jesus as a spiritual model for women. All this is concluded with an idea of how the global body of Christ should empower the women in Christian communities and beyond.

Trinitarian Love as an Ontological Base for Christian Community and Well-Being

The reflection of the being of God needs to be balanced between holiness and love.[10] God is holy and love, but love can also be seen as the relationality of the trinitarian union. Amos Yong has elaborated on the nature of the Spirit as a Spirit of love and presents it as a saving and an energizing element in the body of Christ. "In brief, the Spirit of love is also the Spirit of the Father and the Son who is graciously given to the world so that she might sanctify and redeem the world for the glory of God."[11] Yong writes about Augustine (AD 354–430), who insisted that "happiness derives from desiring and having God, and doing God's will."[12] So, as we participate in Christ and through him, we will be sanctified; we can receive the love from above and enjoy the fullness of life in the Trinity. Augustine also wrote that no human could understand the mysterious love of God without experiencing the love between humans. The love towards neighbor is initiated by the original source of love, God himself. As John wrote, God is love among us (1 John 4:8,12,16).[13]

Yong points out the pneumatological aspect of love flowing from God. This can be approached from experiential and affective but even more so in an ecclesial way to strengthen believing communities. Yong also utilizes thoughts of a more contemporary voice, Paul Tillich, who has explored the nature of love from an ontological perspective. According to Tillich, love is a primordial force and a foundation of being. In itself, it is a counterforce against sin, which is "the existential rupture of being, resulting in estrangement and alienation."[14] This generates, in turn, human anxiety either as "'un-love (lack of faith or belief that separates humans from God as the ground of being) or by selfish love (concupiscence, a self-centeredness that ignores and does not love others)."[15] This pneumatological ontology was revealed to the church in its birth moment, Pentecost, and the outpouring of the Spirit formed something new in humanity and united the believers to love one other and work together.

Love is not the only aspect that matters. John Zizioulas has labored with the mystery of the Trinity, and he insists that the trinitarian communion should be understood through the ontology of the concept of a person. This concept was developed during the early centuries of

Christianity in a conversation between Latin and Greek church fathers. The use of the words *prosopion* (Greek) and *persona* (Latin) modified our understanding of not only God but later also us humans. However, from the philosophical point of view, to be a person in such a way as God is a person is not and cannot be an ontological explanation for the nature of humanity because the original understanding of the nature of a person is tied to its utter freedom. We are never free but remain eternally dependent on God. The only true freedom is hidden in the being of God, who is the only true person. Zizioulas points out how the ontological "principle" of God needs to be traced back to personhood because there is no divine existence, which would be in its "naked" form without the personhood of the Father, who has begotten the Son, and who brings forth the Spirit.[16] The crucial point is to add a layer to the ponderings of the being of God. The essence of God is not like cold energy or unknown darkness, even if it is clothed in a mystery that cannot ever be fully described with words. I argue that the concept of personhood as a metaphysical explanation for the being of God is to secure his majesty and freedom but simultaneously to draw the metaphysical vision of God closer to the narratives of the Bible from the abstract speculations of academic theology. Additionally, while striving to understand the essence of God, we are informed about what should be the essence of the church.[17]

However, the insights into the essence of personhood direct our thoughts to ponder its qualities of it, even if the essence is not applicable to humanity. The Father, who begets his Son in eternity, together with the proceeding of the Spirit, is an early doctrine to support and define the deity of the Son. Athanasius and Cappadocian fathers (Basil of Caesarea, Gregory Nazianzen, and Gregory of Nyssa) were engaged in a debate about Arianism during the fourth century. The Son's divine nature required him to be begotten before the time.[18] But there is another perspective to this eternal generation, which reveals the affective nature of the Father and the divinity. Imagine the moment when a child is born and is placed in the arms of a parent. The love and affection that even we, as limited creatures, can experience are magnificent. How much more is there in the heart of the Father whose love is perfect, and this love flows eternally in this mysterious eternal generation. This love is eternally present among the Trinity because Holy Spirit enjoys the same everlasting existence, and through the Spirit, this love is poured out upon all flesh.

Without taking sides of the old debate concerning *filioque*, it is useful at this point to utilize the old confession of the Trinity, as Father who has begotten and from who the Spirit proceeds.[19] This I write because the divinity wrapped in the mystery of the Father's person can underline the importance of fatherly love. It communicates and embraces the aspects of love and holiness at this moment better than any impersonalized substance of divine essence. We can rest in his love, even if we cannot understand his nature. Gregory of Nyssa (AD 335–395) wrote:

> Following the instructions of holy scripture, we have been taught that [the nature of God] is beyond names or human speech. We say that every [divine] name, be it invented by human custom or handed on to us by the tradition of the scriptures, represents our conceptions of the divine nature, but does not convey the meaning of that nature in itself.[20]

Therefore, it is beneficial to observe the nature of the Trinity from the perspective of persons and their relations. Willian Atkinson has utilized the old perichoretic view, which draws a scene of the divine persons penetrating each other and moving as in a beautiful dance. This is called *perichoresis*, meaning "mutual indwelling." Atkinson clarifies this movement with two perspectives, kenosis, and exaltation. These two actions are the dynamics of the life and heart of the trinitarian relations. He writes: "It is the ultimate expression of selfless love for the living God to undergo genuine kenosis for the sake of the divine other. . . . Thus, what emerges is an enduring dynamic reciprocal "dance" of the persons of the Trinity, in which each ceaselessly empties self in order to exalt the other, and in turn as "reward" is exalted by the other."[21]

I continue Atkinson's idea by pointing to the thoughts of Irenaeus regarding the moments of creation in which Father is revealed as the Creator but creating with "two hands," the Spirit and the Word.[22] Creation is a trinitarian act, but the scriptures point only to *Elohim*; the personalities of Son and Spirit remain hidden. Additionally, God had to remain hidden when dealing with Israelites because of his holy nature, which would have burned them alive (Lev 10). Only Moses was able to meet Him face to face (Exod 33:11). These two actions, kenosis, and exaltation can be seen in Pauline (Phil 2:6–9) and Johannine language (John 16:14; 17:1). Christ emptied himself to become our salvation. Furthermore, Pentecost is the key moment to understand the kenosis of the Father, who pours out his Spirit, and the Spirit is revealed as a person. However, we can see in

Romans 8:26–27 how the Spirit helps us in our weaknesses. Our hearts are searched by the Holy One, and without this willing kenotic act of the Spirit, we could end up like Nadab and Abihu. Therefore, we can see the Trinity giving away space for one other but also in their actions to relate to humanity. Likewise, we can notice the exaltation in the last prayer of Jesus (John 17). This I will take as a leading lesson (in human terms) for the Christian community to guide the practical way towards love, to give space to the other and encourage and lift up each other in love.

Many writers have dreamed of the incarnation of the kingdom of God on earth. Pannenberg wrote how "only in the kingdom of God will human society find the consummation that is freed from all self-seeking and mutual oppression."[23] This kingdom reality should be searched for and desired in the present time. However, as it is written in Vatican II's *Gaudium et Spes*, we should remain in obedience to the Lord and allow his Spirit to nurture on earth the values of human dignity, brotherhood, and freedom, and this will lead to a glorified future because we are reminded that "On this earth that kingdom is already present in mystery. When the Lord returns, it will be brought into full flower."[24] Kärkkäinen writes, "Knowing that the ultimate reconciliation of peoples and groups can only happen in new creation does not lead the church into passivity, let alone apathy. The church is joining the work for liberation and justice exactly because it knows the thereby it participates in the work of the trinitarian God."[25] In order to see this liberation and flourishing happen evenly among humanity, I now turn to observe what could motivate us, women, to embrace it as an equal invitation to abundant and Spirit-filled life as it was above wished-for for the brotherhood.

Spirit-filled Womanhood inspired by Pentecostal Mariology and the Biblical Inspiration for a Mutual Well-being

As in all humanitarian crises, it is women and children who usually suffer the most.[26] The suffering has stormed not only as a fear of illness and lost lives but also in the form of violence[27] and increased poverty.[28] Irwan Gani explains how the pandemic has affected the women in Indonesia and what could be done to help to prevent, for example, the exploitation of women due to poverty.[29] The earlier mentioned *diakonia* is important, and women are often rightfully portrayed both as subjects and objects of *diakonia* and in need of protection in fragile societies. But first, I want to pay attention to the source of Spirit-filled empowerment for women that we Christians have in the Bible, the role model of Mary, the mother of Jesus. This can help us to construct an identity as Christian women who devote their lives to Jesus, embrace a role of an active agent as an enabler of well-being and salvation, and perceive our lives in a community which reflects the Trinity as it has been described above. All this we can learn from the narrative of Mary in the Bible and its use throughout history.

Mary is known in the Gospels as a young woman who needed to make a bold choice, to carry an illegitimate child during a time one could have been stoned because of it. Her strength for that decision came from heaven because she was literally filled by the Spirit. Mary is also presented as a mother, a *theotokos*[30] who carried the incarnated Christ in her womb. Luke especially introduces us to Mary as the one who is willing to take part in the plan of redemption. Mary was not only filled by the Spirit, became courageous to act, and was ready to give her life and flesh to the Christ, but she also acted as a prophet[31] who pronounced the favour of God for the poor, the weak, and the needy (Luke 1:46–55). She was not a passive victim of a cosmic play but was lifted up from the potential and feared disgrace and doom and was transformed to be an active agent who willingly submitted her life for the greater good, and she took part in creating an eternal community. She experienced one of the greatest pains that can strike a mother, losing her child to a cruel death. But that did not prevent her. This is the Mary I offer as a role model for the believing Spirit-filled women in every corner of the globe.

The church tradition holds that Mary remained a member of a Christian community for the rest of her life.[32] According to the early tradition, Mary was regarded as the first disciple and a follower of Christ in salvation. The argument for this view is built with an exegetical interpretation of the Luke 1:28 from the Greek word κεχαριτωμένη, which indicates that Mary had already been transformed by grace.[33] Chris Maunder points out how Mary is the heroine of the salvation history in the nativity scene and how her prophetic vocation in Luke's text is well established through her speeches. Later development in traditional Marian narratives combined these notions with an ecclesiological tone indicating Mary as a prototype and an image of the believing church and in her role as a first disciple.[34]

The key is the motherly love that must have overflowed from her heart for her son. Any mother is willing to do all in their power for their babies. This love, both as a divine presence and in human terms, was another key to transforming her, and this reminds us of the effective part of being a follower and a disciple of Jesus.

Mary's actions and decisions were possible because she was filled with the Spirit and love and therefore did not need to act according to her own human strength. This alone is an important notion for Pentecostals; we long for this, as a baptism of the Holy Spirit, and to live a lifestyle in which we are continuously filled and embraced by the Spirit. Additionally, Mary's experiences of joy and grief were not meant for her alone. Although she rejoiced personally, those moments generated the prophetic words in her, which reminded the world of the need for our collective responsibility. Thus, she became a model of how to endure hardship with the power of God for the good of the others. The lowly and unpleasant circumstances did not make her passive; already, in the beginning, she had the courage to proclaim God's just order, which does not regard the monetary possession as the base for the value of people.

Church tradition along the centuries has generated several ways to characterize Mary. During the first centuries, she was perceived as a virgin mother due to the needs of the developing Christology at that period. Medieval West created a narrative of Mary as a humble servant, and the East emphasized, for example, Mary's role as a defender of orthodoxy and a fierce guardian against Satan.[35] However, Anna-Riina Hakala writes how even in the West, and especially in the medieval monastic tradition, it was common to refer to Mary as a militant figure. She writes. "'Blessed are you among women" (Luke 1:42) is a reference to a greeting received by two Old Testament women, Yael and Judith, who both killed commanders of Israel's enemy by hitting them on the head."[36] This tradition follows the biblical notion of Mary as an active and valiant woman. It needs to be remembered that Mary did not act alone–she was empowered with the Spirit.

The roles and stories of Mary and Eve have been connected since the second century, first by Irenaeus.[37] I do not wish to employ this polarizing placement of Eve against Mary or either woman against any man, but rather I want to point to the Fall as a generating force of oppression and corruption in every level of human existence and relationships. The

Bible shows that this was not the original intention of the Creator. In the beginning, man and woman are portrayed as codependent for agricultural work and for procreating the next generation even if they have specifically different roles for each task.[38] Later stories in the Hebrew canon reveal the dependency on God in both of these matters. It is notable how many important women are barren in the Genesis stories and that there is an immediate need to ask for God's intervention.[39] The pregnancy of Mary was entirely dependent on God. There was no need for man's intervention or involvement, only a need for a subservient woman. However, the welfare of the church, for securing the nurture of its members or bringing in new ones, needs all these aspects, strong and active women and men and codependency of both genders serving in their God-given roles, without any domination or oppression from either side. This differentiation of roles united with the perichoretic cooperation should be the inner core of the church and its relationships and activities. This is the key to the flourishing of life in the Spirit. Additionally, we need to focus on our spiritual lives, earthly bodies, and affective well-being in our communities.

As mentioned, flourishing of life requires the three-dimensional approach to our everyday lives, but which of these is the primary? I present one example from Eastern Syrian fathers. These fathers pondered the secrets of the spiritual life of individuals and a community. They were fully aware of the psychological dimensions of the spiritual experiences, even if the word psychology is anachronistic to be used here. Their teaching was based on the observations and knowledge of the inseparable nature of, on the one hand, a person's inner and purely human experiences and, on the other, divinely originated and, therefore, spiritual ones. The awareness of these two dimensions, human and divinely originated experiences happening and functioning together, was supposed to keep monks humble. Serafim Seppälä explains how the early Syrian understanding of spiritual life included a bodily dimension furthermore as part of a person's spiritual orientation. A human being cannot be divided into separate faculties, and equally, women and men should seek this holistic orientation in their lives as disciples of Jesus.[40]

According to this ancient Syrian wisdom, there is an invisible mirror created in the hearts of humans, which can reflect the divine presence, and this mirror enables people to experience the beauty of being a child of God. Seppälä writes and quotes Simon of Taybutha, who was a monk and a doctor and understood both the spiritual and bodily aspects of humanity.[41] "It is possible for a human to act and orient oneself in a way that his/her inner core is transformed to a state that the influence of the Holy Spirit will brighten the inner being of a human and the way he/she is directed towards the outer world. "By the inner power of the Holy Spirit he/she can behold them [his/her inner being and the world] without any darkness, because Holy Spirit lives and works in that mirror."[42] We ought to allow the secret of the trinitarian love to reside and be reflected in that mirror by the power of the Spirit! That will direct our *kopos, hypomene* and *diakonia* towards the needy world, Christian and other.

It is notable how all those countless generations who have enjoyed the presence and the power of the Holy Spirit have also understood the need to direct the blessing of inner joy to the welfare of the lives at large. This is the secret of abundant life. However, how can we be sure that it is fairly shared in the body of Christ even if the world is not just and not providing sources or having economic or societal stability? Daniela Augustine writes about her observations based on Hebrew and Christian sources:

> Indeed, the protection of human dignity is a fundamental concern of both the Mosaic Law and the rabbinic tradition. An uninvited poverty humiliates and subjugates the person to degrading conditions of existence that could be partially caused by other's charity . . . While humanitarian relief is essential for economic interventions (and . . . is a fundamental Christian mandate, Matt 25), the best form of charity to a healthy adult remains economic empowerment (inseparable from sociopolitical emancipation and demarginalization) through proper employment and related infrastructural prerequisites, such as quality education and professional training, that permanently alleviate hunger and poverty and secure just financial compensation for one's labor.[43]

This inspires me to suggest the following for the global body of Christ.

A Way Forward Among the Global Body of Christ

Trinitarian community is a secret, but our lives need care and nurture, spiritually and in practice. This can be ensured by strong communities. As Moltmann writes, the Christian community is "not just to proclaim the gospel of God's love, but also to live it in community."[44] The body of Christ or the kingdom of God, however, is both local and global. What if the wealthy Global North would commence taking their responsibility for the welfare and flourishing of the Global South members, especially women seriously? We need to be reminded of an example given in Acts 2:44–45 to share our wealth. Veli-Pekka Haarala notifies how Luke emphasized and probably utilized a utopistic view of the early Christian community regarding the idea of selling and sharing. He argues that it was not a probable custom that all sold everything but rather that those who had much sold out of their abundance that everyone had enough. Haarala writes:

> Thus, Hebrew Bible, Second Temple Judaism and early Christian writings include similar features [κοινωνία as a utopia which embraces the idea of sharing the welfare] from harmonious paradise of Eden, theocratic Israel in the Promised land governed by God himself and coming of the promised kingdom proclaimed by Jesus. Surely, the Biblical traditions of assets and ownership fluctuate and deviate, but the fundamental assumptions are quite alike: commitment of the community to cherish the utopistic ideals generates collective happiness, prosperity, and harmony.[45]

This is notable, but according to Daniela Augustine, the way forward is not charity, which is limited to its conventional form of provision of basic needs. Instead, it could be done differently.

The Kashf Foundation is a Non-Banking Micro Finance Company operating in Pakistan, which was set up in 1996. It provides products and services to low-income households and especially women. By creating an enabling environment for women entrepreneurs, it is possible to create stronger communities and provide secure livelihood also for those women who are not protected by their families.[46] Churches could mobilize their members in these types of activities in poor communities, and the provision for this type of microfinance company could come from the wealthy North. Why is the secular world better in this than the global body of Christ? Churches and mission organizations are doing much already, but there is so much wealth in the churches which could be shared by providing this type of business opportunity for poorer communities. Culturally, it would be better that this type of support and service comes from the rich Christian global community to the poorer Christian local communities than altogether from the secular world.[47]

Money is never the final solution, especially in eternal questions. But we cannot neglect the insights of the holistic approach to the flourishing of life, the wisdom is hidden already in the event of creation. Daniela Augustine writes:

God gives the world to humanity in self-sharing as a gift of life so that humanity may, in turn, learn to share it with the other and the different. The world is a gift with a pedagogical function–helping humanity 'grow spiritually'–to grow in the likeness of God . . . the world cannot be kept for oneself–it is made to be shared as a eucharistic communion with the other.[48]

Let this be our inspiration to build a stronger global community of Christ, which is famous in the front of the secular and the fallen world by taking care of every single member, regardless of the location, color, or gender. The Holy Spirit unites the church, and its members should be united in every effort to look after and ensure that all can enjoy the flourishing of life until the kingdom comes in its full splendor.

Notes

1 Jürgen Moltmann, *Theology of Hope: On the Grounds and the Implications of a Christian Eschatology* (New York: Harper and Row, 1965), 6.

2 Moltmann, *Theology of Hope*, 11–14.

3 Simon Chan, *Spiritual Theology: A Systematic Study of the Christian Life* (Downers Grove: InterVarsity Press, 1998), 186.

4 Veli-Matti Kärkkäinen, *Hope and Community: A Constructive Christian Theology for the Pluralistic World*, vol. 5 (Grand Rapids, MI: Eerdmans, 2017), 292.

5 Gunther Wenz, *Introduction to Pannenberg's Systematic Theology* (Bristol, CN.: Vandenhoeck and Ruprecht, 2013), 169. Cf. Wolfhart Pannenberg, *Systematic Theology*, vol. 3, trans. Geoffrey Bromily (Grand Rapids, MI: Eerdman's, 2009), 45. Quoted in Kärkkäinen, *Hope and Community*, 293.

6 Daniela C. Augustine, *The Spirit and the Common Good: Shared Flourishing in the Image of God* (Grand Rapids, MI: Eerdmans, 2019), 45.

7 Theodore Stylianopoulos, "'I Know Your Works": Grace and Judgement in the Apocalypse,' Robert J. Daly, ed., *Apocalyptic Thought in Early Christianity* (, MIGrand Rapids: Baker Academic, 2009), 23.

8 Stylianopoulos, "I Know Your Works," 23–26.

9 Steven M. Studebaker, *From Pentecost to Triune God: A Pentecostal Trinitarian Theology* (Grand Rapids, MI: Eerdmans, 2012), 12. (e-book version)

10 See, for example Dimitar Popmarinov Kirov, "The Way of Holiness," S. T. Kimborough, Jr. ed., *Orthodox and Wesleyan Spirituality* (Crestwood, NY: St Vladimir's Seminary Press, 2002), 121; 117–126.

11 Amos Yong, *Spirit of Love: A Trinitarian Theology of Grace* (Waco, TX: Baylor University Press, 2012), xii.

12 Augustine, "The Happy Life," Boniface Ramsey, ed., *Trilogy on Faith and Happiness*, trans., Roland J. Teske (Hyde Park, NY: New City Press, 2010), in Yong, *Spirit of Love*, 4.

13 Yong, *Spirit of Love*, 5–6.

14 Yong, *Spirit of Love*, 14.

15 Paul Tillich, *Systematic Theology*, vol 2 (Chicago: University of Chicago Press, 1957), 47–55. Quoted in Yong, *Spirit of Love*, 14–15.

16 John D. Zizioulas, *Being as a Communion: Studies in Personhood and the Church* (Crestwood, NY: St Vladimir's Seminary Press, 1985), 18, 35, 40–41, 44.

17 See the discussion offered by Gordon Kaufman, *An Essay on Theological Method*, 3rd ed. (Atlanta: Scholars Press, 1995), 39–41. He argues that the use of metaphysics and metaphysical ideas are essential in the general orientation of life.

18 Charles Lee Irons, "Begotten of the Father Before All Ages: The Biblical Basis of Eternal Generation According to the Church Fathers," *Christian Research Journal* 40:1 (2017), http://www.equip.org/PDF/JAF5401.pdf, accessed May 6, 2021.

19 This was the original confession of Trinity formulated by the Cappadocian Fathers and became a normative for centuries. See Jaroslav Pelikan, *The Emergence of the Catholic Tradition (100–600), The Christian Tradition: A History of the Development of Doctrine*, vol.1 (Chicago: The University of Chicago Press, 1971), 223.

20 Gregory of Nyssa, *That There Are Not Three Gods [Quod non sint tres dii]*, in Pelikan, *The Emergence of the Catholic Tradition*, 222.

21 William P. Atkinson, *Trinity After Pentecost* (Eugene, OR: Pickwick Publications, 2013), 146. Quotation marks original.

22 This notion originates from Irenaeus. See, M. C. Steenberg, *Irenaeus on Creation: The Cosmic Christ and the Saga of Redemption*, vol. 91 (Leiden, Boston: Brill, 2008), 64–65.

23 Pannenberg, Systematic Theology, 523. Quoted in Kärkkäinen, *Hope and Community*, 148.

24 *Gaudium et Spes*, # 39, 23-24, https://www.vatican.va/archive/hist_councils/ii_vatican_council/documents/vat-ii_const_19651207_gaudium-et-spes_en.html, accessed May 17, 2021.
25 Kärkkäinen, *Hope and Community*, 148.
26 See Sustainable Development Goal Report 2020 and key findings, https://www.un.org/sustainabledevelopment/progress-report/, accessed May 27, 2021.
27 See Elisabeth Roesch, et al., "Violence Against Women During Covid-19 Pandemic Restrictions," https://www.bmj.com/content/bmj/369/bmj.m1712.full.pdf, accessed May 17, 2021.
28 See Andrew Sumner, Eduardo Ortiz-Juarez and Chris Hoy, "Precarity and the Pandemic: COVID-19 and Poverty Incidence, Intensity, and Severity in Developing Countries," (Econstor Working Paper no. 2020/77),https://www.econstor.eu/bitstream/10419/229301/1/wp2020-077.pdf, accessed May 17, 2021.
29 Irwan Gani, "Poverty of Women and the Covid-19 Pandemic in Indonesia" *Budapest International Research and Critics Institute-Journal* 4:1 (February 2021),1034–104.
30 Richard Price, "The Virgin as Theotokos at Ephesus (AD 431) and Earlier," Chris Maunder ed., *The Oxford Handbook of Mary* (Oxford: Oxford University Press, 2019), https://www-oxfordhandbooks-com.libproxy.helsinki.fi/view/10.1093/oxfordhb/9780198792550.001.0001/oxfordhb-9780198792550-e-27, viewed May 18, 2021.
31 See, especially, Serafim Seppälä, "Is the Virgin Mary a Prophetess? Patristic, Syriac and Islamic views," *Parole de l'Orient* 36 (2011), 367–373.
32 Andrew Louth, "Mary in Patristics," Chris Maunder ed., *The Oxford Handbook of Mary* (Oxford: Oxford University Press, 2019), https://www-oxfordhandbooks-com.libproxy.helsinki.fi/view/10.1093/oxfordhb/9780198792550.001.0001/oxfordhb-9780198792550-e-19, viewed May 18, 2021.
33 Chris Maunder, "Mary and the Gospel Narratives," Chris Maunder ed., *The Oxford Handbook of Mary* (Oxford: Oxford University Press, 2019), https://www-oxfordhandbooks-com.libproxy.helsinki.fi/view/10.1093/oxfordhb/9780198792550.001.0001/oxfordhb-9780198792550-e-39, viewed May 18, 2021.
34 Maunder, "Mary and the Gospel Narratives," 31.
35 Brian K. Reynolds, "The Patristic and Medieval Roots of Mary's Humility," Chris Maunder ed., *The Oxford Handbook of Mary* (Oxford: Oxford University Press, 2019), 320–322.

36 Anna-Riina Hakala, *Bernard of Clairvaux's Letters and the Anatomy of a Cloistered Man: Gendered Imagery in Letters from the First Decade as an Abbot* (Doctoral thesis, University of Helsinki, 2021), 146. Hakala refers to Curtis Mitch, and Scott Hahn, eds., "Luke 42:1 commentary," *Ignatius Catholic Study Bible* (San Francisco, CA: Ignatius Press, 2010), https://www-oxfordhandbooks-com.libproxy.helsinki.fi/view/10.1093/oxfordhb/9780198792550.001.0001/oxfordhb-9780198792550-e-45, viewed May 18, 2021.

37 Brian K. Reynolds, "Marian Typology and Symbolic Imagery in Patristic Christianity" Chris Maunder ed., *The Oxford Handbook of Mary* (Oxford: Oxford University Press, 2019), 83.

38 Ronald A. Simkins, "Gender, The Environment, and Sin in Genesis," Susan Calef and Ronald A. Simkins, eds., "Women, Gender, and Religion," *Journal of Religion and Society* Supplement series 5 (The Kripke Center: 2009), 45–61.

39 See more about this theme, Janice Pearl Ewurama De-Whyte, "Sarah, Rebekah, and Rachel: Beautiful and Barren" *Wom(b)an: A Cultural-Narrative Reading of the Hebrew Bible Barrenness Narratives* (Brill, 2018) e-book, 81–123. DOI: https://doi.org/10.1163/9789004366305_006.

40 Serafim Seppälä, "Pyhä Henki Itäsyyrialaisessa Mystiikassa," *Pyhä Henki Varhaiskristillisessä Teologiassa* Studia Patristica Fennica 3 (Helsinki: Suomen Patristinen Seura, 2015), 38.

41 See more about the early Syrian understanding of anthropology, Alexey Muraviev, "Mar Isḥaq Ninevita and Possible Medical Context of Eastern Syriac Asceticism," *Parole de l'Orient* 40 (2015), 1–15.

42 Seppälä, "Pyhä Henki Itäsyyrialaisessa Mystiikassa," 37. Quote: Simeon of Taybutha, Early Christian Mystics. WS 7 Cambridge 1934, 315, 194a. (Translated from Finnish by this author) I utilize this old Syrian tradition as an example of an old holistic and charismatic Christian tradition.

43 Augustine, *The Spirit and the Common Good*, 110.

44 Jürgen Moltmann, *The Living God and the Fullness of Life*, trans. Margaret Kohl (Louisville: Westminster John Knox, 2015), 152.

45 Veli-Pekka Haarala, "Omaisuuden Jakamisen Ihanne Alkuseurakunnassa Luukkaan Mukaan: Eksegeettinen tutkielma Apostolien tekojen luvusta 2:44:45," (Pro Gradu Thesis, University of Helsinki, May, 2021), 10. Haarala uses especially Mary A. Beavis, *Jesus & Utopia: Looking for the Kingdom of God in the Roman World* (Minneapolis, MN: Fortress Press, 2006), 29–52; Charles Kingsley Barrett, *A Critical and Exegetical*

Commentary on the Acts of the Apostles (Edinburgh: T&T Clark, 2004), 254–255; James Dunn, *The Acts of the Apostles* (Grand Rapids, MI: Eerdmans, 2016), 58–59.

46 See more about their vision, mission, and core values here: https://kashf.org/vision-mission-core-values/.

47 Private conversation with Javed Gill, May 24, 2021, regarding the situation in Pakistan. Kashf has served well also Christian women, but nevertheless, it is better option also in many cultures, that the support comes from the Christian actors. May 24, 2021.

48 Augustine, *The Spirit and the Common Good,* 130–131.

10 Redeeming the Darkness: A Reflection on How the Pandemic is Bringing Light and Dignity to a Community in a Redlight District of India

Mathew Daniel and Suhasini Daniel

Abstract

This chapter draws from interviews and personal experience of ministry in red light districts of India. Factors perpetuating sex slavery are examined through the lens of global research statistics as well as personal trauma narratives given by former workers in the sex trade in India. The authors' reflection on the Holy Spirit's unique and specific guidance in ministry to women and children trapped in place in a red light district because of Pandemic restrictions is given as a means of encouragement to readers who also listen for the Spirit's voice.

Introduction

This chapter is not light reading. The content isn't about social injustice, loss, or trauma alone. It isn't about the powerful versus the powerless either. Instead, it leads you into the cosmic battles that are being fought and must be waged on behalf of the exploited. This chapter, we hope, will inspire a response of compassion and a desire to join the fight against injustice in your own sphere of influence!

India, the largest democracy in the world, has held a key position in world history for as long as one can explore history. Home to several world religions and tolerant of people from varying cultures, ideologies, and walks of life, India is a colorful and vibrant nation. A nation of 1.3 billion people, Indians are generally hospitable, warm, and peace-loving. Historically, while India may have been invaded by neighboring countries or tribes, it has hardly invaded or annexed any other nation or people. Whether making strides in science, inventions, innovative responses to global crises, military advancement, or educational progress, India has made her mark. She is a fast-developing nation and is quickly shifting into a formidable superpower in the Asian region. At a glance, India has achieved much in global economic, political, social, educational, and international relations. Mark Twain only reiterates India's global position when he said: "So far as I am able to judge, nothing has been left undone, either by man or nature, to make India the most extraordinary country that the sun visits on its rounds. Nothing seems to have been forgotten, nothing overlooked."[1] But Laila and many whose voices you will hear in these pages may disagree with Twain's assessment.

An Overview of Trafficking, Its Extent, and Nature

"A job in the city can help you deal with any family illness. Once your father is discharged, I can meet you." The words brought tears to her eyes as Laila, age sixteen, sat with Suhasini and pieced together her harrowing narrative of trafficking and slavery. "All I wanted to do was ensure my father got his treatment." Laila was just thirteen when she was trafficked. Now sixteen, she sat before me, looking much beyond her years. The oldest of four children, she had to find a way to help her mother make ends meet.

But in her perspective, fate and family conspired and made plans that were for her harm and not for her good. Laila was trafficked from a town in the state of West Bengal, situated on the Indo-Bangladesh border, and sold into Kolkata's Sonagachi red-light district. After an initial week of being there, she was trafficked into Maharashtra and sold into the red-light district in Nashik. Being young and pretty, she was paraded before trusted customers before being exploited every day. This continued for six months. When raids were conducted in the district, she would often be sent off to a separate place on the outskirts of the city. Occasionally, she would be sent out of the city into a new red-light district, where her ordeal began again. On one such occasion, she was drugged and then brought to Pune. Here she was sold again into the red-light district. Within two years, Laila had been re-trafficked ten times and handed over to multiple owners before she was rescued in a raid in Mumbai. By the time she was rescued, she was sixteen, HIV positive, and had had six abortions.[2]

While we may think this is just a story, this is the plight of many women and teens in slavery across the globe. The International Labour Organization estimates that, by their definitions, over 40 million people are in some form of slavery today. 24.9 million people are in forced labor, of whom 16 million people are exploited in the private sector, such as domestic work, construction, or agriculture; 4.8 million persons are in forced sexual exploitation, and 4 million persons in forced labor imposed by state authorities.³ The names, the details, and the circumstances may differ, but the horror of trafficking runs rife. Human trafficking is defined as the recruitment, transportation, transfer, harboring, or receipt of people through force, fraud, or deception, with the aim of exploiting them for profit.⁴ In simple words, it's when people are uprooted, lured, and made to believe that somehow newer options are more viable and then are pushed into exploitation against their will. As one can see, the definition is broad and generalized. However, we are limiting the purview of this chapter to that of trafficking for the purposes of commercial sexual exploitation and sex slavery.

The nature and extent of trafficking and slavery permeates and affects every area of a victim's life. Her body, mind, and spirit are wounded, and it leads to the deep wounding of her soul. Initially duped and lured into a life not of her choosing, she loses trust in people. Broken promises and strong distrust mark her interactions with people. In the red-light district, also referred to as brothel-based prostitution, she has to buy back her freedom by luring men and ensuring she pays back her monetary debt. Mostly uneducated and illiterate, many young girls are unable to count or to realize the amount they have already repaid. In an article by India Today in 2017, Shweta Punj highlights the issue of trafficking and slavery and brings to notice the commerce and income involved.⁵

Vulnerability Factors

The vulnerability factors for victims are numerous and can be broadly categorized into economic, social, and religious factors. One of the most common vulnerability factors that experts cite is poverty. However, poverty alone cannot be said to motivate one to sell one's children. It takes certain desperation combined with a complete disregard for human life for one to sell one's own child. Thus, the authors tend to regard human depravity and greed as key factors in exploitation, as this quote from Teena, a former manager now serving a sentence, illustrates:

> Who are the victims? It can be anyone. We don't differentiate. We see someone whom we perceive as weak, vulnerable, in need or who can be duped and target the child/teen or lady. In some case we even arrange for

their kidnapping if the money is good. But I'm not like that. Every year I go back to my village and bring at least four or five girls. I'm trying to help them come out of debt and help their families.[6]

During the course of over thirty-five interviews[7] prior to this article, women who have long since lost hope cited the material benefits that family or aunts or uncles or neighbors received from selling them. The authors tend to agree. It's when the desire for a better life or better stuff makes you stoop down to disregard human life and its worth. Payal can attest to this theory. She said her family worked hard in the field to make ends meet. Payal and her siblings had even sacrificed their summer holidays so they could help in the field. But nothing they did help as her father had an outstanding gambling debt. The lot fell on her to help redeem his respect and his life. While processing her trauma narrative, she realized it wasn't just the debt but her life that seemed to hold little or no value to the family. Such knowledge seems too heavy to bear for a trauma survivor.

The low status of women, the preference for sons and consequent neglect of daughters, natural disasters and refugee populations, lack of access to education, arranging false marriages, and runaway situations are the factors that pose a threat to the safety of children and teens. But the vulnerability factors don't end here; religious factors too play a critical role in the safety and future of children. Teens who live in certain cultures of the world may be more susceptible as religion and cultural traditions play a certain role in what vocation a child should follow. The *jogini* and *devadasi* (literal "servants of god") systems subject a daughter to the servitude of priests. These young girls are dedicated to goddess, yellamma, in a ceremony akin to a marriage ceremony. Considered an important and revered vocation, the girls are expected to dance and serve people who come to the temple. Several of the young girls are subject to exploitation and then sold to traffickers who finally sell them in red-light districts where they are further exploited. A report by *The Asian Age* in 2017 states: "practice in the southern states of Tamil Nadu and Andhra Pradesh and parts of Western India, the *devadasi* system, which 'dedicates' girls to a life of sex work in the name of religion, continues despite being outlawed in 1988."[8]

Parvati, one of the ladies whom we had the privilege of meeting in one of the red-light districts, narrates a story where she was chosen to carry on her temple duties in the temple town of Miraj, on the Karnataka Maharashtra border. However, she realized very early on that she wasn't chosen for holy and pure acts but for heinous ones. Her family had traveled for three days by bullock cart to drop her at the temple because they felt they were told she was "chosen," and their daughter would lead a very important and blessed life. As she describes the months and years that followed, she claims in her own words: "I was chosen for death, not life."[9]

For the sake of brevity, we will enumerate some additional factors that are critical to helping slavery thrive. The first is a sense of entitlement that pervades society where we think we are deserving of a good life while others aren't. It is the haves versus the have-nots and typically the poor and vulnerable against those who are perceived to be powerful. Second, silence in society regarding issues: we are too afraid to speak up against the exploitation and the trafficking of children and women. We are quite happy with the status quo as long as it doesn't happen to someone within my family and circle of friends. Third, general apathy and judgmentalism on the part of those who are privileged towards those who struggle and suffer from the traumatic past of human trafficking and sex slavery. Finally, a general belief that the onus and responsibility of ending trafficking and sex slavery solely begins and ends with government and law enforcement agencies. This is a myth that seemingly absolves me as an individual from taking responsibility to spread the message and ensuring those around me are safe. From conversations with various stakeholders and victims, the authors think that these four factors play a major role in allowing trafficking and slavery to continue unabated in society.

Understanding the World of Sex Trafficking

So, who are the key players in trafficking? To begin with, the buyer of sex is the main reason women and children are exploited. In 1997, when the first few cases of international trafficking came to the limelight, the authors recall watching an interview of a woman who was exploited in Kamatipura – Bombay's infamous red-light district. When asked by the reporter why she was doing what she did, she said quite candidly something to the effect of, "Contrary to what you're thinking, I did not choose this life. I am here because men want me to be here. If there is no demand, there won't be any need for us to be exploited, right?" Though said in Hindi, the words remained in our minds. The demand truly fuels the supply. Alfred Marshall would never have dreamed that his law of supply and demand would also extend to include exploitation. The "buyer of sex" as opposed to "the client" is the preferred terminology as a client implies that sexual exploitation is permissible and that it does not merit any punishment. It would also lend credibility to selling sex as a profession. This is in stark contrast to what the authors and, we are sure, the readers, too, will consider acceptable.

Traffickers are those agents who are responsible for identifying, transporting, and selling innocents. In one case, there can be several traffickers or agents involved. They are known to have patience and an eye for those who seem discontent with their lot in life, making empty promises, and targeting young girls and luring them with thoughts of a better life. On some occasions, traffickers also resort to kidnapping. The trafficker or trafficking agent may connect with multiple agents who are responsible for transporting and selling young girls, children, and women.

Brothel managers can be a man or a woman who is running the brothel. Most often, it is a senior lady who once upon a time was a victim herself and has long since given up active work in the district. She is in charge of all monies and is the person who collects money and makes various payments. Managers often report to an owner. The owner can be male or female and usually isn't in the district. Most often, many don't know who the owner of a brothel is as s/he may be a respected member of society. The manager stays in touch with the owner and apprises him/her of the day's and week's events. Pimps are individuals or gangs who control and ensure the asset, or the young girl is kept in check. They are also responsible for making sure none run away. The writers have interacted with various managers over the years who themselves narrate horrific stories of exploitation they endured. However, they do it with a certain detachment that has become the coping mechanism for them to endure, live, and become perpetrators of violence. Once victims themselves, they see no harm in victimizing others.

Within such a murky environment, young girls are trafficked and expected to bring in income for the owner. So, what happens to her once she is trafficked from one city to another? We will consider Jhumki's ordeal:

"I was told that I would be going to school, but during the evening, I would need to take care of children who live with their parents. A family was thinking of being with me. I was excited. Here in this village, no girls finished school. I had studied till seventh, but then discontinued since my family believed I had had enough education. We made the bus journey from my hometown near Jaipur to Delhi. I was excited and watched the scenery outside. Auntie and Uncle were known to my family. Auntie gave me a meal, and I ate it happily. That is the last I remember.

When I woke up, there was an odd taste in my mouth. My body felt heavy, and I was so, so tired. I could hear music in the distance and a lot of noise in the background. But I went back to sleep. The next time I woke up, I was told I had been sleeping for three days. Uncle and Auntie were nowhere to be seen. An older lady with a kind face and hundreds of tiny lines etched into her face smiled at me. She called me "Beta," which means child. I took a liking to her instantly. But I didn't know her intentions.

Two days later, I got to know where I was. I was told I had to make men happy. How do I possibly do that? No one told me that. I knew it was bad, so I said "no." But that didn't help me very much. I was tied up and taken to a dark room, kept there for days without food or water. I was reminded again and again that my name was no longer Pallavi but Jhumki. They said they knew where my sister lived, and if I didn't do as they said, she would be sold. They said I was sold. I wondered to whom? Where was I? Where are my mother and my dad? I had no choice. I fought back. But they finally broke my spirit when four older men came and gang-raped me. You have no choice now, they said."[10]

There are several things that occur almost simultaneously with victims of trafficking:

1) She is treated well for a few days, and facts about where she is and why will be kept from her.
2) Following a few days of good treatment then, she is told to dress up for men. Her name is changed, and she is given a generic name that signifies a transfer of control. This is the first step for a victim to begin losing her sense of identity.
3) Simultaneously, she is psychologically coerced and told she is meant for this; she is sold, no one is going to accept her, and this is the only option she has.

4) Most teens fight back in stage two and are then subjected to severe physical torture that takes the form of starvation, kept thirsty for days, shut in a room for days, and isolated from others. If these tactics do not work, she is also kept in a small dark room with no sunshine or fresh air. By the time this is done, the teen is tired and loses the energy to fight. She has no option but to give in.
5) Those who are feistier continue to fight, and the strategy of psychological torture is maximized. However, she may not give in until she is told her family will be killed or that if she does not give in, then her younger sisters/cousins/neighbors will be exploited instead.
6) The last stage is when a teen fights back hard and refuses to give in – she may then be gang-raped and drugged till she complies. This usually is her breaking point.

As opposed to the mid-nineties, when trafficking was seen only as a foreign issue (e.g., Nepali women and Bangladeshi women), trafficking is a domestic issue in India as well. Within a society that attributes one's social standing to the family into which you were born, we often make the glaring error of viewing trafficked survivors as those who chose their lives. Consequently, society almost relegates them to the position of non-entities.

The Response

The extent and nature of trafficking can be overwhelming and quite disconcerting. However, there are many organizations that are spearheading movements across the country to make a greater impact. One must set aside perceptions that can arise from and color the general overview of Indians, Indian government initiatives, and ordinary citizens. Several organizations (NGO's) have collaborated with the government, law enforcement agencies, and government agencies to ensure dignity and hope for victims. But there is a dire need for more networking in response to combat human trafficking. As Beth Grant, author of *Courageous Compassion*, writes: "If organized crime can work together for their shared purpose of greed, exploitation, and injustice, why in the world can't good people – God's people – work together for the sake of accomplishing his purpose of freedom, healing, and justice?"[11] In such scenarios, it is helpful for us to trace the origin and impact of Christianity, in particular Pentecostalism, that has helped shape an adequate response.

Indians tend to be fairly welcoming of new ideas, ideologies, and belief systems. However, lurking within our eclectic society are systemic beliefs that hurt the worth and dignity of women. In the early 1900s, several dissenting voices arose that helped pave the way for education, rights for women, and schools. Allan H. Anderson writes:

> Pentecostals in various parts of the world have always had various programs of social action, ever since the involvement of Ramabai's Mukti Mission in India in the early 1900s and the work of Lillian Trasher among orphans in Egypt from 1911. Early Pentecostals were involved in socio-political criticism, including opposition to war, capitalism, and racial discrimination. African American Pentecostals have been in the forefront of the civil rights movement. Throughout the world today Pentecostals are involved in practical ways caring for the poor and the destitute, those often "unwanted" by the larger society.[12]

Pentecostals as a whole have been people who have a desire to engage compassionately with a hurting world around them. They cannot and could not sit still and watch injustice, hopelessness, and poverty thrive. In fact, the need to respond to the needs of people has been a trademark of Christianity through the ages. Pentecostals were no exception and had the firm belief that missions begins in the heart of God. One cannot sit by and watch the suffering of people. One has to be the hands and feet of Jesus, whatever others' response to you! In his book, Melvin Hodges elaborates on this thought:

> Christians are the salt of the earth. Their presence and influence do affect society.... Christians by their very nature love righteousness and hate iniquity. They will, therefore, be championing every just cause and endeavoring to show "good will to all men." ...We can do no better than follow the words of Jesus and the example of the early Christians. True Christians are a force for righteousness and social betterment.[13]

The authors believe that a response to systemic evils is necessary but a far greater one is striving to respond to the need. Responses to social injustice require shaping and changing perspectives. One cannot break or confront systemic evils without considering the cosmic battle that is being waged on our behalf. Compassionate social engagement, too, is a battle, and most often, it begins very young. Building communities of grace that lovingly invite and include people from all strata of society will influence the responses of young people.

Growing up steeped in Pentecostal tradition, the authors have seen the compassionate work of family, people, and friends around them. One of the writers is the daughter of an Assemblies of God pastor who passed on very early at the age of forty-eight. Following his passing away, her mother and sisters made sure she would not feel the loss of a parent. She recalls that their home, even while her dad was alive, always made room for people. There were people from all walks of life who came around the dinner table. Living in a community of faith, she also experienced the love and compassion of people who loved God and nurtured her. She soon discovered the divine intervention that brought her dad to where he was in life and why he loved Jesus so much. Her father was born into a Hindu royal family that was influenced by superstitions and would have been killed had it not been for a compassionate grandmother (whom we now believe was led by the Holy Spirit). She dropped him off at the door of an orphanage run by Assemblies of God missionaries and instructed them never to send him back to their birth family. She feared for his safety, and the orphanage administration took care of him and brought him up well. From a little orphan boy to a person who completed his Doctorate at Fuller Theological, he made an amazing journey. It took the courage of a grandmother to change the course of his destiny.

The lineage of Mathew, the other author, has also been influenced by generous parents who always had an open home for God's people. Missions was always at the heart of this God-fearing family, and it only intensified as Mathew grew up. By age twelve, under the leadership of a good mentor, Mathew led an entire Vacation Bible School for 1,000 children in his hometown. He then traveled all by himself by age thirteen (in a day when there were only landlines, no cell phones, social media, and the like) to a remote tea estate to conduct a Vacation Bible School for over 100 children. In all these adventures, Mathew was blessed with a supportive and prayerful family. Following his bachelor's and serving children for two years, Mathew went on to complete his master's degree in counseling and felt the Lord calling him to serve in Bombay with an organization that had begun to serve the women and children in the red light district of Mumbai. After they married each other, the authors knew that ministering and bringing hope to women and children would be their lives' call. The authors felt a strong need to respond to the need of trafficked survivors and victims alike and began serving in the city of Pune and Nagpur in 2001.

Understanding the City of Pune

Situated on the leeward side of the Western Ghats on the west coast of India, Pune is a city that holds cultural and political significance. Once the capital city of the kings of the Peshwa dynasty, Pune, has a mix of ancient and modern. Known as the Oxford of the East, it is known for its thrust on education through numerous schools, colleges, and universities. If one were to visit the city, one would find numerous international students who have come to study in the colleges and universities.

As a city, Pune is also the hub of philanthropic work. It is home to the first school for girls that was started by Jyotiba Phule, his wife Savitribai Phule, and Fatima Sheikh. When Jyotiba Pule and his wife Savitribai Phule were forced to leave their home because of opposition, they were given shelter and encouraged by Fatima Sheikh, who partnered in setting up the first school for girls. This was a landmark friendship and, in many ways, a partnership that helped girls receive education in India.[14]

Pandita Ramabai's Mukti mission is also located approximately sixty km away from the heart of the city. Mukti Mission is known globally for the revival that took place in 1900, and the heart of Pandita Ramabai for girls and women who were destitute. Born into a staunch Hindu Brahmin family, her father went against tradition and instead taught her Sanskrit. A reformer and activist at heart, she fought for the rights of women's education and was involved in rescuing children who were neglected during the great famine in 1896.

With a rich legacy of people who spoke for the poor and oppressed, Pune has learned to welcome people from all walks of life and make room for varied cultures to find a safe space. While there are many positive and endearing aspects of the city, there are also some harsh realities. Pune also has a thriving red-light district. In 2017, there was a news article that brought to focus the plight of women and children in exploitation. Three red-light districts were named, and of these, Pune was awarded third place. Five thousand women exploitation in one of the most popular, populous locations in the heart of the city. When the authors saw the staggering numbers, it devastated them.

Many organizations are doing substantial work in ensuring women in the district have access to health care, safe forms of sex, HIV/AIDs education and medications, and education for the children. The authors have registered and provided leadership in an organization that caters to the needs of rescued teen survivors. Their heart is also for the victims of trafficking still enslaved in the red-light district, and so they are also partnering with an NGO on the ground to provide a nutritious evening supper to thirty children in the education program. While providing oversight and leadership to the residential facility in one of Pune's suburbs, they encounter harsh stories of torture, deception, and daily rape of teen survivors. These traumatized young ladies are now safe and are growing as they want to return to society whole and healed.

The authors set about the task of exploring how they could bring their expertise to the table for NGOs serving in the red light district. While there were many organizations serving, their responses and strategies differed. Most of them catered to one need of victims as they lacked either the finance or human resources to provide holistic and comprehensive service to the women and children. But then the pandemic struck. (For more personal impact, the writers would like to share the next section in the first person.)

The Pandemic and its Impact

When the pandemic struck the world, life as we knew it came to a standstill; almost all stratas of society panicked. We wondered how we would make ends meet. With the consequent lockdowns and the panic that ensued to save lives, we, as a society, almost forgot the women and children in the red-light districts. NGOs did their part, but the deathly nature of the disease and the uncertainty it brought led to everyone doing the bare minimum.

As a precautionary measure and in keeping with lockdown requirements, we too had to comply with government norms. No one had encountered such bizarre circumstances, so there was hardly a point of reference. Never before had the world come to a standstill at the same time.

One morning I (Mathew) could wait no longer. I stopped eating breakfast and said, "I cannot eat any longer. We have to do something." Little did we know that the Lord had opened the door for an answer.

Instinctively, we reached out to our outreach partner and offered any help possible. The partner director mentioned that the children needed toiletries. We soon discovered that several women who could leave the district did so during the pandemic and tried to make their way back home. But those with massive debt had nowhere to go.

We consulted our leadership, friends, and well-wishers to see who would be willing to help with sponsoring the needs of the kids. A few friends responded. In response to the children needing toiletries, we put together care packages for the thirty children and their mothers. This included various daily needs like wheat, biscuits, toothpaste, toothpaste, detergent, and bathing soap. One must understand that stores were closed, and there was no transportation for the children or their mothers to buy even these basic necessities.

While distributing these "care packs," we noticed a tall, well-built young man watching us from across the road. Surrounded by excited kids, we missed noticing that he was slowly inching his way to us. He finally walked over to Mathew and asked, "Sir, are you distributing packs for the ladies and children?"

Mathew responded in the affirmative. The young man cleared his throat and said, "Sir, on the other side of the road, there are several senior ladies who need help. They have no food and are starving. Will you come and help?" Mathew willingly offered help in any way possible, and so began a few conversations and information gathering of the ladies who were in need.

That Macedonian call – will you come and help us – plagued us for several days. We knew that the sense of urgency and holy discontent that had been a part of our lives was just the start of a new response. From then on began a survey – conversations with women, their needs, and what could be done – and this data was collated. We made sure we shared the need with our leadership team, and it seemed as if the Spirit had stirred a new revolution.

Deeply impacted by the physical need of hunger and lack of access to hygiene needs, we listed groceries that are needed for a family of three to survive. In this case, it would be a mother and two or three small children.

This included: rice, dal, wheat, salt, sugar, lentils, chickpeas, chili powder, and various masalas and even went on to include washing powder, soap, shampoo, and detergent. These were carefully weighed and packed into a bigger sack. But all this required money. Funds were raised, and we asked people, in hindsight quite unabashedly, to join hands with us to ensure that women and children did not starve. The team of staff who served in the residential program, including Trainees who were above eighteen years old, also helped in packing the rations. It was an "entire family effort," as one beneficiary quipped when asked how she felt after packing things for those in need.

Throughout the subsequent lockdowns and spanning the three waves of Covid-19 from May 2020 to December 2021, a total of seven distributions helped women and their children survive the pandemic. But the story does not end there.

Taking A Step of Faith

The writers realized that something more needed to be done. However, the next logical step was prayer for wisdom. Almost in answer to that prayer, within a few weeks, a lady from the community posed a question: "So, what else can you do to help us? Everyone wants to come and help our children. But no one wants to help us." She is a forty-plus year-old lady who now works as a manager of a brothel. She went on to share the sense of frailty and helplessness which engulfed her and several ladies. The pandemic had taught them that life was transient, and they had no other skills on which they could rely. This seemed to be a second cry for help.

While praying one day, I (Suhasini) was reminded of the question we had raised to the Lord in 2018: "What next, Lord? How do you want us to impact this red-light district which is a death trap for women and children?" The sense of wanting to do something more had opened up a new door, and the need came directly from the community. The Holy Spirit brought to the forefront those dreams and questions that lay dormant and even forgotten and ensured we had open doors to act.

Speaking with leadership we asked their wisdom in next steps. We are blessed to have leaders who recognize and empathize with the victims and who gave us the freedom to follow our hearts and to answer the need in Spirit-led ways. We returned to the community to hear what kind of interventions and facilities would work. As a first step, names were gathered for vaccination drives as this would open the opportunities for government schemes. Thirty-four women got both doses of vaccination through the mobilization of staff teams in the local hospital. The team of staff serving with us made travel arrangements for the ladies. This response helped build trust with the ladies as the staff team was careful that the ladies were treated with dignity and respect throughout their trip to the hospital and back.

Simultaneously the ladies told us that they needed to earn an income. So, a skills program was what we felt the Lord was leading us to implement. For that, we needed a place from which to function. We, along with a team of two staff, began a search. One evening, the gentleman from the community called us saying there was a place available. It had been closed for a while, and the owner was willing to rent it out. A meeting time and day were arranged for us to meet the owner. We met both the owner and his brother several times in the months from December to February 2021.

On the first visit to the place, the building reeked of human stench. It had been closed for two years, but still, the smells remained, almost permeating the walls. Windows were broken, lights didn't work, passages, windowsills, and walls were stained with betel nut juice that men had spat in disgust or boredom, and clothes of women were still hanging on a line. The place echoed with cries of exploitation. It was evident that every inch of space was used up. As soon as we entered, exploitation hit us in the face as we walked through five cabins on the ground floor. Every single room had cabins with a raised platform for women to entertain men. Doors could be locked only from the outside.

We saw the building and decided to take only two floors for rent. However, when we spoke to one of our immediate leaders, he asked if the owner was willing to sell it. The idea had not even crossed our minds. Then began negotiations for sale. As mentioned earlier, the building represented his childhood and his mother, so he took his time (a few weeks) to actually decide whether he wanted to sell it or not.

Towards the first week of February 2021, he decided to sell the entire building. Papers were poured over, verified, reverified, and finally approved for purchase. We have tremendous respect for the previous owner, who decided that he had to change tracks and let this building be used for good. We are deeply grateful to generous donors who have so graciously given to this project. We now finally had space and an address to call our own in the filthiest and most evil part of the city.

The Beginning, in Lieu of a Conclusion

While this section would traditionally be considered a conclusion, we hardly agree. We view this part as the beginning of new hope. Redeeming a place of exploitation can only be a Spirit-led and empowered possibility for those who are called to be salt and light. Matthew 5:13–16 in The Message version portrays our role beautifully:

> Let me tell you why you are here. You're here to be salt-seasoning that brings out the God-flavors of this earth. If you lose your saltiness, how will people taste godliness? You've lost your usefulness and will end up in the garbage. You're here to be light, bringing out the God-colors in the world. God is not a secret to be kept. We're going public with this, as public as a city on a hill. If I make you light bearers, you don't think I'm going to hide you under a bucket, do you? I'm putting you on a light stand. Now that I've put you there on a hilltop, on a light stand—shine! Keep an open house; be generous with your lives. By opening up to others, you'll prompt people to open up with God, this generous Father in heaven.

In an effort to shine and offer hope in the darkness, the writers have designed an after-school education program and a school readiness program for children who are in the district. Nineteen children are part of this program, and fourteen children have completed it and have joined formal school, at the time of writing this article. Thirty-five women come faithfully thrice a week for skills classes, and another twenty-one are waiting for an opportunity to go through the next batch to learn skills and start earning an income.

Today the building has been renovated, and every space is being used creatively and redemptively to change the destiny of people. We are developing a team who will respond compassionately to the community and, in doing so, will bring out the God-flavors and God-colors in their world. We attribute the extent of work only to the glory of God and a Spirit-led response to a cry for help. If you ever have a doubt if the Holy Spirit was at work in the pandemic, we do hope this chapter will only increase your faith. He was and is still at work!

Notes

1. Mark Twain, *Following the Equator* (Stillwell, KS: Digireads Publishing, 2008), 242.
2. Suhasini Daniel, interview with Laila, December 2, 2021, Pune, India.
3. International Labour Organization, "Forced Labour, Modern Slavery, and Human Trafficking," www.ilo.org, accessed December 30, 2021.
4. United Nations Office on Drugs and Crime, https://www.unodc.org/unodc/en/human-trafficking/human-trafficking.html, accessed December 30, 2021.
5. Aroon Purie, "Sex Slaves: The Stomach-Churning Story of Stolen Childhoods," India Today, Nov 13, 2017, https://www.indiatoday.in/magazine/editor-s-note/story/20171113-from-the-editor-in-chief-modern-day-slaves-sex-aroon-purie-1077351-2017-11-03
6. Mathew Daniel and Suhasini Daniel, interview, December 2, 2021, Pune, India.
7. Mathew Daniel and Suhasini Daniel, interviews with victims of trafficking, December 2, 2021, Pune, India.
8. "Devadasi System still Prevalent, 'Naked' Minor Girls in Temples of TN," Reuters, September 27, 2017, https://www.asianage.com/india/all-india/270917/devadasi-system-still-prevalent-naked-minor-girls-in-temples-of-tn.html.
9. Mathew Daniel and Suhasini Daniel, interviews with victims of trafficking, December 2, 2021, Pune, India.
10. Mathew Daniel and Suhasini Daniel, interviews with victims of trafficking, December 2, 2021, Pune, India.
11. Beth Grant, Courageous *Compassion: Confronting Social Injustice in God's Way* (Springfield, MO: My Healthy Church, 2014), chapter ten.
12. Allan H. Anderson, *An Introduction to Pentecostalism: Global Charismatic Christianity* (Cambridge: Cambridge University Press, 2013), 276–277.
13. Melvin Hodges, *A Theology of the Church and its Mission: A Pentecostal Perspective* (Springfield, MO: Gospel Publishing House, 1977), 96.
14. Divya Kandukuri, "The Life and Times of Savitribai Phule," Mint Lounge, December 1, 2019, www.livemint.com/Leisure/DmR1fQSnVD62p4D3eyq9mO/The-life-and-times-of-Savitribai-Phule.html.

11 Christian Justice in a Global Pandemic: The Church's Call to Merciful Advocacy for Roma Communities and Asylum Seekers in Southeastern Europe

Melody Wachsmuth

Abstract

During the early days of lockdown in the COVID-19 pandemic in 2020, there was a misnomer that the pandemic was the great equalizer, a non-respecter of wealth, ethnicity, status, or power. However, it soon became obvious that the pandemic only exacerbated socioeconomic inequalities and even further inflamed racial and ethnic disparities. In Central and Eastern Europe, this can clearly be seen in two marginalized groups of people: the thousands of scattered Roma communities and the long-standing plight of the Middle Eastern and North African asylum seekers trapped in Bosnia-Herzegovina.

As justice is connected to power, marginalized communities have little access to the kinds of power that would ensure their rights and equitable treatment in a time of crisis. However, a Christian witness of biblical justice reveals the compassion of God, manifested through both intentional action and also demonstrated through God's ongoing redemptive work within these communities. This paper will first examine the concept of Christian justice before highlighting the situation of asylum seekers and Roma communities during the pandemic. Finally, it will focus on the ways in which Christian response has exemplified justice and the obstacles preventing a more robust engagement.

Introduction

During the early days of lockdown in the COVID-19 pandemic in 2020, there was a misnomer that the pandemic was the great equalizer, a non-respecter of wealth, ethnicity, status, or power. However, it soon became obvious that the pandemic only exacerbated socioeconomic inequalities and inflamed racial and ethnic disparities. This quickly became apparent when leaders associated with Roma Networks— a grassroots movement whose vision is to network, connect, and research for the sake of sharing the gospel and seeing transformation in Roma communities throughout

Europe— gathered worriedly online to assess the impact of the lockdown on poor and marginalized communities. I took notes on that March 24, 2020, meeting, and Roma pastors from Bulgaria, Romania, and Serbia described the fear and feeling of helplessness. Families dependent on seasonal and migrant work were unsure how to earn money for food and distrusted that the government would be concerned for them because of historical precedent. In some contexts, Roma were prevented from leaving their communities and lacked clean water and proper health services. Others noted that 'scapegoating' had already begun—assuming Roma communities would be greater carriers of disease because of certain societal stigmas related to health and cleanliness.

As the pandemic rolled on, a number of reports were published detailing some of the effects of 2020 on marginalized communities. For example, a 2021 report stated, "The increasing scientific evidence demonstrates that the virus has exerted a disproportionate burden on racialized and ethnic minorities living under detrimental social, economic, political, and environmental conditions."[1] As justice is connected to power, marginalized communities have little access to the kinds of power that would ensure their equitable treatment in a time of crisis. However, the ongoing crisis is also an opportunity to manifest a Christian witness of biblical justice. This occurs not only through intentional action but is also visible through God's ongoing redemptive work within these communities. This paper will first examine Christian justice from a biblical perspective. Next, the paper will introduce Pentecostal and evangelical churches in the Southeastern European context[2] and then highlight the situation of asylum seekers in Bosnia and Herzegovina (BiH) and Roma communities during the pandemic.[3] Finally, I will focus on the ways in which Christian response has both exemplified justice and the barriers that prevent more robust action.

Justice in the Biblical Narrative

The word "justice" possesses many meanings, depending on cultural, theological, and socio-political locations.[4] The additions of certain adjectives in front of the word, such as "social," "retributive," or "restorative," further add complexity. Depending on one's standpoint, "social justice" can have negative or positive connotations, but much of the discussion lacks a holistic picture of biblical justice creatively applied to contemporary challenges.[5]

However, even "reader position" creates different hermeneutical positions by which to interpret the text, as the scripture has been used by both oppressors and the oppressed in very different ways.[6] There can be an inclination to come to the biblical text with a predetermined definition of justice that fits our current socio-political context as it assumes the "infallibility of our current sociopolitical consensus and the inability of the biblical text to correct us."[7]

In the biblical witness, the concept of "justice" is rooted in the very being of God, who, from the "just foundation" (Psalm 89:14; 97:2) of God's throne, ordered the world in a right manner.[8] One can note God's acts of liberation for the oppressed, the mandates to care for the weak and vulnerable, which are described as the fatherless, the widow, the foreigner (Deut 10:12), the poor, and the homeless (Isa 58:6–8). If justice is part of God's essence and, therefore, his engagement with humanity, it must be an essential component of human interaction with God and the world.

In the Bible, justice relates to all aspects of life, framed in the context of relationships so that "Justice means doing all that is necessary to create and sustain healthy, constant, and life-giving relationships between persons."[9] In the Old Testament, *mishpat* (justice) occurs over 200 times in the Old Testament and connotes equitable treatment—foreigner or native-born—regardless if one is talking about punishment, acquittal, or ensuring someone's rights.[10] *Tzadeqah*, which also can be translated "just," connotes the right relationships between God and others—this word has necessary social implications for daily life and interactions. Timothy Keller connects *tzadeqah* and *mishpat* to a rectifying justice (punishing perpetrator) and primary justice (right relational living that makes rectifying justice unnecessary).[11]

In the New Testament, justice is translated as either "right, righteousness, or righteous" or "just, justification, justify," although coming from the same Greek stem. The connotations these words have in modern English are misleading, as "righteousness" alludes to private ethics and "justice" connotes the legal and political realm.[12] However, this public/private distinction is not so distinct in the Bible. Marshall notes that the "righteousness terminology in the New Testament, like its Old Testament counterparts, has a wide semantic range embracing forensic, sociopolitical, ethical, and religious applications," referring to both action and proclamation applied according to what the context requires.[13]

Biblical prophets connect acting "rightly" with relating to God (Jer 9:23–24; 22: 15–16).[14] Jesus, as the incarnate of God's justice (Luke 23:47), draws this same connection between rightly "knowing" God and acting with justice and mercy (Matt 12:14–21), subjecting himself to injustice in order to unleash God's justice. Jesus reordered power by challenging social discrimination (Matt 9:10–13; Mark 7:24–30), economic greed and injustice (Luke 12:13–21; Mark 11:15–19), institutional religious figures (Matt 23), and rejected violence as a means to do this.[15] Jesus' death, in itself, was an example of vicious injustice, but it was also the means whereby God's justice broke the power of sin and death, culminating in God's power raising Jesus from the dead. In a messianic frame, longing for justice is hope for God's just rule over the whole cosmos through his kingship—thus, justice is inextricably connected to both theology and politics.[16]

As the new community in Christ, Christians are to manifest God's justice by "pursuing peace" (Rom 14:19; Heb 12:14; 2 Tim 2:22), overcoming evil by good (Rom 12:14–21; Luke 6:35; 1 Thess 5:15) and being "instruments of justice" in the world (Rom 6:13). Constantineanu explains that believers, "are enabled to live out a new, transformed life of justice, as they share now in the same story of Christ and follow his example."[17] This perspective can be a potent form of Christian witness, particularly in contexts such as Southeastern Europe, where there is cynicism and distrust of government because of blatant corruption. In light of this biblical summary, how could the practice of justice manifest during a global pandemic? Before exploring this question, I will briefly summarize the situation of Pentecostal and evangelical churches in Southeastern Europe.

Pentecostal and Evangelical Churches in Southeastern Europe

The Balkans is a complex geopolitical region with different peoples, cultures, languages, and religions. There are many significant historical factors influencing its current social realities, including the wars in former Yugoslavia, loss of trust in the government, fissure in the social texture combined with "unchecked influences of secularism and consumerism," the challenge of moving from collectivist thinking to individualistic thinking in the free market economies, and the reawakening of traditional religious identities.[18]

The situation of Pentecostals and evangelicals[19] in the Balkans is also diverse, depending on the country and/or region. Although countries are post-Communist and often have a religious identity tied to their political identity—for example, Romania is Orthodox, Croatia is Catholic, Serbia is Orthodox—yet the religious and social context is vastly different. In the former Yugoslavia, Pentecostals and evangelicals make up only a small fraction of the Christian population. For example, in 2020 in Croatia, Protestants made up just .8 percent of the 93.8 Christian percent, and Pentecostal/Charismatics and evangelicals, 2.9 percent and .3 percent of the Protestants, respectively.[20] In Bosnia and Herzegovina, in 2015, there were an estimated 800–900 evangelical and Pentecostals in the country.[21]

Because of the fusion of national and religious identity, Pentecostal and evangelical churches have often been seen as sects by the majority populations, weakening the socio-religious fabric of the nation.[22] Still, in some contexts, evangelicals' past and present humanitarian work, such as the work of *Agape* (Croatia) and *Bread of Life* (Serbia) during and after the war in former Yugoslavia and the work of *Croatian Baptist Aid* during the ongoing refugee crisis in Croatia and Bosnia serves as a witness and relational bridge builder with others. In some contexts, such as Croatia, registered Protestant churches have equal rights to the national church, whereas, in other contexts, official recognition is harder to gain.[23] Regardless, because of the small percentage of evangelicals, many in the majority population practically know very little about evangelicals.

COVID-19 and Roma Communities

The Roma are minority groups living in a wide range of societies and cultures and can be diverse in terms of cultural practices and language.[24] I use "Roma" in this context to refer to a wide umbrella of groups who identify as such. The history of the Roma in Europe is filled with difficult accounts of the relationship between majority cultures and the Roma: state policies intended to forcibly compel Roma into mainstream society, Roma subjected to slavery in Romanian principalities, and slated for extermination in World War II. The more the Roma were "problematized," the more socially and politically marginalized they became, although, in the second half of the twentieth century, a Romani political movement began to build agency on transnational and national platforms.[25] Today, the estimated ten to twelve million Roma in Europe have higher rates of unemployment, poverty, illiteracy, and health problems, and many are socially excluded from mainstream society.[26]

The results of COVID-19 only deepened the issues: poor access to healthcare, a widening education gap during online school because of lack of adequate technology, lack of access to clean water and sanitation, and a loss of employment and inability to access welfare if individuals had informal jobs or housing.[27] Further, the European Roma Rights Centre (ERRC) issued a detailed report in September of 2020, describing human rights abuses such as police violence toward the Roma in Romania, Roma being called "carriers of disease" in Moldova, and public hostility in Italy.[28] The 2020 FRA report related the example of Bulgaria, where six Roma communities with populations of tens of thousands were locked down in March without any cases being found.[29] In Albania, Bosnia and Herzegovina, Montenegro, North Macedonia, Serbia, and Ukraine and found that 73 percent experienced reduced income. Because economic relief is often tied to formal employment, those working in informal jobs were left without relief.[30]

Asylum Seekers and Migrants in Bosnia and Herzegovina

In 2020, 1.4 million people fled their own countries to seek protection elsewhere. The UNHCR reports that displaced people are among those who suffered the most during COVID, in areas of food and economic security and health and protection services.[31] Since 2015, migrants and refugees have been crossing through or attempting to cross through the Balkans en route to Western Europe. Since 2016, when other gateways such as Serbia and Hungary were restricted, Bosnia became a primary hub for people seeking to enter the European Union, and almost 70,000 refugees and migrants coming from South Asia, the Middle East, and Africa passed through or have been stalled in Bosnia over the last three years.[32] Numerous people lost their lives through exposure, accidents, drownings, or even stepping on old landmines from the 1990s Yugoslav wars.[33]

Bosnia and Herzegovina has a complex political system[34] and high rates of corruption, poverty, and unemployment.[35] Bihac is a small city of 60,000 near the border of Croatia. When the migrants began entering

Bihac in 2018, it received little federal help, and the city was left appealing to both international and federal entities. The escalating situation led to a variety of problems, including a growing anti-migrant attitude from locals.[36] In September 2020, locals from Bihac protested the camp near their town, and in December, another nearby camp burned to the ground. In October 2020, the Danish Refugee Council published a report detailing an increase in pushbacks, with 64 percent of people reporting some kind of physical abuse, destruction of property, or abusive and degrading treatment by border authorities.[37] Essentially, the situation is a complex tangle involving the International Organization of Migration (IOM), EU authorities, border guards, smugglers, politicians, humanitarian workers, and the refugees and migrants themselves.

COVID-19 only exacerbated the crisis. Bosnia experienced weak testing and a slow rollout of the virus and reported 7,000 deaths in the population of 3.3 million. Although the pandemic did slow the rate of new arrivals between 2019–2020, the numbers began increasing again after 2020. Although there was testing inside the camps, for the estimated 1,7000 outside the camps, the migrants had no healthcare access with little way to track the COVID spread. As the world grappled with the crisis, the refugees and asylum-seekers were overlooked, deepening the misery and the stalemate. The lack of hygiene and access to vaccines was also a serious problem, putting the local population at risk as well.[38]

Obstacles to Engagement

Within this complex context, I want to suggest specific obstacles that need to be addressed to mobilize the church towards justice for these vulnerable communities. First, because of the history of the evangelical and Pentecostal church in this part of the world, the gospel is sometimes framed only as a personal acceptance of salvation from sins without exploring the ramifications of Jesus' death and resurrection to the wider domains of society, politics, economics, and culture. This all too often results in a sacred/secular split for Christians. Such a split is particularly problematic regarding a theological understanding of justice that would translate to praxis in society. This requires not only reducing the dualistic gap between private ethics (personal "righteousness") and public justice, as mentioned earlier, but also fostering concrete relational acts of caring and advocating for marginalized groups. It is this key "relational" piece that acts as a connector between social, religious, and political domains, which begins to move us into alignment with the biblical view of justice.

Second, in a region that has had a difficult history of being dominated by empires and war, issues of ethnicity, identity, and religion are prominent. Although the evangelical and Pentecostal churches have been successful in integrating together, there are still groups excluded from this.[39] Miroslav Volf describes different forms of exclusion: elimination, assimilation, domination, and abandonment.[40] Throughout Europe's history, each of these forms depicted the Roma people's relationship with the majority cultures around them, from harsh assimilation policies and enslavement to their inclusion in Hitler's final solution. Sadly, the church was often complicit in fostering exclusionary attitudes, a practice that continues in many churches. This ongoing prejudice blinds the eyes of the church to be able to "act justly" in the present circumstances. Again, fostering relationships is key to challenging walls of exclusion. There are many testimonies of non-Roma and Roma developing friendships that eventually broke down walls of prejudice and stereotypes. In recent years, there have been small steps toward the inclusion of the Roma church in mainstream Christian events, such as the European Evangelical Alliance "Hope for Europe" conference in 2018, and the Lausanne Europe "Dynamic Gospel, New Europe" conference in 2021.

Third, because many individuals in churches have their own socioeconomic struggles or are themselves suffering, it is easy to focus on one's weakness, lack of skills needed for the situation, or compassion fatigue. For example, although initially there was compassion for the situation of the refugees and migrants in Bosnia, particularly since many Bosnians experienced being a refugee during the war (1992–1995), empathy dwindled as the situation shows no signs of resolving.[41] Since the economic situation for many Bosnians remains very challenging, compassion fatigue will likely only continue to increase.

Birthing Hope in Weakness

If churches already felt weak and marginalized in relation to society, COVID-19 abruptly reminded the whole world of its fragility and mortality. This can be a critical paradigm shift in how the church understands and participates in God's mission if the church relinquishes its ideas of power and success that it all too often adopts from the world. John Taylor (1914–2001), bishop and theologian, reflected on the idea of cherishing the "weakness of limited means" in terms of mission because this leaves one open to creativity and the Holy Spirit.⁴² Christ both modeled and enabled the releasing of God's justice through his confrontation and victory over the powers in his death and resurrection. If weakness can be seen as an asset in mission, perhaps this can reframe how small churches think of themselves in relation to the West, to the majority society around them, and to those who have been excluded. Therefore, a theological reshaping of power is necessary for the local church's conceptualization of mission and its own self-identity.

Further, hope is critical to compelling action. Esau McCaulley uses the story of the birth of John the Baptist in Luke— in the midst of a community oppressed by Roman rule— to question where God is birthing hope in other situations of injustice in his context, "For Zechariah and Elizabeth, the miracle child is John. For the African American Christian, the miracle is the Black Church born of truly miraculous circumstances and whose witness to Jesus has served as something of a forerunner preparing America to accept a truer and fuller gospel."⁴³ In fact, then, circumstances of suffering are exactly where the Christian can hope to find God "birthing hope."

Both shifting conceptions of power and seeds of hope can be seen in a few different initiatives that took place in 2020 and 2021. When the lockdown measures began in early 2020, Roma Networks, mentioned in the introduction, began meeting virtually. Roma Networks is fueled by a volunteer Board of six people in Finland, Croatia, Romania, Bulgaria, Hungary, and Serbia, and around forty country representatives. The virtual meetings were first held to gather information regarding how Roma communities were being affected by the lockdowns and pandemics. Early on, in April 2020, people shared concerning reports similar to what was discussed earlier by Roma advocacy groups: fear of food shortage, loss of jobs related to not being able to travel for agricultural or other work, scapegoating, loss of education due to not having stable access to Wi-Fi. Staying connected to church also became more challenging, as not everyone had the tools or access to online services. Some Roma pastors felt paralyzed, not knowing how to help their communities. In addition,

Roma leaders reported an upsurge of "false teachers" since anyone could create their own platform on social media.

However, there were also reports of new and creative things happening, with leaders forced to reconceptualize church and ministry. In Hungary, in April 2020, for example, one Pentecostal mission serving with the Roma reported that the situation activated the churches, and many served, prepared food packages, and trained to distribute governmental aid. They also used the situation to begin online Bible classes for their Roma members, who were usually working. In Serbia, many, particularly those who had migrated outside Serbia, re-connected with the Roma Pentecostal churches in Serbia, and new conversions were reported, in addition to more prayer and fasting in an online community. In Bulgaria, one Roma leader began to do online leadership training resulting in some very encouraging developments.

Roma Networks, in relationship with partners in Canada and the United States, began to fundraise to send money to the most critical places of need, primarily in Eastern and Southeastern Europe. In addition, they also began to think creatively regarding how to strengthen the network and encourage the church. They began doing regular live prayer events in different languages, hosting live special events to encourage people and share news, and conducted more online meetings with their country coordinators than they had in the past. Attention was brought to the added injustices happening in some Roma communities through writing, short videos, and live feeds.

In terms of the migrants and asylum-seekers in Bosnia, Evangelical Relief Agency (ERA) (formerly acting as *Ruke Nade*, Croatian Baptist Aid) has been active since 2015 in both Croatia and Bosnia, delivering food and aid, setting up sanitation stations, and advocacy. Currently, they are active in all six camps in Bosnia and have a mobile outreach team that visits groups that are not in the camps. They are working on setting up a sanitation station involving eight wash stations for the camp that was burned and is currently being rebuilt. Other churches and individuals have also been involved in delivering aid or helping specific individuals and/or families. However, the leadership of ERA says most of the evangelical and Pentecostal churches are not involved. Although the complex socio-political situation that the refugees find themselves in will not be able to be solved by the small churches, the ERA argues that the most powerful way to engage socially is to advocate for the refugees and contribute to the public discussion from a Christian justice point of view.[44]

Concluding Remarks

As shown by the summary of justice in the biblical narrative, acting justly, both reactively and proactively, is a mode of being rooted in a Christian ethic based on the character of God. In contexts when the church itself feels weak and vulnerable, enacting justice for those most vulnerable becomes even more challenging. However, this position of vulnerability in the middle of a global pandemic allowed a rare opportunity for the communities who are open to the Holy Spirit to be empowered by the Spirit as advocates for justice and thus present a witness of God's impartial righteousness to a fearful world.

Keller helpfully encapsulates the biblical narratives of justice into four themes which offer insights into orthopraxy in this context.[45] First, practicing radical generosity—viewing our economic resources as belonging to God and stewarding them with wise generosity. This involves an economic reframing for the small churches in Southeastern Europe, a move from viewing one's economic status through the lens of having "less than the West" and instead through God's capable provision. In this case, it is challenging the church toward a radical generosity toward those whom the surrounding society may think do not "deserve" help.

Second, having the attitude of universal equality—rooted in the idea that humanity is created in the image of God, not showing partiality based on ethnicity, gender, or class. Evangelical and Pentecostal churches can be fertile grounds for this unity, as demonstrated in the past. Thus, practicing justice involves developing a contextual theology of justice by identifying those in society who are excluded and abandoned. If our entry into God's mission is shaped by the Bible's message of salvation, liberation, and reconciliation, then our particular context brings its hopes and despair to interact with that message to present a contextual kind of justice.[46]

Third, practicing advocacy—on behalf of the poor and marginalized through supplying material needs, empowerment, and challenging problematic social structures. This is part of what Roma Networks was doing by releasing video updates of the Roma situation in different countries and facilitating live events, inviting people to talk about what was happening in their community. In terms of the refugees and migrants in Bosnia, the director of ERA noted that many do not know how to be involved with advocacy, or they fear negative consequences if they become too vocal. In addition, they lack the financial resources to help pay for lawyers or paperwork fees to help people navigate the complex requirements. Thus, the director related the need for new education since the context in Bosnia changed from the immediate post-war context when churches were involved with peacebuilding and justice. The ERA is also beginning to make videos and share information about the situation in which people are finding themselves. As McCaulley articulated: "In the end, the pandemic test has made plain this truth: The church is not socially or politically ready for all that our modern, interconnected world demands of us."[47]

Finally, by assuming responsibility, both corporate and individual,[48] this sense of responsibility must be built into the way in which disciples are taught and formed in the church. Small groups that are practicing justice in the current situation should share their work and the theology that undergirds their work with the wider church. Although the hope fostered by John the Baptist's birth started first just within his home, the hope gradually spread to the community and beyond as they watched with wonder the events unfold.

In Pentecost in Acts 2, the lavish gift of the Holy Spirit without regard to nation, ethnicity, social position, or gender images the idea of a "one humanity" in Christ, made up of a diversity of language, culture, and ethnicity. Pictures of the final kingdom, justice, and righteous kingdom, portray nations and kings gathering around God (Isa 60:1–7; Rev 21:4). This is the image that undergirds our hope moving us toward intentional justice towards excluded and vulnerable communities. Our own vulnerability and powerlessness should be treasured as a catalyst for the Holy Spirit's creative empowerment toward righteousness and justice.

Notes

1 Maja Saitovic and Marek Szilvasi, "Should Governments Consider Roma a Priority in Their COVID-19 Vaccination Roll-Out Plans?" (Open Society Foundations' Roma Health Project, 2021), https://epha.org/wp-content/uploads/2021/02/should-roma-be-a-priority-in-vaccine-rollout-plans.pdf, accessed July 20, 2021.

2 Although I do draw on information from the larger Central and Eastern European context (CEE), the case studies are primarily focused on countries in Southeastern Europe.

3 Although other Christian traditions in the Balkans are engaged in justice work, such as the Jesuits in Bosnia, this scope is too large for this paper.

4 Christopher D. Marshall, *The Little Book of Biblical Justice: A Fresh Approach to the Bible's Teaching on Justice* (Intercourse, PA: Good Books, 2005); Karen Lebacqz, *Six Theories of Justice: Perspectives from Philosophical and Theological Ethics* (Minneapolis, MN: Augsburg PubHouse, 1986), 10.

5 Stanley Hauerwas, *After Christendom?: How the Church is to Behave if Freedom, Justice, and a Christian Nation are Bad Ideas* (Nashville, TN: Abingdon Press, 1991), 58.

6 Karen Lebacqz, *Justice in an Unjust World: Foundations for a Christian Approach to Justice* (Minneapolis, MN: Augsburg PubHouse, 1987).

7 Esau McCaulley, *Reading while Black: African American Biblical Interpretation as an Exercise in Hope* (Downers Grove, IL: IVP Academic, 2020), 73.

8 Marshall, *Little Book*, 25.

9 Marshall, *Little Book*, 36.

10 Timothy Keller, *Generous Justice: How God's Grace Makes Us Just* (London: Hodder & Stoughton, 2010), 3.

11 Keller, *Generous Justice*, 9,11.

12 Constantin Constantineanu, "'Instruments of Justice:' Biblical Contributions to a Public Theology of Engagement in Eastern European Context," *International Journal of Public Theology* 14:3 (2020), 361.

13 Christopher D. Marshall, *Beyond Retribution: A New Testament Vision for Justice, Crime and Punishment* (Grand Rapids, MI.: Eerdmans, 2001), 37.

14 Constantineanu, "Instruments," 359.

15 Marshall, *Little Book*, 49–50

16 McCaulley, *Reading*, 47–70.

17 Constantineanu, "Instruments," 9.

18 Milkov, Kostake. "Macedonia: The Witness of Evangelical Communities in Contested Balkan Identities," *Evangelical Interfaith Dialogue Journal* 5:1 (2014), 8.

19 I define both Pentecostals and evangelicals in this context rather broadly, thus, evangelicalism can sometimes be related to or sometimes interchangeable with Pentecostalism. Pentecostals are Christians with an ongoing dynamic experience with the Holy Spirit, based in the person of Jesus Christ, resulting in an openness to the supernatural and an orientation toward mission and evangelism. See Wonsuk Ma, "'When the Poor Are Fired Up': The Role of Pneumatology in Pentecostal/Charismatic Mission," in *The Spirit in the World: Emerging Pentecostal Theologies in Global Contexts*, Veli-Matti Kärkkäinen ed. (Grand Rapids, MI: Eerdmans, 2009), 40–52. I draw from Bebbington's classic evangelical definition which highlights the authority of Scripture, human depravity, salvation through Christ, gospel proclamation, and eschatological hope. David Bebbington, *Evangelicalism in Modern Britain: A History from the 1730s to the 1980s*, Ebook Central, (London: Unwin Hyman,1989).

20 Todd M. Johnson and Gina A. Zurlo, eds. *Encyclopedia of World Christianity*, 3rd Ed. (Edinburgh: Edinburgh University Press, 2020), 230.

21 Johnson and Zurlo, *Encyclopedia*, 128.

22 Milkov, "Macedonia," 9; Branko Bjelajac, "The Challenges and Opportunities of Diverse Backgrounds in the Evangelical Churches," *Evangelical Interfaith Dialogue Journal* 5:1 (2014), 16–20.

23 After Croatia became an independent nation, a Protestant-Evangelical Council was formed in 1992, involving different denominations, in order to advocate for Protestant rights equal to the Catholic rights in the newly formed government. Finally, in 2002, an agreement was signed. Julijana Tešija, "Be Salt on Earth: Can Evangelical Churches Make a Difference in Croatia?" *Evangelical Interfaith Dialogue Journal* 5:1 (2014), 27.

24 Kovats, Martin, "Problems of Intellectual and Political Accountability in Respect of Emerging European Roma Policy," *Journal on Ethnopolitics and Minority Issues in Europe* (2001), 7.

25 Huub van Baar, "The European Roma: Minority Representation, Memory, and the Limits of Transnational Governmentality," (PhD Diss. Amsterdam School for Cultural Analysis, 2011), 15.

26 80 percent of EU Roma live below the poverty line, 30 percent have no running water, 46 percent have no indoor toilet or shower. European

Union Agency for Fundamental Rights (FRA), "Second European Union Minorities and Discrimination Survey-Main Results," https://fra.europa.eu/sites/default/files/fra_uploads/fra-2017-eu-midis-ii-main-results_en.pdf, accessed March 17, 2019; FRA, "Fundamental Rights Report-Roma Integration," http://fra.europa.eu/en/theme/roma, accessed March 17, 2019.

27 See Warsaw/Vienna: Organization for Security and Co-operation in Europe, "Persistent Roma Inequality Increases COVID-19 Risk, Human Rights Heads Say," April 2020, https://www.osce.org/odihr/449668?fbclid=IwAR1lSy5oHshRKVhvR8VDf2wz9npwp1ZTTM0v1-3cZAqE6Do9jQEpoCCc5IA, accessed July 7, 2021; FRA, "Coronavirus Pandemic in the EU - Impact on Roma and Travelers," August 2020, https://fra.europa.eu/sites/default/files/fra_uploads/fra-2020-coronavirus-pandemic-eu-bulletin-roma_en.pdf, accessed July 7, 2021; European Commission, "Overview of the Impact of Coronavirus Measures on the Marginalized Roma Communities in the EU, https://ec.europa.eu/info/sites/default/files/overview_of_covid19_and_roma_-_impact_-_measures_-_priorities_for_funding_-_23_04_2020.docx.pdf, accessed July 7, 2021. The FRA 2020 report was built on evidence from Belgium, Bulgaria, Croatia, Czechia, France, Greece, Hungary, Ireland, Italy, the Netherlands, Portugal, Romania, Slovakia, Spain, and Sweden.

28 Bernard Rorke and Jonathan Lee, "Roma Rights in the Time of COVID" (Belgium: European Roma Rights Centre, September 2020), http://www.errc.org/uploads/upload_en/file/5265_file1_roma-rights-in-the-time-of-covid.pdf, accessed July 15, 2021.

29 FRA, "Coronavirus," 11.

30 Craig Willis, "Economic Effects of the COVID-19 Pandemic on Roma Communities in Albania, Bosnia & Herzegovina, Moldova, Montenegro, North Macedonia, Serbia, and Ukraine," (Research Paper, European Centre for Minority Issues, 2020), https://www.ecmi.de/publications/ecmi-research-papers/122-economic-effects-of-the-covid-19-pandemic-on-roma-communities-in-albania-bosnia-herzegovina-moldova-montenegro-north-macedonia-serbia-and-ukraine, accessed July 20, 2021.

31 UNHCR, "Global Trends: Forced Displacement in 2020," (Denmark: The United Nations High Commissioner for Refugees, 2021), 56, https://www.unhcr.org/flagship-reports/globaltrends/, accessed July 20, 2021.

32 Elisa Oddone, "For Migrants in Bosnia, the 'Game' Is a Perilous Journey to a Better Life," NPR (March 27, 2021), https://www.npr.org/2021/03/27/976648642/for-migrants-in-bosnia-the-game-is-a-perilous-journey-to-a-better-life, accessed July 22, 2021; International Organization on Migration, "Flow Monitoring," Displacement Tracking Matrix," https://dtm.iom.int/, accessed July 22, 2021.

33 Lucy Papachristou, "Drowning in the Balkans: 'His Body Went Away with the Water,'" *Aljazeera*, July 14, 2021, https://www.aljazeera.com/amp/features/2021/7/14/his-body-went-away-with-the-water-refugees-drownin?__twitter_impression=true&fbclid=IwAR3e59S4Axkm7ZQadNE790FblSSentK6ksq0-TikAShUPAVvK7Nk3TwTVPg, accessed July 20, 2021.

34 Since 1995, Bosnia and Herzegovina have had two autonomous governing entities, and the presidency rotates between three people, representing the three largest ethnic groupings in the country, every eight months. Nina Strochlic. "At the EU's Doorstep, a War-Scarred Country Pushes Migrants to the Fringes, "*National Geographic*, May 12, 2021), https://www.nationalgeographic.com/culture/article/at-europes-doorstep-war-scarred-country-pushes-migrants-tofringes?fbclid=IwAR0lfBmdYbkJp3us_F5X3J5KAKHcRfKwtKhPadap_PxSdOLga0D13i40tZg.

35 Oddone, "Migrants;" Papachristou, "Drowning."

36 Amir Husak, "Welcome to Bihac!: A conversation with Amir Husak," https://migrationmapping.org/may-june-newsletter/?fbclid=IwAR08Qt-9l4ycBJ4yczdauBY4a_Brky1umC48NyIq1OOlNiX-MAxTnRaHHk0, accessed July 23, 2021.

37 Pushbacks refer to when stated intentions to request asylum are ignored and individuals are returned to BiH without assessment or due process. Barbara Joannon, Selma Mešić, Stephanie Pope, and Marta Welander, "Pushbacks and Rights Violations at Europe's Borders: The State of Play in 2020," Refugee Rights Europe, https://endpushbacks.com/wp-content/uploads/2020/11/pushbacks-and-rights-violations-at-europes-borders.pdf?fbclid=IwAR06qNPNDIsj_z0FkckefmdfN_wBSvBaGgB6sKI986cq2AnnnYSk2Eu8lLQ, accessed July 22, 2021.

38 Elvis Džafić, interview with author, July 16, 2021, Zagreb, Croatia.

39 Tešija, "Be Salt."

40 Miroslav Volf, *Exclusion & Embrace: A Theological Exploration of Identity, Otherness, and Reconciliation* (Nashville, TN: Abingdon Press, 2019), 69,70.

41 Strochlic, "EU's Doorstep."

42 Jonny Baker and Cathy Ross, *Imagining Mission with John V. Taylor* (London: SCM Press, 2020).

43 McCaulley, *Reading*, 84.

44 Džafić, interview.

45 Timothy Keller, "Justice in the Bible," Life in the Gospel, https://quarterly.gospelinlife.com/justice-in-the-bible/, accessed July 14, 2021.

46 McCaulley, *Reading*, 71–95.

47 Esau McCaulley, "The CRT Debate Distracts from God's Justice," *Christianity Today*, July 28, 2021, https://www.christianitytoday.com/ct/2021/july-web-only/critical-race-theory-debate-distracts-from-racial-justice.html.

48 Keller, "Justice."

12 The Inequitable Silencing of Many Tongues: A Critical and Pastoral Response to the Economic, Political, and Racialized Dimensions of the Pandemic in American Pentecostal-Charismaticism

Amos Yong and Aizaiah G. Yong

Abstract

It is well known that the COVID-19 pandemic has caused the most harm to under-resourced communities around the world, and this is also true for marginalized groups within the United States of America as race and socio-economic factors have been significant determinants in both personal and collective suffering. In this chapter we seek to comprehend how US-based pentecostal-charismatic churches have responded and whether there are possibilities of reacting differently in the days ahead. The three parts that follow overview the disproportionate impact of the pandemic on lower-income groups and communities of color in the USA, contrast that to the responses of predominantly White evangelical Christians to highlight how pentecostal-charismatic churches generally have reacted similarly (with some reasons why), and provide a pastoral exhortation for a modified response (based on the evangel).

Introduction

It is well known that the COVID-19 pandemic has caused the most harm to under-resourced communities around the world, and this is also true for marginalized groups within the United States of America as race and socio-economic factors have been significant determinants in both personal and collective suffering.[1] In this chapter, we seek to comprehend how US-based pentecostal-charismatic churches[2] have responded and whether there are possibilities of reacting differently in the days ahead. The three parts that follow overview the disproportionate impact of the pandemic on lower-income groups and communities of color in the USA, contrast that to the responses of predominantly White evangelical Christians to highlight how pentecostal-charismatic churches generally have reacted similarly (with some reasons why), and provide a pastoral exhortation for a modified response (based on the evangel). Note that we write and speak as those embedded within the pentecostal-charismatic movement.[3] Obviously, we cannot claim to speak for all so affiliated, but wish to invite our fellow siblings who seek to be led by the Holy Spirit to a deeper consideration of and self-examined response to the pandemic, which effects will persist for a long time yet to come.

COVID-19 in the USA: A Multi-Dimensional Mapping

The world has surpassed five million deaths due to the COVID-19 pandemic, a bleak reality and outlook indeed.[4] Despite the economic prosperity of the United States, we lead the world in the number of deaths: nearly three-quarters of a million people! What is even more troubling about our national situation are the ways in which low-income communities and communities of color are yet again bearing the brunt of the pain and tragedy from disaster. There are multiple windows into understanding these realities.

While we can begin at various places, focusing on places of employment provides an appropriate first step. In the early stages of the pandemic, low-income workers were immediately deemed "essential" and were called to work, risking their lives every day to keep others "safer at home." In these same settings, when coronavirus outbreaks ensued, these same workers were blamed. In reality, many of their workplaces were not providing or ensuring adequate health and safety protocols, thus facilitating exposure to disease that, in the worst cases, resulted in some work environments turning into "super spreader" hotspots.[5] Thus, to keep basic human services running (agriculture, factory work, and truck driving), low-income people (who were also primarily people of color) faced impossible choices: either keep their job and risk their safety, or leave their jobs and lose their basic source of income for the necessities of life.

As the months wore on, long-term COVID-19 impacts were increasingly felt more acutely in low-income communities. Economic reports made visible how the poor were up to three times more likely to undergo food insecurity, be laid off, or persist in unemployment, thereby plunging these communities into further crisis and deepening pre-existing social inequities.[6] Then, when vaccines were developed and distributed, public health leaders discussed the "privilege gap" that made it increasingly difficult for marginalized communities to access recommended public health resources. There remain correlations between income, insurance status, education, and internet access with vaccination rates: those with more of these indicators were more likely to get vaccinated, and those with fewer, less to.[7]

The proverbial elephant in the room, so to speak, concerns the racialized dimension of the pandemic and how it has ravaged communities of color. Data has revealed especially the disparateness of the pandemic's impact on Black and Latino/a communities, wherein groups that represent about twelve and 18.5 percent of the national population respectively have experienced double the loss: about one-fourth and over one-third (respectively again) of coronavirus-related deaths.[8] When we realize that the dawn of the pandemic in the winter of 2020 also unleashed a national consciousness of this nation's underlying racism, particularly as illuminated just a bit later through the murder of George Floyd and other incidents of police brutality into the spring-and-summer months, the confluence of these realities means that Black and Brown persons were now threatened across multiple fronts. As a post-pandemic world will only very gradually emerge, these communities will continue to be excessively plagued, so much so that some have named the COVID-19 crisis as a modern-day "class war."[9]

When one takes an even closer look at specific groups within these same communities, such as Black and Latina women, they were found to be of the most vulnerable. Reports showed they were least likely to have jobs that could be worked "safely from home," and when the economy shuttered, they were the ones first and most likely to be laid off.[10] On top of the loss of income, these same women were thrust into full-time child care roles as shelter in place orders were announced and child care facilities closed.[11] In this predicament, even those who had not lost their jobs were now forced to quit, and all of these were somehow expected to find income and provide full-time child-care simultaneously. For some women who were in domestic partnerships, the burden intensified as cases of domestic violence reportedly rose up to thirty-five percent half a year into the pandemic.[12] All of these issues have also resulted in mental, physical, and spiritual exhaustion for women of color.

While attempting to adjust to the confines of the pandemic and reckoning with #GeorgeFloyd and Black Lives Matter protests during the summer of 2020, we here in California and those in other parts of the Western region of the country were also experiencing a record year of intense and widespread fires.[13] Environmental degradation related to inattentiveness to these matters over recent decades has fueled (no pun intended) these blazes. What these additional experiences of ecological devastation have prompted, however, is also the realization that communities of color are, again, exceptionally impacted even though they arguably have had little to do with the urgency of the problem in the first place.[14] Many communities of color were located in greater percentages in areas of more extreme air pollution or excess heat (without access to air conditioning), or closer to hazardous waste sites (without the luxury of moving), or exposed to pollutants of various sorts (without the availability of more green spaces or compensating resources).[15] There are now multiple layers of intensification then of the marginalization already felt by communities of color: socio-economic, medical, political, and environmental. The pandemic has exacerbated the lived pre-existing conditions of people of color and effectively deepened the felt inequalities.[16]

The preceding barely scratches the surface of how the COVID-19 pandemic is another revelatory moment illuminating the historical legacies of the "interlocking evils" of systemic racism, poverty, militarism, and ecological devastation that continue to haunt and destroy our collective life.[17] As we know, the politicization of the pandemic has occurred across multiple fronts. While generalizations are just as often misleading as they are helpful, it is also widely recognized that "red" portions of the nation continue to contest the systemic and interlocking character of these aspects of our collective life while "blue" segments are in turn often unconvincing in their admonitions in part due to a broad platform of positions even across this portion of the spectrum, with disagreements between moderates and progressives often complicating, if not confusing, possible ways forward.[18] Ecclesially speaking, it is also well known that evangelical portions of the church in the United States are more inclined to shade "red" while mainline Protestant ones tend toward the "blue" postures, but many are not easily categorizable. In any case, White evangelicals have remained solidly "red" while non-Whites have been more distributed across the political spectrum. Regardless, blame has been cast across all registers, to be sure.

What about pentecostal and charismatic communities, and what have been responses from across these churches and their networks? While there are surely more progressively inclined elements among these (about which we will say more later), by and large, those that have become more pronounced during this pandemic era have been predominantly White pentecostal-charismatic churches, and these have been aligned politically in the "red" with their broader White evangelical counterparts. From our perspective, the responses of this section of churches have been disheartening. There were stories of pastors and leaders who sought to use their public platforms to convince the communities they served that COVID-19 was a "hoax" of the government intending to commit mass murder to the citizens of the United States.[19] Others simply acknowledged the existence of COVID-19 but, presuming a false binary between science and faith, insisted that congregants should not stop gathering in person or it would be a sign of "lack of faith." Beyond this but for similar reasons and purposes, there was also a handful of pastors and leaders who touted "religious freedom" as the basis to admonish people to neglect social distancing protocols and mask recommendations, not least because they claimed to have air-purifying mechanisms that kills the coronavirus![20] As the pandemic wore on and public health leaders made pushes to encourage vaccination as one of the best ways to stop the spread of the virus, ministers made "faith-based arguments" to discourage getting vaccinated and made it an issue of personal piety rather than love for and of the neighbors who are most vulnerable.[21] In other cases, Christian nationalism was wedded to these rallies that called for a "revival" that involved dismissing the pandemic and instead fixing attention on acquiring automatic rifles in order to signal (and perhaps also act on) the belief – based on misinformation, it must be stated – that the election of President Joe Biden was "stolen" and thus a preparation for violence may be necessary to defend the "truth."[22]

Lastly, and perhaps most importantly, there were a large number of many other pastors who took a so-called "neutral" position that recognized the intensity of the pandemic but did not acknowledge the acute ways in which marginalized communities were experiencing suffering inequitably. There is a difference between intention and impact. While this seemingly harmless approach attempts to unify the church by essentially communicating "we are all suffering," what it does in actuality is invisibilize the particular ways in which oppression is manifesting throughout the church body politic. This response for all intents and purposes dismisses and denies the realities that need to be confronted if justice and healing were to take place and ultimately supports the status quo—this is a sin of omission. The prominence of these responses surely drowns out and obscures other actions taken by other pentecostal-charismatic churches from non-predominantly White segments of the movement, yet beg for deeper analysis.

Pentecostal-Charismatic Responses across the Ethnic Spectrum: Whences and Whithers

Clearly, there is no space for any comprehensive explanation for this briefly characterized set of (predominantly White) pentecostal-charismatic responses to the pandemic but given our foci on the pandemic's impact on racial and ethnic minority groups, it may be helpful to also elaborate vis-à-vis these connections. The following are well-rehearsed themes: that the origins of the modern pentecostal movement at Azusa Street features a multi-racial and multi-ethnic sensibility that, even if it did not persist long thereafter, promised a community of many peoples, tongues, tribes, and nations in an era of Jim Crow; that the growth of Christianity as a world-religion across the twentieth century has been marked by pentecostal-charismatic expansion and growth; and that the shift of the center of gravity for the world Christian movement from the European-American West to the so-called global South has been facilitated by pentecostal-charismatic renewal and revival across Asia, Africa, and Latin America.[23] With these historical developments, why has it been that primarily White pentecostal-charismatic personalities and churches have made the news in our pandemic times (above), and how have their responses been replicated across or countered among these other mostly non-White groups and churches?

We hazard three broad and overlapping sets of considerations in response to this query: the socio-historic populism of the movement, the intensely expressed spirituality, and the contemporary lure of political power and in each case, we seek to proceed descriptively as much as possible, saving our more normative (and pastorally motivated) convictions for the last part of this essay. As importantly, we shall note that while there have been a differentiated set of reactions to the pandemic across pentecostal-charismatic communities of color, these have been shaped and informed by similar impulses we have seen featured among White churches.

First, the populism of the Azusa Street revival and networks continues to shape pentecostal-charismatic sensibilities regardless of race and ethnicity factors.[24] This populism has been variously expressed: a suspicion of human capacities, intellect, and achievement perceived as touted by societal elites, and an embrace of divine initiative, tongue-speaking piety, and simple faith instead; by extension a distanciation from the medical-and-scientific establishment undergirded by divine healing prerogatives that bypass human interventions, a fairly pervasive so-called anti-intellectualism (better: anti-rationalism)[25] that also poo-pooed formal higher education in favor of receiving spiritual empowerment and divinely imparted knowledge, and a persecuted-minority self-understanding honed from being the perceived laughingstock of the middle and upper-middle socio-economic classes that in turn pit the remnant of the faithful against the world, not least its governments.[26] We can see that many of these historic emphases have translated to contemporary political practice, not least suspicion of vaccines and the insistence on freedom of assembly even during tumultuous and pandemically-infectious times.

It is understandable that people of color within pentecostal-charismatic communities are no-less distrustful about vaccines given the historic discrimination these groups of persons have experienced at the hands of medical and other experimentation. On the other hand, it is also surely the case that part of the reason the pentecostal movement at its genesis was attractive to people of color had to do with its capacity to empower the voice and agency of those already on the so-called underside of society: ethnic minority groups, migrant communities, and other marginalized populations have continued to find a haven in pentecostal churches.[27] To the same degree that the demographics of the movement continue to include such communities of color, it is usually more the case than not that they continue to embrace these historic themes, so much so that even Black and Brown pentecostal-charismatic churches continue to adopt similar postures to their White colleagues even if their rhetoric might evince some tempered differences. The result is that pentecostal scholars and theologians of color who wish to encourage vaccination, consider criminal justice reform, or advocate for responsiveness to climate change, etc., find themselves now increasingly marginalized from their own ecclesial constituencies.[28]

There is, however, a shadow side of the movement's potent spirituality: its own emboldened and elitist form of triumphalism. On the one hand, pentecostal-charismatic spirituality is presumptive about its full-gospel character: Jesus as savior, sanctifier, healer, Spirit-baptizer, and soon-coming-king – a theological imaginary that nurtures confidence among believers pressed on every side. On the other side, this produces a supernaturalism and otherworldliness that minimizes the material and social dimensions of life, a focus on the benefits of the faith for the individual versus that of the collective, and a fortification mentality of the faithful against its spiritual and other (alleged) oppressors. Pentecostal-charismatic believers are hence less appreciative of other expressions of Jesus-discipleship and generally adopt a rigid exclusivism that otherizes, denigrates, and even demonizes those not deemed born-again with the relevant markers.[29]

What is ironic is that for those (especially but not only White) pentecostal-and-charismatics who have climbed up the social-and-political ladder, the elitism is now on the other foot, so to speak. Those who are bereft of tongues, other *charismata*, or their own conventional manifestations of the fruit of the Holy Spirit are the enemies, although now politicized as the ones inhibiting the gathering of the saints in worship or who are believed to be Marxists and radical socialists that wish to secularize us and our children with demonic ideologies. Most importantly, the privileging of *charismata* forgets the purpose of all spiritual gifts, which is to be in loving and right relationship with all of life (this necessarily means to be committed to social justice). It is surely too much to tar all pentecostal-charismatic communities of color with the same (White) brush, but it is not an over-exaggeration to say that these historical features of pentecostal-charismatic spirituality persist across the spectrum of churches, regardless of racial and ethnic composition. Contemporary pentecostal-and-charismatic churches across the racial-and-ethnic spectrum continue to wrestle with otherworldliness, eschatological expectation, sectarian tendencies, and decontextualizing the aims of spiritual gifts apart from love.[30] Hence, African American, Latino/a, and Asian American pentecostal-charismatic churches also still grapple similarly with the pandemic and its aftermath of emergent partisanship even if their rhetoric is distinct and their accents are in some ways divergent.[31]

We must understand the lure of political power that extends from White evangelical spaces into pentecostal-charismatic nodes against all of this backdrop. This horizon has been looming over the last half-century and as evangelical Christians have attained greater and greater access to political power, so have especially White pentecostal-charismatic believers also attained glimpses of such influences. This spiritualized exclusivism informs political partisanship: God is for us and our (theological and political) convictions, and so God is against our opponents (theologically and politically)![32] The current White nationalism that is pervasive across the country is backed in large part by (White) evangelicalism and thus also supported by (White) pentecostal-charismaticism. If the historical pentecostal movement was apolitical in part due to its commitments to the impending divine reign, the movement's upward political mobility has not included a renewed political analysis to investigate how social and structural power can actually impede the divine reign. Rather, pentecostal Christians have interpreted their newfound political power as "God's will" for hastening the coming kingdom to earth, and this has encouraged deployment of whatever political tools might be accessible to continue to acquire and accumulate more power.[33] This obviously is the opposite of the *agape* and *kenotic* love of Christ that continually gives so that all might have life.

Pentecostal-charismatic congregations and communities of color might be thought of as those attempting to navigate away from these lures. However, especially immigrant groups within these movements, surely a significant contributor to the so-called "browning" of the church in North America,[34] are consistently on assimilationist trajectories difficult to resist. What we mean is that the persons and groups of color within pentecostal-charismatic orbits are pulled into dominant U. S. culture not only religiously and theologically (through their pentecostal beliefs) but also linguistically, socially, and politically (through their accompanying practices). Hence, Asian American pentecostal-charismatic Christians, for instance, are continuously drawn into the (White) evangelical and cultural center and away from their own experiential perspectives.[35] It is not that Asian Americans (and other groups of color) in the pentecostal-charismatic sphere are incapable of adopting counter-cultural postures, but that their ability to do so has been often compromised through behaviors and practices designed to move them away (spiritually, emotionally, socially, and materially) from their marginalized sites to begin with.

A Call to Repentance and to the Promise of the Resurrection

To be sure, there has also been a contingent of spiritual voices and leaders who identify as pentecostal and charismatic that have taken the pandemic seriously, recognized the disproportionate impacts of the pandemic upon marginalized communities, and used their public platforms to encourage others to adhere to public health leadership (including to get vaccinated to stop the spread of the virus) as well as advocate for solidarity with those who are most vulnerable.[36] Unfortunately, however, they are a minority voice. Many Pentecostals and charismatics with the most cultural and social influence seem to be aligned with the White Christian nationalist practices we have observed. As Asian American and mixed-race theological educators embedded within evangelical and pentecostal-charismatic movements, our hearts are broken: for our nation, for our churches, and for our theological institutions. Will we become a people who embody a message of good news for those who are suffering from poverty and the legacies of racism? Will we proclaim freedom for those enslaved to systems of oppression, and will we work towards recovery for those who are sick? Will we be committed to living in solidarity with marginalized communities longing for liberation? Will we reclaim the intercultural spirit that characterized the Azusa Street revival that at least for a brief moment and in localized spaces in the early twentieth century fostered relationships of mutuality and reciprocity? Affirmative responses to these questions, we suggest, will need to include both repentance and a spirituality of compassion that opens the door toward resurrection life.[37]

As pentecostal believers ourselves, we understand both repentance and the embodiment of resurrection life to come through the spiritual practice of testimony.[38] We hope that in this final section of pastoral exhortation, it is received both as our own testifying act as well as encouraging others to testify to the suffering taking place in our time and to God's redemptive power at work in the midst of it towards love and justice.

We begin our testimony with repentance. The act of repentance begins by first naming the wrongs. As we have historically identified, pentecostal theologizing tends to overlook the particular sufferings of persons and instead has stressed the universal healing available to all. While we affirm God as our healer, we want to recognize that there can be no ideal model of how healing occurs. If there were, it would risk ignoring the particularly shaped oppressions of marginalized bodies and communities and subsequently prescribe a monocultural remedy. The repentance we are inviting is one that involves acknowledging the intersectionality of our collective and personal identities as gendered, racialized, and historically-socially constructed. While the majority of pentecostal-charismatic communities after the civil rights have practiced a consciousness of color-blindness, we must recognize how such an approach continues the privilege enjoyed by White persons and obfuscates the challenges that many others continually navigate.[39] Color-blindness has been theologically justified from apostolic texts about there being neither Greek nor Jew, but these have provided excuses for alignment with the dominant (White) culture – including ecclesial cultures – and alleviated responsibility from dealing with the historic injustices of Native American genocide and the scourge of African slavery in American history.[40] If we are to fully embrace the promise of the New Heaven and New Earth, that it will be adorned with the gifts of those from many tribes, peoples, kings, and nations, then we must cherish how human experience derives out of the differentiatedness of our cultures, languages, and experiences, and remain hospitable toward and in community with those rejected by dominant society.[41] This preferential option for those who are suffering from oppression is not an erasure of White realities and challenge but seeks to subvert monocultural interpretations of the *evangel* and establish attention toward the multiplicities of witnesses, each from out of their own experiences, and in their own tongues, that herald the coming divine reign. It is, in fact, thoroughly consistent with the community of love manifest in the Azusa Street revival, where those filled with the Holy Spirit were able to love one another in and through the differences of their racial and ethnic backgrounds.[42]

Second, those in the pentecostal-charismatic movement must repent from not persisting on the fine line between prophetic boldness on the one side and servant-like humility on the other. Our prophets must be cautious of the hazards of their vocation: the scriptures are clear that not all who call themselves prophets are truly so (e.g., 1 John 4:1–3). Our churches should continually test the prophets and ask if their words produce the fruit of the Spirit or serve to perpetuate Christian political power, privilege, and domination. Prophecy, for all Jesus-followers who believe in and are open to Spirit-inspired speech, must turn from the self-aggrandizement of the few to the recognition that the one body has many members, each with the Spirit's gifts enabling edification of others (1 Cor 12). Genuine prophetic messages often also follow from authentic repentance from injustice that results in the shalom the ancient prophets anticipated.[43]

Last but not least, our repentance must renounce the politicization of the gospel by anthropocentric, nationalistic, militaristic, and nation-building impulses. The problem here is not the *evangel* that is the good news of Jesus Christ who sets the captives free, but the *icalism* that thinks we are building an earthly kingdom of comfort wherein we decide who is included and prioritized and who is not.[44] U. S. citizenship (which includes an assumption of U. S. history as neutral at best and thus denies the oppressive realities foundational to the expansion of power therein) has trumped (pun intended) commitments to the coming kingdom (Heb 11:13–16, 12:18–28); modernist individualism has not only elevated and focused on individual rights while marginalizing and even ignoring all-together social justice; and neoliberal capitalism has sucked us all into the never-ending quest for economic growth that overlooks our interdependence with the environment, driven our accumulation of property instead of apostolic giving (Acts 2:42–47), and prioritized an ethic of productivity that ignores the call to Sabbath and the need for personal and planetary rest and renewal.[45] In all of this, our evangelical (and pentecostal-charismatic) piety has over-emphasized an individualized outworking of God's redemptive work, which lacks the interpersonal, ecclesial, and cosmic character of the divine intention for life's all-encompassing flourishing. Repentance will require acknowledgment of how our theological education has not inoculated us from all these seductions, resulting in our (mono)cultural captivity instead of a church capable of speaking truth to power and co-creating a world of mutuality where all thrive.[46]

We are continuing to cry out to God for deliverance from these errors and recognize God's mercy in the midst of it, calling us to a more authentic, even proleptic, embodiment of Jesus' heralding of the reign of God by the power of the Holy Spirit. As we consider the particular sufferings and deaths wrought by the pandemic for many within marginalized communities, we ask what response the church shall offer? We are compelled to testify to the Spirit who brings life out of death. As the Apostle Paul wrote, "the Spirit of him who raised Jesus from the dead lives in you . . ." (Rom. 8:11, NRSV), and we see impulses of this resurrection life beginning to emerge.

Whereas many among us (not least Asian Americans) may be deferential to majority (White) culture as part of their survival and desire for upward socio-economic movement, we have recognized the abundance of life available when we intentionally divest from any practices that promote flourishing for some at the expense of others. We are calling for other pentecostal and charismatic Christians to awaken to the greatest gift and miracle of all, that of love. For it is through love of God and love of neighbor that all commands, gifts, and miracles reach maturity. A love for all things can only be forged in deep resonance with those who occupy the margins, surely beginning with Indigenous and Black American communities but also with migrant sojourners, whether from south of the border or elsewhere around the world. On the other side of repentance, we invite others beyond the Asian American and mixed-raced communities to consider new solidarities of Resurrection communities: less cozying up with those in power and more communion with our siblings who have been on the underside of history, the poor toward whom the divine Spirit has directed the proclamation of the *evangel* (see Luke 4:18).

The way we have experienced the *evangel* is through the invitation to healing and resurrection life. For us, this is glimpsed when we have disrupted our internalized forms of oppression, resisted hierarchies that form within and without, and given ourselves to let go of our own "dreaded and cherished illusions" so that new ways of being are found.[47] We recognize that many of our pentecostal theologies and ecclesiologies within the U. S. have for too log been fashioned by Christian and White supremacy (especially anti-Black racism and anti-Indigeneity), preventing any proximity to the lives of those who suffer disproportionately through particular oppressions that thus render healing impossible. Now is the time when the Spirit is calling us to lay aside the seductions of privilege and ethnocentrism and instead pursue relationships of mutuality with those who are dispossessed. If we so choose, the Spirit promises healing and resurrection.[48]

While we realize there are many ways in which healing occurs and varying effects of how healing impacts us, we admit that any healing can only be a work done in partnership with the divine and emanates from the suffering and broken-hearted of the world (including the suffering of human as well as other than human life). Wholeness then is not about distance from suffering but about how we respond to it with the knowledge that Love alone has the ultimate authority and the final word on things.[49] In pentecostal-charismatic traditions, the healing of suffering is central, and if there was ever a moment needed for healing, it is now amidst such widespread arrogance, self-centeredness, division, and confusion.[50]

We again want to again be clear: any hope for resurrection can only be possible when we first acknowledge and meet death with repentance and compassionate acceptance. This is a paradoxical stance that requires faith and asks of us to stay with the suffering and join God in holding it with transformational love.[51] We are calling for more leaders from the church to center in and face the suffering of the world that we might allow the Spirit to usher collective healing into our personal lives and into the whole world.[52]

A reclamation of the power and practice of testimony is sorely needed in our time as it imbues all with a way to acknowledge our own suffering as well as the hope and confidence we experience in living empowered in the Spirit. We challenge the notion of testimony as a practice that declares triumphalistically "victory" over our suffering; it is rather a way of living from the disarmed and humble posture of compassionate love that seeks to touch the places we hurt the most and receive the gift of new life. We hope that what we have presented demonstrates the realities of human frailty and also finds solace in the Spirit, who cannot be contained or tamed by any one individual, family, cultural group, institution, or spiritual tradition. Thus, although we see death abound, as theological educators, pentecostal ministers, and fellow human beings, we invite you to respond to this death-dealing pandemic by testifying to and with the most vulnerable in the hope that echoes the words of the apostle Paul, "Where, O death, is your victory? Where, O death, is your sting?" (1 Cor 15:55).

Notes

1 This is even acknowledged on the federal leadership level, as seen in the recent statement made by Rochelle Walensky, the Director for the Centers for Disease Control and Prevention, acknowledging the racialized dimensions of the pandemic and the need to identify systemic racism as a serious public health threat on the par with the deadly COVID-19 pandemic; "Media Statement," April 8, 2021, https://www.cdc.gov/media/releases/2021/s0408-racism-health.html, accessed November 6, 2021.

2 This chapter utilizes lower-case "pentecostal-charismatic" when used as adjectives.

3 The elder has carried ministerial credentials with classical pentecostal churches all of his adult life while the younger is, in the course of writing, in the process of transitioning his from a classical pentecostal to a mainline Protestant denomination.

4 Jaclyn Diaz, "The COVID-19 Pandemic Has Now Killed 5 Million People Around the World," *NPR*, November 1, 2021, https://www.npr.org/2021/11/01/1051020063/the-covid-19-pandemic-has-killed-5-million-people-globally, accessed November 6, 2021.

5 One such example of this issue was in the many outbreaks that took place at meatpacking plants across the country, e.g., Smithfield, Nebraska; see Maira Mendez and Michelle Martin, "She's Advocating for Her Meat Plant Worker Parents," June 6, 2020, in *All Things Considered* by *NPR*, MP3 audio, podcast, https://www.npr.org/2020/06/06/871536123/shes-advocating-for-her-meat-plant-worker-parents, accessed November 6, 2021.

6 See one such study discusses the "pandemic precarity" (and its similarities to other national disasters) affecting residents of Indiana, a state still suffering from the devastation of the 2008 great recession; Brea L. Perry, Brian Aronson, and Bernice A. Pescosolido, "Pandemic Precarity: COVID-19 is Exposing and Exacerbating Inequalities in the American Heartland," *Proceedings of the National Academy of Sciences* 118:8 (2021), https://doi.org/10.1073/pnas.2020685118.

7 Tori Marsh, "The Privilege Gap of the COVID-19 Vaccine Roll Out," GoodRX Health, May 19, 2021, https://www.goodrx.com/blog/covid-19-vaccine-rollout-privilege-gaps-between-states/, accessed November 6, 2021.

8 Daniel Wood, "As Pandemic Deaths Add Up, Racial Disparities Persist – and in Some Cases Worsen," *NPR*, September 23, 2020, https://www.npr.org/sections/health-shots/2020/09/23/914427907/as-pandemic-deaths-add-up-racial-disparities-persist-and-in-some-cases-worsen, and Cliff Despres, "Coronavirus Case Rates and Death Rates for Latinos in the United States,"

Salud America! updated November 3, 2021, https://salud-america.org/coronavirus-case-rates-and-death-rates-for-latinos-in-the-united-states/, both accessed November 6, 2021.

9   Les Leopold, "COVID-19's Class War," *The American Prospect*, July 28, 2020, https://prospect.org/coronavirus/covid-19-class-war-death-rates-income/, accessed November 6, 2021.

10 Elise Gould, Daniel Perez, and Valerie Wilson, "Latinx Workers—Particularly Women—Face Devastating Job Losses in the COVID-19 Recession," *Economic Policy Institute*, December 3, 2020, https://www.epi.org/publication/latinx-workers-covid/, accessed November 6, 2021.

11 See Soo Youn, "Quitting was Her Only Option," *The Lily*, October 7, 2020, https://www.thelily.com/quitting-was-her-only-option-she-is-one-of-865000-women-to-leave-the-workforce-last-month/, Paola F. Gleghorn, "One Year into This, Women Still Bear the Brunt," *Sojourners* (March 11, 2021), https://sojo.net/articles/one-year-pandemic-women-still-bear-brunt, and Caroline Kitchener, "A Shocking 156,000 Women Left Jobs in December. Here's what's behind that number. Black women and Latinas were hit hardest," *The Lily*, January 10, 2021, https://www.thelily.com/a-shocking-156000-women-left-jobs-in-december-heres-whats-behind-that-number/, all accessed November 6, 2021.

12 Shalini Mittal and Tushar Singh, "Gender-Based Violence During COVID-19 Pandemic: A Mini-Review," *Frontiers in Global Women's Health*, September 8, 2020, https://doi.org/10.3389/fgwh.2020.00004, accessed November 6, 2021.

13 Alan Buis, "The Climate Connections of Record Fire Year in the U.S. West," *NASA Global Climate Change*, February 22, 2021, https://climate.nasa.gov/blog/3066/the-climate-connections-of-a-record-fire-year-in-the-us-west/, accessed November 6, 2021.

14 See James Cone, "Whose Earth is it Anyway?" *Crosscurrents* 50:1 (2000), 34–46.

15 E.g., Brian Mastroianni, "How Climate Change Disproportionately Affects People of Color," *Healthline*, April 22, 2021, https://www.healthline.com/health-news/how-climate-change-disproportionately-affects-people-of-color, accessed November 6, 2021.

16 See Bishop William J. Barber's sermon entitled, "Light a Candle Tonight for All the Coronavirus Victims,"April 9, 2020, video, https://twitter.com/RevDrBarber/status/1248778038763876354?s=20, and Kristin Soares, "An Inequitable Pandemic: How Environmental Racism Has Worsened COVID-19 in Communities of Color," *Climate Change*, September 23, 2021,

https://climate-xchange.org/2021/09/23/an-inequitable-pandemic-how-environmental-racism-has-worsened-covid-19-in-communities-of-color/, both accessed November 20, 2021.

17 The phrase "interlocking evils" comes from the Poor People's Campaign (which is a contemporary social movement) that has sought to renew the work of Rev. Dr. Martin Luther King Jr. around spiritually rooted social change. See the demands of the Poor People's Campaign that describes these evils succinctly: https://www.poorpeoplescampaign.org/about/our-demands/, accessed November 6, 2021.

18 We have provided an earlier assessment from a more general evangelical perspective in Aizaiah G. Yong and Amos Yong, "Seeking Healing in an Age of Partisan Division: Reckoning with Theological Education and Resounding the *Evangel* for the 2020s," in Miguel A. De La Torre, ed., *Faith and Reckoning after Trump* (Maryknoll: Orbis, 2021), 214–27; the present essay focuses on the pentecostal-charismatic overlay (or undercurrent, depending on one's perspective) of the evangelical Christian movement.

19 James Wilson, "The Rightwing Christian Preachers in Deep Denial over Covid-19's Danger," *The Guardian*, April 4, 2020, https://www.theguardian.com/us-news/2020/apr/04/america-rightwing-christian-preachers-virus-hoax, accessed November 6, 2021.

20 See Andre Gagne, "Coronavirus: Trump and Religious Right Rely on Faith, Not Science," *The Conversation*, March 29, 2020, https://theconversation.com/coronavirus-trump-and-religious-right-rely-on-faith-not-science-134508, and Ruth Graham, "The Phoenix Megachurch Where Trump Is Speaking Says Its Air Purifiers 'Kill 99.9 Percent of COVID'," *Slate*, June 23, 2020, https://slate.com/human-interest/2020/06/dream-city-church-phoenix-trump-young-americans-air-purifiers-covid.html, both accessed November 6, 2021.

21 See Elizabeth Dias and Ruth Graham, "White Evangelical Resistance Is Obstacle in Vaccination Effort," *The New York Times*, updated October 7, 2021, https://www.nytimes.com/2021/04/05/us/covid-vaccine-evangelicals.html, accessed November 6, 2021.

22 Bob Smietana, "America's Revival Features Calls to Prayer, Jesus Trumps COVID Claims and Mike Lindell Conspiracy Theories," *Religious News Service*, August 7, 2021, https://religionnews.com/2021/08/07/americas-revival-christian-nationalism-greg-locke-mike-lindell-joshua-feuerstein-trump-conspiracy-theories/, accessed November 6, 2021.

23 All of this is well-documented, but for those wishing more detailed perspectives provided by a project one of us has been involved in, see

Amos Yong, et al., eds., *Global Renewal Christianity: Spirit-Empowered Movements Past, Present, and Future*, 4 vols (Lake Mary, FL: Charisma House Publishers, 2016–2017).

24 The historical work is Grant Wacker, *Heaven Below: Early Pentecostals and American Culture* (Cambridge: Harvard University Press, 2003); a more recent treatment is Christl Kessler and Jürgen Rüland, *Give Jesus a Hand! Charismatic Christians – Populist Religion and Politics in the Philippines* (Manila: Ateneo de Manila University Press, 2009).

25 See here the argument by Dale M. Coulter and Amos Yong, *Finding the Holy Spirit at a Christian University: Renewing Christian Higher Education* (Waco, TX.: Baylor University Press, 2022), ch. 4.

26 See Erica Ramirez, "Who's Laughing Now? Pentecostal Disrespectability Politics," *Political Theology Network*, July 8, 2021, https://politicaltheology.com/whos-laughing-now-pentecostal-diss-respectability-politics/, accessed November 6, 2021.

27 The classic study is Robert M. Anderson, *Vision of the Disinherited: The Making of American Pentecostalism* (Peabody: Hendrickson, 1992).

28 E.g., Sammy Alfaro, "Latino Pentecostal Democrat: Oxymoron or Prophetic Voice?" *Political Theology Network*, July 22, 2021, https://politicaltheology.com/latino-pentecostal-democrat-oxymoron-or-prophetic-voice/, accessed November 6, 2021.

29 David J. Courey, *What Has Wittenberg to Do with Azusa? Luther's Theology of the Cross and Pentecostal Triumphalism* (New York: T & T Clark, 2015), illuminates the triumphalism that infects pentecostal-charismatic spirituality. Put another way: pentecostal-charismatic supernaturalism understandably and even rightly emerged in reaction to the limitations of the immanentistic naturalism of the modern world, but precisely because subject neither to human manipulability nor rational comprehension, more often promises more than what is delivered, which in the end results in undermining rather than nurturing faith; see Amos Yong, *The Spirit Poured Out on All Flesh: Pentecostalism and the Possibility of Global Theology* (Grand Rapids: Baker Academic, 2005), ch. 7, for more on this theme.

30 E.g., Frederick L. Ware, "On the Compatibility/Incompatibility of Pentecostal Premillennialism with Black Liberation Theology," in Estrelda Alexander and Amos Yong, eds., *Afro-Pentecostalism: Black Pentecostal and Charismatic Christianity in History and Culture* (New York: New York University Press, 2011), 191–207.

31 We highly recommend consulting especially the chapters of David Daniels in this volume, reprinted from Daniels, "COVID-19, Science, and Race: A Black Pentecostal Engagement," *Spiritus: ORU Journal of Theology* 6:1 (2021), 141–55.

32 For instance, René Holvast, *Spiritual Mapping in the United States and Argentina, 1989–2005: A Geography of Fear* (Leiden: Brill, 2008), and Abimbola A. Adelakun, *Powerful Devices: Prayer and the Political Praxis of Spiritual Warfare* (New Brunswick: Rutgers University Press, 2022), among other works that explore how pentecostal-charismatic practices regarding spiritual warfare are politicized.

33 One example is how early pentecostal pacifism gave way to militarism as more and more pentecostal believers came to work in this sector; see Paul Alexander, *Peace to War: Shifting Allegiances in the Assemblies of God* (Telford, PA: Cascadia, 2009).

34 See Robert Chao Romero, *The Brown Church: Five Centuries of Latino/a Social Justice, Theology, and Identity* (Downers Grove: IVP Academic, 2020).

35 Amos' own very gradual coming to grips with this reality is documented in various of his essays, some of them gathered in his *The Future of Evangelical Theology: Soundings from the Asian American Diaspora* (Downers Grove: IVP Academic, 2014).

36 A few such exemplars of this are: Dr. Barbara Holmes, a core faculty of the Center of Action and Contemplation (https://youtu.be/e4qfQckPJWE), The Fellowship of Affirming Ministries and the series of webinars entitled, "The COVID writings," led by Bishop Yvette Flunder (www.facebook.com/tfamworld), and the Pentecostals and Charismatics for Peace and Justice (https://www.facebook.com/pcpeacejustice) who have spoken openly against many of the behaviors we previously reviewed; e.g., Michael Grenholm, "The Five Worst Christian Responses to the Coronavirus Pandemic," PCPJ, March 18, 2020, at https://pcpj.org/2020/03/18/the-five-worst-christian-responses-to-the-coronavirus-pandemic/, accessed November 6, 2021.

37 Aizaiah wrote on the need for a "radical presence" to be practiced that embraces both resistance as well as creativity as essential for healing and restoration to occur amidst multiple crises in "Overcoming Social Demoralization Together: A Call to Communal Care," *Sharing the Practice* 43:4 (2020), 3–7.

38 E.g., Mark J. Cartledge, ed., *Testimony in the Spirit: Rescripting Ordinary Pentecostal Theology* (Burlington: Ashgate, 2017).

39 See Jesse Curtis, *The Myth of Colorblind Christians: Evangelicals and White Supremacy in the Civil Rights Era* (New York: New York University Press, 2021).

40 As documented across the essays of Love L. Sechrest, Johnny Ramírez-Johnson, and Amos Yong, eds., *Can "White" People Be Saved? Triangulating Race, Theology, and Mission*, Missiological Engagements (Downers Grove: IVP Academic, 2018).

41 See Raimon Pannikar, *Cultural Disarmament: The Way to Peace the Way to Peace* (Westminster: John Knox Press, 1995).

42 See Dale T. Irvin, "'Drawing All Together into One Bond of Love': The Ecumenical Vision of William J. Seymour and the Azusa Street Revival," *Journal of Pentecostal Theology* 6 (1995), 25–53.

43 See, for instance, the repentance from racism by historic White pentecostal churches, as documented by the so-called "Memphis miracle" in October 1994 that birthed a new multi-racial Pentecostal-and-Charismatic Churches of North America via its prophetic "Racial Reconciliation Manifesto;" see https://pccna.org/documents/1994manifesto.pdf, accessed November 20, 2021.

44 See Mark Labberton, ed., *Still Evangelical? Insiders Reconsider Political, Social, and Theological Meaning* (Downers Grove: IVP Academic, 2018).

45 One set of constructive responses by evangelical-friendly voices can be found in Jonathan P. Walton, Suzie Laboud, and Sy Hoekstra, eds., *Keeping the Faith: Reflections on Politics and Christianity in the Era of Trump and Beyond* (Middletown, DE: KTF Press, 2020).

46 See our previously referred to co-authored chapter where we seek to begin some of this work: "Seeking Healing in an Age of Partisan Division."

47 Christian mystic and spiritual teacher James Finley, *The Contemplative Heart* (Notre Dame: Sorin Books, 2000), 208–9, describes spiritual healing as discovering our true identity and "learning from God how to let go of and die to your dreaded and cherished illusions that anything less than infinite union with the infinite love of God has the authority to name who you are." This reality is of utmost importance if we are to heal the ways our hearts are easily given to despair amidst the contemporary crises.

48 A recent event led by the California Poor People's Campaign focuses on these very specific challenges that prevent us from the liberation we collectively long for: https://actionnetwork.org/events/rsvp-for-the-california-poor-peoples-campaign-christian-nationalism-event/, accessed November 6, 2021.

49 This thought echoes the words of Rev. Dr. Martin Luther King Jr., who received the Nobel Peace Prize, saying that, "I believe that unarmed

truth and unconditional *love will have the final word* in reality"; https://www.nobelprize.org/prizes/peace/1964/king/26142-martin-luther-king-jr-acceptance-speech-1964/ accessed November 6, 2021. It also inspired a sermon Aizaiah preached at City of Refuge UCC (a historically black and pentecostal church in Oakland, California in April 2021) https://youtu.be/S3tV3w9am7s.

50 Aizaiah has sought to imagine new Spirit-informed pedagogical approaches that overcome the inherited individualism of the United States as a professor teaching spirituality and spiritual care and describes the ways in which re-connecting with the interior world, the divine, and the cosmos can support healing in "Decolonizing Pastoral Care in the Classroom: An Invitation to a Pedagogy of Spirit Experience," *Teaching Theology and Religion* 24:2 (June 2021), 107–16.

51 Aizaiah taught a course called "Healing from White Supremacy: Critical Race Theory and the Contemplative Mind" through the Newbigin House of Studies, which sought to both admit the ways in which racism plagues communal life in the United States and identify possibilities for transforming those patterns through contemplation and action; see https://www.facebook.com/newbiginhouse/photos/a.3262966380448440/3607369896008085/, accessed November 20, 2021.

52 We combine here the spiritual and the mystical that is deeply embedded within the pentecostal-charismatic imaginary: e.g., Mark J. Cartledge, *Encountering the Spirit: The Charismatic Tradition* (New York: Orbis, 2007), and Daniel Castelo, *Pentecostalism as a Mystical Christian Tradition* (Grand Rapids: Eerdmans, 2017); see also Amos Yong, *Spirit of Love: A Trinitarian Theology of Grace* (Waco: Baylor University Press, 2012).

13 COVID-19, Science, and Race: A Black Pentecostal Engagement[1]

David Douglas Daniels III

Abstract

A Black Pentecostal engagement of COVID-19, science, and race points towards a rapport between the Spirit-empowered movement and health sciences where religious and secular (science) actors are respected agents in the public arena with each offering valuable perspectives and resources to pivotal conversations about public health in this case. In this chapter, it is argued that the Church of God in Christ (COGIC) represented in the episcopal letters of Bishop Charles Edward Blake, Sr., the presiding bishop of COGIC from 2007 to 2021, demonstrate a theological position that possesses a critical perspective on engaging health science during the COVID-19 pandemic. Through his establishment of a COVID-19 taskforce of physicians and clergy, Bishop Blake has published episcopal statements on the pandemic that advanced public health by promoting scientifically informed and medically sound measures that are consistent with Scripture and COGIC theology.

Introduction

The United States has entered a leadership vacuum regarding the COVID-19 pandemic during 2020 and early 2021. To switch metaphors, the country has entered a war zone marked by social catastrophes such as nearly 500,000 deaths between March 2020 and March 2021, devastation to families affected by the virus and the related economic crisis, loss of learning by urban public-school students, the projected closure of 5 percent of Christian congregations, and the disproportionate negative social impact of the pandemic on communities of color. Major sectors of U.S. society are reeling in reaction to the pandemic.

Clarity about the role of science in advancing public health has been contested. Situated within a polarized American society and church on the role of science, the debate about science's role in society is compounded by the reality that the society and churches grapple with living within an era of post-truth, alternative truths, alternative facts, and alternative realities that fuel the "infowars," or information wars. This reality hinders the U. S. government along with denominations and congregations from addressing the COVID-19 pandemic in a constructive, systematic manner. Rather than being united in the pursuit of ending the pandemic, an intellectual fight has broken out between the different camps reflecting opposing positions on the role of science in addressing the pandemic.

The debate within congregations, homes, and other institutions is framed by different views. Is COVID-19 just like the flu or a more deadly virus? Should we defend the science or fight science in advancing public health in regards to the COVID-19 pandemic? Are we to interpret the deaths associated by the pandemic as a means to "herd immunity" or avoidable deaths? Should race-related healthcare disparities exacerbated by the pandemic be ignored by the government and healthcare institutions? Or should government and public health funds be directed to reducing these disparities in regard to the pandemic specifically and improving the overall health outcome for Black and Brown Americans in general? Does a person's individual civil liberties trump public health or must public health place limits on one's civil rights? Does the U.S. constitutional religious right to assemble in-person as a congregation prevail over the government's public health responsibility to contain a pandemic by requiring the suspension of in-person religious gatherings? Are Christians to frame this debate as an issue of obeying government or serving God?

Science and COVID-19: A Spirit-Empowered Engagement

While secularization appeared to truncate the religious sphere of the United States with "faith in science" replacing "faith in God" during the second half of the twentieth century, post-secularity might be a better descriptor of the religious context of the twenty-first century and of the context of a Black Pentecostal engagement of COVID-19, science, and race. On this topic, this perspective might point towards a rapport between Pentecostalism and health sciences where religious and secular (science) actors are respected agents in the public arena with each offering valuable perspectives and resources to pivotal conversations about public health in this case.

Collaboration could occur between secular (science) institutions that recognize the civic and intellectual significance of religion in general and Spirit-empowered Christianity in particular. Spirit-empowered

Christianity is deemed to possess a critical perspective on life, hold a valuable wisdom, and play a vital role in society. As the scholar Jurgen Habermas argues, societies, especially western ones, need religion to thrive. So, Spirit-empowered organizations could unashamedly and unabashedly participate as vital institutions in the public arena. Following the thesis of sociologists Donald Miller and Tetsunao Yamamori, there is present in Pentecostalism something more than sociological factors like economics, culture, and identity. What Pentecostals call the Holy Spirit, Miller and Yamamori identify as "the S Factor."[2]

How have Black Pentecostals who engage the scientific discussion of the COVID-19 within the public arena as Christians testify to the power of the Holy Spirit? How do they speak in Christian terms and content? How do they speak on experiences and practices that are "untranslatable" to a secular audience such as the Holy Spirit and divine healing?

How do they avoid perpetuating the culture wars along the lines of the U.S. Christian Right and Left? To engage the secular arena as Christians without culture war politics, Spirit-empowered Christians can cease mirroring cultural wars of the religious versus secularist combatants and co-lead a campaign of Christians and healthcare scientists in both communities to learn together how to respect, appreciate, and celebrate the constructive role that each is able to play in society.

In Michele Dillon's study of a post-secular Roman Catholicism, she proposes for Christianity and the secular an "appreciation of the mutual relevance." This "mutual relevance" could offer the Spirit-empowered Movement a pathway to greater "public relevance" by producing "culturally useful resources for addressing contemporary social ills" in dialogue and collaboration with secularism. These resources could include a constructive engagement of science, especially health care sciences. With a "contrite modernity" of a secularism that is cognizant of its excesses and of a Spirit-empowered Movement aware of its problematic triumphalism, they both can be open to "mutual self-critique." More broadly, these are joined by the inalienable rights of the U.N. Charter of Human Rights with additional commitment to healthcare justice and by Pentecostalism's democratization of the Spirit as well as its theology of holistic healing, including the role of medicine. These perspectives could deepen practices of holistic healing promoted by the Spirit-empowered Movement that respect the integrity of the human body, life, and the family. Together they could enrich citizenship within society and in the Christian household of faith. While difference is acknowledged, it is engagement rather than combat. Consequently, new forms of Spirit-empowered civic engagement could emerge.[3]

Borrowing from Dillon, we stress that Spirit-empowered Christians could introduce their vocabulary of healing and the content of the biblical healing narratives in the public arena. Rather than translating their speech and arguments "into an accessible secular vocabulary" as Jurgen Habermas advocates for all religious arguments, it might be better for the secular sphere to become bi-lingual by learning the Christian language. More than a mere intellectual exchange, a Spirit-empowerment Movement with post-secular sensibilities could express a robust vision of flourishing life that embraces healthcare justice for people of color and others limited by healthcare inequities.[4]

Within the Spirit-empowered study of theology and science, Frederick Ware, a Church of God in Christ clergyperson, is among a select group of Black theologians, including Barbara Holmes, for whom science is a topic of their theological exploration. According to Ware, "Pentecostals have to make a choice of alignment with dominant theological and scientific paradigms." He adds:

> The old alignment with fundamentalist attitudes seems no longer to be a viable option for a robust engagement with modern science, given the evasion and rejection spawned by this kind of alignment. Recently, Pentecostals have associated more closely with both Evangelical organizations (e.g., the BioLogos Foundation) and mainline Protestant groups (e.g., Metanexus Institute and the Center for Theology and the Natural Sciences).[5]

Ware appears to seek a new alignment beyond the Fundamentalist, Evangelical, and Mainline Protestant options that foster a Pentecostal engagement with science that will increase "scientific literacy" among Pentecostals on one hand and "address both the intellectual problems and moral crises posed by modern science and its distortions." Internally within the Spirit-empowered Movement, he spotlights how "the lack of scientific literacy is being exploited" by certain ministries seeking financial gain through concocting "toxic brew(s)" that they advertise as "'healing water,' 'sacramental protocols,' and 'miracle mineral solution'" when consumed "in large doses can result in serious injury or death." A

Pentecostal engagement with science and education in scientific literacy is needed to help more people live amidst lethal misinformation.[6]

Science and COVID-19: The COGIC Engagement

During these first decades of the twenty-first century, Spirit-empowered denominations like the Church of God in Christ (COGIC) have occupied a unique place within the American religious landscape by having among its national leadership from the 1920s physicians and scientists who were either bishops, pastors, or women officials. These leaders created a space within COGIC to pursue a constructive, albeit limited, dialogue between faith and science.

The Church of God in Christ acknowledges the role of medicine as part of God's plan of healing. While some Pentecostal traditions reject medicine on theological grounds, juxtaposing faith with belief and medicine with doubt, limiting healing to divine agency, COGIC understands the role of divine and human agency in the biblical plan of healing. Providing theological support for medicine and vaccinations, COGIC has expressed support for members being vaccinated against COVID-19.

"The general welfare of all people," including healthcare, has been a long-term concern of COGIC. In its official theological document, the denomination states: "We believe that Christ, through his redemptive power, has enabled us and called us to help relieve human suffering created by sin, and we are to use whatever available resources in the restoration of [hu]man [beings] to physical, mental and spiritual health." Accordingly, prescription pharmaceuticals are to be used "under medical supervision for one's health and well-being." While prayer is recommended as the first "treatment" for illness, medical treatment is encouraged. Under a rubric of "Medical Care," COGIC expresses a dedication to "principles and practices in wholesome living, as a sound mind must reside in a sound body. . . ."[7]

Communiques called "Presiding Bishop's Statement on COVID-19" were authored by Bishop Charles Edward Blake, Sr., presiding prelate of the Church of God in Christ from 2007 to 2021, and disseminated to the Church of God in Christ during the first year of the COVID-19 pandemic beginning in March of 2020. In addition, by May 2020, Bishop Blake convened a taskforce, the "COGIC COVID-19 Advisory Commission," and appointed as the commission's co-chairs two COGIC physicians who are bishops, Elton Amos and Terence Rhone. The commission was comprised of physicians, attorneys, scholars, pastors, and bishops.

In his first episcopal letter on COVID-19 dated 11 March 2020, Bishop Blake placed in conversation "considerable prayer" and consultation with "trusted medical professionals." He noted: *"After considerable prayer and direct consultation with trusted medical professionals from around the country, the following is our response to the growing concerns over the rapid spread of the coronavirus disease epidemic (COVID-19) that is currently impacting the world"* (italics original). He stated that "the Church of God in Christ is providing and adhering to the Centers for Disease Control (CDC) & Prevention guidelines, in addition to fervent, believing prayer." He included a link to the CDC website in his letter so that the COGIC leadership and membership could access current information about the virus and the guidelines. He saw a need for a "joint effort" between the congregations and the CDC in order to "reduce the risk of exposure as much as possible." While this joint effort expressed concern about individual transmission of the virus. He also acknowledged the role of risky decisions of organizations like denominations that could collectively increase transmission. He asked the "more than 10,000 congregations" of COGIC "to aggressively monitor the epidemic as it develops and take all necessary and recommended measures provided by the CDC."[8]

> Prayer opened and concluded the communique:
> Lastly, let us continue to pray for the speedy recoveries of all who have been affected by COVID-19. Please also pray for the many healthcare workers who faithfully serve in numerous patient care settings as essential personnel, for our Church, the nation, and the entire world. The Church of God in Christ trusts in the miraculous healing and protective power of the Lord Jesus Christ. As He alone is our Keeper, we will continue to wholly put our trust and faith in Him.

There is a call for the church to enter into intercessory prayer on the behalf of frontline workers and prayer for "miraculous healing" and "protective power" found in Jesus Christ.[9]

In the second episcopal letter on COVID-19 dated 18 March 2020, Bishop Blake continues the conversation. He inquires in response to the pandemic, "What are the saints to do?" He proposes:

First, needless to say, we are living in perilous times, but certainly not without a divine remedy to survive, overcome and to emerge safely and victoriously. In fact, the same way God exercised His power to save Israel from every disease which struck the land of Egypt, even so did our Lord and Savior Jesus Christ demonstrate Himself to be the Son of God in accomplishing the healing of every widespread outbreak and pandemic affecting the regions wherever He traveled. For this reason, it is my desire to share some practical guidelines for elevating our awareness while fully engaging our faith.

He emphasized that COGIC congregants and leaders should "stay fully informed, well-prepared and safely empowered." They should "remain connected to good counsel" coming from CDC and "'be not deceived' nor vulnerable" to the virus through misinformation and risky behavior.[10]

Bishop Blake stated in this second episcopal letter on COVID-19 that "during this crisis, our faith in God is most responsibly exercised in trusting those voices whose entire lives and professions have been dedicated to the awesome task of ensuring our public health.... Strategic planning is the key to warfare. Therefore, to win, you must remain connected to good counsel." He grounds his perspective in the sovereignty of God. For Bishop Blake, God "is in control and is He [who] is ready to come to our rescue in critical times" such as during this pandemic. He also confesses God as the healer who "has sent His Word to heal." Bishop Blake understands healing in terms of miracles on one hand and preventive public health measures on the other, measures that relieve and mitigate against the public dimensions of the virus.[11]

In the third episcopal letter of 25 March 2020, Bishop Blake issues a call to the Church of God in Christ.

> Fervent prayer is our biblical response to any and all societal challenges. For this reason, your Presiding Bishop and General Board are calling all saints to observe a day of "GLOBAL FASTING AND INTERCESSORY PRAYER." This coming Friday, MARCH 27, 2020, we will intercede on behalf of all nations and people for Heaven's help in mitigating this dreaded disease—and for healing the bodies, minds and spirits of a fallen and fearful humanity. Please observe fasting from midnight, Thursday, March 26th until 4:00 p.m. on Friday, March 27th—and continue in fervent prayer throughout the day. Ultimately, we trust in the great physician, Jesus Christ.

During the day of global fasting and prayer, prayers that "wise decisions will be made by international, national and state leaders" were offered up to God. There were prayers "for all that are in authority" extending from political offices to "the compassionate vanguard of those in harm's way," ranging from medical personnel to teachers and police to pharmacy staff and grocery store workers. In addition, prayers were offered for "the mission-critical manufacturing supply chain." Amidst increasing infection and death rates, prayers were said for the affected families "grappling with the illness or loss of loved ones," requesting "divine comfort," and for "total health and healing" for those infected by the virus as well as "other medical conditions."[12]

Bishop Blake noted in his April 2020 episcopal letter on COVID-19:

> The Church of God in Christ does not support or condone any actions that defy the collective wisdom and recommendations of government leaders, both federally and locally, including scientific experts. In fact, the leadership of our church has communicated directly, on multiple occasions, with pastors and church leaders, encouraging all to abide by the directives and stay-at-home guidelines set by city, state, and federal officials.

He made clear that "Church of God in Christ remains committed to prioritizing the welfare of people over the economy" as government and civic leaders debate whether to prioritize profit or people.[13]

In the 1 May 2020 episcopal letter on COVID-19, Bishop Blake addresses what he identified as "premature re-openings" of churches. In the debate of whether to follow the government in reopening sectors of cities, towns, and states, Bishop Blake proposes caution regarding the premature re-openings until there is "tangible, persistent flattening of the curve" related to the rates of infection, hospitalizations, and deaths from the virus. He states:[14]

> We do not recommend the reopening of COGIC churches at this time. Although our current circumstances are not ideal, the Church of God in Christ is resolute in our stance that the reopening of churches, prior to the number of new COVID-19 cases significantly declining, and prior to a tangible, persistent flattening of the curve could prove detrimental to our congregant populations as a whole.

In the 23 May 2020 episcopal letter, he implored:[15]

> We urge you, our pastors, to adhere to the recommendations of the CDC and NIAID [National Institute of Allergy and Infectious Diseases] and to refrain from prematurely opening your churches and congregating in your buildings

before we have credible and substantiated evidence that it is safe to do so. In addition, we urge you to establish a protocol to safely reopen your church to prevent any risk to the health and safety of our members and communities at large *before* you reopen your churches.

In the 29 December 2020 episcopal letter, Bishop Blake and the co-chairs of the Commission addressed the issue of COVID-19 vaccinations:

Appealing to "trusted" medical doctors, Bishop Blake expressed confidence in their "advising COGIC adherents in a safe, scientifically sound and God-guided manner" regarding "medically sound counsel." While noting "the unprecedented acceleration of research, development, and approval (EUA) also contributes to the unease that some share regarding vaccination," Bishops and Doctors Amos and Rhone argue that since the "vaccination is the only medical option for the prevention of COVID-19" it should be taken. They offer three reasons to be vaccinated against this coronavirus.[16]

First, the "coronavirus vaccines do not contain live virus." Therefore, the vaccine itself cannot potentially infected people with the virus. Second, "the benefits outweigh the risks." They note that by being vaccinated you receive "a 95 percent chance of eradicating the virus in your system before it can make you sick! The result to be expected is that you LIVE and not DIE!" Third, there is the benefit of reaching herd immunity by "at least 70–80 percent of the population" being vaccinated and becoming immune to the virus; thus, the pandemic will end and the virus will be eradicated.[17]

In different cities and towns, COGIC congregations are partnering with county health departments, hospital systems, and pharmacies to distribute the COVID-19 vaccine in underserved communities from Los Angeles (CA) and Durham (NC) to Arkansas (KS). These COGIC congregations demonstrate their support of the vaccination efforts. In Los Angeles, West Angeles Cathedral, pastored by Bishop Charles Edward Blake, Sr., is partnering with the Los Angeles County Public Health Department to provide COVID-19 vaccinations to the Crenshaw neighborhood where the congregation is located. In Durham, Nehemiah Church is partnering with Duke Health, allowing its facility to be utilized as a COVID-19 vaccination center to administer the first shot on 11 February 2021 and the second shot on 11 March of 2021. According to Dr. Herbert Davis, the pastor, the congregation provides volunteers to assist as well as recruit people from the area churches to apply for appointments to receive the vaccine in addition to the people recruited by Duke. In Arkansas (KS), St. James Church is partnering with Graves Drug, a regional pharmacy. West Angeles Cathedral, Nehemiah Church, and St. James actively recruit vulnerable populations from underserved communities of people of color in the vaccination efforts.[18]

Science and COVID-19: Divine Healing and Medicine

Bishop Blake and the Commission build on the COGIC history of holding in creative tension divine healing and medicine. The Church of God in Christ acknowledges the role of medicine as part of God's plan of healing. While some Pentecostal traditions reject medicine on theological grounds, juxtaposing faith with belief and medicine with doubt, limiting healing to divine agency, COGIC understands the role of divine and human agency in the biblical plan of healing. Providing theological support for medicine and vaccinations, COGIC has expressed support for members receiving the COVID-19 vaccine.

"The general welfare of all people," including through healthcare, has been a long-term concern of COGIC. In its official theological document, the denomination states: "We believe that Christ, through his redemptive power, has enabled us and called us to help relieve human suffering. . . ."[19]

The relieving of human suffering is a calling of the church that is enabled by the redemptive power of Christ. Since human suffering is understood as being a product of sin and Christ's redemption frees from sin, Christians are to utilize all relevant resources in restoring people in a holistic manner, including "physical, mental and spiritual health."[20]

Accordingly, prescription drugs or pharmaceuticals are to be used with "medical supervision for one's health and well-being." While prayer is to be the first "treatment" for illness, medical treatment is encouraged.[21] Under the heading of "Medical Care," COGIC expresses a dedication to "principles and practices in wholesome living, as a sound mind must reside in a sound body. . . ."[22] Counseling ministries by certified professionals are encouraged to be made available to congregations in order for members to be able to receive referrals for "medical information" as well as other services.[23]

Science and COVID-19: Engaging Racial Disparities

The COGIC expressed commitment to "the equal access of all [hu]mankind to the goods and service of this earth," which conceptually could include "equal access" to healthcare services for all people regardless of income or race.[24]

Government and public health funds should be directed to initiatives that will reduce the race-related healthcare disparities that have been exacerbated by the pandemic. These initiatives should provide better healthcare in treating and preventing the infections from the coronavirus for African Americans, Latinx, and First Nations (Amerindians) as well as improve the overall health outcomes of these populations.

In the "COGIC Doctors' COVID Response" (1 May 2020) co-authored by Bishops Terence Rhone, MD, and Elton Amos, MD, they note the issues of race-related healthcare disparities in their communication to the denomination as they reviewed the recommended guidelines from the Centers for Disease Control and Prevention and the National Institute of Allergy and Infectious Diseases. They state that "the experts have admitted the health disparity that results in more deaths in people of color than whites. Centuries of social and economic inequality most likely have caused Black Americans to suffer additional consequences of this pandemic, increasing the vulnerability of our members and worshippers." They stress that "especially distressing is that the rates of COVID19 infections and deaths remain disproportionally high among African Americans." They relate this phenomenon to "the U.S. government's history of experimentation, disparate healthcare services, and willful blindness to the social determinants of health that contribute to people of color's health status."[25]

Key to understanding race-related healthcare disparities and appropriate Spirit-empowered Christian responses is possibly to re-engage the Memphis Miracle of 1994 and the "Racial Reconciliation Manifesto" sponsored the Pentecostal Charismatic Churches of North America (PCCNA). A serious, critical, and constructive re-engagement of the Memphis Miracle of 1994 and its "Racial Reconciliation Manifesto" that promoted racial reconciliation could introduce new vocabulary, sensibilities, and ethics into the discourse of North American Pentecostals of all races as well as Spirit-empowered Christians on all continents. The re-embrace of the Memphis Miracle and the Racial Reconciliation Manifesto could lunge North American Pentecostal-Charismatic denominations into the future as leaders in advocating the reduction of race-related healthcare disparities and the advancement of healthcare justice for all people.[26]

Re-engaging the Racial Reconciliation Manifesto could re-introduce the topics of racial equality, reconciliation, and equity as subjects and identify healthcare justice for people of color as a priority in promoting racial equity. This perspective would challenge discourses that espouse "colorblindness" in healthcare delivery by recognizing racism as an institutional reality that negatively impacts health systems and the life outcomes of people of color. A re-engagement of the Manifesto could commit Spirit-empowered Christians to supporting the call to end racist structures that produce healthcare disparities among the races as they "work against all forms of personal and institutional racism." By adopting the distinction between personal and systemic racism made in the Manifesto, Spirit-empowered Christians and congregations could advance analyses of racism in healthcare institutions. Identifying racism as a sin expands racism from being merely a moral flaw or social problem, providing a framework to address issues such as race-related healthcare disparities.[27]

Understanding racism systemically would frame race-related healthcare disparities as intertwined with racial privilege, prejudice, and power in the allocation of healthcare resources. Racism, according to William J. Wilson, leads one racial group, often white people, to garner the power to impose its racial prejudices on other racial groups; these non-white groups function in a subordinate manner within the society, ruled invisible in research on disease, pharmaceuticals, and public health initiative as well as underserved in the healthcare delivery system; hospitals, clinics, and physicians are fewer per capita than in majority white communities.

The race-related healthcare disparities exacerbated by the pandemic should garner government and public health funds in reducing these disparities in regards to the pandemic specifically and the overall health outcome indexes for African Americans, Latinx, and First Nations (Amerindians) from leading Black Pentecostal perspectives.

In support of the establishment of health clinics in communities underserved by the medical establishment, COGIC congregations and the denomination itself have illustrated the partnerships between faith and science. Clinics have been sponsored in urban centers like Detroit (MI) by New St. Paul, in towns like Hayward (CA) by Glad Tidings International COGIC, and rural communities in the global South. Within the global South, COGIC has also sponsored medical mission trips staffed with doctors and nurses to countries in the Caribbean, South America, Africa, and Asia.

Conclusion

The concerted efforts of COGIC in addressing the pandemic can be a factor in containing "the spread of COVID-19 pandemic and decrease morbidity and mortality." COGIC facilitates preventive behavior "changes based on faith motivations and worldview" by ensuring that the public health recommendations they support square with COGIC's moral "values and religious practices." Therefore, in providing "relevant health messaging" from a Spirit-empowered Christian perspective, COGIC advances public health by promoting scientifically informed and medically sound measures that are consistent with Scripture and COGIC theology.[28]

In "leading by example" in its denominational and congregational modification of its religious practices in compliance with public health measures related to the pandemic, COGIC participates in the civic arena as a "transformational" leader. It models best practices in preventing the transmission of the virus. It defuses "fear and mistrust" by engendering hope and fostering trust amidst the pandemic. It enters the public arena as a national and global institution constructively engaging science and promoting public health, serving as "a trusted intermediary between the government and local communities." It illustrates the vital role congregations and denominations can play in educating people about where to locate reliable scientific information about best public health practices regarding preventing and limiting the transmission of the virus as well as about vaccines to protect against the virus. Within the context of "infowars," or information wars, a greater chance for reliable information to be heard and believed exists when more institutions like COGIC disseminate reliable information and counter misinformation.

This reliable information can "facilitate" preventive behavior that lessens the spread of the virus.[29]

By being located in communities underserved by medical establishments and other institutions, COGIC congregations are crucial intermediaries between the government and the people because of its "close proximity" to the people most infected and affected by the virus and many of these congregations themselves being comprised of people from these vulnerable populations. By being "embedded in local communities" and maintaining "relationships of trust and familiarity," COGIC congregations offer a "comparative advantage" in conferring credibility to public health initiatives addressing the COVID-19 pandemic. By COGIC congregations serving as COVID-19 testing and vaccination sites, they are part of the healing infrastructure that connects prayer and medicine.[30]

Bishop J. Drew Sheard, Bishop Blake's successor in the office of presiding bishop of COGIC, has continued to engage faith and science in addressing the COVID-19 pandemic during his first two years in office. The leadership of Bishop Charles Edward Blake, Sr., and the Church of God in Christ during the first year of the pandemic has offered an exceptional model of Pentecostal engagement of science, public health, and faith that is theologically based, medically informed, and scientifically sound, presenting a powerful Christian witness in the public arena.

Notes

1. An earlier version of this study appeared under the same title in *Spiritus: ORU Journal of Theology* 6:1 (2021). Used with permission of the publisher.
2. Jürgen Habermas, "Notes on Post-Secular Society," *New Perspectives Quarterly* 25:4 (Fall 2008), 17–29; Donald E. Miller and Tetsunao Yamamori, *Global Pentecostalism: The New Face of Christian Social Engagement* (Berkeley: University of California Press, 2007), 219–221.
3. Michele Dillon, *Post-Secular Catholicism: Relevance and Renewal* (New York: Oxford University Press, 2018), 7, 11, 9.
4. Dillon, *Post-Secular Catholicism*, 8.
5. Frederick L. Ware, "Theology and Science: Disciplines at the limits of Pentecostal Discourse," in *The Routledge Handbook of Pentecostal Theology*, ed. Wolfgang Vondey (New York: Routledge, 2020) 461, 460, 461.

COVID-19, Science, and Race 245

6   Ware, "Theology and Science," 461, 460, 461.

7   *Church of God in Christ Official Manual* (Memphis, TN: Church of God in Christ Publishing House, 1973), 131, 135, 136.

8   Charles E. Blake, Sr., "Presiding Bishop's Statement on COVID-19," 11 March 2020, n.p., https://www.cogic.org/covid19/files/2020/03/Bishop-Blake-letter-Covid-19-2.pdf, February 12, 2021.

9   Blake, "Presiding Bishop's Statement," March 11.

10 Blake, "Presiding Bishop's Statement," March 11.

11 Charles E. Blake, Sr., "Presiding Bishop's Statement on COVID-19," March 18, 2020, n.p.

12 Charles E. Blake, Sr., "Presiding Bishop's Statement on COVID-19," March 25, 2020, n.p., https://www.cogic.org/covid19/presiding-bishops-covid-19-update-3-25-20/, February 12, 2021.

13 Charles E. Blake, Sr., "Presiding Bishop's Statement on COVID-19," April 23, 2020, n.p., https://www.cogic.org/covid19/presiding-bishops-covid-19-update-4-23-20/, February 12, 2021).

14 Charles E. Blake, Sr., "Presiding Bishop's Statement on COVID-19," May 1, 2020), n.p., https://www.cogic.org/wp-content/uploads/2020/05/COGIC-COVID-FINAL-2.pdf, February 12, 2021.

15 Charles E. Blake, Sr., "Presiding Bishop's Statement on COVID-19," May 23, 2020, n.p., https://www.cogic.org/covid19/files/2020/05/COVID-Blake-9.pdf, February 12, 2021.

16 "Presiding Bishop and Expert Doctors' Statement on COVID Vaccine," 29 December 2020, n.p., https://www.cogic.org/wp-content/uploads/2020/12/COVID-Newsletter-Dec-2020-2.pdf, February 12, 2021.

17 "Presiding Bishop and Expert Doctors' Statement on COVID Vaccine," n.p.

18 Dr. Herbert Davis, interview by author, 13 February 2021; Rev. C. Edward Watson, atty., interview by author, 17 February 2021.

19 *Church of God in Christ Official Manual*, 131.

20 *Church of God in Christ Official Manual*, 131.

21 *Church of God in Christ Official Manual*, 135.

22 *Church of God in Christ Official Manual*, 136.

23 *Church of God in Christ Official Manual*, 138.

24 *Church of God in Christ Official Manual*, 137.

25 "COGIC Doctors Contribute Responses to COVID-19," May 1, 2020, https://www.cogic.org/wp-content/uploads/2020/05/COGIC-COVID-FINAL-2.pdf.

26 Leonard Lovett, Cecil Robeck, Harold Hunter, and Ithiel Clemmons, "Racial Reconciliation Manifesto," *Pentecostal Charismatic Churches of North America*, 1994, n.p., http://pctii.org/manifesto.html, April 20, 2020.

27 Lovett et al., "Manifesto," n.p.

28 "Church Agencies and Faith-Based Organizations in COVID-19 Humanitarian Response," *Can Do*, April 2020, n.p., 200401 Role of Churches and FBOs in COVID response FINAL [2].pdf (icvanetwork.org), February 12, 2021.

29 "Church Agencies," n.p.

30 "Church Agencies," n.p.

14 Pentecostalism and Coronavirus: Reframing the Message of Health-and-Wealth in a Pandemic Era[1]

J. Kwabena Asamoah-Gyadu

Abstract

One of the global effects of the COVID-19 pandemic is the religious responses that it has generated. For contemporary Pentecostalism in particular, which is a religion that preaches and teaches a theology of human flourishing through the principles of prosperity, the negative effects of the coronavirus on people proved a theologically challenging endeavor. Pronouncing curses on evil or blaming Satan for it in human life has always been part of the means to achieve health and wealth for contemporary Pentecostals. This is very much the case in Africa where the instrumentalist use of religion as a means of personal and communal survival and wellbeing already exists. Thus, the contemporary Pentecostal health-and-wealth gospel, although appeals to the Bible for theological legitimacy, also resonates very much with the African worldview. In the midst of the pandemic, however, the monolithic understanding of flourishing preached by some Pentecostals came unstuck. In this article, we discuss African contemporary Pentecostal responses to the pandemic in order to show how the reality of evil can challenge existing understanding of life's challenges and the need to be holistic in our responses to them.

Introduction

This chapter reflects on Pentecostal-charismatic responses to the outbreak of the COVID-19 pandemic. The discussions are situated within the African context where contemporary Pentecostalism is flourishing both in numerical strength and in public presence because of the extensive use of modern media technology. There is a strong affinity between Charismatic Christianity and media and in the last year in which in-person meetings have had to be restricted as a result of the COVID-19 pandemic. The use of media technology by religious organizations has been moved several notches up from where things were just about a year ago. The outbreak of the pandemic, I point out elsewhere, coincided with the celebrations of major Christian events.[2]

In the year 2020, the Christian seasons of the Passion, Resurrection, Ascension, Pentecost, and Christmas were all celebrated either in lockdown mode or under restrictions. The celebrations in the year 2021 are likely to be the same, at least in most non-Western contexts, where vaccination against the virus is unlikely to take place until past the midpoint of the year.

The coronavirus pandemic triggered a world crisis of monumental proportions and as Klaus Schwab and Thierry Malleret point out, "deep existential crisis also favors introspection and can harbor the potential for transformation."[3] The pandemic has created "a dangerous and volatile period on multiple fronts—politically, socially, geopolitically—raising deep concerns about the environment and also extending the reach of technology into our lives," Schwab and Malleret note.[4] When the two authors add that no industry or business will be spared these changes brought upon the world order by the pandemic, it definitely includes the business of the church. In this article, we first learn about the nature of contemporary Pentecostalism before pointing out how its theology of prosperity and interpretations of reality are brought to bear on a public health issue—the COVID-19 pandemic—helping us to appreciate the importance of religion, and in this case, the religious and theological responses of Pentecostal Christianity to existential evil.

Contemporary Pentecostalism

The designation contemporary Pentecostal or Charismatic church/ministry is usually deployed in the African context to refer to those urban-centered prosperity-preaching churches and ministries that emerged across Christian Africa from the middle of the 1970s. The well-known characteristic features of contemporary Pentecostal churches/ministries include an emphasis on the critical place of charismatic manifestations in the lives of believers and the worship of the church; urban-centered mega-size congregations; hermeneutics of success and prosperity; prayer and proactive attacks on the sources of evil; ministries of healing, exorcism, and deliverance; belief in the powers of positive declarations and the cursing of evil; and a focus on spiritual warfare as a means of human flourishing. Contemporary Charismatic churches have built or aim to build modern and imposing worship auditoriums that are fitted to accommodate a strong and innovative media culture and a taste for religious internationalism and globalization of faith. Their modern outlook, media technology driven religious services, and messages of motivation appeal strongly to Africa's upwardly mobile youth.

Contemporary Pentecostal churches and ministries are led by highly influential and charismatically gifted leaders. Many of them have a public ministry because of their strong and powerful media activities that reach millions of followers around the world. The adoption of a motivational approach to preaching, their knack for breaking down biblical narratives and applying them within a context of personal development and economic empowerment and their existential and pragmatic approaches to faith that use the Bible to speak to real-life situations in times of peril has endeared the average contemporary charismatic pastor to a wider public in a way that the historic mission churches have not been able to do. The responses to the outbreak of the pandemic that we discuss in this article are based on data obtained from the media sources of contemporary Pentecostal-charismatic pastors such as their live televised worship services, and especially You Tube videos circulating on various social media platforms. At the height of the pandemic these are the locations from where religious resources of supernatural succor were obtained by many people. The contemporary Pentecostal-charismatic culture of mobilization of prayer for the public good—whether it means positive declarations of prosperity or the cursing of evil—is something that proved very relevant in how this wave of Christianity has dealt with the pandemic.

Preaching Prosperity in the Context of the Spread of an Evil Virus

The discussion of the negative effects of COVID-19 in the light of contemporary Pentecostal-charismatic Christianity is important for theological reasons too. These are churches that emphasize a theology of health-and-wealth. The general thrust of the message is that Christians must believe God for success, wellbeing, prosperity, emancipation, positives, elevation, and empowerment for various endeavors in this life. The preaching of prosperity is not necessarily inconsistent with the promises of God in Scripture. One of the many biblical passages one heard over and again at the height of the pandemic was Jeremiah 29:11, "For surely I know the plans I have for you, says the Lord, plans for your welfare and not for harm, to give you a future with hope." The problem is therefore not with the message of wellbeing and prosperity, but rather, it is with the simplistic emphasis on a formulaic theology of success that does not leave room for self-denial, pain, and suffering as outlined in a proper theology of the cross.

This gospel of prosperity, in several of its aspects, came unstuck in the face of what in sermons and prophetic declarations has been described as an "evil virus." This has been very much the case, at least in African Pentecostal-charismatic homiletics and rhetoric. In the theology of many of the charismatic figures that lead these churches and movements, the presence and persistence of evil would normally be explained in terms of the work of the devil and other principalities and powers. What creates the spiritual spaces for evil to thrive, in the charismatic prosperity discourses under scrutiny here, range from living in sin to the non-fulfillment of tithing obligations to the church. In Africa, the general belief among Christians, but in particular Pentecostals, is that traditional religious practices of libation-pouring to deities and ancestral sacrifices and celebrations of festivals have become sources of spiritual contamination and setbacks to the fortunes of a continent that is otherwise very materially blessed by God.

On the world stage supernatural evil, it is believed, comes upon humanity as a result of social deviations like the endorsement and toleration of alternative sexual lifestyles—the LGBTQI agenda—and these are considered to be a source of affliction as it goes against the teachings of the Bible on proper human sexuality and marriage. Contemporary Pentecostal-Charismatic Christianity propounds a reciprocal theology, in which Christian giving in particular is transactional in nature because not only does God bless those who give to their pastors and prophets, but he also withdraws his cover and protection form those who do not give. This is a Christianity that also believes very much in the authority possessed by Spirit-filled believers to curse evil, cancel curses, and to principalities and powers generally to neutralize their powers and effects on people's lives and situations. In contemporary Pentecostal-charismatic Christianity, spiritual and material prosperity follows the cursing of evil and so the coronavirus was problematized as an "agent of Satan" inflicted on the world not just to upset our lives, but also to trouble seriously the people of God.

Contemporary Pentecostal Responses to COVID-19

How are Africa's contemporary charismatic pastors with this prosperity mindset, authoritative approach to prayer, and belief in the prophetic and supernatural evil, responding to a pandemic that has defied their theological logics? There are many influential charismatic preachers in Africa who have founded very large or mega-size ministries with public influences unparalleled in the history of Christianity on the continent. Their religious media empires, as we have noted, enable these charismatic figures to speak to global audiences. The ones whose responses to the pandemic are discussed in this article include Archbishop Nicholas Duncan-Williams of the Action Chapel International (ACI) and Pastor Mensa Otabil of the International Central Gospel Church, both based in Ghana. Pastor Chris Oyakhilome of Christ Embassy, a Nigerian based in South Africa, receives mention for buying into conspiracy theories surrounding the outbreak of the pandemic. Pastor Oyakhilome shares that position with the American prosperity preacher Kenneth Copeland, who at the height of the spread of the pandemic declared it nullified. Prophet Emmanuel Makandiwa of Zimbabwe predicted the outbreak of a pandemic about five years ahead of the coronavirus pandemic and we discuss what he prophesied as an example of the Pentecostal-charismatic emphasis on the deployment of spiritual gifts in public life.

Pastor Otabil is a motivational speaker who usually takes a pragmatic approach to existential issues. Archbishop Duncan-Williams leans towards mobilizing prayer to deal with crisis and Pastor Oyakhilome is known for his miracle working ministry and in particular for his emphasis on healing and deliverance. Pastor Makandiwa functions as a charismatic prophet. This is to say that although we categorize all these pastors and their ministries under the general rubric of contemporary Pentecostal-charismatic ministry, there are differences in the way their ministries operate or function. In spite of these differences one can say that, to a very high extent, they all belong to the prosperity believing and preaching category of Pentecostalism and that orientation shows to various degrees in the ways they have preached, prayed, or prophesied in relation to the pandemic.

Religious Responses to the Pandemic

Pentecostalism is an experiential religion with a very forceful oral culture and so the data for discussion is accessed mainly from sermons, statements, and prophetic declarations made during the lockdown and restriction periods through various media outlets. There are a number of things to note from the outset: first, many of the sermons and declarations were very inspirational as they sought to bring hope to hearers through various media networks; secondly, some have bought into religious conspiracy theories relating to the pandemic with Pastor Chris Oyakhilome even claiming that the whole thing was a hoax perpetrated by media technology companies seeking to install a new 5G network facility that would harm the world; thirdly, the trajectories of the messages also showed how the pandemic was challenging contemporary Pentecostal-charismatic triumphalist assumptions on faith and evil in human life; and fourthly, the element of the prophetic has played a key role in the religious responses to the pandemic.

The COVID-19 pandemic has, among others, challenged the faiths of many people with Christians calling for concerted prayer to defeat a virus that some thought had been inflicted on the world by the devil. In many sermons, especially from the charismatic sector, the coronavirus was "cursed" as demonic, and as an agent of the devil, is out to destroy God's people and this was particularly on account of the fact that it disrupted the nature of church as we have come to understand it. In not a few cases there were submissions speculating that perhaps this was the beginning of the apocalyptic times about which the Bible talks. Pastor Chris Oyakhilome of Christ Embassy has also indicated that the virus attack is a way in which technological giants are diverting human attention to facilitate the setting up of their 5G infrastructure around the world.[5]

One the most important biblical passages that served as the foundation of prayer in the COVID-19 period was Psalm 91. It begins with the words, "You who live in the shelter of the Most High, who abide in the shadow of the Almighty, will say to the Lord, 'My refuge and my fortress; my God, in whom I trust'" (Ps 91:1–2).[6] The psalmist's reference to God's deliverance from "the snare of the fowler and from the deadly pestilence" in verse 3 provided the appropriate discourse for many seeking to invoke the name and power of God in dealing with the pandemic. A lot of prayers circulating in the media used verses from this particular Psalm. Of the various Christian churches in Africa, I found the responses of the contemporary Pentecostal or Charismatic churches to the outbreak of the pandemic very instructive and revealing. This is because as churches that focus on the charismatic experience in the power of the Holy Spirit, their theology has an interventionist orientation; they take the theology of evil seriously and how to deal with evil features prominently in their ecclesiology.

Lockdown and Contemporary Pentecostal Theology

The COVID-19 era came as a test of a situation that provided an alternative context within which to articulate Charismatic motivational messages. Pastor Otabil is one among a very few charismatic pastors who decided, when the government increased the numbers of people gathering in a single location from twenty-five to one hundred, to continue services online. In the face of depressive spirits, failing businesses, empty pockets, family dislocations, sicknesses, bereavements, and so on and so forth, many, like Jesus on the cross, felt forsaken. Pastor Mensa Otabil seized the moment to repackage his messages on the principles of success, positives, promotion, and wealth creation to suit the spirit of the times. A number of charismatic pastors returned to eschatological messages, a theme that is normally missing from prosperity discourses.

That is not to say Africa's Charismatic church leaders do not believe in judgment, hell, the second coming of Christ, and the like; no, they do. However, that sort of message was simply inconsistent with the regular emphasis on health, wealth, and material prosperity that had become part of the charismatic self-definition in terms of religious emphasis. Whether articulated in terms of the power of Jesus or that of the Holy Spirit, Charismatic Christianity speaks the language of power in which God turns impossibilities into possibilities. The depressive circumstances that the COVID-19 pandemic situation created offered the virtual perfect fit for the sort of motivational and inspiring messages associated with contemporary Pentecostalism. Thus, the responses to the pandemic also brought to the fore contemporary Pentecostal-charismatic religious cultures of the mobilization of prayer for the public good in the light of their strong hermeneutics of evil as spiritually caused.

Its prosperity message had often sounded a bit monolithic and myopic in the sense that although it is preached in full knowledge that suffering and evil are real, those sorts of human circumstances have often been ignored. The American prosperity gospel exponent, Kenneth Copeland, even responded to the pandemic against the backdrop of the American elections that eventually President Joe Biden was to win. He wrote on his Facebook page on October 17, 2020, as follows:

> The COVID-19 pandemic has been used as a pretext for the election to force all of us into fear. When we are fearful, we are willing to sacrifice our peace and prosperity for security, but it is a false security. We need to stand firm in our faith and have dominion over fear. Resist fear, and the devil will flee from you.

The emphasis on the power of triumph, success, promotion, life, health, victory, and overcoming has blinded many Charismatic, especially prosperity touting, preachers to the real-life circumstances of their patrons. With businesses, domestic economies, and the personal health of many people taking a hit, the messages of prosperity were simply confronted with a reality check in the midst of the COVID-19 pandemic. Until the onset of the pandemic, it was the triumphalist stories of those who are winning the battles of life that we often heard about in Pentecostal testimonies. The lots of those going through challenges were often treated as if they did not apply the right principles of success, which would usually mean the faithful fulfillment of tithing obligations. In the particular circumstances of the pandemic, everyone to some extent was confronted with the realities of evil and suffering with even the wealthiest of nations and their economies being crippled.

Suddenly, the messages of prosperity had to be repackaged due to the onset of affliction with the outbreak of COVID-19. In contrast to the regular messages that those who fulfill certain religious obligations would be successful and win the battles of life, this particular demon of a coronavirus was affecting the fortunes of everyone including pastors and prophets who had assured us that faithful Christians were beyond the logic of suffering. Many took to social media to question the inability of the African Charismatic prophets to foretell the onset of the coronavirus and if not deal with it, at least get the world to prepare. The world was locked down through Good Friday and the Easter periods of 2020. Archbishop Nicholas Duncan-Williams claimed that the virus was a demonic attack from satanic and demonic wombs and incubators.[7]

He further declared that the virus would disappear by the Passover, but this did not materialize with another Passover upon us in 2021.[8] The lockdowns did not afford African Pentecostal-charismatic pastors their usual opportunities to advertise the "benefits of the cross," "the blood that speaks," or the "power of the resurrection" during Lent and Holy Week.

Here for instance is a selection of a combination of prayer and declarations made by Archbishop Nicholas Duncan-Williams in the early weeks of the pandemic:

> The Coronavirus is a name, is a person without body and in the name of Jesus, as we bow our knee and we pray, in the name of Jesus, this plague, pestilence and virus will bow the knee and will stand down and go back from whence it came in the name of Jesus. The Lord is good, a stronghold in the day of trouble and he knoweth them that trust in Him. I challenge you, within these thirty days, to trust in the Lord like never before. Show the enemy that your faith is in God. If we only trust God when everything is good and in good times when everything is alright, then it is not faith and it is not trust. But it is the times of trouble and moments like this that we know whether we trust God, or we don't trust God. It is times like this that your faith and my faith is renewed, it takes times like this, trying situations like this, to reveal the strength of our faith. Trust in God, I challenge you to trust in God, to have faith in God, as never before.
>
> This is not the end of the world, there are people who are saying that this virus is judgement from God and that it is the sign of the end of the world. They are entitled to their opinion. And others believe it is from the enemy but whatever these schools of thought are, doesn't bother me. The most important thing is for you to have right standing with God because if you have a right standing with God, if it is from the enemy, the Bible says, "no weapon formed against you shall prosper and every tongue that rises in judgement against you, you shall be condemned." And if it is judgement from God, in the day of judgement, God has promised to deliver and to exempt His chosen, His children from the judgement. So, whatever it is, you are covered. And I don't want you to entertain fear, don't entertain any fear because the blood of Jesus has covered us, the Bible said, "when I see the blood, when I see the blood, when I see the blood, I will pass over you."
>
> We invoke the blood of Jesus over this nation, we invoke the blood of Jesus over our borders, our airwaves, our high seas and the land, and every family of this country and nation and all the members of our church. We invoke the blood of Jesus that this virus and this angel of death will pass over our dwellings, will pass over our loved ones, will pass over all that concerns us and that there will be no loss of any father, mother, wife, husband, boy or girl

or grandson or granddaughter. There will be no loss of any life among us and that our wives will not be widows and our children will not be fatherless. And no father or mother will bury their children by any means in the name Jesus. . . . In the face of adversity, in the face of disaster and in the face of tragedy, you are an overcomer.[9]

In this mix of discourses on hope, demonization of the virus, and the declaration of protection from evil, Archbishop Duncan-Williams very clearly confronts an issue that had become a problem for the otherwise prosperity theology that he has been propagating. As with the first Passover and the first Crucifixion and Resurrection days in the Bible, everyone was locked down at the height of the pandemic and churches were closed. That was a reality away from which no one could run as it was the reality the world was facing. The messages were still empowering; preachers were challenged by the circumstances to tweak them a bit to account for what the world was going through.

"The Man Who Could Not Be Locked Down"

During the 2020 Resurrection Day televised church services, one of the sermons came from Pastor Mensa Otabil. The word "lockdown" featured quite prominently in his Easter Sunday message. The text for the day was Matthew's account of the resurrection and the theme was "The Man Who Could Not be Locked Down." There were three instruments that the authorities used to lock Jesus down, according to Pastor Otabil. These were the physical, legal, and political. The physical instrument was the stone that was used to seal the tomb in which Jesus was laid. The legal one was imposed when the chief priests and the Pharisees gathered before Pilate and asked him to issue a "command for the tomb to be made secure until the third day" because "the imposter," when he was alive, had said he was going to resurrect after three days. Pilate complied and gave the request legal backing (Matt 27:62–63). The third instrument of lockdown was the political one in which soldiers were sent to guard the tomb of Jesus: "Pilate said to them, 'You have a guard of soldiers; go, make it as secure as you can.' So, they went with the guard and made the tomb secure by sealing the stone" (Matt 27:65–66).

In spite of these three instruments of lockdown, Pastor Otabil averred, Jesus resurrected from the dead: "God wants to breakdown something that has locked you down," Pastor Otabil assured his hearers. There were three instruments of lockdown used to restrain Jesus, but God needed only two instruments to release him. These were the natural and the supernatural instruments of God and both are listed in Matthew 28:2, "And suddenly there was a great earthquake; for an angel of the Lord, descending from heaven, came and rolled back the stone and sat on it." Pastor Otabil explained that God has his own way of intervening when we are locked down by the circumstances of life. In the case of Jesus, God deployed the natural instrument of an earthquake and a supernatural instrument of the intervention of angels. The stone was rolled away for us to see what God had already done, and that is, he had raised Jesus from death. Pastor Otabil illustrated his point using parts of the Pentecost day message preached by Peter: "But God raised him up, having freed him from death, because it was impossible for him to be held in its power" (Acts 2:24).[10]

The Eschatological Gear

Until the COVID-19 pandemic outbreak, one would have struggled to hear sermons on the second coming of Christ among contemporary Pentecostal preachers. One scarcely hears sermons about eschatological events in the contemporary charismatic world. This is because a preacher cannot, in prosperity fashion, encourage members to make as much money as they could, build big and palatial homes, buy the best in luxurious cars and at the same time preach that, but anyway, Jesus could appear like a thief in the night.[11] Contemporary Pentecostals believe in God's end time judgement and the second coming of Christ, but they simply do not preach it. Paul Gifford also mentions this in his book, *Ghana's New Christianity*, noting that the recurring emphasis in this form of Christianity "has to do with success, wealth and status."[12] If these are the recurring themes of contemporary Pentecostalism, what changed in the first quarter of the year 2020?

Prosperity preachers were forced to respond to a pandemic that revealed the realities of life. In the period of the coronavirus consternation, there was certainly a change in mood and several preachers took on eschatological issues that had hitherto been placed on the back burner. Archbishop Nicholas Duncan-Williams of the ACI claimed on Palm Sunday that this was a wakeup call for the church to realize that "we have a place to go." The reason for the born-again experience was for us to prepare for eternity, he noted. In his words: "this is the time for purity, holiness, righteousness in heart and motive; this is not the time to make money but to give and be a child of God like never before. This is not the time to bear grudges." These "worldly things" would be obstacles when Jesus returns to judge the world. This message was a complete antithesis to his proposals in the book *You Are Destined to Succeed* in which the archbishop claimed that the use of luxurious material things were divine rights and not options for "a man of God."[13]

On the Sunday of the Triumphal Entry, Archbishop Duncan-Williams preached on the works of the flesh (1 Thess 5:2–3). "This is the time for people to get saved . . . if we do not get into the ark now, we will be left behind." This coronavirus is a "pestilence and a plague," he noted. The only thing that can save humanity is to get into the ark of our salvation, which is Christ. It was instructive to hear Archbishop Duncan-Williams saying people must "endure" trials and temptations. All the prophecies are falling into place, he further noted, for the Son of Man is coming again. He refers to Matthew 24:22, "And if those days had not been cut short, no one would be saved; but for the sake of the elect those days would be cut short."

In the particular sermon, Archbishop Duncan-Williams preached that in the COVID-19 situation, we have seen nations evacuate their citizens. It is the same way in which "heaven will evacuate its own," that is, the elect at the imminent return of Jesus: "God will send an aircraft with Jesus as its captain and every believer will be evacuated home." He explained that only "citizens of heaven" would qualify for the evacuation and made a direct appeal in his broadcast for listeners who did not know Jesus to embrace him as Lord and Savior. The days of suffering would be shortened for the sake of the elect, he emphasized. God said, "I will spare the elect" and so, all the citizens of heaven will be evacuated; you cannot go to the airport if America sends an aircraft to evacuate her citizens if you do not have an American passport; even your spouse, if they are American would be evacuated and you will be left behind; the rapture is an aircraft," the Archbishop noted.

The terms and expressions that were deployed in this thoroughly eschatological message by Archbishop Duncan-Williams were striking: heaven, hell, redeemed, sanctification, preparedness, purity, uprightness, rapture, and these as compared to the recurring emphasis on material success that Gifford talks about. Archbishop Duncan-Williams concluded with the story of the ten virgins (Matt 25:1–13). At the announcement of the arrival of the bridegroom, only those with adequate oil in their lamps were able to meet him. In the same way, "if you are not a citizen of a country, it does not matter who you are married to, you will not be evacuated when the rapture takes place." It was striking because this is a preacher who, like many others in his category, often centered his sermons on tithing and offerings as seed-sowing for blessing: wealth, health, and upward mobility as the right of the Christian. "This is not the time to make money" the archbishop said, rather, "this is the day to show compassion; you can have all the money in the world, but it cannot save you; a day is coming when all these material things will mean nothing."

The Prophetic Gear

A video recording still circulating on social media shows Prophet Emmanuel Makandiwa prophesying the appearance of the coronavirus about five years before its emergence in China. Prophet Makandiwa has a thriving international ministry in Zimbabwe.[14] He is the Founder and General Overseer of the United Family International Church (UFIC).[15] Prophet Makandiwa is about the only known charismatic voice to have prophesied the onset of the pandemic and that was in 2015. He delivered about five prophecies in total on different occasions pointing then to an incoming pandemic that was going to throw the world into confusion. In the first prophetic utterance made in January 2015, Prophet Makandiwa held a Sunday service at the City Sports Centre in Harare, Zimbabwe, where said, "we need really to pray," noting that an ailment was coming out of China that would not compare to anything we have witnessed before in world history. He compared what was coming then to a nuclear weapon, noting however that it was not going to be about an explosion, but rather a catastrophic contamination of the atmosphere that was going to be chaotic. "It was going to take the world time and days to gather the dead bodies together," he prophesied. He likened it to a demonic spirit on rampage that was going to stop at nothing, except prayer: "only prayer can save us now."[16]

In the second prophecy delivered in November 2016 at a Sunday Service at the City Sports Centre in Harare, Zimbabwe, Makandiwa declares among others:

> I saw also . . . another disease more deadly. I saw it coming from the sea. They will investigate and find it will come from the ocean. More deadly than HIV

and cancer. Very fast. Very aggressive . . . and thousands, if not millions, will die. . . . It is a plague, so we must pray against it. God preserves. God gives life.[17]

Prophet Makandiwa put out a third prophecy in February 2017, also at the City Sports Centre in Harare, Zimbabwe. In this third one, he prophesied among others that the disease was going to kill more people than any disease that the world had fought previously. He claims to have been given a divine revelation that showed people falling like leaves and dying: "they will do everything to investigate where its coming from they will not find it, but eventually, they will confirm what I am telling you. . . . It is a plague that only God can stop."[18]

The fourth prophecy was delivered just before the onset of the pandemic in Africa in early March 2020. At the Sunday service at Chitungwiza Basilic. Prophetic Makandiwa stated in part:

> I say our intelligent people will break down. Doctors will cry. Leaders of our nations will cry. Now at this rate if (it) goes on for 3 months, it will be terrible. But you know that God has given us grace over every flying evil. . . . God will give power to his people. Power to do what? As you are praying now, you are pronouncing a curse over this curse. You will open your mouth and command every flying insect to die. As long as the insect is a virus, as long as it is a disease, you have to take charge over every flying insect which is a disease. . . . The fear of the Lord is the beginning of knowledge. He will deliver you from this plague and when you become proud again, he will give you other (another) one. Until you know that God reigns in the Kingdom of [humanity].[19]

Prophet Makandiwa's final prophetic utterance was delivered in February 2020 at his Chitungwiza Basilica.[20] In this final one the prophet seemed to have prescribed hydroxychloroquine, which had been discredited in some quarters as one possible pharmaceutical intervention to the disease. Our concern though lies in the fact that at least Prophet Makandiwa predicted a lurking disaster that he referred to as a plague and also framed its emergence in terms of the demonic, although in the same breath both prayer and hydroxychloroquine were pointed to as possible cures to the pandemic.

Reframing the Message of Health-and-Wealth in a Pandemic Era

The religious responses to the outbreak of the COVID-19 pandemic, especially what I have referred to in this article as the "mobilization of prayer" against evil, are not new. At the beginning of the twentieth century, when the worldwide influenza epidemic broke out, African Pentecostal prayer and spiritual healing groups, as Lamin Sanneh calls them, mobilized prayer to fight the pandemic even resisting the use of modern scientific medicine in the process.[21] The prophetic element that surfaced with Prophet Emmanuel Makandiwa's ministry was itself a reinvention of something that was present in the ministries of the early African prophetic movements of the early twentieth century. The mobilization of prophetic prayer in African Pentecostal Christianity has always been inspired by the worldview that the enemy, lodged in the numerous maladies that afflicted the flesh, must be muzzled. It is usually up to the prophet or charismatic leader to channel the forces of healing and protection into the community and sustain prayer "as the essential supply-line of the struggle" against evil.[22] In the particular case of the COVID-19 pandemic, Prophet Makandiwa served both as the one through whose ministry the revelation came and also the one who mobilizes for prayer against the plague.

We also see from the narratives that in the midst of the COVID-19 pandemic, people who previously preached about prosperity suddenly found the space in the times to talk about the issues of heaven and hell. These examples we have cited from charismatic preaching, prophecy, and prayer within the COVID-19 period shows how difficult circumstances, the reality of evil, and the unpredictability of the future can affect one's understanding of the church and the message that is carried in the name of Jesus Christ. On the one hand, we see how the coronavirus situation has led to the delivery of very pragmatic sermons, such as the one preached by Pastor Otabil, that confront evil as an existential reality. On the other hand, we see from Archbishop Duncan-Williams how the realities of evil led to a rethinking of a gospel that had become so materialistic that the things of eternity had been dislodged from their central place in contemporary charismatic ecclesiology. The eschatological messages of the COVID-19 era resonate very much with what happened to the American apostle of the prosperity gospel, Jim Bakker, who after his fall from grace due to imprisonment for federal crimes returned to write a very instructive book, *Prosperity and the Coming Apocalypse,* in which he denounces his earlier message that materialism was a prime indicator of God's favor. In that book he uses his own context to criticize a one-sided prosperity gospel devoid of any eschatological significance:

> By and large, most of the church . . . does not want to hear an apocalyptic message. It wants a message of health and wealth, hope, healing, and financial prosperity. . . . Rarely does anyone talk about sacrifice, repentance of sin, or our failure to be what God wants us to be. When, for example, was the last time you heard a message on the cost of discipleship? When was the last time you heard someone preach on the judgment of God or the horrors of hell?[23]

It is noteworthy that just as his personal troubles led him to return to an eschatological message, the COVID-19 pandemic literally led most African Charismatic pastors along similar paths as we saw, for example, in the preaching of Archbishop Duncan-Williams.

The messages of prosperity preached by contemporary Pentecostal pastors are not entirely unbiblical, for there is such a thing as biblical prosperity (Psalm 1; John 10:10). And indeed, the born-again experience itself has in the lives of many people led to a redemptive uplift in both its spiritual and material senses. When the born-again convert from lives of vanity and carnality, critical material resources become available for constructive uses and investment in personal and family lives are enhanced. What we criticize is therefore not material prosperity as part of God's blessing, but the fact that materialism—the love of money—is the root cause of all evil. Besides, the materialistic gospel of prosperity fails to account for existential evil and those whose lives are impacted by it are left without answers regarding their afflictions. Many of the principles of prosperity come unstuck in the face of misfortune, calamity, and evil, and the hope is that the coronavirus has among other things exposed the areas of deficiency.

Conclusion

There has not been a monolithic response to the outbreak of the COVID-19 pandemic among African Pentecostal-charismatic figures. The responses have ranged from mobilizing prophetic prayer to deal with the outbreak to inspiring hope in people in these times of despair and using the opportunity to return to messages that warn that eternity is not a figment of anyone's imagination. It is a reality for which people must prepare. This is a call for things to be rectified using the very biblical resources that are used to justify what it means to prosper in an uncertain world in which everything else is temporal and God alone remains sovereign. When we defer to his wisdom, we will walk through the valley of the shadow of death and still fear no evil, because God is with his people. That was the crux of the matter in Pastor Mensa Otabil's sermons of the pandemic era.

Notes

1 An earlier version of this study appeared under the same title in *Spiritus: ORU Journal of Theology* 6:1 (2021). Used with permission of the publisher.
2 J. Kwabena Asamoah-Gyadu, *Christianity and Faith in the Pandemic Era: Lockdown Periods from Hosanna to Pentecost* (Accra: Step Publishers, 2020).
3 Klaus Schwab and Thierry Malleret, *COVID-19: The Great Reset* (Geneva: Forum Publishing, 2020), 11.
4 Schwab and Malleret, COVID-19, 11.
5 Juliet Tochi, "Pastor Chris Oyakhilome Speaks on COVID-19 and 5G Network," August 7, 2020, n.p., https://clacified.com/religion/news/pastor-chris-oyakhilome-speaks-on-COVID-19-and-5g-network.
6 All Bible quotations are from *The New Oxford Annotated Bible: New Revised Standard Version* (Oxford/New York: Oxford University Press, 1994).
7 K. Effah, "COVID-19: Duncan-Williams Declares 30-days Fasting and Prayer for Ghanaians," March 17, 2020, n.p., https://www.msn.com/en-xl/africa/ghana/COVID-19-duncan-williams-declares-30-days-fasting-and-prayer-for-ghanaians/ar-BB11hMZQ.
8 Bernice Bessey, "Duncan Williams: COVID-19 Pandemic Has Nine Days to Vamoose," April 22, 2020, n.p., https://thechronicle.com.gh/duncan-williams-COVID-19-pandemic-has-nine-days-to-vamoose/.
9 Nicholas Duncan-Williams, "Duncan-Williams Declares 30-days Fasting and Prayer against Coronavirus," March 16, 2020, video, 5:40, https://www.youtube.com/watch?v=TthFqQCAEFs.
10 Mensa Otabil, "The Man Who Couldn't Be Locked Down," video, 2:02:29, April 12, 2020, https://www.facebook.com/watch/live/?v=1031844287216686&ref=watch_permalink.
11 J. Kwabena Asamoah-Gyadu, *Sighs and Signs of the Spirit: Ghanaian Perspectives on Pentecostalism and Renewal in Africa* (Oxford: Regnum, 2015), 163–76.
12 Gifford, Ghana's *New Christianity*, 44.

13 Nicholas Duncan-Williams, *You Are Destined to Succeed* (Accra: Action Faith Publications, 1990).
14 Emmanuel Makandiwa, "Who Is Emmanuel Makandiwa," January 2020, n.p., http://emmanuelmakandiwa.com/who-is-emmanuel-makandiwa/, accessed 16 August 16, 2020).
15 Makandiwa, "Ministries—Emmanuel Makandiwa."
16 For His Glory, "Prophet Emmanuel Makandiwa Compilation of COVID-19 Prophecies (From 2015–2017 & 2020)," 20 July 2020, n.p., https://www.youtube.com/watch?v=xgJQVMIDHYE&feature=youtu.be.
17 For His Glory, "Prophet Emmanuel Makandiwa Compilation."
18 For His Glory, "Prophet Emmanuel Makandiwa Compilation."
19 For His Glory, "Prophet Emmanuel Makandiwa Compilation."
20 Christ TV, "Coronavirus Chloroquine Prophecy—Prophet Emmanuel Makandiwa," April 13, 2020, n.p., https://www.youtube.com/watch?v=PygVx9qKfgg.
21 Lamin Sanneh, *West African Christianity: The Religious Impact* (Maryknoll, NY: Orbis Books, 1983), 184.
22 Sanneh, *West African Christianity*, 195.
23 Jim Bakker, *Prosperity and the Coming Apocalypse* (Nashville, Tennessee: Thomas Nelson Publishers, 1998), 8.

15 Pentecostal Hope in the Age of COVID-19

Peter Althouse and Audrey McCormick[1]

Abstract

This research sought to identify how Pentecostals and Charismatics responded to the Coronavirus pandemic. Specifically, what role did eschatology play in provoking hope, and how did theologies on healing influence responses? Data revealed that Pentecostals were generally not casting their responses to the pandemic as a millennial expectation of a better future but were grieving their losses and seeking to provoke hope amidst suffering. While minimal miraculous healings were reported, healing was cast primarily as the ongoing presence of defiant hope amidst trauma, grief and suffering. We propose that grief and grieving is an eschatological response to loss and death.

Introduction

On the eve of 2020, the world was about to change. An unknown, virulent coronavirus was in the air and would quickly spread throughout the world. COVID-19 was a harbinger of the death of countless lives, would overrun hospitals, disrupt economic livelihood, educational settings, and social structures such as families and churches. What was expected to be a short-term situation that would end as quickly as it started is still ravaging the world. As of this writing, more than 5 million deaths have been reported worldwide,[2] with over 807,000 deaths in the United States.[3] Despite the fact that we now have vaccines, the first half of 2021 reported more deaths from COVID-19 than all of 2020.[4] The untold costs to the survivors of COVID-19 have yet to be reported. Many survivors have experienced long-term health effects, families have buried their loved ones, and people have lost their livelihood, not to mention the mental and physical deterioration of those who remain behind.

Churches in the United States and abroad have been hit hard by COVID-19. Stay-at-home orders and quarantines have forced churches to close their sanctuaries or to significantly curtail the number of people allowed to congregate. Congregants have become sick, and some have died. In some instances, ministers have contracted the disease and passed away. Many churches have struggled with a loss of revenue. Churches have experimented with digital technology to offer media-based services and liturgies with varying degrees of success. What is lost, however, is the relational interaction that is so important for what it means to gather as a body of believers. This is true of Pentecostal-charismatic churches as well. But what theological resources and practices have Pentecostal-charismatic churches drawn on, or developed, to help them navigate through the pandemic?

This research is guided by the following questions: What theological resources, if any, do Pentecostals and charismatics employ to support their responses to the COVID-19 Pandemic? Does eschatological hope play any part in the Pentecostal and charismatic responses to the pandemic? If so, what mode of discourse is used? How is the Pentecostal-charismatic theology of healing related to its response(s) to the pandemic? Rather than presupposing a speculative Pentecostal response that is then applied to how the Pentecostal church should respond, we conducted a document analysis of selected Pentecostal denominational websites and official publications to determine how Pentecostal churches responded to the pandemic. We examined websites and online content dealing with the pandemic as well as official statements, documents, and publications either in digital or print form. The period of examination ran from January 2020 to August 2021. The organizations sampled included historic Pentecostal denominations such as The Church of God in Christ (COGIC), The Assemblies of God (AG), Church of God, Cleveland (CG), and The Pentecostal Assemblies of Canada (PAOC). We also sampled network churches such as Bethel Church, Redding, CA (Bethel), The International House of Prayer (IHOP), and Hillsong Church. Although many of these organizations were located in the United States, we included Pentecostal-charismatic churches from English-speaking countries such as Canada and Australia. What we found was unexpected. As will become evident, both eschatological and healing theologies were either muted or absent, and the focus was on the personal and social grief Pentecostals and charismatics were experiencing as they dealt with the effects of COVID-19. It should be noted that our findings are illustrative in nature rather than representative.

Hope in the Face of Despair

Fundamental to eschatology is Christian hope. While the details of eschatology can differ substantially, Christian hope is at the root of faith in the ultimate coming of Christ. With the exception of IHOP, which cast its discussion in dispensational millenarian terms, the discussion of eschatology in relation to the pandemic was rather muted, except for references to hope in the face of despair, fear, and anxiety. PAOC writer George Werner stated, "People's hearts are more open than ever before as they are searching for hope in the face of disaster."[5] The editor of *Testimony* referred to the situation as "deferred hopes" in the face of COVID-19, politics, national disaster, and gross injustice (in reference to the George Floyd murder). She says, "what we are experiencing during COVID-19 resembles the discomfort—even despair—that people in the margins have been enduring. . . loss of freedom. The lack of structure. The heightened sense of despair. The hovering threat of illness. Insecurity about what will happen tomorrow."[6] As one writer for the *Testimony* claimed, "We have all experienced the overwhelming feelings of chaos in life through illness, loss, pain, and our own choices."[7] "Unpredictable friendships. Loneliness. Strife. The pure loss of opportunity."[8] Bethel Church advocated for faith for healing but also encouraged wisdom by following the heath protocols implemented by city officials. Bethel also advocated for hope. ". . . [w]e do not partner with fear, but choose to lean into faith and hope, as well as practice wisdom and safety."[9] For Hillsong, holding onto hope was a way to cope with the pandemic as the church encouraged people to live in gratitude and rely on Jesus to gain strength in times of pain.[10] The most overtly eschatological millenarian position was offered by IHOP, which saw the pandemic as a "sign of the times" of the Lord's return, provoking eschatological hope and an urgency to prepare for greater tribulations to come.[11]

While an overt eschatology is mostly muted, an implicit eschatology threads the discussion of the pandemic through a discussion of hope and despair. At this point, it is germane to state that eschatology is a term that was first coined in seventeenth-century Protestantism. However, its meaning has never been clear. On the one hand, eschatology points to the belief in the future and afterlife. On the other, it refers more specifically to an older theology of the *eschata* (Greek) or *de novissimus* (Latin) of the last things: death, judgment, heaven, and hell. The nineteenth century witnessed a new and controversial development by adding an historical millennium or chiliastic component that was more in tune with popular Protestant piety than theology proper.[12] And yet, eschatology is not just about the future, but it is about present hope as well. The whole of theology is perceived from the perspective of hope, a hope that has transformative implications for the present.[13] In the midst of despair, suffering, and grief, the hope is for new beginning and new life.[14] That being said, the last things remain still a constituent part of eschatology. "What happens when I die?" is an existential question that probes one's personal eschatology, but one can also talk about the consolation of grief that lingers in the orb of death as the penultimate to death. Moreover, death is not, strictly speaking, solely an individual matter, but takes on social, historical, and cultural forms in the context of the pandemic so that one can speak about the death of the way things used to be, and the new reality in the middle of a pandemic (and hopefully post-pandemic) world.

Scholars of Pentecostal-charismatic Christianity have highlighted the importance of eschatology in the ethos of the movement. Harvey Cox argues that the genius of Pentecostalism is its recovery of primal spirituality, in which primal hope is a constituent aspect. For Cox, Pentecostal hope is rooted in Pentecostalism's millennial expectation for a better future.[15] Steven Land locates Pentecostal eschatology in its spirituality and eschews a dispensational fundamentalism for an anticipatory millennial hope of the not yet.[16] However, in the context of the pandemic, Pentecostals appeared to hope for a better future, but this hope was not placed in a dispensational millenarian framework. What does it mean, though, to expect a better future in the throes of a global pandemic when millions have died and those who remain are left to pick up the pieces? Damian Thompson convincingly argues that Pentecostal eschatology is not about predicting the future, but about explaining the present using eschatological and apocalyptic symbolism.[17] Eschatological imagery were ways in which people were able to make sense of the world in which they lived. Jon Bialecki makes a cogent point in his analysis of the Vineyard, but applicable in this context:

> On the one hand both past and future are only available in the present, but likewise the present encompasses both a "becoming future" and a "becoming past." This is because the past is never past, and the future does not [yet] exist.

For either the past or the future to have effects, they must be active in the present despite the fact that the present is always splitting into past and future.[18]

In other words, anticipatory hope is focused on present realities. Our data revealed that Pentecostals were generally not casting their responses to the pandemic as a millennial expectation of a better future. The data revealed that Pentecostals were grieving their losses to the pandemic. Death was at the forefront, and those who remained were trying to cope with the trauma—loss of loved ones, loss of safety and security, loss of job and economic well-being, loss of familial and religious networks that sustain and comfort in times of grief. Yet, hope remained despite trauma and grief.

Grieving Losses

Throughout our analysis of official documents, the expression of grief and the desire for relief from despair was constantly in the background. Bob Jones, for instance, wrote on the place of lament in the pandemic. He asked, "Is it OK not to be OK at your church?"[19] Jones cautioned about using church worship, or shallow forms of compassion and empathy, to make people feel better. Citing Ed Stetzer positively, Jones encouraged the church to ". . . allow space for people to lament—to wonder why, to ask questions, and to work through grief."[20] He proposed that lament leads to "deep transformation in our perceptions of suffering," and "engenders healing and intimacy," because "community is built on real-life joy and pain."[21] Lament, argued Jones, was critical support to raising awareness of mental health.[22]

Church of God in Christ (COGIC) Bishop Anthony Gilyard joined other COGIC leaders to discuss how church life has shifted during the pandemic. Bishop Gilyard stated that he lost four members of his church to COVID-19 and twenty-six individuals in his jurisdiction.[23] He said, "There was so much death, disease, and hospitalizations that people of faith became weary and tired. They didn't want church or even worship music because they were too depressed from the season."[24] The bishop talked about how he found it necessary to rebuild the people by simply reading scripture over them for up to thirty minutes at a time in an effort to bolster them without any programs or expectations. After doing this for some time, some of the worship leaders felt encouraged enough to ask to start leading musically again, but he explained how this was a slow process of grieving that needed to occur before rushing onward in the work of ministry.

Similarly, Allen Hood of the International House of Prayer admonished the leaders and members to take time to grieve, saying that any other response could reveal a disconnected, untouched heart. He said, "God's desire in times like these is that the eyes would cry before the mouth would speak. Hollow words from faces that shed no tears bring no true change."[25] He encouraged people to embrace the pain, let it touch the heart, and avoid "false comfort and false bravado." The acceptance of pain was quickly partnered with hope and purpose. He wrote, "We must use this crisis to prepare the way of the Lord. We have a mighty calling to be in this world yet not of it. We must do more than alleviate the shock of the moment with quick public statements, sermons, and prophecies. We must let this crisis touch us to the core, embrace the fear of the Lord, repent, and bear fruit!"[26]

Grief is a human response to irretrievable loss that consists of various feelings, both transitory and enduring. Grief is complex in that it is constructed from a multiplicity of other emotions such as sorrow, disbelief, numbness, fear, shame, and relief, to name a few. Grief can range between weak and strong intensity, the former including unsettled feelings, sadness, regret, and anxiety, and the latter provoking mental and physical distress that disrupts and destabilizes.[27] Grief is known to pass through different stages, including denial, anger, bargaining, depression, and acceptance.[28] However, these stages are seldom linear but ebb and flow, weaving forward and backward and turning in on themselves. Although grief is most often associated with death and dying, grief can also be a response to other losses such as the loss of employment, security, living quarters, childlessness, or friendships. What appears to be the case with Pentecostal and charismatic responses to the pandemic is that people are grieving real physical, social, cultural, and symbolic death and loss. The Assemblies of God produced an article that focuses on the multi-faceted layers of grief within churches during the pandemic.[29] In analyzing the choice of some leaders to meet in large gatherings during the pandemic despite public health orders to refrain from doing so, the author speculates this could be a form of denial. He says, "What seemed like bold faith turned out to be denial and presumption. Even the most cursory reading of the Bible makes it clear that our faith doesn't make us immune to suffering. Yet denial in grief can cloud our thinking and trump rationality."[30] The article gives tips for how to deal with each stage of grief at both the personal and corporate levels. The author emphasizes the importance of leaders and churches in processing grief because it is when one successfully maneuvers through these dark waters of grief that a sort of rebirth of hope can occur.[31]

Grief and despair are intricately related to eschatological hope, however. Moltmann argues that hope is rooted in love, but love is only possible at the risk of vulnerability. People experience loss and grief because they have loved and because they have hope. Even the spiritually strong can be overwhelmed by the pain of death and the grief and despair this event produces. "Often, the pain comes over grieving in waves. If this is so, the ability to weep is better than dumb frozen calm. Even to lose consciousness can be a blessing in the pain of mourning."[32] To downplay or reject the reality and effects of the pandemic, or to eschew the use of medical intervention and technologies to treat the virus, points to a deep denial in people who are experiencing overwhelming grief. To turn back to the question of eschatology, we propose that grief and grieving is an eschatological response to loss and death, whether personal, familial, physical, or symbolic in nature.

Trauma and Hope

According to Serene Jones, an event is considered traumatic when persons perceive that they or others are threatened by annihilation from an external force that they cannot resist and are overwhelmed to the point of being unable to cope. Trauma must also be differentiated from stressful or disturbing events.[33] An event is considered traumatic when a person perceives it as such. Trauma is an injury to the body, mind, and/or emotions. However, while a bodily injury is evident, psychological and emotional injuries, which may include a range of psychological ailments, are more difficult to ascertain.[34] The experience of the pandemic is not only death but can at times be experienced as traumatic death. This death is not just personal death, or death in the context of families, but a death that is social and global in scope. Trauma, and the grief it elicits, presents a challenge to those who are left to make sense of the senseless of death.

We cannot simply return to a normal course of life, but we must persist in life as we now know it.

The Assemblies of God was more explicit in identifying the link between grief and trauma. *Influence,* one of the denomination's official publications, published several articles that connected the pandemic to trauma. Beth Grant, for instance, bluntly stated, "Like everyone else, Christians are facing the raw uncertainties of life, the loss of loved ones, family tensions, and unemployment. People everywhere are dealing with overwhelming challenges, fear, and trauma."[35] This statement was framed in the context of the pandemic, racial tension, political chaos, and natural disasters. Similarly, Matthew D. Kim discussed the role of lament during the pandemic, and writes, "Within every congregation, there is grief, physical pain, emotional trauma, stress, depression, anxiety, and even suicidal thinking."[36] Later, he concluded, "Pain comes in waves. Chances are many of your people are experiencing a tsunami of trauma."[37] In response to this tsunami of trauma, the AG placed a special emphasis on bolstering counseling services for ministry leaders. In one article, Robert C. Crosby, the president of Emerge Counseling Ministries, was quoted saying, "The fallout from the pandemic is emotional trauma. The intensity of this season is more multi-faceted and challenging than the Great Recession of a decade ago."[38] He also speculates that COVID-19 will result in a myriad of post-traumatic stress disorder diagnoses. The grief is overwhelming, ". . . [families] have lost loved ones during the coronavirus and couldn't say goodbye face to face."[39] According to Crosby, the COVID-19 therapeutic fallout is yet to come.[40]

The theological relationship between death and trauma is addressed by Shelly Rambo in *Spirit and Trauma: A Theology of Remaining.* According to Rambo, "Trauma is described as an encounter with death. This encounter is not, however, a literal death but a way of describing a radical event or events that shatter all that one knows about the world and all the familiar ways of operating within it."[41] Trauma is not just personal but includes multiple levels of historical trauma, institutional trauma, and global trauma. Rambo focused on the middle ground between death and life. In this middle ground, trauma is that which exceeds categories of comprehension in the human capacity in taking in and processing the external world. Trauma grapples with the relationship between death and life. Life and death are not opposites, and therefore theology must account for what remains of death in life. To cast this insight into theological terms, there is no linear path between death and resurrection, but one must remain in the in-between of Holy Saturday. Triumphant predictions of life's victory over death fails to account for the traumatic suffering of those who remain. This remainder or middle ground is the locale of trauma.[42] There is a difference, however, between suffering and trauma. Suffering is eventually integrated into one's understanding of the world, while trauma remains as a disintegrated and open wound.[43]

Note that the trauma of death is not focused on those who have died. Trauma is experienced by those who perceive an event, or series of events, as traumatic. But trauma is experienced by those who witness the event as well.[44] The trauma of death is focused on those who remain in their grief and grieving. "The dynamics of traumatic experience press Christian discourse beyond the site of the cross to think about what it means to live in the aftermath of death."[45] Rambo's theological focus is on the followers and disciples of Jesus who remained after his crucifixion, the time in between Good Friday and Easter Sunday. Those who remain alive yet in a stupor regarding death—neither alive nor death but death in life—experience the trauma: a mother's loss, a disciple's despondency, a follower's confusion. ". . . [D]eath pervades life: it entails attesting to the temporal distortions, and epistemological ruptures of an experience that exceeds a radical ending yet has no pure beginning."[46] In this way, trauma has a double structure in both the occurrence of the violent event(s) and the later awakening to the event. "Trauma is not solely located in the actual event but, instead, encompasses the return of the event, the way in which the event has not been concluded."[47]

Returning to Robert Crosby, "Even when we are able to breathe a sigh of relief as the pandemic abates, we still need to be vigilant regarding emotional, spiritual, and mental health needs."[48] He recalls spending several days counseling pastors who had lived through the decimation of West Florida with Hurricane Michael in 2018, and many of them were not ready to discuss the matter until sixteen months afterward.[49] This comment gives perspective to the way trauma traps us between the loss of the way it was and an inability to imagine the future.

Jones suggests but does not propose a potential eschatological response to the crisis of trauma. The vision of the world to come told through stories and images insists that the Christian lives in the tension between this world of pain and the utopian expectation of a world without tears. However, she proposes a different theological path aimed at reconstructing the collective imagination through creative storytelling in order to reconstruct the world that we inhabit.[50] The problem is that those who suffer trauma are no longer able to tell their stories. However, scripture is a critical resource for imaginative storytelling that can speak to trauma as we find our life stories reconstrued within the grand story of the Christian faith. Through story, the imaginative crafting and recrafting of the world has the potential to heal the rupture and disorder of trauma. This is what Jones calls the "healing imagination."[51] Rambo concurs. Christian hope that is founded in the Spirit of resurrection is the promise of new beginnings that has a forward pull. However, when hope is filtered through the perspective of trauma, it requires an emphasis on the imagination.[52]

The Assemblies of God looks to have been deliberate in emphasizing hope in stories of healing and community outreach. The COVID-19 website for AG includes 257 short stories telling of healings from COVID-19, provision, outreach, acts of kindness, and highlighting good deeds.[53] This effort to help people to process their trauma was a way of moving people toward a path of healing while admitting it would be a long process. Many of the stories emphasized the importance of prayer and holding onto hope for healing despite bad reports and dismal circumstances. One story in particular tells of a woman, Sharon McClennan, who was rushed to the hospital by ambulance after collapsing in the middle of the night. Upon arrival at the hospital, X-rays revealed she had "COVID-19 pneumonia" in both lungs.[54] She was transferred to the ICU with the expectation of a long, critical road to recovery. The McClennan family began to pray and declare scripture over the hopeless situation. To the surprise of medical staff, a new set of x-rays revealed no trace of COVID-19 or pneumonia. The story encouraged prayer despite bad reports. However, this report was the exception. Other stories described longer paths of healing but emphasized the importance of faith, prayer, and worship through a severe illness. One missionary described how the Holy Spirit urged her to praise God through the night while she sensed a spirit of death lingering in her room during the peak of her illness.[55] While praising God, she sensed strength enter her body, and she described the victory over COVID-19 that was gained through spiritual warfare and praise. Each story of healing is unique, but each carries the common thread of defiant hope in the face of bad reports and a looming sense of death. Also, it must be noted that only three of the 257 stories included descriptions of "supernatural healing." Most reports emphasized hope, care, outreach, and acts of kindness amidst grief and suffering. Similarly, Bethel Church focused on provoking hope in the midst of suffering by encouraging people to "partner with heaven's perspective" and to "stand on the promises of God" amidst suffering.[56]

To be clear, healing in the context of traumatic grief is not a shallow homage to the supernatural and unexplained. Nor is healing, strictly speaking, a therapeutic response though the therapeutic is a part of the response. Healing is hope in the face of loss and despair. The documents only peripherally mentioned healing, and when it was mentioned, healing was not linked to the instantaneous, physical cessation of the disease (known as the divine cure) but to the slow process of recovery as the body through the aid of medical science regained health. Healing was also associated with recovery through the process of grieving. The healing hinted at in the documents is more akin to what Francis MacNutt defines as inner or emotional healing.[57] Space is afforded to allow people to "be okay that they are not okay." The pandemic and its effects have traumatized the world. The question that remains is how a healing imagination might allow people to tell their stories of grief and hope to recraft the world as part of the story of the faith.

Conclusion

COVID-19 is a global virus that will likely be with us for many years to come. At this point, people are navigating mitigation measures that lessen mortality rates and long-term health effects. The crisis presents a theological challenge to Pentecostal and charismatic Christians in that triumphalist tendencies will not soothe the world's pain. More to the point, expectations of triumph over the coronavirus may be a form of denial in the face of grief. Yet, despite the grief and trauma triggered by the pandemic, hope remains. This hope is borne of the ashes of grief, when we can finally look up to the sky and smile at the radiant sun/Son, while carrying the burden of the departed and the loss of the way things used to be in our hearts.

Notes

1. Special thanks to Betty Gilliam, who conducted some initial research into the responses of the historic Pentecostal denominations.
2. "WHO Coronavirus (COVID-19) Dashboard," World Health Organization, last modified December 22, 2021, https://covid19.who.int/.
3. "United States at a Glance," COVID Data Tracker, Centers for Disease Control and Prevention, last modified December 21, 2021, https://covid.cdc.gov/covid-data-tracker/#datatracker-home.
4. John Kamp, Jason Douglas, and Juan Ferero, "Covid-19 Deaths This Year Have Already Eclipsed 2020's Toll," The Wall Street Journal, Microsoft Start, June 10, 2021, https://www.msn.com/en-us/health/medical/covid-19-deaths-this-year-have-already-eclipsed-2020-s-toll/ar-AAKUG3Y?ocid=msedgdhp&pc=U531.
5. George Werner, "Raising Up a Generation of Leaders: A New Church in Italy," *Enrich* (Summer 2020), 29.
6. Stacey McKenzie, "From the Editor," *Testimony* 1:4 (Fall 2020), 3.
7. Kim Quigley, "The Discipleship of Spiritual Gardening: Cultivating Promise from Chaos," *Testimony* 2:1 (Winter 2021), 6.
8. Stacey McKenzie, "From the Editor," 3.
9. "Bethel's Response to Coronavirus," Bethel Coronavirus, https://www.bethel.com/coronavirus-response/#pray, accessed May 12, 2021.
10. "Day 7 - Hold On To Hope. Live From Love Not Fear," Coronavirus Constructive Thoughts, *Hillsong Collected* (blog) Hillsong Church, March 24, 2020, https://hillsong.com/collected/blog/2020/03/day-7-hold-on-to-hope-live-from-love-not-fear/#.YK7TVy2z3Up.
11. Mike Bickle, "A Letter Regarding COVID-19," *International House of Prayer* (blog), March 16, 2020, https://www.ihopkc.org/resources/blog/letter-regarding-covid-19/. See also, Mike Bickle, "Putting This Season into Perspective," *International House of Prayer* (blog), July 28, 2020, https://www.ihopkc.org/resources/blog/putting-this-season-into-perspective/.
12. Markus Mühling, *T & T Clark Handbook of Christian Eschatology*, Jennifer Adams-Maßmann and Daniel Andrew Gillard, trans. (New York: Bloomsbury T & T Clark, 2015), 4–6.
13. Jürgen Moltmann, *Theology of Hope: On the Ground and Implications of a Christian Eschatology*, James W. Leitch, trans. (London: SCM Press, 1967), 16.
14. Jürgen Moltmann, *In the End—The Beginning: The Life of Hope*, Margaret Kohl, trans. (Minneapolis: Fortress Press, 2004), x, 93–94,

15 Harvey Cox, *Fire from Heaven: The Rise of Pentecostal Spirituality and the Reshaping of Religion in the Twenty-first Century* (Reading, MA: Addison-Wesley Publishing Company, 1995), 82–83.

16 Steven Land, *Pentecostal Spirituality: A Passion for the Kingdom* (Cleveland: CPT Press, 2010).

17 Damian Thompson, *Waiting for Antichrist: Charisma and Apocalypse in a Pentecostal Church* (New York: Oxford University Press, 2005).

18 Jon Bialecki, *A Diagram for Fire: Miracles and Variations in an American Charismatic Movement* (Oakland, CA: University of California Press, 2017), 75.

19 Bob Jones, "Making Space for Lament: It's OK not to be OK," *Enrich* (Winter 2021), 30.

20 Jones, "Making Space," 31.

21 Jones, "Making Space," 31.

22 Jones, "Making Space," 31.

23 Anthony Gilyard, panel discussion moderated by Myron L. Williams and Cathey Owens Oliver, "Pandemic Paradigm: Shifting the Way We Lead Worship," *COGIC International Music Department Applied Studies Institute*, July 1, 2021, on Youtube, video, 50:32, https://www.youtube.com/watch?v=X_S3H8pyLmI.

24 Gilyard, panel discussion, "Pandemic Paradigm," (10:06–12:00).

25 Allen Hood, "Responding to the Crisis: Turning to the Words of Jesus," *International House of Prayer* (blog), April 28, 2020, https://www.ihopkc.org/resources/blog/responding-to-crisis-turning-to-words-of-jesus/.

26 Hood, "Responding to the Crisis."

27 Kathy Charmaz and Melinda J. Milligan, "Grief," in *Handbook of the Sociology of Religion*, Jan E. Stets and Jonathan H. Turner, eds. (New York, NY: Springer, 2006), 517–519.

28 Elisabeth Kübler-Ross, *On Death and Dying* (New York: MacMillan, 1969), 34–121; Elisabeth Kübler-Ross and David Kessler, *On Grief and Grieving: Finding Meaning of Grief through the Five Stages of Loss* (New York: Scribner, 2005), 7–28.

29 Joseph Castleberry, "Leadership During Times of Loss and Grief," Church Leadership, Assemblies of God Response to COVID-19, https://covid19.ag.org/en/Resources/FR-Church-Leadership/Leadership-during-Times-of-Loss-and-Grief, accessed July 16, 2021.

30 Castleberry, "Leadership During Times of Loss and Grief."

31 Castleberry, "Leadership During Times of Loss and Grief."

32 Moltmann, *In the End*, 124. See Althouse, "In Appreciation of Jürgen Moltmann: A Discussion of his Transformational Eschatology," *Pneuma: The Journal of the Society for Pentecostal Studies* 28 (Spring 2006): 21–32.

33 Serena Jones, *Trauma + Grace: Theology in a Ruptured World*, 2nd ed. (Louisville, KY: Westminster John Knox, 2019), 13.

34 Jones, *Trauma + Grace*, 12–13.

35 Beth Grant, "In Step with the Spirit: Authentic Pentecostal Leadership in Disorienting Times," *Influence* 34 (April-June 2021), 40.

36 Matthew D. Kim, "Preaching Where It Hurts," *Influence* 34 (April-June 2021), 49.

37 Kim, "Preaching Where It Hurts," 54.

38 John W. Kennedy, "No Counseling Downturn," Assemblies of God: Response to COVID-19 https://covid19.ag.org/sharedcontent/penews/No-Counseling-Downturn?D=F34D07D1EBE14A51856DAC58C9148CBA&BAPI={B74DA9C0-FDF4-43DE-8A13-82AEC2E280BA}, accessed July 16, 2021.

39 Kennedy, "No Counseling Downturn."

40 Kennedy, "No Counseling Downturn."

41 Shelly Rambo, *Spirit and Trauma: A Theology of Remaining* (Louisville, KY: Westminster John Knox Press, 2010), 4

42 Rambo, *Spirit and Trauma*, 6.

43 Rambo, *Spirit and Trauma*, 7.

44 Jones, *Trauma + Grace*, 13–15.

45 Rambo, *Spirit and Trauma*, 7.

46 Rambo, *Spirit and Trauma*, 15.

47 Rambo, *Spirit and Trauma*, 7.

48 Kennedy, "No Counseling Downturn."

49 Kennedy, "No Counseling Downturn."

50 Jones, *Trauma + Grace*, 37–38.

51 Jones, *Trauma + Grace*, 19–20.

52 Rambo, *Spirit and Trauma*, 168.

53 "News," Assemblies of God, https://covid19.ag.org/en/news, accessed July 16, 2021.

54 Dan Van Veen, "A Miraculous 24-Hours of Covid-19," Assemblies of God Response to Covid-19, News, https://covid19.ag.org/sharedcontent/penews/A-Miraculous-24-Hours-of-COVID-19?D=%7BF34D07D1-EBE1-4A51-856D-AC58C9148CBA%7D&BAPI=%7BC76497A0-901D-46E0-8449-F87D36881695%7D, accessed July 20, 2021.

55 LaVonna Ennis, "Prayers and Praise Bring Healing to Missionary," Assemblies of God Response to Covid-19, News, https://covid19.ag.org/en/SharedContent/PENews/Prayers%20and%20Praise%20Bring%20Healing%20to%20Missionary?D=%7BF34D07D1-EBE1-4A51-856D-AC58C9148CBA%7D&BAPI=%7BA1C1F50C-0D96-4FD4-A102-BC7CD6B93B1D%7D, accessed July 20, 2021.

56 "How to Pray," Bethel's Response to Coronavirus, Bethel Coronavirus, https:/www.bethel.com/coronavirus-response/#pray, accessed July 20, 2021.

57 Francis MacNutt, *Healing* (Altamonte Springs, FL: Creation House, 1988). MacNutt describes four different types of healing: physical healing, spiritual healing, inner or emotional healing, and deliverance. Inner healing is more consistent with recovery from grief and sorrow than then other three.

16 Triumphalist Theologies and Pentecostal Responses to COVID-19

Hanna Larracas

Abstract

How have Pentecostals responded to the experiences of suffering related to the COVID-19 pandemic? Analyzing Pentecostal responses to COVID-19 regarding experiences of suffering and grief produced two central themes: 1) emphasized triumphalism which failed to integrate experiences of sickness and suffering in the lives of faithful Christians, and 2) spiritualistic worldviews which prioritized interventions including prayer, worship, and expressions of faithfulness as means to eradicate experiences of sickness and suffering. To the extent that Pentecostals respond to suffering with petitions for deliverance through prayer and worship, it is concluded that there is a need for Pentecostal responses to suffering that include remaining attentive and present to experiences of suffering.

Introduction

How have Pentecostals responded to the experiences of suffering related to the COVID-19 pandemic? Existing research from the last two years concerning the response towards COVID-19 from Pentecostal communities explores themes of resourcing these triumphalist theologies with the intention of instilling hope and denouncing suffering related to the pandemics as well as evils also associated with the pandemic. Encouraged practices in these Pentecostal communities include a reliance on prayer, worship, and expressions of faith in God in light of challenges presented by the pandemic.

In reviewing research produced in the last two years concerning Pentecostal responses to COVID-19 regarding experiences of suffering and grief, I propose that two central themes emerge out of this analysis: 1) emphasized triumphalism which failed to integrate experiences of sickness and suffering in the lives of faithful Christians, and 2) spiritualistic worldviews which prioritized interventions such as prayer, worship, and expressions of faithfulness as means to eradicate experiences of sickness and suffering. Ultimately, notions of triumphalism present a challenge to sitting with tension in the midst of suffering. To the extent that Pentecostals respond to suffering with petitions for deliverance through prayer and worship, it is concluded that there is a need for Pentecostal responses to suffering that include remaining attentive and present to experiences of suffering.

Experiences of Grief & Suffering During Pandemic Times

The current landscape of research on grief during pandemic times primarily focuses on grief related to death and dying despite the prevalence of losses and griefs that transcend these categories.[1] Non-death losses have become invisible relative to grief and losses related to death, although the grief of non-death losses "often may be equally substantial."[2]

Grief has become its own epidemic within the COVID-19 pandemic, affecting mental health in addition to physical health. A popular working definition of grief in the social sciences conveys grief as a response to loss within the realm of spiritual, social, cognitive, behavior, emotional, and physical notions of well-being.[3] To that end, ambiguous loss is a loss that is physically absent and simultaneously psychologically present.[4] For instance, doctors from Japan demonstrate the negative impact of the pandemic on the mental health of Japanese communities. In addition to disruptions to social and economic norms, their research reports increased levels of anxiety primarily related to fears of the unknown.[5]

In a different study that references a North American context though remaining applicable to various localities around the world, individuals lost access to available support systems due to imposed, and necessary, social distancing measures. Scheinfeld et al. reported phenomenon of individuals feeling exhausted by their own grief and without access to normal coping strategies and sources of resilience.[6] This research explores how ambiguous loss can become traumatizing when there is no closure or way of resolving grief; such was the case with non-death losses experienced during the pandemic including, but not limited, to a prolonged loss of community and a sense of normalcy.[7] In lacking access to typical sources of resilience for the individual during pandemic times and the perpetual existence of the source of grief, I posit that contemporary events warrant responses from Pentecostal theology regarding suffering that goes on and grief without resolution.

Pentecostal Responses to COVID-19

The criteria utilized in this research for selecting samples of Pentecostal responses corresponds with how Pentecostal communities define and understand themselves. Spickard reflects on a phenomenological approach to religious experience which coincides with the previously provided description; "phenomenology seeks to describe experience as it presents itself to subjective consciousness."[8] A phenomenological approach to religious experience "allows one to enter into an aspect of the informants' religious world as it presents itself to their consciousness."[9] In addition to a phenomenological approach to understanding Pentecostalism, it is important to mention characteristics and contours specific to Pentecostalism and Pentecostal spirituality. In the midst of this embarking on this project of nuancing a Pentecostal identity lies the challenge that Pentecostalism lacks cohesive doctrinal and theological commitments in the various expressions of this movement across communities around the world. With this caveat in mind, Neuman presents four features of Pentecostal spirituality that attempt to capture a definition of the movement while recognizing its global identity across the waves of Classical, Charismatic, and Neo-Pentecostalism. Neuman presents Pentecostal spirituality as "(1) experiential, (2) biblical/revelatory, (3) holistic, and (4) missional/pragmatic."[10] It is with this working definition that the following Pentecostal communities were selected for this research.

After having set the stage by providing a brief description of experiences of grief and suffering during the pandemic, illustrating the experiences to which Pentecostals responded and even felt themselves, this research moves into identifying responses from various Pentecostal communities towards the pandemic. Perez explores the theological significance of worship in Pentecostal communities in a North American context as responses to experiences of suffering, arguing that worship accesses God's power for the purpose of facilitating spiritual work for communities and individuals.[11] This posture towards worship originates from a theology of praise and worship emerging from the Latter Rain Revival movement in the 1940s.[12] For Latter Rain theologians and communities, the belief that "God inhabits praise," inspired by Psalm 22:3, which captures a prominent message behind this theology of worship, finds continuity in two locations in scripture.[13] The Tabernacle of David's restoration as mentioned in Amos 9:11 and again in Acts 15:16 is associated with Israel's worship practices. Hebrews 13:15 interprets worship and singing as a kind of "sacrifice of praise with our lips."[14] As theological reflections on praise and worship gained momentum in the from the late 1970s and into the 1980s, praise and worship became recognized as the primary means for restoring the Tabernacle of David, leading to a consideration of singing praise and worship, more so than prayer and spoken praise, as the predominant practice in services.[15] Worship expressed through music-making was "associated with access to God's power in the life of Israel, a power that could also be accessed in the present day."[16] After gaining traction in Pentecostal communities such as the Word of Faith movement, Vineyard Church movement, Hosanna! Music, and other spaces, worship became a spiritual intervention invoked in response to suffering. During pandemic times, a sense of suffering ensued alongside lockdown mandates imposed by the government in some Pentecostal communities.[17] Praise and worship as spiritualized interventions responded to a perceived spiritualized interpretation of COVID-19.[18]

Although Perez's research is located within a North American context, Asamoah-Gyadu's account of Pentecostal responses to COVID-19 in Africa bears striking thematic similarities worth highlighting, including but not limited to enacting worship and other interventions invoking spiritualized interventions of the pandemic as responses to grief and suffering.

First, Asamoah-Gyadu's observations of contemporary Pentecostal communities in Africa recognize the emphasis on theologies of health-and-wealth. Belief in God in this theological framework corresponds with receiving "success, well-being, prosperity, emancipation, positives, elevation, and empowerment for various endeavors in life."[19] Whereas belief and explicit affirmations of faith in God invoke these realities in a Christian's life, lack of faith, failing to tithe, among other practices, not only disrupts receiving these gifts in one's life but can also invite further evil and suffering.[20] With regard to the pandemic affecting Pentecostal communities, the coronavirus was received as an "agent of Satan" wreaking havoc on the world and the lives of faithful Christians, revealing a spiritualized worldview and interpretation of the pandemic.[21] Pentecostal sermons viewed the virus as an agent of the devil and demonic, aiming to harm the church and God's people.[22]

The function of prayer in these African Pentecostal communities endorsing health-and-wealth theologies sought to invoke the power of God to remove the pandemic.[23] Asamoah-Gyadu observed the frequency with which Psalm 91:1–2 was referred in sermons, specifically mentioning parallels between God's ability to deliver from danger in scripture and in present times.[24] The purpose of these prayers and invocations can be summarized as seeking to resource the Holy Spirit through prayer in order to intervene with perceptions of evil working through the pandemic.[25]

However, ensuing life difficulties corresponding with the pandemic challenged expectations shaped by theologies of health-and-wealth, creating a novel sense of frustration for faithful Christian adherents. Although Pentecostals continued to express their faithfulness to God through worship and prayer, "the lots of those going through challenges were often treated as if they did not apply the right principles of success."[26] The paradigm for locating the origin of evil, here associated with experiences of suffering from the pandemic, failed to adequately address experiences of Pentecostals.[27]

Kagtle discusses suspicion from African Independent Pentecostal communities towards the COVID-19 vaccine and its perceptions of reliability, introducing a latent dualistic spiritual worldview or framework utilized to interpret the pandemic or make sense of the pandemic.[28] Demonizing the COVID-19 vaccine corresponds with a Pentecostal eschatology where vaccines are signs of the end times, perhaps as the mark of the beast, and resisting vaccines are expressions of faithfulness.[29] In spiritualizing the pandemic, suffering and sickness were moralized as evil or manifestations of evil and sin in one's life.[30]

Doležalová's account of Romani Pentecostals reveals salient themes that exist in continuity with Pentecostal communities in Nigeria and the United States. Her research seeks to observe and understand the continued practice of holding in-person meetings by Roma Pentecostals in England within the context of lockdown measures/restrictions.[31] In one account, she reports instances of individuals in the Light and Life Church who believe the devil was responsible for the pandemic.[32] A pastor of this community also shared his concern that following government-endorsed lockdown restrictions, which would involve shifting in-person services to an online medium, would communicate a lack of faith and trust in God to his congregants.[33]

At the same time, Doležalová provides important insights into the complexities of Pentecostal responses towards experiences of grief and suffering during COVID-19, offering a judicious and hospitable reading of Pentecostal responses to the pandemic from a Roma community in the UK. The Romani community commonly experiences lack of access to housing, sanitation, and inadequate infrastructure to facilitate remote learning during lockdown.[34] In other words, COVID-19 exacerbated already existing health inequalities for the Roma population and lack of access to public and common goods.[35] In this scenario, where the state fails to provide, the church becomes an important community of care meeting material, relational, and spiritual needs.[36]

In addition, her research identifies a personal relationship with God as a source of peace and comfort in response to existing uncertainty regarding Romani's access to common goods, an experience made much more fraught during the pandemic. While her observations reflect a specific Romani Pentecostal community, I suggest these themes are also present in Pentecostal communities in other regions.

Triumphalism in Pentecostal Theology

The provided accounts of Pentecostal responses to the pandemic indicate shortcomings in Pentecostal theologies and praxis to address grief and suffering. While the offered vignettes reveal limitations within Pentecostal theologies for seriously grappling with grief and suffering experienced during the pandemic, a deeper excavation reveals theological claims undergirding themes of triumphalism in Pentecostal theologies and communities. This phenomenon within contemporary Pentecostal communities exists in continuity with observations from Pentecostal theologians previously exploring the limitations of triumphalist theologies, including the prosperity gospel and theologies of health-and-wealth, in grappling with suffering that continues in the face of prayer and worship seeking deliverance.

Courey frames this conflict as a crisis within Pentecostalism located within tensions between expectations of power and realities that involve disappointing experiences.[37] In Courey's observation of this conflict, he identifies the expectation of a victorious life after experiencing salvation and Spirit baptism. Similar to how Pentecostals experienced dissonance when suffering from the pandemic did not end in response to their expressions of worship and prayer towards God, crisis ensues when reality fails to meet this expectation of a victorious life in existential and historical dimensions.[38]

Triumphalism as a worldview leaves little room for questions.[39] Themes of triumphalism are evident, for example, in the Pentecostal eschatological vision of Christ's second coming, saturated with a sense of a spiritualized immediacy, motivating missions and revivals.[40] An inherent issue within this triumphalist worldview is the struggle to incorporate realities which contradict its promises of power and grandeur. To the extent that there is no room for suffering in the coming kingdom, where Christian victory appears inevitable, suffering challenges triumphalism.[41] Butler takes up a similar argument as Courey in exploring how themes of victorious triumphalism discourage serious considerations of suffering.[42] Triumphalism also appears in notable streams of theologies of healing which endorse expectations of deliverance from sickness and illnesses as forms of suffering.[43]

Theologies of Healing

In introducing prominent theologies of healing within Pentecostalism, I make the connection between theologies of healing and experiences of suffering because, as the next section will demonstrate, similar to illnesses and ailments, experiences of suffering must be eradicated within these theologies. This section demonstrates the pervasion of triumphalist theologies that conditions expectations of healing and deliverance in Pentecostal contexts. Understanding theologies of healing reveal implicit commitments that undergird worship and prayer as responses to the pandemic.

Warrington explores the connection between expectations of miraculous healing from the church and the power of the Holy Spirit, believing in the "possibility of divine healing as a legitimate expression of the ministry of the church."[44] Expectations and theologies of divine healing are present in streams of Pentecostalism around the world where communities rely on scripture to corroborate these claims.[45] Warrington presents two operating views of healing in Pentecostalism. First is the belief that because of Jesus' death, healing remains available to those who believe. The second is that healing is made available to believers after death, and that atonement is not fully actualized in this life.[46] After presenting narratives of God as healer in the Hebrew Bible, Jesus as healer in the New Testament, and Holy Spirit as healer in the world after Jesus' ascension, beyond conveying miracles of healing, these healing narratives reveal the identity and character of the healer, specifically regarding Jesus' messiahship and the miracles of healing as opportunities for faith from witnesses.[47] Ultimately, Pentecostals will benefit from viewing healing in expansive and inclusive terms and to rethink categories of illness and healing, beyond envisioning healing in one's after life.

In inquiring how Pentecostals navigated the tension between COVID-19 and commitments to divine healing, Ma emphasizes physical healing as an important hallmark within the Pentecostal tradition, highlighting various locations in scripture where physical healing is foundational for other forms of healing (e.g. spiritual, moral, and national).[48] This emphasis is reinforced in the face of the erasure of healing as an expression and practice of Christian faith.[49] However, given the reality of non-healing that remains, Ma makes sense of the non-healing in the present in light of an inaugural eschatology where the kingdom of God is both present and still unfolding.[50] While works and miracles of healing function as a nod towards an inaugurating eschaton, Pentecostals are called to maintain hope for healing through the eschaton within the present such as when healing has not transpired and suffering is still at hand.[51]

Alexander also identifies two predominant models of healing practices and theologies within the North American context, the "Wesleyan-Pentecostal Stream" and "the Finished Work Pentecostal Stream."[52] The theology of the healing movement is also known as the "Faith-Cure Movement" as identified by Chappell, and in this framework, illnesses are cured when God, out of a response to prayer, responds supernaturally.[53] To the extent that the gospel preached by Pentecostals included "healing for the whole person," expectations were directed towards healing and for God to demonstrate power in people's lives.[54]

Clifton fleshes out Pentecostal theologies of healing and their impact and relationship with disabilities, specifically mentioning these theologies as alienating and the phenomenon of disability as a kind of "unhealing."[55] The consequences of the intense inclination towards miraculous healing and Spirit baptism specifically towards "people with permanent illnesses, injuries, and disabilities" yields the experience of individuals feeling disaffected and disenfranchised from the community of faith.[56] After outlining ways that Pentecostal theologies of healing fall short of addressing disenfranchisement and alienation of those who don't experience miraculous healing according to traditional expectations, Clifton suggests a revision of a Pentecostal theology of healing, one oriented with values that emphasize flourishing.[57]

Similarly, Yong argues that Pentecostal theologies of healing appear to run counter to experiences of disability scholars who see themselves "not as problems to be resolved (or healed or cured) but as part and parcel of their identity as human beings."[58] The Pentecostal movement emphasizes notions of healing rather than exploring the experiences of people with disabilities under hegemonic and disenfranchising ideologies.[59] Yong challenges assumptions around healing in Pentecostal contexts, that rather than eradicating disabilities, perhaps that stigmas around disabilities will be transformed. In this claim is the conviction that Pentecostal studies' engagement with disability studies contains powerful implications for Pentecostal theologies of healing and suffering which can widen an understanding of a Spirit-filled community.[60]

Pentecostal Theodicies

Theodicy is an ongoing conversation eking out causes and sources of suffering and where God is present in those circumstances. In the context of this research, theodicies provide an explanation for the source of suffering, illness, or ailment, and explore reasons and causes for a lack of healing even in the face of petitions to God for healing. Competing commitments present within the problem of theodicy was first presented by Leibniz: "How can an omnipotent and, at the same time, just and benevolent God allow so much suffering in the world?"[61] God's goodness and God's power exist as competing goods in this presentation of the problem.[62] The following section will present arguments from Pentecostal scholars who navigate these competing commitments within a Pentecostal framework and subsequently identified the need for robust theologies of suffering that embrace continued suffering in Pentecostal theology.

Engelbert asks the question, "When God does not intervene in the midst of suffering, how do Classical Pentecostals understand and/or interpret their experiences and relationships both with God and with others?"[63] First, suffering is defined as a multifaceted experience of pain that is inconsistent with expectations.⁶⁴ Reflecting on experiences of suffering from Classical Pentecostal communities through the lens of psychology, culture, Pentecostal theology, and narratives in scripture, Englebert demonstrates how these communities experienced extended suffering and did not receive their expected divine interventions. Instead, they experienced an absence of God, a phenomenon which Engelbert describes as nothingness.⁶⁵ Recognizing a gap in research and in practice between beliefs around God's presence during suffering and lacking a comprehensive theology of healing and suffering when suffering is not alleviated, Engelbert lifts up the importance of community and presence who embody God's expressions of empathy in the face of suffering.⁶⁶

Fettke and Dusing survey criticisms regarding the absence of responses to chronic suffering and concepts of evil within the Pentecostal tradition.⁶⁷ Social hierarchies and social perceptions influence experiences such as blessings, health, and affliction. For example, if afflictions are not healed through prayer, Pentecostal communities may consider the unhealed as second-class citizens rather than continuing to wrestle with the reality of chronic suffering.⁶⁸ God's faithfulness to facilitate healing and deliverance through miracles appears to be reserved only for the most faithful and most prayerful in the community. A lack of experiencing healing is translated to the adherent exhibiting laziness or a lack of faith.⁶⁹

Taking his cues from Job, where God states to Job's friends "that they had 'not spoken of me what is right, as my servant Job has,'" Torr states his primary research question as: "What does it mean to communicate rightly of and to God in the face of seemingly innocent, meaningless suffering when God appears to be absent, in a way that is conducive to Pentecostal/Charismatic theology?" Resourcing biblical theology and Pentecostal hermeneutics to explore best practices for responses to suffering, Torr finds inspiration in the theo-dramatics of scripture (script) and the religious adherent who enacts the script to explore Pentecostal/Charismatic responses to suffering.⁷⁰ Similar to Fettke and Dusing, Torr's project involves navigating expressions of lament in tandem with embracing the Pentecostal faith and the Spirit's work of healing with the goal of reconciling the disparity between Pentecostal/Charismatic adherence to and reverence for scripture and their understanding of scripture, especially regarding humanity's experience of suffering and God's presence in suffering.⁷¹

This section illustrates the growing symphony of voices within Pentecostalism who recognize the absence of responses or theologies of suffering, where conventional practices involve prioritizing prayers of healing and seeking miracles through worship and expressions of faithfulness. In response to these presented observations, rather than grappling with definitions or causes for evil and suffering, this chapter prioritizes responses that emphasize pastoral care towards the afflicted.[72] Fettke and Dusing opt for a "'practical' Pentecostal theodicy" which considers "peace and light and comfort" as works of the Spirit.[73] This practice involves validating expressions of lament and argues for churches to carve space for this practice alongside testaments and testimonies of miracles, healing, and deliverance. At the center of Pentecostal theology should be the invitation to "love God and neighbor as the center of faith and faithfulness," rather than prioritizing miraculous healing within a supernatural worldview.[74]

A Historical Perspective on Pentecostal Responses to Suffering

Amidst the demonstrated issues in Pentecostal responses rooted in triumphalism and the theological claims scaffolding spiritualized interventions in response to the pandemic, I argue that Pentecostal theologies already demonstrate the capacity to identify suffering expressed in material and embodied dimensions and generate relevant material and embodied responses. The following section traces the expressions of social ethical commitments within Pentecostal communities to demonstrate how Pentecostals already possess the tools to adequately develop responses that meet latent emotional and material needs, and address experiences of suffering within a pandemic context, in addition to the spiritual needs of the community.

Miller and Yamamori focus on the growing phenomenon of Pentecostal churches providing social ministries, a movement the authors are defining as Progressive Pentecostalism.[75] The ministries observed included growing indigenous churches in the developing world that facilitated ongoing social programs meetings needs within their respective communities.[76] This movement holds in tension the eschatological vision of Jesus' return along with meeting material and social needs of their neighbors. These practices contrast the tendency for Pentecostals, who out of a spiritualized worldview, emphasize "personal salvation to the exclusion of any attempts to transform social reality."[77] Progressive Pentecostalism demonstrates how Pentecostalism, at its roots, has the capacity to be an agent of social change and transformation and to identify the presence of suffering in their communities and to draw near.

Cecil Robeck traces the history of Protestant, specifically evangelical, spirituality and its expressions of social justice.[78] Robeck identified commitments to social transformation and civil rights issues within Revivalism and the Holiness Movement around the mid-twentieth century. The extension into Pentecostalism becomes apparent upon recognizing Revivalism and the Holiness Movement as part of the Pentecostal lineage/heritage.[79] Robeck offers accounts of early Pentecostals who were inspired to enact social programs to address material and physical needs in society. One such instance recounts the early 1900s when, Finis E. Yoakum, out of encountering a Pentecostal experience, established the Pisgah Home Movement which "provided help to the homeless, the poor, and such social outcasts as alcoholics, drug addicts, and prostitutes."[80]

However, Robeck recognizes the discontinuity between expressions of social transformation in Pentecostal's predecessors, in the North American context, and Pentecostalism's apolitical temperament.[81] Citing Jesus' prophetic declaration of Isaiah 61:1 in Luke, Robeck describes Pentecostals' application of a spiritualized hermeneutic rather than applying these verses in a literal sense. This tension is best captured by Robeck's observation. "While Pentecostals have ministered freely to those enduring spiritual poverty, they have often ignored the plight of the economically or socially deprived of our society."[82] One of the consequences of this spiritualized hermeneutic has been the tendency to ignore physical and material problems and to the promise of a heavenly reward, and "the development of deviant theologies of health and wealth."[83]

Similar to Robeck, Dempster recognizes the need for Pentecostal communities to enact a praxis of compassion which accompanies theological commitments, and argues for a biblically informed practice of social care that can be integrated into church social ministries from a Pentecostal perspective.[84] According to his framework, dispensational eschatology in Pentecostalism provides an impetus for Christian social engagement, thus resisting critiques of Pentecostal social disengagement and apolitical temperament, giving the example that Jesus' own ministry was inspired by expectations around God's imminent reign.[85] Jesus' eschatological vision empowered his message and ministry in community, and Jesus's teachings and actions on morality and ethics represent God's character.[86] Embodying Jesus' life is an extension of responding and committing to the Good News. Consistent with the Pentecostal belief that Spirit baptism empowers global mission and witnessing for the gospel, Pentecostals, inspired by eschatological commitments, expressed these values through social engagement responding to suffering in the world.[87] Dempster argues this eschatological character brings to fruition an "affirmative community," where "strangers are incorporated into the circle of neighbor love; peace is made with enemies; injustices are rectified; the poor experience solidarity with the human family and the creation."[88]

Dempster describes the importance of social action within the life and function of Pentecostal churches and communities.[89] He supplements the Pentecostal praxis of acting on social concern with a robust Pentecostal social ethic in order to sustain its continued practice within the context of Pentecostal communities and churches, and to demonstrate that social action and evangelism, an important concern for Pentecostal communities, need not be competing values.[90]

Building on Stronstad's notion of the transfer of the Spirit, Dempster claims that the theology of church mission in Luke extends to the empowerment and function of the contemporary Pentecostal church.[91] Pentecost for the apostolic church in Luke-Acts contains important implications for the modern church. The church is empowered by the Holy Spirit to participate in the ministry Jesus began, specifically the ministry of responding to social, physical, emotional, and material needs of the community.[92]

Isgrigg considers parallels between the COVID-19 pandemic and the Spanish Influenza outbreak of 1918, and how Pentecostals responded to both of these historic events.[93] During the 1918 pandemic, prayer was a prevalent practice for and with the sick from Pentecostal ministers such as A. J. Tomlinson and G. F. Taylor who routinely spent time with inflicted individuals. Other accounts recall congregants gathering around sick members to facilitate prayer and subsequently experiencing divine presence and intervention. Pentecostals also acknowledged death through testimonies and obituaries through papers and periodicals. These stories shared experiences of tragedy and loss through the death of loved ones such as children left motherless and parents grieving the loss of newborns. Grief was not interpreted as weakness or faithlessness but was encountered as an experience held in common for all to navigate in community. Publicly sharing and holding the ubiquitous experience of grief and loss within community existed in tension with hope that those who were suffering were soon after found with peace and comfort with the Lord. Ultimately, these vignettes invite consideration in how the Pentecostal response to the 1918 Spanish Influence pandemic could inform Pentecostal responses to the COVID-19 today, especially in how early Pentecostals modeled both faith towards healing while demonstrating compassion in light of death and healing that did not transpire after prayers.

This section portrays the importance of the Pentecostal ethos or the spirit of action and proactivity in the world. How the Pentecostal spirit is texturized bears important implications for a Pentecostal response to suffering. Pentecostal theology and communities, as empowered by the Spirit, are adequately resourced to identify suffering and meet latent needs in their communities. Inspiration from the Holy Spirit empowers Pentecostals to identify and respond to spiritual, physical, and social needs of others, practices which are considered to be expressions of social justice.[94] With the Bible and history as resources Pentecostals can access to catalyze and understand this praxis of transformation, Pentecostals are adequately resourced to enact transformation towards wholeness in personal and social dimensions.[95]

Conclusion

This research sought to demonstrate implicit themes of triumphalism within Pentecostal responses to the pandemic expressed through worship, prayer, and expressions of faith in God. Triumphalist theologies prioritize expectations of God's demonstration of power, especially that God can and desires to deliver faithful Christians from experiences of suffering.

After providing case studies illustrating the context of the pandemic to which Pentecostals responded and even experienced themselves, this research illuminated the prevalence of triumphalism in Pentecostal responses to COVID-19 and the recurrence of triumphalist commitments in theologies of healing and Pentecostal theodicies. Pentecostal theologians recognize the negative impact of triumphalist theologies on alienating, disaffecting, and disenfranchising those within communities of faith who do not experience expected healing.

However, exploring the history of Pentecostal social ethics demonstrates that Pentecostal communities have historically exhibited the capacity to identify suffering in their communities. They have responded in embodied ways that take seriously manifestations of suffering in material, social, and personal realms in addition to understanding suffering in spiritual terms or instead of as a predominantly spiritual reality. Therefore, the possibility remains open for future research on exploring and constructing a Pentecostal social ethic of remaining with suffering within pandemic times.

Notes

1 Harjinder Kaur-Aujla, Kate Lillie, and Christopher Wagstaff, "Prognosticating COVID Therapeutic Responses: Ambiguous Loss and Disenfranchised Grief," *Frontiers in Public Health* 10 (2022), 1.

2 Kaur-Aujla, et al., "Prognosticating COVID," 1.

3 Emily Scheinfeld et al., "Please Scream Inside Your Heart: Compounded Loss and Coping during the COVID-19 Pandemic," *Health Communication* 37:10 (2022), 1316.

4 Scheinfeld et al., "Please Scream," 1317.

5 Jun Shigemura et al., "Public Responses to the Novel 2019 Coronavirus (2019-nCoV) in Japan: Mental Health Consequences and Target Populations," *Psychiatry and Clinical Neurosciences* 74: 4 (2020), 281.

  I propose that Pentecostals must recognize the presence of grief and suffering in diverse contexts in order to be adequately equipped to respond to needs in public and pluralistic spaces.

6 Scheinfeld et al., "Please Scream," 1317.

7 Scheinfeld et al., "Please Scream," 1317.

8 James V. Spickard, "Phenomenology," in *The Routledge Handbook of Research Methods in the Study of Religion*, eds., Steven Engler and Michael Stausberg (London: Routledge, 2011), 333.

9 Spickard, "Phenomenology,"333.

10 Peter D. Neuman, "Spirituality," in *Handbook of Pentecostal Christianity*, ed., Adam S. Stewart (DeKalb, IL: Northern Illinois University Press, 2012), 124.

11 Adam A. Perez, "'It's Your Breath in Our Lungs': Sean Feucht's Praise and Worship Music Protests and the Theological Problem of Pandemic Response in the U.S.," *Religions* 13:47 (2022), 7.

12 Perez, "'It's Your Breath,'" 5.

13 Perez, "'It's Your Breath,'" 5.

14 Perez, "'It's Your Breath,'" 5.

15 Perez, "'It's Your Breath,'" 5.

16 Perez, "'It's Your Breath,'" 6.

17 Perez, "'It's Your Breath,'" 7.

18 Perez, "'It's Your Breath,'" 5.

19 J. Kwabena Asamoah-Gyadu, "Pentecostalism and Coronavirus: Reframing the Message of Health," *Spiritus* 6:1 (2021), 160.

20 Asamoah-Gyadu, "Pentecostalism and Coronavirus," 160.

21 Asamoah-Gyadu, "Pentecostalism and Coronavirus," 160.

22 Asamoah-Gyadu, "Pentecostalism and Coronavirus," 162. "Archbishop Duncan-Williams claimed that the virus was a demonic attack from satanic and demonic wombs and incubators."

23 Asamoah-Gyadu, "Pentecostalism and Coronavirus," 162.

24 Asamoah-Gyadu, "Pentecostalism and Coronavirus," 162.

25 Asamoah-Gyadu, "Pentecostalism and Coronavirus," 162.

26 Asamoah-Gyadu, "Pentecostalism and Coronavirus," 162.

27 Asamoah-Gyadu, "Pentecostalism and Coronavirus," 160.

28 Mookgo S. Kagtle, "Demonology, Eschatology and Vaccinology in African Independent Pentecostalism," *In Die Skriflig* 56:1 (2022), 2.

29 Kagtle, "Demonology," 1,3.

30 Kagtle, "Demonology," 2.

31 Markéta Doležalová, "Praying Through the Pandemic: Religion, Uncertainty, and Care," *Romani Studies* 31:2 (2021), 277.

32 Doležalová, "Praying Through the Pandemic," 292.

33 Doležalová, "Praying Through the Pandemic," 291.

34 Doležalová, "Praying Through the Pandemic," 288.

35 Doležalová, "Praying Through the Pandemic," 287.

36 Doležalová, "Praying Through the Pandemic," 286. "[The church] uses practices of care to create a sense of collectivity. In addition, the church uses a narrative of a God and Jesus as caring entities, because Jesus "suffered on the cross" to lift other's suffering. Converts should place their faith into the caring hands of Jesus, like Iveta did after her cancer diagnosis," Doležalová, 291. "The Life and Light Church creates a sense of collectivity among Roma and it does so by attending to both the practical and the emotional aspects of care, the caring *for* and the caring *about* others," Doležalová, 285.

37 David J. Courey, *What Has Wittenberg to Do with Azusa?: Luther's Theology of the Cross and Pentecostal Triumphalism* (London: Bloomsbury, 2015), 2.

38 Courey, *What Has Wittenberg*, 3.

39 Courey, *What Has Wittenberg*, 5.

40 Courey, *What Has Wittenberg*, 6.

41 Courey, *What Has Wittenberg*, 7.

42 Geoffrey Butler, "Plague, Pentecostalism, and Pastoral Guidance: Luther's Wisdom for the Contemporary Church," *Pneuma* 43 (2021), 5.

43 Butler, "Plague, Pentecostalism, " 8. Butler argues not for the eradication of hope towards divine healing, but that a more nuanced balance is needed in mediating expectations and responses for when suffering is not immediately removed via worship and prayer practices, 9.

44 Keith Warrington, *Pentecostal Theology: A Theology of Encounter* (London: T&T Clark, 2008), 265.

45 Warrington, *Pentecostal Theology*, 268.

46 Warrington, *Pentecostal Theology*, 271.

47 Warrington, *Pentecostal Theology*, 269.

48 Wonsuk Ma, "The Holy Spirit, Human Suffering, and Healing: An Initial Pentecostal Reflection," in *Christianity and COVID-19: Pathways for Faith*, Chammah J. Kaunda et al. eds. (Routledge, 2022), 60.

49 Ma, "The Holy Spirit," 58.

50 Ma, "The Holy Spirit," 65.

51 Ma, "The Holy Spirit," 64.

52 Kimberly Alexander, *Pentecostal Healing: Models in Theology and Practice* (Blandford Form, Dorset: Deo Publishing, 2006), 7.

53 Alexander, *Pentecostal Healing*, 9.

54 Alexander, *Pentecostal Healing*, 2.

55 Shane Clifton, "The Dark Side of Prayer for Healing: Toward a Theology of Well-Being," *Pneuma* 36 (2014), 204.

56 Clifton, "The Dark Side," 210.

57 Clifton, "The Dark Side," 218.

58 Amos Yong, "Many Tongues, Many Senses: Pentecost, the Body Politic, and the Redemption of Dis/Ability," *Pneuma* 31 (2009), 169.

59 Yong, "Many Tongues, Many Senses," 169.

60 Yong, "Many Tongues, Many Senses," 171.

61 Marius Nel, *God, Suffering, and Pentecostals* (Eugene, OR: Wipf & Stock, 2022), 13.

62 Nel, *God, Suffering, and Pentecostals*, 13.

63 Pamela F. Engelbert, *Who Is Present in Absence? A Pentecostal Theological Praxis of Suffering and Healing* (Eugene, OR: Pickwick, 2019), 15.

64 Engelbert, *Who Is Present*, 14.

65 Engelbert, *Who Is Present*, 18.

66 Engelbert, *Who Is Present*, 19.

67 Steven M. Fettke and Michael L. Dusing, "A Practical Pentecostal Theodicy?" *Pneuma* 38 (2016), 160.

68 Fettke and Dusing, "A Practical Pentecostal Theodicy?" 164.

69 Fettke and Dusing, "A Practical Pentecostal Theodicy?" 163.

70 Stephen Torr, *A Dramatic Pentecostal/Charismatic Anti-Theodicy: Improvising on a Divine Performance of Lament* (Eugene, OR: Wipf & Stock, 2013), 27.

71 Torr, *A Dramatic Pentecostal/Charismatic Anti-Theodicy*, 12, 29.

72 Fettke and Dusing, "A Practical Pentecostal Theodicy?" 168.

73 Fettke and Dusing, "A Practical Pentecostal Theodicy?" 169.

74 Fettke and Dusing, "A Practical Pentecostal Theodicy?" 164.

75 Donald E. Miller and Tetsunao Yamamori, *Global Pentecostalism: The New Face of Christian Social Engagement* (Berkeley: University of California Press, 2007), 2.

76 9/19/2023 11:07:00 AM

77 Miller and Yamamori, *Global Pentecostalism*, 2.

78 Cecil Robeck, "Pentecostals and Social Ethics," *Pneuma* 9:1 (1987), 103.

79 Robeck, "Pentecostals and Social Ethics," 103.

80 Robeck, "Pentecostals and Social Ethics," 105.

81 Robeck, "Pentecostals and Social Ethics," 103.

82 Robeck, "Pentecostals and Social Ethics," 104.

83 Robeck, "Pentecostals and Social Ethics," 104.

84 Murray Dempster, "Social Concern in the Context of Jesus' Kingdom, Mission and Ministry," *Sage Publications* 16:2 (April 1999), 43.

85 Murray Dempster, "Eschatology, Spirit Baptism, and Inclusiveness: An Exploration Into the Hallmarks of a Pentecostal Social Ethic," in *Perspectives in Pentecostal Eschatologies*, Peter Althouse and Robby Waddell, eds. (Eugene, OR: Wipf & Stock, 2010), 155.

86 Dempster, "Eschatology," 156, 168.

87 Dempster, "Eschatology," 158.

88 Murray Dempster, "Evangelism, Social Concern, and the Kingdom of God," in *Called & Empowered: Global Mission in Pentecostal Perspective*, Murray Dempster, Byron D. Klaus, and Douglas Petersen eds. (Grand Rapids, MI: Baker Academic, 1991), 20.

89 Dempster, "Evangelism," 19.

90 Dempster, "Evangelism," 19.

91 Dempster, "Evangelism," 20.

92 Dempster, "Social Concern in the Context of Jesus' Kingdom, Mission and Ministry," 47.

93 Daniel Isgrigg, "Pentecostals and Pandemics: A Historical Perspective" (E21 Scholars Consultation, Dubai, UAE, October 13, 2021).

94 Michael Wilkinson and Steven M Studebaker, *A Liberating Spirit: Pentecostals & Social Action in North America* (Eugene, OR: Wipf & Stock, 2010), 14, 11.

95 Wilkinson and Studebaker, *A Liberating Spirit*, 16. Sources in scripture referenced include passages of transformation in creation myth and empowering Israel's liberation from hegemonic powers; narratives of Jesus' actions demonstrate impact on physical, spiritual, and social dimensions of human lives. Liberation and transformation by Holy Spirit in Acts 2 and Joel 2, important texts for the Pentecostal tradition, carry implications for social and material needs.

17 Pentecostal Power and Pandemics: The Impact of the COVID-19 Pandemic on the Practice of Baptism in the Holy Spirit in Ghana

S. Ofotsu Ofoe

Abstract

This study uses a mixed design within the Church of Pentecost to show how the pandemic influences the baptism in the Holy Spirit with respect to the means by which the baptism is imparted by human agents. The study reckons that the pandemic had a negative bearing on this Pentecostal distinctiveness and argues that it is due to the restrictions to bodily contacts, which invariably undermines the traditional means by which this experience with the Holy Spirit is sought by Ghanaian Pentecostals. It recommends that the Holy Spirit and Christ, the baptizer in the Holy Spirit, cannot be undermined by the COVID-19 pandemic's limitations on touch and social distancing. This study argues for emphasis to be placed on other means of receiving the baptism in the Holy Spirit by drawing from the Bible and from other cases such as praying without touching. This would enable the Pentecostal practice of the baptism in the Holy Spirit for continual Pentecostal power notwithstanding pandemics of this nature.

Introduction

Pentecostalism since its renewal at the turn of the twentieth century has grown to become a force to reckon with in world Christianity. The outburst of the Pentecostal movement really took off at Azusa in 1906, and the movement has known no bounds since that time.[1] With reference to Christianity in Africa, Allan H. Anderson, the respected scholar in Pentecostal studies, has noted how Pentecostalism in its diversity has become the representative face.[2] Scholars even struggle to define what "Pentecostal" is. Walter Hollenweger asserts, "I do not know anybody who could convincingly define what 'mainstream Pentecostalism' is."[3] In Ghana, Cephas Narh Omenyo could talk of "Pentecost outside Pentecostalism."[4] Alfred Koduah also talks of pentecostalization of Christianity in Ghana having realized the penetrance of marks of

Pentecostal fervor into various churches in Ghana.[5] This Pentecostalization includes the various strands of the "Pentecostal." Harvey Cox identifies the African Independent Churches (AICs) as part of the Pentecostal breed.[6] This seems to augur well with Philip Jenkins.[7] Really, the AICs were there before the phenomenon known as "pentecostal" caught up with Africa. Asamoah-Gyadu in classifying indigenous Pentecostal movements in Ghana, apart from "Western Mission-Related Pentecostal Denominations" and "The Neo-Pentecostal Movements," also considered AICs as Pentecostal.[8] John S. Pobee and Gabriel Ositelu did a similar thing in their *African Initiatives in Christianity*.[9] This means that not all Pentecostal movements around the world have links with the Azusa revival of 1906.[10] Essentially, the complexity in defining mainstream Pentecostalism is even more heightened in Africa.

The Pentecostals-charismatics keep on growing. Scholars, both in and out of Africa, recognize that the heartland of Christianity has shifted from the West to the Southern hemisphere,[11] much of the growth is to be found within Pentecostalism.[12] Thus, especially in Africa, the South of the Americas, and Asia, Pentecostals-charismatics, especially from the global South, are on the move preaching the gospel to the ends of the earth. In fact, they are giving hope to the Euro-American West due to their efforts in "reverse mission" to the Western places.[13] Asamoah-Gyadu has reported that an African-led church, which is a Pentecostal-charismatic denomination, was once Europe's largest church. He pointed that "quite a significant number of the African churches in the diaspora tend to belong to the Pentecostal-charismatic stream of Christianity."[14]

Aware of the complexity or diversity in Pentecostalism,[15] this essay is concerned with classical Pentecostalism in Ghana. This is the movement that had diverse erstwhile names including "Fourfold or Foursquare Gospel," "the Apostolic Faith," and "the Latter Rain of the Holy Spirit or the Holy Ghost Revival."[16] However, this essay will use the Church of Pentecost (CoP) in Ghana. The CoP, like other classical Pentecostals, holds an unwavering view of baptism in the Holy Spirit with the physical evidence of speaking in tongues. This has driven its missionary enterprise. Their fervency towards missions and evangelism is coupled with the baptism in the Holy Spirit. David Maxwell cites the confession of a Pentecostal who has been baptized in the Holy Spirit thusly: "After that, I received baptism in the Holy Ghost and fire and now I feel the presence of the Holy Ghost, not only in my heart but in my lungs, my hands, my arms and all through my body, and at times I am shaken like a locomotive steamed up and prepared for a long journey."[17] This experience called baptism in the Holy Spirit evidenced by speaking in tongues and operation in spiritual gifts has generally been the heartbeat of modern Pentecostals since the beginning of 1900.[18] The dictum of belief in this regard goes like this: "that in the apostolic times, the speaking in tongues was considered to be the initial physical evidence of a person having received the baptism in the Holy Spirit."[19]

This essay shall take a brief look into the Pentecostal teaching of Holy Spirit baptism, consider the praxis of the baptism in the Holy Spirit, and its implication for the current global pandemic. Data was collected using written interviews with seven classical Pentecostal pastors of the CoP. The years 2018, 2019, and 2020 field statistical progress reports on the baptism in the Holy Spirit collected from twenty administrative districts of the CoP in the Greater Accra region of Ghana were gathered. Other primary data was collected via participant observation. All these would be analyzed towards assessing the progress of the baptism in the Holy Spirit in the face of COVID-19. The 2018 and 2019 reports would be compared to that of 2020, the year the pandemic hit Ghana. Using cases from the Bible and church history other means of receiving the baptism in the Holy Spirit against the traditional methods of practice are explored as the usual ways have been seriously compromised by the pandemic. I shall not delve into the history (emergence and progress) of the Ghanaian classical Pentecostal movement here. "Baptism *in* the Holy Spirit" and "Baptism *with* the Holy Spirit" have been used interchangeably in this essay.

"Second Blessing"

Pentecostal pneumatology is a fast-developing field of theology. This is significantly a result of the special attention given to the Holy Spirit by Pentecostals. It may seem at first glance that in salvation, Pentecostals place more importance on the Holy Spirit. However, it can be said that Christ is the center of Pentecostal teaching. Pentecostal theological thinking revolves entirely around Christ through the empowering presence of the Holy Spirit which is bestowed by Christ. For example,

Grant Wacker identifies emphasis on "heartfelt salvation through faith in Jesus Christ" as a noticeable mark of the Pentecostal movement.[20] Similarly, Roger Stronstad observes, "having become the exclusive bearer of the Holy Spirit at his baptism, Jesus becomes the giver of the Spirit at Pentecost."[21] Jesus is the baptizer with the Holy Spirit.

For Pentecostals, the role of the Holy Spirit in salvation does not end with the rebirth experience. Beyond the conversion-initiation of a person into Christ, there is another experience with the Holy Spirit. This Pentecostal theology emanates out of the setting of the Holiness Movement in which Spirit baptism was seen as a sanctification experience towards perfection in Christ. This baptism in the Holy Spirit took a new understanding in the classical Pentecostal movement. This overshadowed its erstwhile interpretation as sanctification. In the new understanding, baptism in the Holy Spirit empowers the disciple of Christ for ministry in the kingdom of God.[22]

In salvation, the Holy Spirit enables the regeneration of a person who has repented, come into faith in Christ, and confessed the Lordship of Christ. The Spirit is bestowed upon the person to transform the person into a new creation.[23] Subsequent to this is a post-conversion experience with the Holy Spirit. Here, the Christian noticeably encounters the Holy Spirit. This "second blessing" is a core of Pentecostal thought and practice. How Ghanaian Pentecostals seek this blessing in practice will engage our attention next.

The Pentecostal Distinctive Practice of Baptism in the Holy Spirit in Ghana

In classical Pentecostal churches, special times are set aside for prayers to seek the experience. This is announced at the church gathering earlier on. It is sometimes accompanied by fasting. In addition to and separate from these special times, baptism in the Holy Spirit may become necessary in any church meeting due to the leading of the Holy Spirit. The church leaders may be moved to lead the church to pray for the experience. This Pentecostal practice is an automatic part of conventions, gospel crusades, and rallies. These are reported on by church leaders to their immediate superiors. Those who do not have a show of an appreciable number of people receiving the baptism for the period under review are queried. The power that the experience brings, and the accompanying evidence incites many people to seek the experience. In this practice, "tarrying meetings" are used to engage the Holy Spirit in deeper depths. The mindset of Pentecostal Christians, their expectation, and the consequent result is well captured in this Pentecostal classic by E. C. W. Boulton:

> Tarry for the Spirit
> He shall come in showers,
> Energizing wholly
> All your ransomed power;
> Signs shall follow service
> In the Holy Ghost,
> Then the Church of Jesus
> Prove a mighty host
> On, then, Church of Jesus,
> Claim your Pentecost;
> God shall now baptise you
> In the Holy Ghost.[24]

The meetings proceed with relevant sermons expounding on the baptism. These sermons are usually accompanied by testimonies. The sermons are interjected with spontaneous singing and shouts of "hallelujah." A key aspect of this ministry is to explain to the congregation that the baptism gives the Christian power to witness and enables the Christian to live a holy and victorious Christian life. It is taught that the physical evidence of the baptism in the Holy Spirit is speaking in tongues or other languages. These tongues may be known languages as in Acts 2:4–12, or mysteries according to 1 Corinthians 14:2. Enthusiastic preachers would inform the congregation that their tongues would change when they receive the baptism.

The sermon is followed by Pentecostal songs about the Holy Spirit amidst drumming and clapping. The way the singing is done in these services seems to suggest that it is in this ecstatic environment that the Holy Spirit moves and gets people baptized in him. Was this the case in the upper room on the Day of Pentecost? The prayer leader in many instances would invite the congregation, especially persons that are yet to receive the experience to leave the pews and move forward. This is usually to give more space for people to comfortably pray. Frenzied happenings are expected during the prayer sessions, so space is needed. The people are instructed to queue up in an orderly manner. This is to allow the church leaders to move among them freely to minister the baptism. Those who have received the baptism are encouraged to pray for themselves and for the ones who now seek the experience. The seekers are, in many instances, urged to pray and also keep on saying "Jesus, Jesus . . ." in anticipation of the baptism.

After much prayer, the leaders of the church, especially the elders, go and walk among and people to pray for them. They go to impart the baptism in the Holy Spirit. This ministration comes in diverse ways. One would often hear the prayer leader say, "the elders would now come and lay their hands on you." The laying of hands as a means by which the baptism is done is not exhaustive. Other actions are seen being used for the ministration. Key methods used include breathing on seekers, putting fingers in their ears, pointing a finger on the forehead, holding the shoulders with two hands, putting hands on the eyes, raising the chin, placing the hands over the ears, holding the hands, rubbing the face with the hands, and putting hands on the chest. Many fall under the power of the Holy Spirit with shouts, groaning, and speaking in tongues.

While we can say that all these resonate with African primal religion, they are found in the Holy Spirit baptism sessions of classical Pentecostals not only in Africa but elsewhere.[25] When the Holy Spirit descended at Azusa Street in the United States in 1906, similar scenes were witnessed. The media portrayed the phenomenon at Azusa as "Weird Babel of Tongues."[26] This is not limited to the African continent. Consequently, this way of life is to be identified with classical Pentecostals no matter the geographical area they find themselves especially during the formative years. These usual methods mentioned, used in the Pentecostal practice of baptism in the Holy Spirit, are opposed to the protocols of the present global pandemic.

Baptism in the Holy Spirit and Medical Science Concerns in the Pandemic

The current global pandemic has gravely affected our everyday life. In Ghana, restrictions were imposed on the usual church meetings. On March 15, 2020, the president of the republic, H. E. Nana Addo Dankwa Akuffo-Addo, in an address concerning the fight against the global pandemic, imposed restrictions on gatherings including church meetings. Prior to this, the CoP in a circular letter dated March 13, 2020, encouraged its churches worldwide to among others "minimize church and congregational practices that encourage body contact such as hugging /embracing." Some others mentioned include "handshaking" and not "touching nose and mouth with unwashed hands."[27] The imposition of hands during prayers, a major form of body contact during church meetings of the CoP was not specifically mentioned. However, just two days later, the presidential address that closed down the churches came through. The restrictions were eased in another address on May 31, 2020. Accordingly, the CoP directed its churches to reopen for public worship starting on or after June 19, 2020.[28] Thus, for about three months, churches did not physically meet.

Humans are highly sociable beings. However, the means of transmission of the SARS-Cov-19 virus which causes the corona virus disease breaks down the human social system. The virus gets into the human body via the mucosal lining in the eyes, nostrils, and mouth. These parts of the human anatomy are opened to the air. From an infected human, the air becomes contaminated with the virus through droplets. The structure of the virus enables it to attach itself to receptors on the cell surface when it gets into the human body. It later penetrates the cell surface, replicates, and multiplies.

Considering how the COVID-19 virus is spread from one person to another, the various methods used in imparting the baptism in the Holy Spirit, as observed from practice, are negatively affected. Medical sciences preventive measures of keeping a social distancing of not less than two arm's length, and not touching the eyes, nose or mouth among other protocols eliminated the highly used bodily contact methods in the impartation. Meanwhile, these supposed means of receiving the baptism are deeply rooted in the minds of Ghanaian Pentecostals.

Data Analysis

Seven classical Pentecostal pastors selected from five different administrative regions of Ghana; Northern, Eastern, Volta, Bono East, and Greater Accra regions have been interviewed. The interview questions were ten in all; five closed-ended and the other five open-ended. All of the interviewees were very much aware of the COVID-19 protocols (100 percent). During this pandemic, all the pastors organized sessions of Holy Spirit baptism. This points out the important place of the baptism in the Holy Spirit in Pentecostal thought and practice. All of them observed the protocols in their practice of the baptism. Classical Pentecostal church leaders are increasingly becoming considerate of medical sciences though divine healing is a center of Pentecostal theology. They have given a place for the medical sciences in their doctrine of divine healing. In heeding the protocols, the prayers for the baptism were done by the leaders for the seekers from a distance. Concerning how the baptism was imparted, all the pastors responded that it was done by "praying for the seekers of the baptism from the platform as they [the seekers] stand in their pews."[29] Four of the interviewees were of the view that the laying of hands impacts on whether a person gets baptized or not. The other three responded otherwise.

Reports from twenty administrative districts of the CoP selected in the Greater Accra region, the cumulative number of persons who received the baptism in the Holy Spirit was 2,707 in 2018. In the year 2019, the reports from the same districts totaled 2,688. This shows a reduction by nineteen (0.7 percent). In the year 2020, these twenty districts show 1,010 as the number of people who have received the baptism. Evaluating 2020, a COVID-19 pandemic-stricken year, against the year 2018, a reduction by 1,697 (62.7 percent) is observed. A reduction of 1,678 (62.4 percent) is also seen when the figure for the year 2019 is used for comparison.

There has been a significant reduction in the number of persons who received the baptism in the Holy Spirit. Has the frequency of the baptism services been reduced? Almost all the interviewees organized a fewer number of the baptism sessions. They attributed this to the COVID-19 protocols. One of them responded that "We are mindful of the COVID-19 protocols and the fact that at times people will have to be supported by strong deacons to avoid injuries when they are touched by the Holy Spirit."[30] Also, can this be pinned down on the reduction in church attendance? To a much less extent, restrictions to church meetings for a number of weeks would influence this reduction. However, this study realizes that the protocols accompanying this pandemic is a more significant factor. This suggests that if the parameter of church attendance remains constant, there would be a significant reduction in cases of the

Spirit baptism. This would be due to not praying very close to seekers, laying of hands, breathing upon seekers, and putting fingers in the ears of seekers by church leaders in accordance with the protocols.

Case Studies of the Practice of Baptism in the Holy Spirit

Cases in the Acts narrative that apprise the Pentecostal teaching of baptism in the Holy Spirit with evidence of speaking in tongues present with diverse circumstances under which the baptism takes place. In the first instance in Acts 2, it was within a corporate tarrying meeting that the Spirit descended. In obedience to the instruction of Jesus in Acts 1:4–5 to wait in Jerusalem for the promise of the Father God, the believers waited in prayer until they had the phenomenal experience. The immediate event which led to the baptism was most intriguing. A noise sounded like a mighty rushing wind was heard. They sighted what appeared to be tongues of fire that separated and rested on each of them. It is recorded that all those gathered were filled with the Holy Spirit and began to speak in other tongues. Here, no hands were laid on the recipients of the baptism, not on their heads, shoulders, eyes, or any other part of the body.

The baptism in the Holy Spirit that took place in the home of Cornelius as recorded in Acts 10:44–46 presents with a similar case in which the family was filled with the Holy Spirit during Peter's preaching. The Apostle Peter did not use any special method that involved touching the recipients. Nevertheless, they received the baptism. To show that they had received the baptism, Peter in his narration of the event said, "As I began to speak, the Holy Spirit fell on them just as on us at the beginning. And I remember the word of the Lord, how he said, John baptized with water, but you will be baptized with the Holy Spirit" (Acts 11:15–16, NIV). Thus, Peter connected the event at the home of Cornelius with the "you will be baptized with the Holy Spirit" word given to the disciples by Jesus.

In Acts 19:1–6, at Ephesus, Paul encountered a group of disciples who were not aware of the Holy Spirit, not to speak of the baptism with the Holy Spirit. Paul explained the issues to them and placed his hands on them. This saw these Ephesian Christians speaking in tongues and prophesying. This case as well as in Acts 8:14–19 in which the Christians in Samaria received the Holy Spirit after Apostles Peter and John laid their hands. This shows that laying on of hands is also a means by which baptism with the Holy Spirit can be ministered. But it is not an exclusive means, of course.

Many continue to be baptized in the Holy Spirit. Church history globally and locally provides cases. One Methodist preacher narrates:

> We Methodists were praying together when we heard a noise, like the sound of a rushing wind in our prayer room, whereupon we gazed with wonder as cloven tongues of fire actually appeared upon our heads. In awe and worship of God, we were caught up in a heavenly atmosphere, speaking and singing in other languages.[31]

This experience with the Holy Spirit was not made possible by the placement of hands on those Christians.

In the CoP, there have many instances in which people received the baptism with the Holy Spirit without the physical bodies of church leaders serving as bridges through which the baptism happens. John Mensah, one of the earliest "divine healers" in the CoP (then Ghana Apostolic Church) received the baptism which he very much desired during his personal prayers. It is said that he personally fasted and prayed fervently for the baptism. His day of joy came one day when he woke up around 1:00 a.m. to pray. As he prayed, he suddenly began to speak in tongues. The empowerment that came with this experience caused him to also operate in spiritual gifts and establish a number of prayer groups in and outside Ghana until he became recognized by the CoP as a full-time worker.[32]

Opoku Onyinah, the fifth chairman of the CoP also received the baptism through personal prayer. He narrated with joy how he got baptized as a young Christian. Then a Roman Catholic, he desired the baptism and got the experience eventually. He joined in a CoP prayer session to pray for the baptism.[33] He did not receive the experience immediately. He did not give up but continued his pursuit of the pneumatic encounter with fasting and prayer. On the last day of a seven-day fast, he went to a hide-out in a bush to pray. On his way to the place, he met another Roman Catholic who, like Opoku, was also seeking the baptism in the Holy Spirit. He requested this person to join him to pray in the bush. The two found themselves in a time of prayer. During the prayers, as he puts it, "suddenly my tongue changed, and I started speaking in tongues."[34]

In 1931, James Kwaku Gyimah of Akroso, Ghana (then the Gold Coast), became the first Ghanaian to receive the baptism in the Holy Spirit through personal means. Then a Presbyterian, James' only connection with Pentecostalism was periodicals he had been receiving from the Apostolic Faith in the United States. He might have read of the baptism in the Holy Spirit from these magazines. His tongue-speaking was not accepted by his denomination, so he left. He preached Christ in the power of his new experience. He drew many followers as a result.[35]

Another person, Stephen Owiredu of Brekumanso received the baptism with the Holy Spirit and spoke in tongues in 1932, through personal prayer for his ailing child.[36] These cases among others indicate diverse ways in which the baptism can happen. Other ways include the prayerful reading of the Bible, praying for seekers of the baptism from a distance without any bodily contact, and listening to the preaching of the word of God.

It is evident from the above that in the practice of the baptism, the Bible, and evidence from the continual work of the Lord in history show that Christ, the baptizer with the Holy Spirit employs varied ways to cause one to get the encounter. The methods that have become popular and the norm in Ghanaian Pentecostalism have swept under the carpet the other ways in which the Lord can empower his people.

The laying of hands has been revealed in the Bible as a means by which graces can be bestowed. The Old Testament presents examples of this. For instance, Moses laid his hands on Joshua (Deut 34:9). Some patristic theologians including Tertullian, Cyril of Jerusalem, Athanasius, and Chrysostom took up the issue of the Spirit being given through the laying on of hands. Cyril of Jerusalem for example indicated that power has been designated by Christ to the Apostles to convey the Spirit through the laying of hands. Athanasius held a similar view. The interest of the church fathers on this issue was largely in the area of who qualified to lay hands. Meanwhile, the laying of hands in Ghanaian Pentecostalism has become a baptismal rite, almost sacramental, that one who needs baptism in the Holy Spirit has to go through. This method as a means of imparting the baptism in the Holy Spirit emerged in part from the cases in Acts 8 and 19.

Other methods evolved from diverse interpretations of biblical phenomena and perhaps from African primal religious practices. For example, John 20:22 in which Jesus breathed on his disciples to receive the Holy Spirit is sometimes used to justify breathing on seekers of the baptism in the Holy Spirit. On the contrary, this act by Jesus does not define a format for the baptism. Putting fingers in the ears is understood by some who minister the baptism as a way of getting the ears of the seekers opened so they could hear from God and speak mysteries. This may have been picked up from Mark 7:32–35. More so, and here too, Jesus putting his fingers in the ears of a man to heal him of deafness does not define a pattern for getting the ears of people opened whether spiritually or physically.

Conclusion

This essay has shown that baptism in the Holy Spirit, a distinctive classical Pentecostal practice, has been impacted negatively by the present pandemic. This seems to put in crisis Pentecostal power. The study points to the normative use of bodily contact between church leaders and seekers of the baptism in the Holy Spirit as underlining this impact. These popular methods used to minister the baptism have been undermined by the COVID-19 preventive protocols. The methods also obliviate other ways by which the Lord used to baptize people with the Holy Spirit. Other means of receiving the experienced must be explored and built up in the minds of Christians. The Christian must come to grips with the fact that the Holy Spirit per his ontological nature cannot be limited by time and space. He cannot be undermined by the protocols of the present pandemic. One can be immersed in unlimited ways into the Holy Spirit by Christ. Restrictions the pandemic placed on other aspects of church life should not limit Christ, the baptizer in the Holy Spirit. Pentecostal power must be on the go during any pandemic that may hit the world.

Notes

1 Walter J. Hollenweger, *Pentecostalism: Origins and Developments Worldwide* (Grand Rapids: Baker Academic, 1997), 20; William W. Menzies and Robert P. Menzies, *Spirit and Power: Foundations of Pentecostal Experience* (Grand Rapids: Zondervan, 2000), 16–17.

2 Allan H. Anderson, "Stretching Hands to God: Origins and Development of Pentecostalism in Ghana" in *Pentecostalism in Africa: Presence and Impact of Pneumatic Christianity in Postcolonial Societies*, Martin Lindhardt, ed. (Leiden: Brill, 2015), 54.

3 Walter Hollenweger and Neil Hudson, "Pentecostalism, Past, Present and Future," *Journal of the European Theological Association* 21:1 (2001), 46.
4 This is the title of his book that presents his research on the spread of Pentecostal-charismatic spirituality into the mainline churches in Ghana. See Cephas Narh Omenyo, *Pentecost Outside Pentecostalism: A Study of the Development of Charismatic Renewal in the Mainline Churches in Ghana* (Zoetermeer: Boekencentrum, 2002).
5 Alfred Koduah, *Christianity in Ghana Today* (Accra: Advocate Publishing Ltd., 2004), 178. See also Kwabena Asamoah-Gyadu, "Migration and the African Diaspora Mission and the Changing Christian Landscape of the West," *Pentecost Journal of Theology and Mission* 1:1 (2016), 67; J. Kwabena Asamoah-Gyadu, *African Charismatics: Current Developments within Independent Indigenous Pentecostalism in Ghana* (Leiden: Brill, 2005), 14.
6 Harvey Cox, *Fire from Heaven: The Rise of Pentecostal Spirituality and the Shaping of Religion in the Twenty-First Century* (Reading: Addison-Wesley Publishing Company, 1995), 15.
7 Jenkins, *The Next Christendom*, 68.
8 Asamoah-Gyadu, *African Charismatics*, 19–29.
9 John S. Pobee and Gabriel Ositelu III, *African Initiatives in Christianity: The Growth, Gifts and Diversities of Indigenous African Churches: A Challenge to the Ecumenical Movements* (Geneva: WCC Publications, 1998), 33–44.
10 See Asamoah-Gyadu, *African Charismatics*, 11.
11 Philip Jenkins, *The Next Christendom: The Coming of Global Christianity* (New York: Oxford University Press, 2002), 2; Kwame Bediako, Christianity in Africa: The Renewal of a Non-Western Religion (Edinburgh: Edinburgh University Press, 1995), 3; Ogbu U. Kalu, "African Christianity: An Overview" in *African Christianity: An African Story*, Ogbu U. Kalu, ed. (Trenton: Africa World Press, 2007), 23.
12 Cox, *Fire from Heaven*, 14–15.
13 See Afe Adogame, *The African Christian Diaspora: New Currents and Emerging Trends in World Christianity* (London: Bloomsbury Academic, 2013), 172.
14 Asamoah-Gyadu, "Migration and African Diaspora," 65–67. See also J. Kwabena Asamoah-Gyadu, "African Initiated Churches in Eastern Europe: Church of the 'Embassy of God' in Ukraine," *International Bulletin of Missionary Research* 30:2 (2006), 73–75.
15 Nimi Waroboko, *The Pentecostal Principle: Ethical Methodology in New Spirit* (Grand Rapids: Eerdmans, 2012), 107.

16 See David Maxwell, *African Gifts of the Spirit: Pentecostalism and the Rise of a Zimbabwean Transnational Religious Movement* (Athens, Ohio: Ohio University Press, 2006), 17.

17 See Maxwell, *African Gifts of the Holy Spirit*, 17.

18 Menzies and Menzies, *Spirit and Power*, 16.

19 See James D. G. Dunn, *Baptism in the Holy Spirit: A Re-examination of the New Testament Teaching on the Gift of the Spirit in Relation to Pentecostalism Today* (Philadelphia: Westminster, 1970), 2.

20 Grant Walker, Heaven Below: *Early Pentecostals and American Culture* (Cambridge: Harvard University Press, 2001), 2.

21 Roger Strongstad, *The Charismatic Theology of St. Luke: Trajectories from the Old Testament to Luke-Acts*, 2nd Ed. (Grand Rapids: Baker Academic, 2012), 55.

22 See Frank D. Macchia, "The Kingdom and the Power: Spirit Baptism in Pentecostal and Ecumenical Perspective" in *The Work of the Spirit: Pneumatology and Pentecostalism*, Michael Welker, ed. (Grand Rapids: Eerdmans, 2006), 109–110.

23 Dunn, *Baptism in the Holy Spirit*, 2. See also Macchia, "The Kingdom and the Power," 114–115.

24 "Tarry for the Spirit."

25 See Wacker, *Heaven Below*, 101–102.

26 See Cecil M. Robeck, Jr., *The Azusa Street Mission and Revival: The Birth of the Global Pentecostal Movement* (Nashville: Thomas Nelson, 2006), 75.

27 Eric Nyamekye, "The Church of Pentecost General Headquarters March-2020-Circular," March 13, 2020.

28 Eric Nyamekye, "The Church of Pentecost General Headquarters: Guidelines for Re-opening Assemblies for Church Services," June 6, 2020.

29 Interview by the author, March 17, 2021, Accra, Ghana.

30 Interview by the author, March 17, 2021, Accra, Ghana.

31 Quoted in T. L. Osborn, *The Purpose of Pentecost* (Tulsa, OK: T.L. Osborn Evangelical Association, 1963), 12.

32 The Church of Pentecost, *A History of the Church of Pentecost*, vol. I, E. Kafui Asem ed. (Accra: COP Literature Committee, 2005), 114–116.

33 Those types of prayer session that Pentecostals call "tarrying meetings." See Robeck, *The Azusa Street Mission and Revival*, 140.

34 See S. Ofotsu Ofoe, *The "Newness" Theology of Opoku Onyinah: For Christian Spirituality, Mission, and Thinking* (London: MSI, 2018), 30–31.

35 The Church of Pentecost, *A History of the Church of Pentecost*, 18–19.

36 E. Kingsley Larbi, Pentecostalism: *The Eddies of Ghanaian Christianity* (Accra: Centre for Pentecostal and Charismatic Studies, 2001), 101–103. See also The Church of Pentecost, *A History of the Church of Pentecost*, 18.

18 COVID-19, the Church, and the Pneumatological Challenge[1]

Jean-Daniel Plüss

Abstract

The COVID-19 pandemic has raised questions about how churches respond to an extraordinary situation where not only health and economic issues are at stake, but also the understanding of what church is all about and how ecclesial life is practiced. Furthermore, how do the experiences made, reflect our understanding of how the work of the Holy Spirit is understood? This article introduces the issues raised by first reviewing how Christians in past centuries have faced pandemics. Secondly, the text will look at recent responses by large church bodies and organizations. Thirdly, a small survey will focus on the responses by local churches across the globe as to the benefits and challenges associated with the coronavirus crisis. Finally, the paper addresses what the various reactions tell us about a reassessment of the nature of the church and how the work of the Holy Spirit is appreciated, both in the local context and with regard to the wider Body of Christ.

Introduction: There is Nothing New Under the Sun

These words, taken from the Book of Ecclesiastes (1:9)[2] may hint at the somber reality that the cycle of life and death is a given. Generations come and go. Embedded is the reality that a variety of widespread diseases have affected humanity over millennia. To contextualize, it may be useful to look back at how severe illness and epidemics have impacted biblical writers and Christian churches through the ages. In Old Testament literature the triplet of famine, war, and virulent disease are commonly referred to as signs of judgment (Lev 26:25–26; Jer 24:10; Eze 14:21). The horsemen of the Apocalypse (Rev 6:3–8) also announce a cataclysm of war, famine, and death. What is of interest in this study is not the fact that Christians, who considered themselves as saved and healed[3] by the blood of Christ, had to face outbreaks of deadly contagious diseases, but rather how they responded to these scourges.

As an early example[4] one can take the pandemic that ravaged the Roman Empire in the years 249–262 AD. It is commonly referred to as the Plague of Cyprian, because Cyprian, the Bishop of Carthage, wrote about its effects. In paragraph fourteen of his *De Mortalitas* he graphically describes the disease with all the suffering associated and contrasts it with the steady faith of the believer who can stand upright and rejoice in the life promised in Crist. But in this situation, Cyprian is also reflecting critically when he writes:

> And further, beloved brethren, what is it, what a great thing is it, how pertinent, how necessary, that pestilence and plague which seems horrible and deadly, searches out the righteousness of each one, and examines the minds of the human race, to see whether they who are in health tend the sick; whether relations affectionately love their kindred; whether masters pity their languishing servants; whether physicians do not forsake the beseeching patients....[5]

Cyprian admonishes his audiences to examine themselves. Are they living up to their ethical benchmark given to them by their Christian faith? Are they caring towards their neighbors and family relations? Are they merciful toward their employees? Do believers live up to their responsibilities? What one notices here is a clear emphasis on the common good. Individualism as it is widespread in the Western world today did not enter Cyprian's mind.

Three hundred years later Emperor Justinian, ruler of the Byzantine Empire, experienced in 541–549 AD an inbreak of the Bubonic Plague. It would be a pandemic that would eventually affect all of Europe, kill millions and severely weaken the Byzantine Empire. Justinian, who had led numerous military campaigns and had heavily invested in building projects (e.g. Hagia Sofia) was desperately needing funds. If the historian Procopius is to be believed, the emperor was ruthless towards his subjects:

> But trouble did not stop here; on the contrary, when the plague came, seizing in its grip the whole civilized world and especially the Roman Empire, and wiping out most of the farmers, and when for this reason the lands, as one might expect, had become deserted, the emperor shewed no mercy to the owners of these lands. For he never relaxed his exaction of the annual tax, not merely as he imposed it upon each separate person, but also exacting the share which fell to his deceased neighbors.[6]

Justinian had survived an attack of the plague on his own body and was a witness to the incredible death toll the pestilence caused in

Constantinople as thousands died daily.⁷ One would surmise that the severity of the disease would lead him to be compassionate. But in spite of his merits to Eastern Christianity, Justinian is an example of how a leader, to that a religious one, reacted selfishly in this situation.⁸

Of course, one cannot overlook the Black Death when talking about pandemics. It brought death from one third to half of the population in different parts of Europe,⁹ and in its wake famine, economic hardship, and general upheaval in the Late Middle Ages. How did Christians and their institutions respond to this pandemic? The middle of the fourteenth century, when the Plague first broke out (1347–51), was also a time during which mysticism as an expression of Christian spirituality flourished. The desire to be Christ-like, to love as he loved, to suffer as he suffered, favored initiatives that paid attention to the plight of the sick and the poor. Lay religious orders, like the Beguines in Northern Europe, saw it as an expression of practical spirituality to bring relief to the marginalized.

Another example is Catherine of Sienna, who as a child experienced the devastation brought about by the Black Death. Coupled with mystical experiences was her social engagement, the care for all citizens she called her "family," and a passion for the salvation of all.¹⁰ As people at that time had little or no understanding how viral infections spread and how important hygiene and physical distancing was in combatting a disease, they frequently exacerbated the problem by bringing the sick into their homes. The Plague was especially deadly where people lived together in cramped spaces like cities, fortresses, monasteries, and convents. At the Benedictine convent in Engelberg, Switzerland, 116 sisters died in the period of four months. For many monasteries, the large number of deaths meant a break in fellowship and an economic collapse.¹¹ Clearly, Christian compassion, fueled by their spiritual communion with God, played an important role in the life of the religious.

The next pandemic in this historical review is related to outbreaks of smallpox. A vaccine was accidentally discovered in the late eighteenth century in England, as the relatively mild cowpox virus provided immunity against the deadly smallpox virus. The Spanish King Charles IV, whose daughter had died of the smallpox, promoted an expedition by the court physician Francisco Javier de Balmis to bring the vaccine to all parts of the world (1803–1806). Twenty-two young orphan boys were selected to carry the cowpox infection across the ocean to Latin America. Balmis later traveled to the Philippines and China to bring the vaccine there.[12] This philanthropic expedition is considered to be the first international healthcare endeavor. It can also be seen as a successful combination of Enlightenment thought and Christian values to save millions of lives.

A reaction to the Spanish Flu (1918–1920) can serve as last example of how past pandemics influenced Christian responses. In order to curb the spread of the virus, the Swiss government issued in 1918, emergency orders relating to meeting in public places. Festivities, church services, concerts, theater performances and visits to the sick were forbidden and heavy fines were imposed on people who were caught breaking the decree.[13] When the peak of the epidemic seemed to have passed, the Reformed and Catholic State Churches were allowed to resume services, restaurants and inns could reopen, but gatherings of the independent evangelical churches were still forbidden. This unfair situation led to their initiative to unite as an association in order to demonstrate strength and unity in their lobbying with the government.[14] Up to that point, each independent church did its own thing. External pressure forced the leaders to reconsider. As there was more that united than divided them, they saw the need to present themselves as a united front. It can be argued that this decision, brought about by the constraints of the pandemic, was an early ecumenical moment among the churches and communities that normally emphasized their distinctiveness.

This historical review has shown that the responses by Christians to epidemic situations was not limited to prayers, but generally expressed themselves in outward gestures to the benefit of all. The example provided by the Swiss situation during the Spanish Flu provides an inter-ecclesial context. Pandemics can influence our understanding of what church is about. If we talk about the church, then it also makes sense to reflect on the nature of the work of the Holy Spirit in the overall mission of God. With this in mind, we turn to the present situation. How the churches have responded to extraordinary circumstances can be seen from two points of view, an institutional and a parochial one. For this reason, we first pay attention to responses given by church bodies and organizations, then we will look at how particular local churches have reacted.

Responses by Large Church Bodies and Organizations

Many people had to submit to self-isolation as countries across the globe decreed lockdowns as a response to the rapid spread of infections with the coronavirus. Generally speaking, the first reaction was an "we are all in this together" attitude. This popular sentiment was palpable when people began to clap, bang dishes, light candles, hold banners or sing at a given time of the day in solidarity and support for medical staff for their relentless dedication to save lives. More specifically religious responses were manifest when, for instance, sixty-five churches and movements of different confessions united in the British Isles to produce "The UK Blessing" which has been watched online over five million times.[15] Anyone watching this video will notice that this was not just a common project, a professional performance, but also an expression of deep faith that can be attributed to the move of the Holy Spirit. Similarly, Christian churches in India made a video in which a blessing was sung in thirty-one languages spoken on the subcontinent.[16] To give a third example, in the wake of Pentecost a movement began called "Germany prays together." It included churches from different traditions and received support from the government.[17] The same group has since also prayed for peace in Ukraine. In many places there was a common sense of encouragement and hope in spite of the suffering, loss of life and great uncertainty about what would happen next. The basic message was "God is with us."

Thanks to digital communication and social media all major churches, denominational bodies and networks were quick in providing information and issuing help to all who logged in. They made resources available for their church leaders, but also more generally for the believers. The Roman Catholic Church for instance created a COVID-19 Commission on March 20, 2020, to "to express the Church's solicitude and care for the whole human family facing the COVID-19 pandemic."[18] Churches with a strong sacramental tradition, like the Orthodox churches, were facing an existential crisis as to how they could receive the eucharist as this is a fundamental part of their worship. At first, the discussion often centered on the proper administration of the rite. But more fundamental than organizational and clerical considerations was, in the words of the Liturgy of St. Basil the Great, partaking in "the one bread and cup in the communion of the Holy Spirit."[19] At the same time these churches provided a wide number of spiritual and practical resources for the faithful.[20]

Similarly the Evangelical Lutheran Church of America issued a thirty-six page document based on an ecumenical consultation that included Methodist, Episcopal, Baptist, Presbyterian and Roman Catholic participants originally called "Resuming Care-Filled Worship and Sacramental Life During a Pandemic."[21] Advice is given how to properly administrate Holy Communion and Baptism, but, in my opinion just as importantly, frequent reference is made to the empowerment given by the Holy Spirit and encourages the believers to trust in the gifts and work of the Spirit. In the conclusion to that document the authors recall the words of the prophet Micah on what God requires, namely "to do justice, and to love kindness, and to walk humbly with your God" (Micah 6:8); adding, "The COVID-19 pandemic has radically changed our lives and our world. It has not, however, changed what God requires of us."[22] This reminder nicely leads to the COVID resources provided by churches that are characterized less by their sacramental life and more by sharing the Gospel in "word and deed."

The World Communion of Reformed Churches is a communion of 233 churches rooted in the historic traditions of the Reformation, thus comprising Congregational, Reformed, Presbyterian, United and Uniting, as well as the Waldensian churches. It put together an impressive number of resources that its member churches have provided. They range from practical tips on how to stop the spread of COVID-19 to a variety of suggestions on how to live as a church in times of physical distancing. There are suggestions on how to meet in small groups and includes lists of churches offering online services. Other websites point to the need to financially support congregations hardest hit by the pandemic. Pastoral letters, news highlights, and partner resources are listed.[23]

The Anglican Communion also pulled resources together after an appeal by the Archbishop of Canterbury.[24] The Anglican Alliance provides a resource hub with information about COVID-19 as such and how churches can respond in many ways, for instance by providing care for the most vulnerable.[25] Central to their initiatives is the fact that their churches are "Together in Unity."

Then there are the associations that relate beyond a particular church tradition like the World Council of Churches, the Evangelical World Alliance, or the Pentecostal World Fellowship. They all have responded swiftly. The website of the World Council of Churches (WCC), a fellowship of 352 churches representing more than half a billion Christians, has in its resource section, twenty-two questions being answered by a support team. Issues raised include responding to increased domestic violence due to confinement and how to accompany people with mental illness. On occasion of the commemoration of the first year of the pandemic in March 2021, the WCC published a book entitled *Voices of Lament, Hope, and Courage*. It was put together as "a resource for use in prayer groups, congregational services, personal prayer, and in the pastoral accompaniment of those directly affected in different ways by the pandemic" and responded to the spiritual needs of Christians.[26] The World Evangelical Alliance, networking with 143 national alliances, has digitally published resources for church leaders, for national alliances, for business leaders, for health professionals and families. Each section is filled with further links, documents, videos, and apps.[27] Finally, we can mention the efforts of the Pentecostal World Fellowship, a loosely connected association of classical Pentecostal churches relating to about as many as 120 million believers. Next to the relevant information that one could expect on its website there is a webinar that covers medical, pastoral, social, and spiritual aspects on how to respond as disciples of Christ in the face of the challenges posed by the coronavirus.[28] Interesting is not only the scope of concern and width of application, but also the fact that church leaders as well as the general public can benefit from this fifty-four minute video.

As we have looked at various church bodies, organizations, and fellowships one insight is overwhelmingly clear. Without their digital initiatives, it would have been very difficult to respond to such a severe pandemic, to so many churches in such a quick and efficient way. With regard to the IT specialists in charge one could paraphrase Winston Churchill's speech in the wake of the Battle of Britain in the summer of 1940 by saying, "Never in the field of urgent human communication was so much owed by so many to so few." What became clear was the fact that being part of God's church is more than what meets the eye on any given Sunday. This clarity expressed itself through repeated insistence that the Holy Spirit was both indwelling their institutions and the individual believers. More on that and what these recent initiatives may mean to the global Christian church will be addressed later. We will, for the sake of broader perspective, need to shift the focus of attention, namely to insights gained from local and national churches. Were there positive discoveries? How did they meet challenges?

Local Churches Responding to the Coronavirus

In order to receive a first impression a short questionnaire was sent by the author to seventy-two people across the globe. It contained only two questions. The first: was there a positive consequence that the church of the responder experienced due to the challenges imposed by the pandemic? The other question asked whether the present situation impacted the relationship with other churches. Interestingly, a lot more information was volunteered. To be meaningful, men and women were contacted, representing a variety of churches across six continents. Forty-eight of them replied. The analysis that follows does not in any way claim to offer empirical data. Rather, it is intended to give an overview of what has been going on.

Basically, the responses centered on four clusters. First, there was a sense that the churches across the globe had to face the fact that they were living in the context of the twenty-first century. Another insight was that the church could demonstrate its life and relevance to the public. A very strong bundle of responses focused on the family and the home. The fourth cluster centered on serving the needy.

To be Church in the Twenty-First Century

Similarly, to the Christian churches and organizations mentioned before, the pandemic demonstrated the importance of the church's digital presence. This has been evident not only for the sake of worship, but also in terms of community support and education.[29] Some responders also mentioned that online services facilitated worship across larger distances[30] and even across denominational boundaries.[31] What has been the case before to a certain degree is now increasingly happening, namely that parishioners are dual church adherents, formally belonging to one church but frequently also attending (digital) services of other churches. One of the challenges today is to explore the nature and impact of virtual koinonia.[32]

Another discovery widely shared was that in the first months of the pandemic "attendance" grew much larger than in comparison to the usual physical presence at a service taking place in a church building.[33] Examples given were for instance by a Pentecostal church whose attendance grew from ca. 250 persons at in house events to 1000–1400 viewers online in the Chicago area. A seasonal Episcopal church in Florida grew because those living in the North of the United States during the summer months would join online. Their "attendance" doubled due to digital services.[34] To that one could add streamed services that were followed by people from overseas.[35] This may especially be the case for migrant workers abroad and believers in countries where Christian worship is restricted. For such groups online services are the only means of spiritual fellowship. The increased digitalization has made it easier for them to be part of the church. However, this phenomenon did not last. Many got used to spending free Sundays and did not immediately return to church once the restrictions were eased. For those people who so far did not attend services in person but had been awakened by watching online services, the question arose how they could be invited to the physical church community once congregational worship in buildings was the norm again.[36]

A number of responders felt that the COVID-19 situation was an opportunity to seize and that a challenge presented itself to be innovative, especially with regard to evangelism and discipleship.[37] An impressive example was given by the Anglican Rev. Nicky Gumbel, from Holy Trinity Brompton (HTB). He is convinced that the present situation is a great opportunity for the church. In order to illustrate this, he shared that the Alpha Courses offered by HTB, which are usually attended by around 500 persons, where recently reaching 1,900 people because the course had gone online. Nicky Gumbel provided a second example citing the HTB marriage course, usually attended by eighty to 100 couples, had been attended by 8,500 couples during lockdown. Rev. Gumbel added that during their online Holy Spirit weekends, which for obvious reasons did not take place in the context of emotive in-person worship, a good number of conversions took place and charismatic giftings by the Holy Spirit were evident.[38] Some responders mentioned a spiritual awakening as people faced self-isolation and rediscovered their faith, desired to be closer to God and began to request more teaching.[39] There is indeed a greater demand for online learning. Seminaries and colleges had to adapt. Regarding online education and discipleship, the churches, seminaries, and colleges were challenged to respond quickly.[40] At the same time, it is clear that paying attention to best practices in online education is essential.[41]

However, there was also an appeal not to forget those who are not able to "connect" especially the elderly who have not learned to master the internet, and the poor who cannot afford a mobile phone. Taking that into account, parishioners were contacted by phone. One pastor in Ghana called all 900 members of his congregation,[42] sermons were printed out and dropped in mailboxes.[43] Many churches, especially in rural areas, made a lot of progress in getting digitally organized. Some of them received help with digital material from other churches.[44]

Finally, discussions began across different denominations on how best to be church digitally. For instance, the journal of Sárospatak Reformed Theological Academy in Hungary, initiated a conversation including Lutheran, Pentecostal, Adventist, and Roman Catholic contributors.[45]

To Be "Church Outside the Walls"

The heading to this section is of course in reference to the "Basilica of St. Paul Outside the Walls," a church that had first been built outside the Aurelian Wall of Rome in the fourth century AD. It serves as a symbol of the church to be outside its own walls. The coronavirus challenged the church to abandon its usual surrounding and be present in the open and somewhat undefended territory. What is asked for is being church in a creative way. In Germany for instance, as indoor Easter celebrations were not possible due to the lockdown, church members received Easter meditations per mail and were invited to go to the streets and shopping malls to be witnesses of Christ's resurrection. Congregations and brass bands marched through the quarter. They discovered a new way of being church.[46] Churches also united for a common purpose, not immediately tied to their usual roles.[47] They responded to the needs of others, regardless of their religious affiliation or non-religious outlook. This public presence is significant in an increasingly secular and at the same time multi-religious world.[48] Being "church outside the walls" demonstrated to many that the mission of God in Christ and through the Holy Spirit was possible outside the expected frame and usual context. They could not congregate in a dedicated building nor approach a consecrated altar, but the assurance of the presence of the Holy Spirit, wherever they were, was of the essence.

To be Church in the Family and at Home

During the pandemic, many people newly recognized the importance of the family as a nucleus of faith and worship.[49] Some churches with a well-developed IT department not only aired online services for adults but also digital Sunday school classes for children and virtual meetings for young adults. Small groups, generally better known among the newer churches, were now seen as an alternative expression of koinonia by many historic churches. Homes can turn to temples and Zoom meetings become platforms for affirming one's faith and sharing concerns for prayer.[50]

Generally, these micro networks of building faith and human support demonstrated an increase in shared involvement among parishioners and gave them a sense of communion.[51] However, the responders also were aware that Christians should not fall into the temptation of being self-centered.[52] Much emphasis was therefore given to the role of the church in caring for the needy.

To be Church for Those Who are in Need

The first line of support was to those who were economically affected.[53] Street vendors who had to stay in their simple dwellings, migrant workers and low-income employees that were fired as well as small businesses owners whose income suddenly came to a standstill were helped with food and necessities. Often the churches cooperated with aid-organizations and the government to find appropriate ways of working together.[54] Sometimes they did so in cooperation with the major national church organizations.[55]

The other avenue of help was dedicated to the elderly and disabled.[56] Youth groups were going from door to door to do the shopping for people that belonged to a high-risk-group. It took a bit longer for church leaders to recognize that people with disabilities were also severely affected, especially in those areas where government help was completely missing or not well organized.

Finally, churches realized that they had to be emotionally supportive. A good example happened in Hungary. The Reformed Pastoral Service in Hungary had to substantially increase their number of volunteers to respond to the many phone calls of people that felt lonely, had challenges caused by failure, alcoholism, depression, domestic violence, and problems with the workplace, or the absence of employment. Many were afraid of falling ill, suffered or had to cope with loss of life in the family and were glad that they could get in touch with someone who took them seriously.[57] Emotional support was not only important for the laity. For some pastors, changing to mostly digital ministry was arduous work. While some clergy found a work-life-balance and even had time to write,[58] other pastors were faced with an increased workload and realized that they had to look after themselves to avoid exhaustion. [59]

The many practical examples mentioned in the above paragraphs show that being compassionate in the name of Christ is both a physical and a spiritual exercise; it is both communal and personal. The pandemic revealed two common pneumatological misconceptions: a) that the Hoy Spirit is only active in given institutional structures, and b) that the Holy Spirit is only working in the lives of individuals. The former was common within the Roman Catholic Church prior to the Second Vatican Council, the latter is often found among Pentecostal and independent charismatic churches.

The Nature of the Church Revisited

Some churches have a long and strong diaconal tradition. For them, getting engaged in helping the poor, the sick and otherwise disadvantaged is part of their identity. Other churches, especially younger ones, have more of an emphasis on proclaiming the good news and pragmatic fellowship. This pandemic has challenged both kinds to reflect anew on the nature, constitution, and role of the church.[60] For those who have a strong sacramental tradition it includes deliberating on how the central role of the eucharist may be upheld if the physical participation is not or only privately possible. Other churches need to re-think more down to earth matters, for instance, how "works of mercy" can be extended in a secular environment. Both groups are challenged to stretch their understanding of what they took for granted for a long time and are invited to widen their understanding of the church. Rev. Dr. Jacqueline Grey, a Pentecostal theologian, asks if our vision of the church has been too small? She calls for a holistic church with a large vision in the light of Pentecost, in which not only the proclamation of the gospel is important, but also concrete engagement in the world. In her view, the world needs a church that is full of the Spirit and therefore is courageously prophetic, setting people free and speaking truth to power.[61]

This emphasis on the church, in the light of Pentecost, brings us to an important book on the Holy Spirit that was written by the Dominican theologian Yves Congar.[62] In the second volume, he studies three important aspects of the Spirit's work. First, the Spirit animates the church. Second, the Spirit is the breath of God in our lives. And third, the church is renewed by the Spirit. Congar speaks favorably about the Pentecostal and Charismatic renewal movements. What I would focus on is the role of the Spirit in the church; an aspect that Pentecostals often neglect and a reality that has come to the fore during this pandemic because the church is always more than structure, organization, fellowship, and doctrine. Could it be that we need to be more sensitive to the ecclesial dimension in our pneumatology? By implication that would mean that we need to acknowledge that God's church is one because the Spirit of God cannot be divided. In other words, it is the Holy Spirit that calls us from different churches and traditions together to the one body of Christ. The COVID-19 pandemic has, in a practical way, alerted us to that reality.

Widening the parameters of the church is more easily said than done. It is understandable that a number of responders pointed to the fact that their church had to look primarily for their own, they were somewhat in "survival mode,"[63] while other churches consciously reached out to set up programs with other churches precisely because they were in "survival mode" and realized that they had to pull their resources together. They were looking at the church as a global reality.[64] The primary focus was on helping. They looked at the global church as a means to uphold our common humanity as all are equally created in the image of God.[65]

COVID-19 tested large ecclesial bodies like the Roman Catholic Church and the members of the World Council of Churches in their intention to work toward peace, justice, and the care of creation[66] as part of the redemptive work of Christ in the power of the Holy Spirit for the sake of God's kingdom.

A new awareness of belonging to the body of Christ on a global level is indeed growing. It is focusing on what believers of all shapes and colors have in common, their faith in Jesus Christ; it can be expressed in common prayers, their hope in common witness and their love in common concern. This attitude can be subsumed as spiritual ecumenism. It is expressed by praying together with Christians of other denominations, for instance by video conferencing for weekly prayer meetings and support,[67] or having joint church services; online or physically distanced but socially and spiritually united.[68]

Another example of churches coming together in all parts of the world is provided by the Global Christian Forum, a platform for Christian churches, organizations, and movements to meet on equal ground and foster mutual respect as common challenges are addressed. This platform is shared by members of the historic churches like the Orthodox, the Roman Catholic Church, the churches of the Reformation, as well as the younger churches like evangelical, Pentecostal, and independent churches. The Global Christian Forum has produced COVID-19 related interviews, reflections, and other contributions from churches all over the world with the distinct feature that these pieces never have an exclusive character.[69] The church is called to be responsive to God's mission, not its own.

If one takes the potential impact of the global church further, then one must reflect on the plight of people that do not adhere to the Christian faith. This practical step was taken by the World Council of Churches in cooperation with the Pontifical Council for Interreligious Dialogue. They have released a document called "Serving a Wounded World in Interreligious Solidarity: A Christian Call to Reflection and Action During COVID-19 and Beyond."[70] The twenty-page document is a call to the followers of Jesus Christ to love and serve their neighbors. The parable of the Good Samaritan is a reminder that religious communities cannot pass the wounded by, and that help may come from a representative of another faith community. The document lays out the basis for interreligious solidarity, sets up principles and gives recommendations. It is the Spirit of Christ that crosses boundaries because God so loves the world.

Conclusion

[t] The first section of this chapter looked back at the history of the church and how Christians reacted to past pandemics. The impulse to care was there from the beginning. It is common knowledge that the building of infirmaries and hospitals go back in part to a response to these health challenges. The current reactions emphasize the need to help others in the name of Jesus Christ, the Savior who brought healing to humanity.

In the second step, we looked at Christian institutions and how they responded to the crisis. There it was evident that all churches and organizations were quick to connect in an effort to be actively responsible. They took advantage of social media and digital networks like never before. Technology was at the service of our spiritual calling. It is fair to assume that this avenue of communication will further develop and become more important even after this particular coronavirus has mutated to a seasonal epidemic like a flu.

As representatives of local churches were interviewed, the importance of personal contact became the most important feature. Furthermore, COVID-19 has in some sense also been a blessing in disguise because it caused the churches to demonstrate that they are alive and available to serve following the example of Christ. The Spirit bade them go.

Finally, the recent global pandemic has shed a light on the global church. Changes are often driven by necessity; they may include getting out of one's comfort zone. This process often starts with having a greater appreciation of one's national network, then develop from a regional denominational affiliation to a fellowship within the worldwide church and finally across ecclesial boundaries. This may express itself in the context of a common interest group in communication and action with a national government or international agencies because the challenge is simply too big as that it could be met by one group alone. As it was stated in the beginning, "We are all in this together." It might well be that the COVID-19 pandemic will go into the history books as an important puzzle piece that has contributed to a continual move towards greater unity within the global church, the body of Christ, because it is willed by the Spirit who animates the church.

Notes

1 This is a modified and expanded version of an article written at the beginning of the COVID-19 pandemic and published by Sage Journals under the title "COVID-19, the Church, and the Challenge to Ecumenism," Transformation 37:4 (Oct 2020).
2 Bible quotations are all taken from the New Revised Standard Version.
3 Keeping the double meaning of the Greek word σωζειν in mind.

4   The first pandemic that affected Christianity was probably the Antonine Plague (165 – 180 AD). It is commonly argued that Christianity grew during that time because Christians made a point to care for the sick. It is difficult to fact check this claim for the second century AD, but see the Article by Sarah K. Yeomans "The Antonine Plague and the Spread of Christianity" in *Biblical Archeological Society*, https://www.biblicalarchaeology.org/daily/ancient-cultures/daily-life-and-practice/the-antonine-plague-and-the-spread-of-christianity/, accessed March 1, 2023, and Lyman Stone "Christianity Has Been Handling Epidemics for 2000 Years", March 13, 2020, in *Foreign Policy* https://foreignpolicy.com/2020/03/13/christianity-epidemics-2000-years-should-i-still-go-to-church-coronavirus/, accessed March 1, 2023.

5   Cyprian of Carthage, *On the Mortality (or Plague) De Mortalitate*, https://www.ewtn.com/catholicism/library/on-the-mortality-or-plague-de-mortalitate-11412, accessed March 1, 2023.

6   Procopius, *The Anekdota*, Chapter 23, 20–22; https://penelope.uchicago.edu/Thayer/E/Roman/Texts/Procopius/Anecdota/23*.html, accessed March 1, 2023.

7   Procopius, *The Plague*, 542, in *Fordham University, Medieval Sourcebook*, https://sourcebooks.fordham.edu/source/542procopius-plague.asp, accessed March 1, 2023.

8   For a detailed account of the Justinian Plague see: William Rosen, *Justinian's Flea: Plague, Empire and the Birth of Europe* (London: Penguin Random House, 2008).

9   Suzanne Austin Alchon, *A Pest in the Land. New World Epidemics in a Global Perspective* (Albuquerque: University of New Mexico Press, 2003), 21, 29.

10 Donald Attwater, *The Penguin Dictionary of Saints* (Harmondsworth: Penguin Books, 1965), 211f.

11 Schweizerisches National Museum ed., Nonnen, *Starke Frauen im Mittelalter* (Berlin: Hatje Cantz, 2020), 124.

12 For a well-researched fictional account of the Balmis Expedition see: Julia Alvarez, *Saving the World* (Chapel Hill, NC: Algonquin Books, 2006).

13 Katja Schlegel, "Während der 'Spanischen-Grippe' 1918 war vieles wie heute – und doch ganz anders," *Aargauer Zeitung*, April 3, 2022, https://www.aargauerzeitung.ch/aargau/kanton-aargau/waehrend-der-spanische-grippe-1918-war-vieles-wie-heute-und-doch-ganz-anders-137587003#:~:text=Gottesdienste%2C%20Feste%2C%20

Besuche%20bei%20Kranken,die%20Spanische%20Grippe%20ihren%20 H%C3%B6hepunkt, accessed March 1, 2022.

14 "Die Geschichte der Freikirchen," *Freikirchen.ch*, https://freikirchen.ch/ueber-uns/geschichte/, accessed March 1, 2023.

15 "The UK Blessing – Churches sing 'The Blessing' over the UK," https://www.youtube.com/watch?v=PUtll3mNj5U&t=1s, accessed March 1, 2023.

16 "The Blessing – A Taste of Heaven- the Indian way in 31 languages," https://www.youtube.com/watch?v=Eb7g7-IIKVc, accessed March 1, 2023.

17 *Deutschland betet gemeinsam*, https://deutschlandbetetgemeinsam.de/, accessed August 23, 2020. The website has since been updated in view of the war in Ukraine.

18 Vatican COVID-19 Commission, http://www.humandevelopment.va/en/vatican-covid-19.html, accessed March 1, 2023.

19 Dassouras Nicholas, "From One Spoon to Many," *Public Orthodoxy*, https://publicorthodoxy.org/tag/coronavirus/ first accessed 23 August 2020, other contributions have since been added, see "Community or "Comspoonity"? on the same website, accessed March 1, 2023.

20 "COVID-19 Guidelines and Resources," *Orthodox Church in America*, https://www.oca.org/resources-coronavirus, accessed March 1, 2023.

21 Available now as "Care-filled Worship and Sacramental Life in a Lingering Pandemic," Evangelical Lutheran Church of America, https://download.elca.org/ELCA%20Resource%20Repository/Care-filled_Worship_and_Sacramental_Life_in_a_Lingering_Pandemic.pdf, accessed March 1, 2023.

22 *Care-filled Worship*, 31.

23 "Corona Virus Resources," World Communion of Reformed Churches, http://wcrc.ch/coronavirus-resources, accessed March 1, 2023.

24 "Anglican Communion Fund Covid Appeal," The Archbishop of Canterbury, https://www.archbishopofcanterbury.org/about/anglican-communion-fund/coronavirus-appeal, accessed March 1, 2023.

25 "COVID-19 Hub," Anglican Alliance, https://anglicanalliance.org/covid-19-resources-hub/, accessed August 23, 2020, and March 1, 2023.

26 "COVID-19 Resources," World Council of Churches, https://www.oikoumene.org/en/resources/documents/covid-19/questions-and-answers, accessed August 23, 2020.

27 "The Church Responding to COVID-19 with Faith, Hope and Love," World Evangelical Alliance, https://covid19.worldea.org/, accessed March 1, 2023.

28 "COVID-19 Response," Pentecostal World Fellowship, https://www.pwfellowship.org/covid-19. The webinar was moved to the site of the Pentecostal World Fellowship's World Missions Commission, http://pwfmissions.net/covid-19, accessed March 1, 2023.

29 The individual contributors are known to the author. Their names have been anonymized to protect their privacy. NG, United Kingdom (UK); AD, UK; CVL, Netherlands; DD, United States of America (USA); PM, Peru; ST, India; JT, Philippines; GW, Indonesia; ST, Thailand; KC, Australia.

30 KK, Costa Rica; CL, Philippines; SHW, Japan.

31 JT, USA; JG, Australia.

32 JLP, South Africa.

33 GR, Hungary; CVL; Netherlands; DD, USA; DBF, USA; PM, Peru; DB, Uruguay; ST, India; EB, Philippines.

34 DD, USA; DBF, USA, this phenomenon has been reported widely in religious online services across various denominations.

35 MTY, Philippines

36 NG, UK; ST, India.

37 SH, Switzerland; NG, UK; ST, Thailand.

38 Information drawn from an interview with Rev. Martin Stössel, director of Agape, Switzerland, shared on August 21, 2020.

39 LI, Nigeria/Switzerland; PI, India, JT, Philippines; GW, Indonesia; MC, Philippines; MS, American Samoa/ Fiji.

40 This has been a challenge for all institutions of higher education. In India, where for years the infrastructure has been lacking to accommodate and train enough students in theology and pastoral ministry, the need for online teaching was exacerbated due to the pandemic. The institution that is quicker and better will definitely benefit (PI, India).

41 So, for instance, JC, USA/Philippines.

42 SN, Ghana.

43 AD, UK.

44 JT, USA; AD, UK.

45 GR, Hungary.

46 CWO, Germany; SMN, France.

47 CVL, Netherlands.

48 In this regard see Marina Ngursangzeli Behera and Jean-Daniel Plüss, eds., *Conviction in an Optional Society. Pentecostal / Charismatic Christianity and Religious Pluralism* (Oxford, UK: Regnum Books, 2020).

49 SF, UK; JLP, South Africa; DP, India; JT, Philippines, CL, Philippines, TS, New Zealand/Samoa.

50 WGM, USA; GR, Hungary; DF, Samoa.

51 CS, USA; JS, Chile; PI, India; JG, Australia; KC, Australia.

52 The Reformer Martin Luther pointed to sin as being "incurvatus in se," that is being turned on oneself and living only an inward or self-sufficient life, forgetting the outward call to serve God and the others.

53 JBB, UK; DBF, USA; OV, Chile; SN, Ghana; DM, India; JT, Philippines; GW, Indonesia; ST, Thailand; EB, Philippines.

54 NG, UK; GR, Hungary; CVL, Netherlands; SN, Ghana.

55 JLP, South Africa.

56 GR, Hungary; JBB, UK; JG, Australia.

57 GR, Hungary "Crisis Hotline Expanded," *Reformed Church in Hungary*, May 10, 2020, https://reformatus.hu/english/news/crisis-hotline-expanded/. Similarly, "seelsorge.net" the online counseling platform of the Reformed churches in Switzerland recorded in 2020 a 42 percent increase in contacts as compared to the previous year. The staff had to be enlarged from twenty-one to thirty volunteers: Kirchenbote 9 (2020), 20. Meeting emotional needs was also mentioned by JG, Australia.

58 JT, Philippines; AJ, Sweden.

59 KC, Australia; ST, India.

60 SF, UK.

61 Jacqueline Grey, "Is your Vision of the Church too Small?" Alphacrucis, June 17, 2020, https://crucis.ac.edu.au/your-vision-church-too small/?fbclid=IwAR1eyy-f09YPRm57IUM9Xrmf93oaFJMtwNEuIKW9iLClwo1yvvZHmwpd3SsKc.

62 Yves Congar, *I Believe In The Holy Spirit*, 3 volumes in one, (New York: Seabury Press, 1983). The original French publication: *Je crois en l'Esprit Saint* (Paris : Edition du Cerfs, 1979/1980). For my research I have used the German translation, *Der Heilige Geist* (Freiburg: Herder, 1982).

63 SH, Switzerland; SF, UK.

64 JS, Chile; CWO, Germany mentioned this specifically and indirectly it was referred to by many other responders.

65 A point that especially Catholics frequently make, LI, Nigeria/Switzerland.

66 Some people have rightly pointed out that aggressive viruses like HIV, SARS, Ebola, and COVID-19 have all been related to the trade and consumption of wild animals and the transmission of the viruses to humans. Others mentioned the remarkable increase in air quality in urban areas due to the drastically diminished traffic during lockdown. In view of these realities, the current pandemic is also relevant from an ecological point of view.

67 SMN, France; GR, Hungary; CWO, Germany/Southeast Asia; OO, Ghana; DP, India; ST, India; CL, Philippines, MS, American Samoa/Fiji; TS, New Zealand/Samoa.

68 JT, USA.

69 These contributions were available under "recent posts" and "news" at http://www.globalchristianforum.org. However, the website has been reorganized since.

70 "Serving a Wounded World in Interreligious Solidarity: A Christian Call to Reflection and Action During COVID-19 and Beyond," World Council of Churches, https://www.oikoumene.org/en/resources/documents/wcc-programmes/interreligious-dialogue-and-cooperation/serving-a-wounded-world-in-interreligious-solidarity-a-christian-call-to-reflection-and-action-during-covid-19, accessed March 1, 2023.

19 State-Church Partnerships: Opportunities and Challenges in Spirit-Filled Responses to the Global Pandemic

Ulrik Josefsson and Niclas Lindgren

Abstract

In this article, the relationship between Society and Church is discussed, with a special focus on relief and development in the light of the UN goals on sustainable development.[1] Pentecostalism is a major global actor with a strong passion for social action. It is mainly a grassroots movement and has not always had strong connections to official structures. The case studied here is the Swedish Pentecostal relief and development organization PMU, which to a large extent, is run through governmental funding. The conclusion is that, despite some challenges, Pentecostals have great opportunities to cooperate with official partners.

Introduction

The ongoing pandemic has put all people throughout the world in an exposed situation and has shown that we live in deep interdependence. No one is safe until everyone is safe. All of us share responsibility to minimize the harm of the pandemic, but at the same time, to realize that some people are more vulnerable than others. During the time of restrictions and lockdowns due to the current situation, a long-term positive development has come to an end. Poverty is again increasing among the most vulnerable, and the possibilities to reach the sustainable development goals of the 2030 Agenda seem very limited. In this situation, we need to come together and, with joined hands, work for a better future for all. States and global institutions have their roles and responsibilities. However, governmental efforts will not be enough. All good forces must be engaged and cooperate when global challenges are to be tackled.

A growing number of scholars have started to recognize the role of religion in development and the role of religious communities and faith-based organizations. Throughout history, the Church has played a major role in dealing with social problems, and today Pentecostalism is one of the biggest social movements and perhaps the fastest growing one. With access to both individuals and communities, Pentecostal churches can motivate social engagement and community transformation that includes both behavioral change and its ethical foundation. Elisabeth Brusco has shown that the conversion of an individual can start a societal transformation from below.[2] Miller and Yamamori have shown that groups of what they call progressive Pentecostals around the globe are already involved in massive societal development.[3] Dena Freeman argues that Pentecostal churches are probably the most effective change agents based both on their communal understanding of faith and the theological value-based action.[4] In a situation where all good forces need to work together, there is an increasing possibility for cooperation between civil society organizations and churches on one side and official structures, states, and global institutions on the other. This article aims to elaborate on how Pentecostals can cooperate with a wide range of organizations in the common strive for societal development.

In Sweden, the Pentecostal church has a long experience of such cooperation, and we will use the Swedish Pentecostal movement as a case to learn from when it comes to possibilities and challenges in cooperation between church and government. The questions discussed here are: What are the possibilities and challenges in state-church cooperation? How can a Pentecostal theological foundation for wider cooperation be described? What lessons can be learned from the experiences of such cooperation in Sweden?

Background

When starting the discussion on social engagement and global relief and development work the theological foundation needs to be considered. Below we give a short background mainly based on the work done by the Pentecostal Relief and Development Partners network.

Understanding of the Gospel

We believe that the understanding of the gospel affects the identity and the societal role one can play. Pentecostals sometimes struggle with their holistic identity and deal with poverty as primarily a spiritual thing. Others struggle in their role as societal actors due to the teaching about us as strangers on earth and that we, therefore, do not have to care about the societal challenges and the environment but that it is enough to save souls. It is, therefore, important to deepen both theology and practice around societal and political engagement and to link theological processes to deepen knowledge also in other academic disciplines and development theories. Believers do not always have the language for a relevant social analysis and, therefore, need to learn more about society from political, sociological, and economic perspectives. Otherwise, there is a risk that the church will become part of the problem and an easy target for politicians who want to make use of the church for their own political agendas. A too narrow and spiritualized understanding of societal challenges might limit both language and understanding, thus making the church irrelevant to today's challenges. In this process, we also need to shed light on what might be called institutional or structural sin; the structures and systems that keep people in poverty. Pentecostal churches are sometimes too focused on individual sin and salvation, which makes it difficult for them to play a relevant role in responding to the global challenges of our time. It is crucial to deepen the dialogue on a holistic view of salvation, in which all broken relationships are to be restored.

Identification with the Poor

Identification with the poor and vulnerable is at the core of the biblical narrative. In Exodus, we read about a God who sees and hears and who promises to act on the cry of the people (Exod 3:7–10 ; 6:6–8). It is clear that the kind of poverty and captivity, as well as the freedom that was required for the people of Israel, was holistic. It regarded total redemption from political oppression, economic poverty, and even slavery, social exclusion, and spiritual restrictions.

In Matthew 25, we read about how Jesus identifies himself with the vulnerable. For example, Jesus was born into a family that could not afford the stipulated lamb to be sacrificed when a Jewish boy was born (Luke 2:24; Exod 12:8). Throughout Jesus' life, we see that he is on the side of the vulnerable, not only in principle and morally, but he really lives his life there. He belongs to them and not to the powerful and influential. We usually have no problem imagining Jesus identifying with the poor and vulnerable, but he went further than that; he was one of the vulnerable. God thus enters history as one of the powerless, humiliated, and marginalized. The mission of Jesus was to bring light to the darkness, loosen unjust shackles, and give the oppressed holistic freedom (Luke 4:18–19). Like Jesus, the church is not only there for the poor; she is the poor in many countries. She, therefore, is the voice for and by the poor at the same time. The church thus voices the perspectives of the poor and marginalized and can do so even more intentionally on a local, national and international level.

Swedish Pentecostal Mission and Relief Work

Among others, David Bundy has described the important role Scandinavian missionaries have played in the spread of Pentecostalism.[5] The Swedish Pentecostal Mission has throughout history acted in a holistic manner, making no division between social ministry and evangelism. Building clinics was as important as starting Bible schools for the Swedish Pentecostal missionaries. Some missionaries testify to how the two Bible stories "The Prodigal Son" and "The Good Samaritan" became a collective description of the mission call. Individual missionary initiatives could have their identity in one of the two Bible stories, but overall, there was a holistic view of the Swedish Pentecostal mission. The lost would be brought into God's arms, and the beaten would be healed and restored. However, it was not just about helping individuals to a better life. The eagerness to see a change has also taken other forms, aiming for authorities and whole communities to change. When possibilities emerged for funding through the government, the Swedish Pentecostal movement, in 1965, formed an NGO, PMU, through which the churches could get support from Governmental aid money for the social ministry they were already involved.

Religious Actors in Development and Relief

Within secular circles of relief and development aid, religion and the role of faith-based actors are frequently being discussed.[6] There is a growing consensus that the role of religion in development is crucial and that religious leaders are key if we are to succeed in the handling of both local and global challenges. For example, the Minister of Development Aid in the Swedish Government recently said that studies show that 75 percent of the people in Africa trust their religious leaders more than they trust their elected politicians.[7] This shows the importance of religious leaders being conscious and responsible for what kind of messages they convey to their constituency and that Northern politicians are aware of this fact. In most countries of the world, faith and religion are fundamental parts of society and life.[8] Faith is an important aspect of people's identity and everyday life. It is part of their worldview, forming how they relate to one another and society. This means that faith and religion also affect change processes. Faith-based actors and groups, therefore, have great legitimacy to challenge and influence negative norms and systems, and support from religious leaders can be crucial in the process of change. Beliefs are very strong drivers for changing attitudes and behaviors at all levels of society. When West Africa fought the Ebola crisis some years ago, the former Minister of Development Aid in Sweden said that it was not until the aid initiatives cooperated with local religious leaders that they succeeded. The reason for this was that the crisis, to a large extent, was driven by deeply culturally rooted behavior, for example, around funerals and the treatment of the dead. Only the religious leaders had the keys to, in a culturally appropriate manner, address the behavioral changes that were needed.[9]

Pentecostal Relief and Development

Pentecostalism is growing globally and, according to current research, contributes, to social development in many places.[10] This movement has the potential to play a major role in the global work for justice and poverty reduction, as well as in building social capital and a democratic, equal, and inclusive culture. In many countries, it is the church that, to a large extent, gives people access, for example, to health care and education. Furthermore, the church enables rapid response to disaster situations through its local presence. At the same time, as being a major force for transformation, the global Pentecostal movement also sometimes holds attitudes and behavioral patterns that risk hindering the fight against oppression and poverty and the strive for respected human rights.

Pentecostal Voice and Advocacy

The broad Pentecostal network is important for not only changing the situation on the ground and meeting people's needs but also for communication and advocacy. Advocacy is an extension of the biblical responsibility to love and care for others by speaking out against social and structural injustice and calling for restoration and change (Prov 31:8–9). We advocate out of a commitment to love our neighbor and a commitment to identify with the marginalized and oppressed as equals (Heb 13:3; Gal 2:10). The size and the scope of the Pentecostal movement make its advocacy work to reinstate fair, impartial, and accessible systems and structures for the marginalized and oppressed and for equal access to opportunity and resources very important. It is also of great value to listen to studies like *Voices of the Poor* when developing a Pentecostal response to global poverty and injustice.[11]

Church and Society

When Pentecostal churches engage in societal development, the interaction is based on the identity of the church in a specific society. Therefore, we need to briefly discuss the underlying ideas of church and society and how the two of them interact.

What is the Role and Identity of the Church?

In the classical work of Richard Niebuhr, *Christ and Culture*, Niebuhr defines five different ways of being the church in culture or society. The model, "Christ against culture," is where the church lives in opposition to the culture, which is seen as deprived, worldly, and against God. The opposite is the model "Christ of culture," where church and faith are seen to be fundamentally compatible with the surrounding culture and that the kingdom of God is embedded in the culture. These are the two extremes in church and culture relations. "Christ above culture" would see the good in society as an expression of God's presence, but culture could never embrace the fullness and beauty of God as the church could. "Christ and culture in paradox" would argue that the two belong to different realities that never can be compared, whereas "Christ as the transformer of culture" sees a strong connection between two entities where the church forms a kind of counterculture with higher standards and the task of transforming the culture after the image of Christ.[12] How a specific church looks at the relation to a specific cultural context highly defines the role it will take.

Niebuhr's theory is about the relationship between church and society with a focus on the interaction and how different churches view society. That view is partly formed by the historical and sociological context. At the same time, the inner logic of the church, or ecclesiology, forms an identity by which the church is acting in the world. Whereas Niebuhr discusses the relation between church and society, in the book *Models of the Church*, Avery Dulles, deals with different identities of church or types of ecclesiology. In his first edition, Dulles uses five metaphors to describe different ecclesiologies. The model "institution" emphasizes the structure and order of the church that gives clear roles but can, according to Dulles, probably not be the fundamental aim of the church. "Sacrament" sees the church as the visible sign of God's presence in the world and puts emphasis on both the visible and invisible nature of the church. In the model, "mystical relation," focus is put on deep community both with God and between members. That kind of deep community is seen as the true nature of the church. Church as "herald" is more focusing on the proclamation of the church. It is seen as a messenger of God's saving love in the world. Church as "servant" emphasizes the Church's commitment to social justice. The role of the church is seen as doing what Jesus did in caring for the oppressed and thereby building the kingdom of God. In the second edition, Dulles added the model "community of disciples," which, in one way, is an integration of the former models. It emphasizes that the church is a community of people that follow Jesus.[13]

Niebuhr's theory deals with the principles of the relation between church and society, and Dulles has identified six models of ecclesiology. The sociologists of religion Stanley Hauerwas and William Willimon have formed a theory based on the mission and mentality of the church. They call the first one "activist," and here, the focus is put on the social activity of the church, mainly its efforts for social change and justice. The second form they call "conversionist." Here, the focus is on proclaiming the gospel and on individual conversion. The third form of appearance they call "confessional." Here, the focus is on the identity of the church and that all the church does is based on her confession, both the social action and the proclamation.[14]

Pentecostal churches are navigating this landscape, and different groups are taking different positions. All the three theories mentioned above are ideal metaphorical types. At the same time, the different theories show that the church's view on the identity, mission, and interaction with the surrounding society is highly affecting how she thinks and acts. In this regard, we need to remember that Pentecostalism is multi-faced. Pentecostalism is, as Allan Anderson has shown, not one expression but many.[15] Therefore, the discussion on how Pentecostalism interacts with the world must be defined by a contextual understanding of which Pentecostalism we are talking about. One of the more influential descriptions of Pentecostal ecclesiology is the one of Veli-Matti Kärkkäinen in the book *Ecclesiology*. He refers to different observers asking whether it is possible to define a specific Pentecostal ecclesiology. The Pentecostal view of the church could be described as a charismatic, missionary, and eschatological fellowship.[16]

How May We Understand Society?

Now we need to enter the discussion from another angle, asking ourselves how to understand society. One of the leading sociologists, Antony Giddens, states in his book *Sociology* that society is more than a specific people who share territory, language, values, and behavior. Society "also includes institutions [. . .] and the relatively stable relationships between them. The enduring patterns formed by relationships among people, groups, and institutions form the basic social structure of a society."[17] To discuss and develop this multi-dimensional understanding of society requires what Mill calls a sociological imagination, the ability to step outside one's own society precisely to understand the contextual structure of that specific society. That means that society is a complex interwoven entity of relations in a specific context where individual agents form a specific set of behaviors that could be understood, as Giddens frames it in the theory of structuration.[18]

In order to get the different societal relations to work together, there is a need for social capital. Relations are not enough to get a society to work; there is also a need for trust in the relations. The concept of social capital is about how trustful relations are and that trustful relations are essential qualities in a strong society. Robert Putnam shows that social networks and the economic system together form a well-functioning society only when there is a certain amount of trust involved.[19] This means that society depends on the quality of its relations and that society, therefore, is relational. In line with that, the Swedish historian Lars Trägårdh has defined the inner logic of a society as its theory of love. If a society is built on trust, who are you going to trust? Trägårdh shows that trust and dependence are built differently in different societies. In American society, for example, the strong link is between the individual and different parts of the civil society, especially the family. In Germany, the line of dependency instead is built between the state and the civil society. In the Swedish society, Trägårdh writes about state-individualism, where individual independence is strongly promoted, and the axis of dependence is between the state and the individual.[20] This means that even in societies with strong relational trust, that trust can be directed in a different direction. Society is therefore relational, but the question is what relations and between whom.

Many observers of society have shown that the understanding of the role of civil society has exploded during the last decades. With growing globalization and supranational agencies, the different groups of civil society can build a bridge of agency and democratization. That means that the different actors within the global civil society can and must play an important role in the formation of the new global village.[21] Especially groups that share global values can be influential in forming a global societal logic, such as NGOs or different parts of the church.[22]

To summarize this discussion, it is obvious that the relationship between the church and society is contextually formed. It is dependent on the nature of both the specific church and the type of society where it is based. It is also relational in the meaning that social capital and a certain amount of trust are needed in the interaction. Furthermore, it is intentionally based on the identity or ecclesiology of the church. Finally, we can see that the church-society interaction is not only formed by ideas and theories but also by pragmatic actions within the civil society in any given context and that the arena for such actions is growing, not least for the church, as the expectations on the church as a societal actor grows.

Pentecostal Reflection on Church and Society

The field of interaction between the church and society from a Pentecostal perspective has gained more interest during the last decades. Social action, charity, and benevolence have, from the early days of Pentecostalism, been included in the strategy for international and domestic mission. However, there has been a resistance to engaging in societal problems on a more structural level. Lately, Pentecostalism has been thoroughly studied by social scientists, who have explored the rapid growth and the growing societal impact of Pentecostalism. One example is the European research network GloPent, with the digital journal *PentecoStudies*.[23] Another example is the ground-breaking book *Global Pentecostalism* by Donald Miller and Tetsunao Yamamori, where they try to map up and understand the growing group of socially engaged Pentecostals (whom they call progressive Pentecostals).[24] Among theologians in the field, one of the pioneers is the American theologian Douglas Petersen and his book *Not by Might nor by Power*.[25] In recent years, theologians have been engaged in developing a theology for social change. Among them, Amos Yong with *In the Days of Caesar* is important. Yong places Pentecostalism in relation to other political theologies and shows that a Pentecostal contribution must take action based on the theological distinctives of the movement.[26] More recently, the two-volume work *The Holy Spirit and Social Justice* has been published.[27] The articles elaborate on Pentecostalism as a catalyst for social reform. Two major things are obvious in that work: the empowering experience of the Spirit is seen as the driving force, and a radically holistic view of the gospel is the framework. Together this concept of Pentecostalism is forming a strong theological motivation for the church to be a socially engaged change agent in the world. In addition to this, the Pentecostal global theological association World Alliance for Pentecostal Theological Education used its journal Pentecostal Education to publish a thematic issue in Fall 2021 dealing with social engagement and community transformation with articles written from a Global South perspective.[28] With this foundation, we will now move on to discussing the partnership between the Swedish Pentecostal movement and governmental actors and thereafter discuss how such a partnership can be used in handling the ongoing pandemic and in the fight against global poverty and injustice in general.

Pentecostal Partnership

After some sections of theoretical reflections on church and society we now turn to a more practical and empirical perspective. Focus is on how the Swedish Pentecostal movement and its international partner churches have worked with mission in relation to governmental funding.

Experiences from Sweden and churches in the Global South

The Swedish Pentecostal movement has chosen to cooperate and receive funding from the government in many different parts of its ministry. It regards, for example, the children and youth ministry, the folk high schools, the theological seminary, the ministry for drug addicts, and the global relief and development work through PMU. Partnership with the government has many benefits. As for PMU, it has been working with financial support from the Swedish Government since 1965 as one funding stream supporting the work it does together with partner churches and organizations. Obviously, there are opportunities but also risks. On the positive side are the funding opportunities. Another thing is the legitimacy it gives us as a Pentecostal movement and the broad network of like-minded actors working for global justice and social work in Sweden. Networking with others keeps you constantly reflecting on identity, goals, and methods and keeps you from isolation. It also gives a chance to share important perspectives and stories not heard if faith-based actors are not around the table.

Clearly, there are also risks. One would be losing our faith-based identity and our holistic view on both poverty and development. It is something that constantly has to be on the radar for any relief and development agency cooperating with the government. Another risk is to become an actor that comes too close to political power and (maybe without noticing) develops strategies that detour from basic values and foundational documents. Yet another risk is becoming dependent on external financial support for the ministry of the church. PMU has struggled with all these risks over the years but still concluded that they can all be overcome if handled intentionally and that the benefits are greater than the risks. The experience of PMU is also the expectation of being a change agent, both from the constituency of Swedish churches, the partner networks, and other development actors in Sweden, as well as the Swedish government. This is also clearly expressed in many Pentecostal networks today, where Pentecostal churches have been growing fast and now are the majority churches in their respective societies and communities. With size and strength comes responsibility, and many leaders now express that it falls on us to act for justice in the fight against corruption and to be the voice of the people.

There are, according to the Swedish Pentecostal movement, many reasons why broader partnerships with Governments and with multilateral actors like the UN bodies are important. The 2030 Agenda lays a foundation for the fight against global poverty. In the Agenda, the following is stated:

> We are resolved to free the human race from the tyranny of poverty and want and to heal and secure our planet. We are determined to take the bold and transformative steps which are urgently needed to shift the world onto a sustainable and resilient path. As we embark on this collective journey, we pledge that no one will be left behind.[29]

The 2030 Agenda also stresses that "We are determined to foster peaceful, just and inclusive societies which are free from fear and violence."[30] Furthermore, it is stated that:

> [W]e are determined to mobilize the means required to implement this Agenda through a revitalized Global Partnership for Sustainable Development, based on a spirit of strengthened global solidarity, focused in particular on the needs of the poorest and most vulnerable and with the participation of all countries, all stakeholders and all people.[31]

The seventeen sustainable development goals (SDGs) in the 2030 Agenda can only be achieved through global cooperation. SDG 17, therefore, focuses on partnerships and the fact that the state, business, academia, and civil society in all countries of the world need to work together to strengthen the work for sustainable development.

One reason for the importance of Pentecostals responding to this invitation is that our goals, to a large extent, overlap. Pentecostals are all over the world active in the fight against poverty and for justice, being called by God to do so. Other actors are involved for other reasons. One way to explore how the goals fit with the biblical concept of shalom and the faith of the church is explored by World Evangelical Alliance.[32] Another example of this reflection is how The Lutheran World Federation describes how the 2030 Agenda relates to faith and the biblical narrative.[33] When reading through the Cape Town Commitment, it is also clear that the global Christian network of Pentecostals are part of wants to play an important societal role in global challenges that are also mentioned in the 2030 Agenda.[34]

With this background in mind, it should be of great relevance for Pentecostals to find a way to relate to the 2030 Agenda and other global processes. Another reason is the fact that the budget to reach the goals of the Agenda by far exceeds all relief and development funding in all global funding streams. In a meeting with the management of the Swedish Governmental body for relief and development (Sida), it was stated that less than 10 percent of the budget is covered and that, among other things, we need to invest in change processes that do not cost much money. One very interesting example to learn from here is a case study from Malawi.[35] The study presents findings from a research project comparing the cost-effectiveness of a traditional project approach with a church and community mobilization approach (CCM). The research found that CCM had the same level of positive impact on quality of life but at 4 percent of the cost. It also found that CCM communities were almost four times more confident in solving problems themselves, indicating a much greater likelihood of sustainability. To realize the potential advantages of faith in development means funders and faith-based organizations have to mobilize local faith communities and explore the links between institutional aid and change processes within faith communities.

There is also a sociological perspective on this. A strong mistrust between the people and the political leaders is found in many societies and communities. In recent years, both scholars and policymakers have expressed great interest in the concepts of social capital and civil society. A growing body of research suggests that the social networks, community norms, and associational activities signified by these concepts can have significant effects on social welfare, political stability, democratic processes, economic development, and governmental performance. As mentioned earlier, religious leaders and institutions are of particular importance in many contexts, having the possibility of building trust and a peaceful culture in the community between the state, civil society, and individuals. At the same time, civil society organizations, as well as faith-based actors, have an important role of being a watchdog, making sure that the government acts in a way that benefits the people. Today we face weakening democratic development in the world and a lack of trust in political systems (on national and multilateral levels) and in political leaders. The global decline during the past ten years has been steep and continued to decline in 2020. The level of democracy enjoyed by the average global citizen in 2020 is down to levels last found around 1990, according to V-Dem Institute.[36] This shows the importance of the church network to act against conspiracy theories and mistrust and instead be part of building a culture of trust and cooperation, but at the same time holding people in power accountable.

Pentecostal Action in the Pandemic: A Case Study

The 2030 Agenda for sustainable development stipulates that extreme poverty should be abolished by 2030, that all people have the same rights, and that, therefore, no one should be left behind.[37] Economic poverty in the world has more than halved in the last thirty years, and many of the world's poorest countries have shown strong economic growth. However, at the same time, distribution is unfair, and inequality has increased. The world's poverty has increasingly concentrated in sub-Saharan Africa and in countries in war and conflict. The effects of the pandemic now present us with the biggest challenge since World War II, providing us with drastically reduced opportunities to achieve the agreed goals of the 2030 Agenda. For the first time since 1990, the fight against global poverty is going backward. In 2021, 150 million people were estimated to be forced into extreme poverty.[38] The economic and social disruption caused by the pandemic is devastating. Informal economy workers are particularly vulnerable because the majority lack social protection and access to quality health care and have lost access to productive assets. Without the means to earn an income during lockdowns, many are unable to feed themselves and their families. As the pandemic is spreading across developing countries, the eradication of extreme poverty seems nearly utopian. The pandemic has also meant that the number of people in need of humanitarian aid has more than doubled. World Food Program has warned that the world will face famines of biblical proportions if enough funds are not pledged to combat the effects of the pandemic on the world's most fragile countries, where food security was already a problem. In many places, the pandemic has furthermore been taken as a pretext for democratic restrictions, and trust in the democratic system is diminishing. In addition, crime and violence tend to increase when crises strike. Another effect of the pandemic is a global gender backlash, where the effects of the virus have major consequences for the safety, health, and economy of women and girls. Due to school closures, there has, for example, been an increase in child marriages, FGM, and teenage pregnancies. Violence in close relationships has also increased dramatically.[39]

Pentecostal Voices on the Urgency of Taking Action

The pandemic has thus led to a dramatic loss of human life and presents an unprecedented challenge to, among other things, public health, food systems, work opportunities, equality, and education. In many countries, people in need will end up at the stairs of the church, expecting it to act on their behalf since the church is one of the institutions they trust in the community. At the same time, many churches witness about lack of resources and means to meet their needs. Many churches also testify to the mistrust and fear surrounding vaccination programs, with widespread conspiracy theories that the vaccine is intended to spread diseases in order to limit population growth or that the vaccine would contain a microchip to restrict and control people's freedom. There are Pentecostal churches in the Global South who, therefore, ask for joint investments in the future, where we also reach the marginalized with proper information and support.

When the pandemic hit the world in the spring of 2020, the Taskforce for Relief and Development within the Pentecostal World Fellowship decided to act together. The background was the voices from partner networks, describing the lack of proper information but also the fear of not being able to cope with the situation. The task force made a major investment in the form of materials and webinars to stimulate the church networks to spread information about the virus and give concrete tips on how to get involved as a local church.[40] The material produced was distributed to church networks in more than 100 countries, with more than 140 million members. The material (for print and social media) contained information on what Covid-19 is, protective measures to take, why the church should get engaged, and how the local church can respond by limiting the spread of the virus, taking care of the members, mobilizing the church as an actor in the community, and in prayer. The materials also contained links to information from the World Health Organization. Church representatives from more than fifty countries joined in a deeper dialogue in webinars on the material and on the role of the church in dealing with the increased domestic violence during the pandemic.

One voice on the importance of the material came from a partner church in Kenya. The Kenyan church representative said that they got the materials very timely since, during the spring of 2020, they were facing dilemmas in terms of if they could trust what the government was saying and doing. In addition, they wanted to know whether the virus was real or if it was, above all, a spiritual attack from the devil wanting to close down churches and ministries. In the Kenyan church, leaders were also at that time discussing how to get the proper information out to all parts of the country. The leaders say that the materials helped them see and understand important perspectives on how to respond, and the fact that it also came in Swahili made it easy to get it distributed in the countryside. Leaders from the Kenyan church appealed in their feedback for the global Pentecostal movement to be more active in the days to come, responding to global challenges in a way that supports local churches to play an active societal role.

Still today, the need remains high for this type of support. In order to deal with the crises the pandemic has led to, action is needed at different levels and in many different ways. We need to prevent the spread of infection, disseminate accurate information, alleviate the effects of the pandemic, and influence those in power to make wise decisions. The church and its leaders are a power that many people listen to and who need to communicate well-thought-through messages. Some PMU partners also highlight the need for us to raise our voices when it comes to global vaccine justice. A lot is being done on resource mobilization and fair distribution, but we need to continue to affect politicians in the world by making just decisions on the vaccine issue. Besides the importance of working on local and global advocacy to affect governments and multilateral actors like the United Nations, Pentecostal churches are also important actors on the ground. They do not have to go to the poor and vulnerable since the church, to a large extent, is part of poor, marginalized, and vulnerable communities.

The partnership between the government and multilateral actors like the United Nations and religious leaders and institutions has shown to be fruitful in the response. In a report regarding the overarching response to Covid-19, the estimated amount of funds disbursed in relief and assistance until June 2020 was USD 71,155,450.[41] Since then, more has been done. Some of the funding came from governments, and some from local fundraising. During the implementation of programs on the ground, coordination and cooperation with authorities are always important though, irrespective of funding. The Pentecostal response regarded projects and programs in food security, economic relief and development, refugee camps, assistance to pastors and churches, medical equipment and testing kits, psychological support, information in different languages, and basic hygiene and sanitation. The scope of the response, as well as the results, gives some insights as to why it is important that the global Pentecostal movement is an actor in societal transformation, both in its' own right but also in partnership with governmental and international institutions.

Conclusion

In this article, we have discussed how the church can cooperate with governmental actors in the common task of fighting poverty and in reaching the sustainable development goals in the 2030 Agenda. The case has been the Swedish Pentecostal movement and the global challenges raised by the Covid-19 pandemic. We have argued for the importance of a holistic understanding of the gospel, a gospel that is about the restoration of broken relationships, renewal of creation, and reconciliation between the Creator and the created. We have also given examples of the role of faith in development and why churches (as well as religious actors in general) are key actors in the fight against the spread of Covid-19 and when handling other global challenges. This has been shown through stories from pastors on the ground and from learnings from other sources. The responsibility, therefore, falls heavily on the global Pentecostal network and its' leaders due to the movement's size and scope. This is not least in a time when authorities and multilateral cooperation is questioned; even though we face global challenges, we can only solve them together.

A Spirit-filled response to today's global challenges is more needed than ever. We, therefore, have to continue deepening our reflections on the holistic or integral mission and the links to the goals in the 2030 Agenda. In order to succeed, there is a need to actively support one another to act wisely and in a transformative way in our respective communities, bringing sound theology and good development theory together. We need to work together and with others that share our vision of a just world, free from poverty, but without losing our faith-based and Spirit-filled identity. As has been shown in the text, there are several risks connected to relationships between the church and official bodies, but also benefits. It is also a matter of shouldering the responsibility to connect to others. People know about the size and scope of the Pentecostal movement globally but wonder whom to talk to. Our voice is asked for by people in power. An example of the importance of raising our voices together as a global network regards vaccine justice and the importance of vaccines also being distributed to the poorest communities and countries.

Notes

1. United Nations Department of Economic and Social Affairs, "Do You Know All 17 SDGs?" un.org, https://sdgs.un.org/goals, accessed September 1, 2022.
2. Elisabeth Brusco, "Gender and Power" in Allen H. Anderson, Michael Burgunder, Andre Droogers, and Cornelis van der Laan, eds., *Studying Global Pentecostalism: Theories and Methods* (Berkley, CA: University of California Press, 2010), 74–92.
3. Donald Miller and Tetsunao Yamamori, *Global Pentecostalism: The New Faces of Christian Social Engagement* (Berkley, CA: University of California Press, 2007).
4. Dena Freeman, *Pentecostalism and Development: Churches, NGOs, and Social Change in Africa* (London: Palgrave Macmillan, 2012).
5. David Bundy, *Visions of Apostolic Mission: Scandinavian Pentecostal Mission to 1935* (Uppsala: Uppsala University Library, 2009).
6. See, for example, The World Bank, "Faith Based and Religious Organizations," https://www.worldbank.org/en/about/partners/brief/faith-based-organizations, accessed August 30, 2021.
7. See, for example, Lucie Sarr, "Africans Trust Religious Leaders More than Politicians," *La Croix International*, July 3, 2020, https://international.la-croix.com/news/religion/africans-trust-religious-leaders-more-than-politicians-poll-says/12683.
8. World Value Survey, "The New 2020 World Cultural Map has been Released," February 4, 2021, https://www.worldvaluessurvey.org/WVSEventsShow.jsp?ID=428.
9. See, for example, Katherine Marshall, "Religion and Ebola: Learning from Experience" Berkley Center for Religion, Peace and World Affairs, July 6, 2015, https://berkleycenter.georgetown.edu/posts/religion-and-ebola-learning-from-experience.
10. PMU has compiled a brief overview of what some researchers say about our global movement and societal transformation. PMU, "Global Pentecostalism and Agenda 2030" https://pmu.se/wp-content/

uploads/2019/09/39918001-GLOBAL-PENTEKOSTALISM-AND-AGENDA-2030-ENG-word-FINAL-20190906....pdf, accessed August 30, 2021.

11 Deepa Narayan et al. *Can Anyone Hear Us?: Voices of the Poor* (Washington D.C.: World Bank Publications, 2000) was a research initiative to understand poverty from the eyes of the poor. The publication provides a picture of the life of the poor and explains the constraints poor people face to escape from poverty. "Voices of the Poor" concludes that we need to expand our conventional views of poverty which focus on aspects such as income expenditure, education, and health, to include measures of voice and empowerment.

12 Richard Neibuhr, *Christ and Culture* (San Francisco: Harper, 2001).

13 Avery Dulles, *Models of the Church* (Dublin: Gill & Macmillan, 1987).

14 Stanley Hauerwas and William H. Willimon, *Resident Aliens: Life in the Christian Colony* (Nashville: Abingdon Press, 1989).

15 Allan Anderson, "Varieties, Taxonomies and Definitions" in Anderson et al., *Studying Global Pentecostalism*. (Los Angeles: University of California Press, 2010), 13–29.

16 Veli-Matti Kärkkäinen, *An Introduction to Ecclesiology* (Downers Grove: IVP Academic, 2002).

17 Anthony Giddens and Philip Sutton, *Sociology* (Cambridge: Polity Press, 2017), 7.

18 Anthony Giddens, *The Constitution of Society* (Cambridge: Polity Press, 1984), xii–xxxvii.

19 Robert Putnam, *Making Democracy Work* (Princeton, NJ: Princeton University Press, 1993). The concept of social capital is also discussed by Pierre Bourdieu in a more conflict-oriented understanding. In this article, we leave that discussion.

20 Henrik Berggren and Lars Trägårdh, *Är svenskan människa?* [Is the Swede Human?] (Stockholm: Nordstedts, 2015), 33–76.

21 Jean Cohen, "Civil society and Globalization" in Lars Trägårdh, ed., *State and Civil Society in Northern Europe* (New York: Berghahn Books, 2007), 37–66.

22 Filip Wijkström, "Charity Speak and Business Talk" in Filip Wijktröm, ed., *Nordic Civil Society at a Cross-roads* (Baden-Baden: Nomos, 2011), 27–54.

23 *PentecoStudies*, https://journals.equinoxpub.com/PENT/issue/archive, accessed August 30, 2021.

24 Donald Miller and Tetsuano Yamamori, *Global Pentecostalism: The New Face of Christian Social Engagement* (Berkely: University of California Press, 2007).

25 Douglas Petersen, *Not by Might Nor by Power* (Oxford: Regnum, 1996).

26 Amos Yong, *In the Days of Caesar* (Grand Rapids, MI: Eerdmans, 2010).

27 Antipas Harris and Michael D. Palmer, *The Holy Spirit and Social Justice* (Lanham: Seymour Press, 2019).

28 *Pentecostal Education* 6:2 (Fall 2021).

29 UN Department of Social and Economic Affairs, "Transforming our World: the 2030 Agenda for Sustainable Development (Preamble)," https://sdgs.un.org/2030agenda, accessed September 25, 2021.

30 UN Department of Social and Economic Affairs, "Transforming our World: the 2030 Agenda for Sustainable Development (Peace)," https://sdgs.un.org/2030agenda, accessed August 30, 2021.

31 UN Department of social and economic affairs, "Transforming our World: the 2030 Agenda for Sustainable Development (Partnership)," https://sdgs.un.org/2030agenda, accessed September 25, 2021.

32 WEA Sustainability Centre, "The Bible and the Sustainable Development Goals," https://wea-sc.org/en/biblesdgs, accessed August 30, 2021.

33 Lutheran World Fellowship, Waking the Giant, https://wakingthegiant.lutheranworld.org/, accessed August 30, 2021.

34 Lausanne Movement, "The Cape Town Commitment," https://lausanne.org/content/ctcommitment, accessed August 30, 2021.

35 Rick James et al. "Sustainable Value for Money – a Glimpse of the Holy Grail?" *Development in Practice* 5 (2020), 1–10.

36 V-Dem "Global Standards Local Knowledge" https://www.v-dem.net/, accessed August 30, 2021.

37 UN Department of Economic and Social Affairs "Transforming Our World: the 2030 Agenda for Sustainable Development," https://sdgs.un.org/2030agenda, accessed August 30, 2021.

38 World Bank "COVID-19 to Add as Many as 150 Million Extreme Poor by 2021," October 7, 2020, https://www.worldbank.org/en/news/press-release/2020/10/07/covid-19-to-add-as-many-as-150-million-extreme-poor-by-2021.

39 For more on the consequences of the pandemic, see, for example, Christoph Lakner et al. "Updated Estimates of the Impact of COVID-19 on Global Poverty: Looking back at 2020 and the Outlook for 2021," January 11,

2021, World Bank Blogs, https://blogs.worldbank.org/opendata/updated-estimates-impact-covid-19-global-poverty-looking-back-2020-and-outlook-2021.

40 Pentecostal World Fellowship World Missions Commission "Covid-19 Resources for Churches and Global Leaders," http://pwfmissions.net/covid-19/information, accessed August 30, 2021.

41 "Pentecostal Development and Relief Partners Covid-19 response report," PWF World Missions Commission | Relief & Development Partners, pwfmissions.net.

20 Holy Spirit Empowered Teaching: Stories of Teacher Survival During the Pandemic

Kim E. Boyd and Philida Rosalind Ignacio[1]

Abstract

This phenological study investigated Oral Roberts University alum educators' reliance on the Holy Spirit during the COVID-19 pandemic. Four female educators who taught at various elementary, middle, and alternative high schools in Tulsa, Oklahoma, were interviewed to discuss their experiences. The interview was informal, with all candidates and an educational facilitator present. The discussion was recorded using conferencing software to ensure the accuracy of the data collected, as participants answered four questions. Three themes emerged from the answers to the questions: uncertainty, purpose, and revival of their relationship with God. The findings highlight the role of the Holy Spirit in the experience of peace during uncertain times. Yielding to the Holy Spirit during seasons of change can result in the adaptation or adjustment in one's understanding and pursuit of purpose that simultaneously revitalizes faith. Thereby supporting the notion that a relationship with God is not linear but dynamic. Opportunities for further studies can include replicating the methodology in other professions, states, or with male candidates. Additionally, a review of the literature confirms that there is a need for more extensive research on Holy Spirit-empowered educators.

"But we will never advance this heavenly cause if we do not rely on the power of the Spirit. Jesus needed the Spirit's power—what makes us any different?"[2]

Introduction

The U. S. Department of Education describes an educational disruption as the loss of instructional time delivered in a school setting. According to Schleicher, the lockdowns due to COVID-19 interrupted conventional schooling with nationwide school closures, with most closures lasting at least ten weeks.[3] For P–12 students, the change from physical classrooms to an online setting, in many instances, was disastrous. Student motivation took on a whole new level of urgency during the pandemic, including how to get students to participate in remote learning and then, once engaged, how to help them focus remotely amidst the distractions of home. While some students excelled in the online learning environment, most of their decline was evident when they returned to school in person.[4] According to the article "What's Lost, What's Left, What's Next: Lessons Learned from the Lived Experiences of Teachers during the 2020 Novel Coronavirus Pandemic," a majority of parents (60 percent) and teachers (86 percent) expressed concerns about how children were doing during remote learning.[5] Teachers reported having a more challenging time doing their job remotely (83 percent) and believed that children (76 percent) were falling behind due to "distance"/remote learning.[6] Researchers further stated that the full effect of COVID-19 has yet to be seen.

While the educational community made concerted efforts to maintain learning continuity during this period, several students have had to rely more on their resources to continue learning remotely through the internet, television, or radio. Only 12 percent of teachers reported covering their full curriculum during Spring 2020 remote teaching.[7] Teachers also had to adapt to new pedagogical concepts and modes of delivery of teaching, for which they may not have been trained.[8]

In addition to the challenges educators faced professionally during the pandemic, they also faced many personal challenges. Educators who were also parents found themselves having to teach and care for their own families, sometimes choosing which of the two was most important. Moreover, teachers were learning conferencing software while simultaneously teaching their students how to use the same software. Educators had to create and adjust the curriculum to adapt to online teaching, using asynchronous and synchronous instruction while also being challenged to establish a connection with their students, their families, and colleagues.[9] To further complicate matters, teacher absenteeism due to their health concerns stemming from COVID-19 escalated the stress on their colleagues, students, and families.[10]

What occurred during March 2020, and its subsequent fallout has left the educational system in a crisis, resulting in many educators exiting the profession. During the pandemic, 79 percent of teachers either taught fully remote or a hybrid of both remote and in-person. As a result, the RAND survey found that nearly one-quarter of teachers indicated that they desired to leave their jobs by the end of the school year 2021. This figure compared to pre-pandemic results over the previous school year of 16 percent.[11] The survey also found that after teaching during the pandemic, more teachers could not confirm that they would work their entire careers in the classroom. Further, 42 percent of teachers considered retiring or leaving during the 2020–2021 school year.[12] In her article, "How Bad is the Teacher Shortage? What Two New Studies Say," Will states that teachers have indicated that they will leave their jobs as educators because of high stress, low pay, and disrespect.[13]

Schools that typically have no challenge filling vacant positions even experienced the residual effects of COVID-19. According to Fortin and Fawcett, one such school in Phoenix, Arizona, that serves approximately 3,000 students had to open the Fall 2022 semester with three mathematics teachers missing; this was unprecedented for the school.[14] There are currently 36,500 teacher vacancies in thirty-four of the fifty states, as documented by Will.[15] The reason educators desire to leave the profession is not only due to the pandemic; salary and location are also a consideration. Teachers struggled before, during, and after the pandemic to maintain their desire and willingness to teach the nation's children. However, since the pandemic, data indicates that the desire to teach continues to diminish.[16] Teachers who profess to have a personal relationship with Jesus Christ had the same challenges as all teachers had during the pandemic.

The mission of Oral Roberts University (ORU) is to develop Holy Spirit-empowered leaders through whole-person education to impact the world. A whole-person education includes an ORU identity: spiritual integrity, personal resilience, intellectual pursuit, global engagement, and a bold vision. The educational product is further enhanced through opportunities for students to grow in their faith to become Spirit-empowered leaders.[17] These Spirit-empowered leaders include those that are preparing for the teaching profession. The vision of the ORU College of Education is to prepare professionals to go into every person's world as transformed educators who transform society. The transformation described in Romans is foundational in preparing professionally skilled and credentialed teachers who can work in any field of education while impacting their students' lives. Romans 12:2 states: "And do not be conformed to this world, but be transformed by the renewing of your mind, that you may prove what *is* that good and acceptable and perfect will of God."[18]

In keeping with the University's Statement of Purpose, the College of Education is rooted in the philosophical position that education shapes the whole person: Spirit, mind, and body. At the center of the education program at Oral Roberts University is the understanding that true wisdom and knowledge come from God. The Bible is God's inspired word and is upheld as the standard and central point of reference. Therefore, the College of Education prepares administrators and teachers for public, private, and Christian schools to go into every person's world as transformed educators to transform society. The College of Education's desire is to develop and train future educators who have been transformed by the power of Jesus Christ and demonstrate the character and dispositions of Christian values, ethics, and moral integrity. These transformed educators are Spirit-empowered leaders who have a relationship with Jesus Christ and are filled with the Holy Spirit. As such, they have learned to rely on the Holy Spirit for guidance, direction, and peace in their chosen profession.[19]

Background to the Study

Daniel Isgrigg's review of "Spirit-empowered Leadership Definition and Characteristics" surmises that there has not been an abundance of research on Holy Spirit-empowered Leadership. However, a few authors are close to tapping into what it means to be a Spirit-empowered Leader.[20] Referencing several books on the topic, Isgrigg highlighted the work of Truls Akerlund.[21] Isgrigg maintains that Akerlund's book contents closely and clearly identify a Spirit-empowered leadership model.[22] Despite the limitations of a small group of Pentecostal leaders, Akerlund's work identifies traits in spiritual leaders to determine commonalities in characteristics within the group. The following list represents a few common characteristics of Pentecostal leaders compiled by Akerlunad: 1) They led from a calling from God and operated out of a worldview that sees the Holy Spirit as active. 2) They recognized that the Holy Spirit operates everywhere and engages in both the sacred and secular spheres of life. 3) These leaders treat the Pentecost as a resource, not a source.[23] While Akerlund's study is encouraging, Isgrigg noted that Timothy Geoffrion proposes a promising model of spiritual leadership in his work, *The Spirit-Led Leader*.[24]

Geoffrion summarizes that Spirit-led leaders seek to 1) know and love God deeply in a personal way; 2) follow Jesus Christ faithfully and wholeheartedly; 3) live and lead by the power, love, and self-discipline that comes from the Holy Spirit, and 4) draw others into Spirit-led living and Spirit-led leading in ways that build up the whole body of Christ.[25] Geoffrion provides nine leadership practices for those seeking to become Spirit-led leaders:

1) Envision your leadership following out of a deep spiritual life.
2) Actively cultivate your own spiritual life.
3) Develop specific spiritual disciplines.
4) Always seek to serve God's purposes first.
5) Create a vital spiritual environment within your workplace.
6) Make change a personal priority.
7) Lead by listening well.
8) Always trust God.
9) Open yourself fully to the love and grace of God.[26]

There cannot be Spirit-empowered leadership without the Holy Spirit. He is the essential part. The Holy Spirit is the third person of the Godhead; he is God. Before Jesus ascended, he promised to leave us with a comforter. John 16:7 states: "Nevertheless I tell you the truth; It is expedient for you that I go away: for if I go not away, the Comforter will not come unto you; but if I depart, I will send him unto you." Jesus needed the Holy Spirit while he lived on earth. For the same reason, we need the Holy Spirit's help to survive the challenges of everyday life.

The Holy Spirit is ever present to function in many of the same roles he did for Jesus. He is our helper and reminds us of the word of God (John 14:26). He is a source of wisdom and revelation (1 Corin 2:10–11) to build relationships and give guidance and power (Acts 1:8). Further, the Holy Spirit is referred to as the Spirit of Truth because in the believer's life. He guides them to all truth, including knowledge of what is to come. Likewise, a Spirit-empowered educator realizes the need to depend on the Holy Spirit for guidance in all aspects of his or her personal and professional life.

Purpose of the Study

While the ORU College of Education seeks to prepare Spirit-empowered professional educators who are uniquely equipped to positively impact student learning, evidence regarding the role the Holy Spirit played in the lives of its graduates during the pandemic has yet to be examined. Therefore, this research highlights lived experiences of reliance on the Holy Spirit during the pandemic, by Christian educators, who are ORU COE alumni.

Methodology

Qualitative research was the methodology used to determine the Holy Spirit's role in the lives of four ORU College of Education alums during the pandemic. Creswell and Creswell define qualitative research as exploring and understanding the meaning individuals or groups ascribe to a social or human problem. The research involves collecting information or data from participants and analyzing the information consistently to create themes. These themes are then interpreted to glean the meaning of the data.[27] The specific qualitative research used for this article was phenomenological research. It emphasizes the ethos of lived experiences of phenomena described by the participants. The information was collected as an interview, where participants could share their stories without external control or bias, allowing them to express their experiences on their terms.[28] Phenomenological research is not only pictorial in nature but also an interpretive process where the researcher can seek clarity on the participants' lived experiences.[29]

The Sample

Four Oral Roberts University alumni were chosen to provide insight into their lived experiences during the COVID-19 pandemic. The interviewees were identified through the process of purposeful sampling. The researcher emailed COE faculty members to ask for assistance in identifying alums in the Tulsa area, who were currently active in the education profession, and who were educators during the COVID-19 pandemic. As a result of the faculty responses, four alumni were identified and contacted. All agreed to participate in the study. Additionally, a graduate assistant, who is also an educator in the P–12 setting, and a current doctoral candidate in the COE helped to facilitate the interview process. The doctoral candidate served as an assistant researcher to help guide the discussions and validate ideas expressed by the interviewees.

Merriam identified attitudes and orientation as key variables in effective interaction between researchers and informants (interviewees).

Beyond these variables, Merriam maintained that information obtained from informants is predicated upon a researcher's sensitivity to verbal and non-verbal messages conveyed by informants. This sensitivity proved beneficial to the interview process.[30] The four participants were all female College of Education alums. Three were Caucasian, and one was African American. The assistant facilitator was also an African American female.

The Setting

The institutions represented were private, religious, and public schools in South Tulsa. The educational settings in which the participants worked played a significant role in how free they were to openly rely on the help of the Holy Spirit to provide peace, comfort, and understanding during the pandemic. Two participants worked in Christian nondenominational elementary schools, overseen by their church board, providing education from preschool through twelfth grade. Another participant worked in a public elementary school that serves students from preschool through fifth grade. The final participant taught at an alternative high school located in Tulsa County.

Moody states that alternative high schools take on many forms for differing purposes. However, most are defined as high schools with a curriculum that differs from the standard curriculum that usually serves students who have behavioral challenges that prevent them from receiving education in traditional educational settings.[31] The alternative high school of our participant is unique. As outlined on the school's website, this particular setting offers 9–12th grade students another option to complete their education. School is not a punishment program. Instead, it is intended to lead students toward success in mainstream education by using innovative teaching techniques, greater access to counseling services, more individualized course study, flexible scheduling, lower student/teacher ratios, and a more supportive classroom atmosphere.

Research Questions

The interview took on the form of an informal discussion during dinner at a local restaurant. The meeting was recorded using conferencing software. Each participant was asked four questions and allowed to volunteer their responses. They were also free to expound on their answers as they relived the memories of the pandemic, specifically during the period from March 2020 to December 2021. It was, at times, very emotional as they grappled with the reality of their lived experiences. The goal of the interview was to seek answers to the following four questions:

1) How did you rely upon the Holy Spirit during the pandemic?
2) How did your relationship with the Holy Spirit inform your decisions, both personally and professionally, as an educator during COVID-19?
3) What does it mean to be a Holy Spirit-empowered educator?
4) How did your relationship with the Holy Spirit provide strength in dealing with your family situation during this time?

Results

To analyze the data, interview recordings were transcribed and coded. Numerous themes emerged from the interview process. However, three overarching themes succinctly summarized participants' lived experiences during the pandemic: uncertainty, purpose, and revival of their relationship with God. In summation, the uncertainty of the pandemic compelled participants to lean into the leadership of the Holy Spirit for direction and insight. Each practice of reliance was marked with subsequent growth in the spiritual lives of informants. Thereby reigniting their sense of purpose and faith in God. The following discourse highlights responses to the research questions while simultaneously supporting the emergence of themes.

Question One

Times of uncertainty compelled reliance on the Holy Spirit. Reliance on the Holy Spirit requires dependence on Him through good and bad times. Dr. Peppler states that relying on the Holy Spirit is understanding our own inability. It means a person must trust, obey, be led by the Holy Spirit, and embrace the calling over their life.[32] Leaning into the Holy Spirit was expressed in statements made by interviewees as they addressed the question: How did you rely upon the Holy Spirit during the pandemic?

Participant A responded that at her Christian school, leadership relied on the Holy Spirit for the best plan for students to be healthy and to attend school in person as much as possible. She stated, "teachers prayed individually and in groups to support the administration's decisions." Participant B commented that she was patient and had peace, even though she did not know what would happen. She knew it would be okay. She stated, "so I just relied on my experience with the Holy Spirit to give me peace and comfort."

Participant C admitted that relying on the Holy Spirit was challenging for her. She disagreed with the school's decisions. She stated, "I just relied on the Holy Spirit for guidance as I was not in the seat of authority. I followed the directions from my leaders and tried to be the best teacher I could and support my students' families." She stated that she remembered the mindset that God gave her when she became a teacher: "I am here to serve the families."

Participant D said that she relied on the Holy Spirit to understand and define her passion for teaching. She stated: "It was difficult teaching during the pandemic as student learning was difficult to achieve. Consequently, the Holy Spirit helped break down her mindset about what teaching should look like; "it looks different, but it is still teaching." Additionally, this participant took time to memorize the Fruit of the Spirit. She began declaring it, as guided by the Holy Spirit, every day while driving to school because she needed strength to face the day with all its uncertainties. Participant B expressed that there was a lot of pressure and unknowns. However, the Holy Spirit provided the peace that [surpasses] all understanding, and he guards our hearts. She stated that the Holy Spirit, with his peace, shielded her from many difficult situations.

Question Two

As individuals, we make thousands of decisions every day. Some are very small such as what to wear or eat, and others are life-altering. No matter the weight of the decision, it all requires thought and discernment. The Holy Spirit is there to provide resources that will assist us in this process. These resources include, but are not limited to: prayer, reading scripture, wise counsel from mature individuals, and spending time in worship. Hudson states that in critical times, the decisions we make help shape our lives.[33] These truths show up in our interviewees' statements in response to the question: How did your relationship with the Holy Spirit inform your decisions, both personally and professionally, as an educator during COVID-19?

Participant D stated that she questioned when did she stop seeking after the Lord? She stated: "God meant it to be a daily walk, a daily ritual with the Holy Spirit. Your walk with God is for him to meet with your spirit so you can pour out into others. We were never meant to live this life alone." Through this revelation, the participant adjusted her teaching style led by the Holy Spirit, which allowed her to become an asset to her students. With a refined sense of purpose, she gave students what they needed, not what she felt they needed.

Participant C validated a previous statement she had made by querying the use of the word "normal." She remarked: "People kept saying that this situation was not normal, or we were returning to normal. What Jesus did was not normal; He raised people from the dead and fed five thousand on two loaves and three fishes!" As she wrestled with deciding what her students needed, she decided that she would take it daily and trust God that she would know what her students needed to know and what the standards say should be taught. She declared: "I am here to be the hands and feet of Jesus." This participant mentioned the revival of her daily devotions during the pandemic. She realized that she could break free of legalism about her devotion. Changing her time and not feeling guilty if she did not do it in the morning was a new freedom expressed by the participant. She commented that her "walk with Christ did not have to look like everyone else's." An understanding of the personal nature of one's spiritual journey led her to exclaim that her "relationship was with the Holy Spirit, Jesus Christ, and God. No one else!"

Reliance also requires compliance with the prompting of the Holy Spirit. Participant A stated the Holy Spirit helped her move from a place of contentment and comfort to another path during the pandemic. He called her to a new place and required her "to use her faith to walk where he wanted her to be." She remarked that God was rocking her boat and spent much more time reading the word, praying, and worshiping God. So, he could reveal what he needed her to accomplish. Consequently, in her classroom, God had her focus on 1 Corinthians 13: 4 – 8:

> Love is patient, love is kind. It does not envy, it does not boast, it is not proud. It does not dishonor others, it is not self-seeking, it is not easily angered, it keeps no record of wrongs. Love does not delight in evil but rejoices with

the truth. It always protects, always trusts, always hopes, always perseveres. Love never fails. But where there are prophecies, they will cease; where there are tongues, they will be stilled; where there is knowledge, it will pass away.

She prayed this scripture over her students and her relationships with coworkers in her school building. Because she was at a Christian school, the participant had her student repeat daily: "God is kind, I am kind …" reflecting on the attributes of God.

Participant B stated that her foundation grew deeper in him. "Personally, I needed the Holy Spirit when I was about to quit teaching." However, she trusted him for direction because she had a strong foundation. He guided her with a feeling of peace. She described peace as a "fuzzy feeling" and the absence of peace as a "scratchy feeling." His guidance eventually led her to a new teaching position where her passion for education was restored. The participant stated that she could have just done what she wanted, but the decision to trust God because of her relationship with the Holy Spirit kept her on the path to her purpose.

Question Three

Richard Foster declares in his book, Celebration of Discipline: "The desperate need today is not for a greater number of intelligent people, or gifted people, but for deep people."[34] To be a Holy Spirit-empowered educator is to draw on the tools of faith that God has given us. These are simple yet effective tools to grow deeper in Christ: reading the word of God, worshiping, spending time with God, and praying. These are some of the tools used by our alum and what they believe makes them Holy Spirit-empowered educators. The third question examined their personal view of their profession as an educator: What does it mean to you to be a Holy Spirit-empowered educator?

Participant C stated that she is very intentional: "While driving to school, I prayed in tongues." She stated that it was supernatural warfare: "I do not know what will happen today, but I want to be ready." She plays instrumental worship music, prays over her students' assigned seats, and calls them by name: "I do not know what is going on in their lives, but Jesus does." During the day, she will stop and ask the Holy Spirit for guidance on what direction to go with her lesson. Furthermore, she concluded: "It is simple. I feel like, as a Spirit-empowered educator, you rely on the Holy Spirit for peace to know what to do."

Participant D stated: "It is about the union between God and us; it is all about relationship. I believe it is a daily walk, everyday walking with your best friend. In every situation you are in, your best friend is with you. The Holy Spirit is right there with you, bringing comfort and peace." Several participants echoed the same sentiments. Establishing and building that relationship will help with interaction with students, families, and coworkers.

Question Four

A paraphrase of an old Burmese proverb states: "in times of test, family is the best." In the most general sense, this is true, and this was the intention of the family, but it is also a fact that the source of some of our most significant pain comes from family members. Whether our family is great or troubling, family is essential. Psalm 68:6a says God sets the lonely in families. God is relational in that he designed humans for connection and desires connection with his children. In Genesis, God stated that it is not suitable for man to be alone, and he created a help meet for him. From its inception, God saw the need for man to find support and connection. This subject sparked a more profound connection in conversation among participants, who then vulnerably shared challenging family situations they were in and, in some instances, still navigating. The emotions and vulnerability further enhanced the safe space for participants to grapple with the final question: How did your relationship with the Holy Spirit provide strength in dealing with your family situation during this time?

Participants talked about their struggles with their parents and siblings, mending relationships, and loneliness because they were away from family. Participants also talked about purpose, knowing that while they may have wanted to be with their families, they understood that God purposefully had them planted. They spoke of the desperate need to trust God to work all things out for their safety and the safety of their family members. Participants spoke of walking through forgiveness and knowing how powerful it is for God to bring healing to their families. Some participants thanked God for his preserving power, as none of their family members contracted COVID even though the educators had to go to school daily.

Conclusion

There was much uncertainty during the early stages of the pandemic. School administrators were desperately trying to figure out what to do. The interviewees spoke about understanding and respecting earthly authority as the Holy Spirit guided them. The Holy Spirit guided our teachers in re-establishing, confirming, and re-evaluating their purpose. Several teachers stated that the Holy Spirit had them look at their functionality as a teacher and lay it before the feet of Jesus, trusting Him to show them how to teach and connect with their students and families.

Our participants discussed how the Holy Spirit guided them to become vulnerable and open to learning or relearning pedagogy they thought they knew. He encouraged them to understand their students' needs, focusing on teaching and emotionally connecting with their students and families. He also admonished them to become more spiritually prepared to meet with their students by praying in tongues, praying over seats, and growing in their faith, transitioning them from a place of comfort and very relaxed to a place of purpose and becoming intentional.

The pandemic affected the world, and as we emerge from its throngs, we are left with the aftermath. As we focus on education, students are struggling with learning loss. The Measure of Academic Progress (MAP) score shows that reading and math levels have dropped considerably, especially in low-income schools.[35] Many teachers are undecided on whether teaching is a profession they want to pursue. Amidst all this ambivalence, one person remains constant: the Holy Spirit. The stories of the participants confirm the consistency and steadfastness of the Holy Spirit. Hebrews 13:5 says, in part, "He himself has said, 'I will never leave you nor forsake you.'" As one participant said, he is a close friend that goes with you wherever you go.

A relationship with the Holy Spirit is essential to function successfully in this world. God has given us this comforter. Proverbs 18:24b teaches: "but there is a friend who sticks closer than a brother." Through their unwavering dependence upon the Holy Spirit, these graduates of the Oral Roberts University College of Education successfully navigated teaching during the pandemic.

While this brief research study is certainly not generalizable, it does provide evidence through the participants' lived experiences that the COE's mission has been realized. They are transformed educators who have transformed their educational settings. By staying the course and a reliance on the Holy Spirit, these educators have grown personally and professionally as they navigated their lived experiences through the COVID-19 pandemic. While there were times of uncertainty, as Spirit-empowered educators, their reliance on the Holy Spirit was a central theme throughout the interview. Those who participated in this study specified that the Holy Spirit was present to provide relief and comfort.

Further research in other professions, states, Christian Universities, and with a male population can provide additional insight on the subject. Although the findings of this study add to the body of research on Holy Spirit-empowered education, there is a growing need for more extensive research on the subject.

Notes

1. The authors are indebted to the editor of this chapter, Candera Lomax.
2. John Bevere and Addison Bevere, *The Holy Spirit: An Introduction* (Palmer Lake, CO: Messenger International, 2013), 81.
3. Andreas Schleicher, "The Impact of COVID-19 on Education Insights: Education at a Glance," https://www.oecd.org/education/the-impact-of-covid-19-on-education-insights-education-at-a-glance-2020.pdf, accessed August 3, 2023.
4. United States Government Accountability Office, "Pandemic Learning: Less Academic Progress Overall, Student and Teacher Strain, and Implications for the Future," June 8, 2022, https://www.gao.gov/products/gao-22-105816.
5. Justin Reich, Chris Buttimer, Dan Coleman, Richard Colwell, Farah Faruqi, and Laura Larke, "What's Lost, What's Left, What's Next: Lessons Learned from the Lived Experiences of Teachers During the Pandemic," September 10, 2020, https://edarxiv.org/8exp9.
6. Reich et al., "What's Lost."
7. Reich et al., "What's Lost."
8. Kavitha Cardoza, "'We Need to be Nurtured, Too': Many Teachers Say They're Reaching a Breaking Point," National Public Radio, April 19, 2021,

https://www.npr.org/2021/04/19/988211478/we-need-to-be-nurtured-too-many-teachers-say-theyre-reaching-a-breaking-point.

9 Gema Zamarro, Andrew Camp, Dillon Fuchsman, and Josh B. McGee, "Understanding How COVID-19 Has Changed Teachers' Chances of Remaining in the Classroom," August 16, 2021, https://scholarworks.uark.edu/edrepub/127/.

10 Schleicher, "The Impact of COVID-19 on Education Insights."

11 Elizabeth D. Steiner and Ashley Woo, "Job-Related Stress Threatens the Teacher Supply: Key Findings from the 2021 State of the U. S. Teacher Survey," RAND Corporation, https://www.rand.org/pubs/research_reports/RRA1108-1.html, accessed June 26, 2023.

12 Zamarro et al., "Understanding."

13 Madeleine Will, "How Bad is the Teacher Shortage? What Two New Studies Say," Education Week, September 6, 2022, https://www.edweek.org/leadership/how-bad-is-the-teacher-shortage-what-two-new-studies-say/2022/09.

14 Jacey Fortin and Eliza Fawcett, "How Bad is the Teacher Shortage? Depends Where You Live," New York Times, August 29, 2022, https://www.nytimes.com/2022/08/29/us/schools-teacher-shortages.html.

15 Will, "How Bad?"

16 Will, "How Bad?"; Zamarro et al., "Understanding."

17 "Whole Leaders for the Whole World," Oral Roberts University College of Education, https://oru.edu/academics/coe/index.php, accessed June 26, 2023.

18 New King James Version (Nashville: Thomas Nelson, 1982).

19 Oral Roberts University, "Whole Leaders."

20 Daniel Isgrigg, "Spirit-empowered Leadership Definitions and Characteristics: A Literature Review for the Taskforce for Spirit-empowered Leadership," October 4, 2019, unpublished review, n.p.

21 Truls Akerlund, *A Phenomenology of Pentecostal Leadership* (Eugene, OR: Wipf and Stock, 2018).

22 Isgrigg, "Spirit-empowered Leadership."

23 Akerlund, *A Phenomenology*.

24 Isgrigg, "Spirit-empowered Leadership."

25 Timothy C. Geoffrion, *The Spirit-Led Leader: Nine Leadership Practices and Soul Principles* (Lanham, MD: Rowman & Littlefield, 2005).

26 Geoffrion, *The Spirit-Led Leader*.

27 John Creswell, and J. David Creswell, *Research Design: Qualitative, Quantitative, and Mixed Methods Approaches*, 5th Ed. (Newberry Park, CA: SAGE Publications, 2018).

28 John Creswell, *Educational Research: Planning, Conducting and Evaluating Quantitative and Qualitative Research* 4th Ed. (Boston: Pearson, 2012), 76.

29 A. Alase, "The Interpretative Phenomenological Analysis (IPA): A Guide to a Good Qualitative Research Approach," *International Journal for Education and Literacy Studies* 5:2 (2017), 9-19.

30 Sharon B. Merriam, Case Study Research in Education: A Qualitative Approach (Hoboken, NJ: Jossey-Bass, 1988).

31 Josh Moody, "How Attending an Alternative School Impacts College Admission," U.S. News, August 9, 2019, https://www.usnews.com/education/best-colleges/articles/2019-08-09/how-attending-an-alternative-school-impacts-college-admissions.

32 Christopher Peppler, "Dependence on the Holy Spirit," SATS, December 2, 2019, https://sats.ac.za/blog/2018/02/05/dependence-holy-spirit/.

33 Trevor Hudson, *Holy Spirit Here and Now* (Nashville: Upper Room Books, 2013).

34 Richard Foster, *Celebration of Discipline: The Path to Spiritual Growth* (Hertogenbosch, Netherlands: Van Haren Publishing, 1998).

35 Megan Kuhfeld, Jim Soland, Karyn Lewis, and Emily Morton, "The Pandemic has had Devastating Impacts on Learning. What Will it Take to Help Students Catch Up?" Brookings, March 3, 2022, https://www.brookings.edu/blog/brown-center-chalkboard/2022/03/03/the-pandemic-has-had-devastating-impacts-on-learning-what-will-it-take-to-help-students-catch-up/.

"A Shared Story of Future Hope"[1]: Postscript

Rebekah Bled and Polly Tjihenuna

"Lament is the appropriate biblical response to loss."[2]

Introduction

Throughout the pandemic, the losses are staggering. Reeling from one loss to another, how may an individual, a community, respond? Together with the authors of this book, Scott Cormode calls for a practice of biblical lament, citing the Psalms as the primary model, and distinguishing lament from other forms of complaint because of the one to whom the complaint is made. "We need models for lament because it would be easy to draw the wrong conclusion about our complaints by thinking that God is like the other authority figures we have in our lives. It is often not safe to speak honestly to a human authority figure – especially if you want to accuse that authority figure of neglecting his promises."[3] But God is not like other authorities (Psalm 89:8–13). Instead of being threatened by our lament, he invites us to "pour out our hearts like water" in his presence (Lam 2:19a). Unlike many other authority figures, God provides refuge (Psalm 91; 62:8) rather than rejection in response. Our voices, rather being diminished by pain and loss, find space and resonance in biblical lament.

Yet, what of comparing griefs? Do some have more right to mourn than others? I (Rebekah) once listened to a man reflect on a group of teenagers in the context of a North American youth group, going around the circle at the end of the evening, sharing prayer requests for the upcoming week. A teenager who had recently been homeless listened in disbelief and mounting rage as another teenager shared her distress at what seemed to him to be minor inconveniences, if they could even be considered at all. When the second student finished, the first muttered an agitated comment about the ease of life and "made up pain" of "some people." The youth minister took the first student aside after the others had left and said, in effect: "everyone's deepest pain gets to be their deepest pain." While in this story the depth and impact of ongoing teenage homelessness is not equal to the situational distress of a teenager, the invitation to lament is extended to both characters, as it is extended to each of us. The offer to share our losses, small and staggering, is made ever available by the one who keeps track of sparrows (Matt 10:26–31) and before whom the mountains melt like wax (Micah 1:4; Nahum 1:5).

Through case studies both current and historical and through examination of theology both practiced and proclaimed this book takes a critical and necessary look at responses of Pentecostal-charismatic communities to the pandemic. This Postscript suggests a framework borrowed from Scott Cormode called a "shared story of future hope"[4] through which to read this collection. A shared story of future hope is, in brief, a story anchored in the past which encompasses present experience and extends a vision into the future. While Cormode discusses a shared story of future hope in the context of innovation, we believe this framework can serve well as an interpretive lens through which to read this book on lament's movement to hope and healing. Indeed, the two movements of innovation and lament are not exclusive to each other, and the pandemic and post-pandemic church finds herself simultaneously doing both. Applying Cormode's framework includes first identifying those entrusted to your care, empathizing with "longings and losses," teasing out the "big lie" that may be hampering the people identified in step one, making spiritual sense of those longings and losses, and expressing spiritual meaning as a shared story of future hope.[5]

Longings and Losses

It is, of course, easiest to discuss the first step of identifying those entrusted to our care in this book's case studies. Kim Boyd and Philida Ignacio's interviews with teachers who taught through the pandemic focus explicitly on care for individual classes in predetermined contexts.[6] Mathew Daniels and Suhasini Daniels write about the Spirit's expansion of care to include certain women and children in the redlight district of Pune, India, who were facing starvation as a result of COVID-19 protocols.[7] Both of these focus on specific leaders (teachers, Daniels and Daniels) with clearly defined groups (students, sex workers). Robert McBain, Melody Wachsmuth, David Daniels, Amos Yong, Aizaiah Yong, and Hanna Larracas expand the delineation, calling the Spirit-empowered movement's attention to people "entrusted to our care," yet too often disregarded. Wachsmuth details the experience of Roma communities and asylum seekers in Eastern Europe,[8] Yong and Yong and Daniels of people of color within the United States.[9] McBain points to the depressed;[10] Larracas to the grieving.[11]

If one part of the body suffers, the whole body suffers (1 Corin 12:26). The pandemic has laid bare a sense of global trauma. As Hanna Larracas states, "Grief has become its own epidemic within the COVID-19 pandemic."[12] The people entrusted to our care are in fact members of the same body and thus the longings and losses represented by the body are also shared. To move to the second step in Cormode's framework, perhaps there is also a "big lie" or fear that the Spirit-empowered stream of the body also shares.

A "Big Lie"?

Stephen Ofotsu Ofoe describes a pre-pandemic service in Ghana designed to encourage participants to be filled with the Spirit. Ofotsu Ofoe surmises, "The way the singing is done in these services seems to suggest that it is in this ecstatic environment that the Holy Spirit moves and gets people baptized in him."[13] McBain provides a contrast, describing the early weeks of the pandemic: "Isolated in their homes, people felt vulnerable as they realized that their old way of living was not as stable as they thought."[14] Wonsuk Ma states that "Pentecostal spirituality is best expressed and experienced in a community context."[15] What happens then to Pentecostal spirituality when the context of Pentecostal community is removed? The central question many of the authors here interrogate is how the Spirit has worked and is working in the pandemic. The "big lie" or pervasive fear to which this book provides counter testimony is that removed of the familiar ways in which the Spirit moves in gathered community, the Spirit may not move at all.

Making Spiritual Sense of Loss

To go back to Cormode: "Understanding the longings and losses of the people entrusted to our care is the necessary beginning, but it cannot be all that we do. We Christians will need to make spiritual sense of the longings and losses of the people entrusted to our care, and in doing so, we will join a great cloud of biblical witnesses."[16] We also join a cacophony of noise. As several authors have pointed out, the pandemic brought to light the proverbial good, bad, and ugly of the church, Pentecostal-charismatic or otherwise. Many in the world are working to make spiritual sense, some shouting louder than others in their certainty. Alex Mayfield states, "Unexamined positions on health and hyper-individualist framings of infectious disease were just as common in 2020 and 2021 as they were in 1908."[17] J. Kwabena Asamoah-Gyadu, Peter Althouse and Audrey McCormick, Hanna Larracas, and Stephen Ofotsu Ofoe wrestle with the implications of varied Pentecostal theologizing during the Pandemic.[18] Making spiritual sense of longings and loss does not happen in a vacuum, and there are a multitude of narratives that seek to describe the pandemic, it's roots, and the correct response.

YWAM Missionary, Andy Byrd, says that one of the sure markings of being a mature believer of Jesus is being able to take responsibility of someone else's actions. Being part of the body comes with a responsibility to own up to mistakes made by the global church. Often, as Christians, we become someone's point of reference to what they see and hear is happening in and through the church. As a student in the United States, I (Polly) have easily become the point of reference to many families and friends in my home country, Namibia, who have seen the rise of Christian nationalism during the pandemic. During the height of the COVID-19 pandemic, the term "Christian" (specifically in the United States) became associated with anti-vaxxers, anti-masks, COVID hoax, January 6th, Donald Trump, etc. Videos of prolific Pentecostal leaders praying and prophesying that Trump would win the election amongst other viral videos paint an idea of evangelical Christians having the final authority in these matters. Caricatures have arisen within the frenetic and public competition for interpretation during the pandemic, heightening polarization, and confusing "scapegoating"[19] for sense-making. Beyond the public noise, troubling theology has been revealed.

J. Kwabena Asamoah-Gyadu points to prosperity as part of the promise of God, but notes however, its overemphasis, can serve as a form of escapism to present realities of pain and suffering.[20] As someone who grew up in a Pentecostal context, I (Polly) have a framework for the experiential aspects of the tradition and have seen the, at times, dismissive nature of "naming it and claiming it" made popular by the prosperity gospel. Although there is truth that life and death is in the power of the tongue (Prov 18:25), there is also the promise of trials and assurance of peace (John 16:33). McBain points this out beautifully by stating that Jesus's crucifixion achieved "the peace that originates from restored relationship" between humanity and God.[21]

Another element of troubling theology is that of taking scriptures out of context or proof texting. Scriptures such as John 15:7 and Mark 11:24 that say to "ask and receive," but it is easy to forget James 4:3 that tells us "You ask and do not receive, because you ask wrongly, to spend it on your passions." Although many have prayed against COVID-19, Ma, Althouse, and McCormick state that the pandemic might be here to stay.[22] As evidenced not only through the COVID-19 pandemic but throughout the centuries, Spirit-filled believers have not been exempted from the sufferings of the rest of the world but are expected to respond differently.

Daniel Isgrigg reminds us of how the Pentecostals of the last century responded during the Spanish-flu with compassion.[23] May and Plüss likewise note the compassion of believers during the Plague of Cyprian from 249–262 AD,[24] and the black death of 1347–51, often to their own detriment.[25] Plüss contrasts the compassionate care for others during these pandemics with political selfishness displayed by Justinian during the bubonic plague from 541– 549 AD, despite his religious affiliations.[26] Of the responses to the Plague of Cyprian and the Black Death, Plüss surmises: "Clearly, Christian compassion, fueled by their spiritual communion with God, played an important role in the life of the religious."[27]

Compassion is a great marker of being filled with the Spirit of God as it removes fear of others and of bodily harm (i.e., sickness, threats). However, compassion may sometimes look like retreating in order to protect others. Ma notes that although we believe that healing can take place when we pray, prevention is part of that healing.[28] Isgrigg points out that Pentecostals in the early twentieth century also took preventative measures to protect those in their communities.[29] This historical posture of compassionate protection poses a contrast to some loud voices in the current pandemic shifting the lens from preventative measures for the vulnerable as personal and corporate persecution.[30] Amos Yong, Aizaiah Yong, Ulrik Josefsson, Niclas Lindgren, and Hanna Larracas reminds us of the eschatological conspiracies and mistrust that formed around the vaccine amongst Christians.[31] It has been interesting for me (Polly) to observe some people stop going on missions trips because of the vaccine requirements in some of the countries. When I had the chance to go to a missions training school during the summer of 2021, I remember one of our instructors saying that taking a "stupid vaccine" is worth preaching the gospel to the lost in other nations. While the second example is technically of government compliance, it lacks the compassion of the early Pentecostals described by Isgrigg.[32]

Ma reminds us that we live in this tension of the "already not yet" kingdom of God whereby Jesus has already paid the full price for our healing and redemption, yet we still await the day when all tears will be wiped away and pain will be no more (Rev 21:1–4). Ma expounds that until that day, we are to demonstrate the coming kingdom by praying for the sick regardless of whether we see immediate healing or not.[33] The compassion of Jesus is demonstrated in part by actions towards the vulnerable and the sick. That may look like going to visit with them and praying with them in-person or being aware of people who may have preexisting conditions that exposure to COVID may cause serious health challenges or death. Jun Kim is incisive on the need for Spirit-empowered discretion in truly loving one's neighbor:

> . . . the most critical violation of God's commandment is not missing the Sunday services but not loving God by not loving our neighbor (Matt 22:36–40) intentionally or unintentionally. As this issue may continue, we need to consider if Jesus would be pleased with our sacrifice that has sacrificed someone's life, not ours.[34]

For scapegoating, dismissing, ignoring, and otherwise devaluing,[35] the members of the same body entrusted to our care, Yong and Yong together with Opoku Onyinah call us to repentance.[36] Cormode ties repentance into lament, saying "When we learn to practice lament, we develop the habit of [. . .] self-reflecting on the ways we may even contribute to the pain in our world."[37] Sanna Urvas adds her voice, reminding the church: "The permanent division of condemnation between the light and darkness has not yet happened. Thus, we need to pay attention to our works and deeds until the coming of Christ."[38]

Just as the pandemic made visible the "bad and the ugly," it also highlighted strengths of the Spirit-empowered movement's response, notably an enduring eschatological hope with immediate implications.

Asamoah-Gyadu points out that the pandemic almost forced Pentecostal preachers to confront the realities of pain and suffering within their church body. "Prosperity preachers were forced to respond to a pandemic that revealed the realities of life" and contribute to the overall understanding of hope and the Christian journey.[39] Sometimes the mountain doesn't move when you speak to it, but we are promised the companion of the Spirit and, if we look around, the companionship of others to climb over it.

Through their study, Peter Althouse and Audrey McCormick discovered not triumphalism, but a focus on appropriate grieving made possible by implicit eschatological hope.[40] Althouse and McCormick found that "Eschatological imagery were ways in which people were able to make sense of the world in which they lived."[41] Urvas also points to the eschatological future, then returns to the here and now: "Therefore, to balance the perspective of hope for the future, it is necessary to focus on the question, how should we understand the kingdom of God at present, which is linked to the eternal, and should we do something about it?"[42] Balfour points out the Lukan precedent of empowerment for immediate action.[43] Far from limiting the work of the Spirit, the pandemic has provided a window into some of the fresh movements of God's Spirit, among these, a new opportunity for Spirit-empowered believers to turn towards the public good in the face of a public crisis. As noted by May, Mayfield, Isgrigg, and Plüss, this is not the first such opportunity.[44] It is, however, a fresh invitation.

David Daniels discusses a path of "mutual relevance" between Pentecostals and secular health sciences. Citing the leadership of Bishop Charles Edward Blake Sr., Daniels argues for the Spirit-empowered stream to continue to "express a robust vision of flourishing life that embraces healthcare justice for people of color and others limited by healthcare inequities."[45] Josefsson and Lindgren comment on the sheer numbers represented by the Spirit-empowered movement, stating that "With size and strength comes responsibility."[46] Josefsson and Lindgren encourage Spirit-empowered leaders in public partnerships for the common good. Asamoah-Gyadu reflects on the role of prayer in this: "The contemporary Pentecostal-charismatic culture of mobilization of prayer for the public good—whether it means positive declarations of prosperity or the cursing of evil—is something that proved very relevant in how this wave of Christianity has dealt with the pandemic."[47] Daniel and Daniel end their chapter with a beginning in lieu of a conclusion, pointing to the Spirit's new work of advocacy for otherwise destitute women and children.[48]

In the introduction to his book of lament, Poet Lo Alaman roots lament itself in hope: "Biblical lament stems from hope that God has more in mind for his people than the brokenness they find themselves in."[49] Lament cries out about injustice, rooted in the hope of response by the one who is himself justice. Wachsmuth states, "If justice is part of God's essence and, therefore, his engagement with humanity, it must be an essential component of human interaction with God and the world."[50] May echoes this from the perspective of history, saying of Christians during the Plague of Cyprian: "Fragments of the eschatological fulfillment and kingdom of God were partially experienced by those who laid down their life for others in need."[51]

Conclusion: A Shared Story of Future Hope

Arthur Frank asks: "If recovery is taken to be the ideal, how is it possible to find value in the experience of an illness that either lingers on as chronic or ends in death?" Though Frank writes as a Sociologist, this question is pertinent when posed to a religious stream who proclaims divine healing. Frank's answer is surprisingly at home in Spirit-empowered theologizing: "The answer seems to be in focusing less on recovery and more on renewal."[52] Frank continues, discussing the intertwined narratives of those suffering from illness, concluding that "Renewal is easiest if it is a shared process."[53] Indeed, a shared story of future hope is one shared in history,[54] experienced together in the present,[55] and extending into the eschatological future.[56] As Althouse states, "The whole of theology is perceived from the perspective of hope, a hope that has transformative implications for the present."[57] As Spirit-empowered believers, our shared story of future hope can be found in the movement of lament. Our story is one of being heard and answered, by the one who self describes as unchanging (Rev 1:8). We share both story and hope in lament's final act, the vow of praise.

Cormode describes a proto-typical lament as being composed of five sections[58] and Lee Roy Martin identifies seven sections which fit into a four-part structure.[59] Regardless of the number of sections our lament, either personal or communal, the movement is one from despair or complaint to a vow of trust and/or praise.[60] The hinge or turning point for both authors seems to be the assurance of God's answer. Indeed, Martin describes hope in this context as a justified assurance based on the person of God: "Israel has grounds to hope in Yahweh because 'with Yahweh is commitment,' a theological conviction rooted in Yahweh's self-revelation."[61] Lament's invitation is two-fold: to boldly "pour out" our complaints while clinging to the reminder that the one to whom our complaint is addressed is worthy to be trusted, though it may be he whom we are accusing. Thus, in concert with Pentecostal-charismatic streams, lament, like testimony or intercessory prayer, can be an experiential, embodied, practice of faith that takes place in and on behalf of communities through the power and comfort of the Spirit. Balfour looks back to the early church's story in the Spirit describes, saying: "The first generation of believers had to learn how to adapt and apply their faith in new and unimaginable situations." Balfour then looks with continuity to the future: "And now it is *our* turn to create pathways for open access and participation in the redemptive, transformative, healing, saving power and presence of the Holy Spirit!"[62]

Notes

1 Scott Cormode, "A Shared Story of Future Hope," Fuller Studio: The Next Faithful Step, https://www.fuller.edu/next-faithful-step/resources/a-shared-story-of-future-hope/, accessed July 13, 2023.

2 Scott Cormode, "The Practice of Lament," (paper presented at Fuller Youth Institute MIYA cohort, 2018, Pasadena, CA), 1.

3 Cormode, "The Practice of Lament."

4 Cormode, "A Shared Story of Future Hope."

5 Cormode, "A Shared Story of Future Hope."

6 See chapter 20.

7 See chapter 10.

8 See chapter 11.

9 See chapters 12 and 13 respectively.

10 See chapter 8.

11 See chapter 16.

12 See chapter 16.

13 See chapter 17.

14 See chapter 8.

15 See chapter 6.

16 Cormode, "A Shared Story of Future Hope."

17 See chapter 4.

18 See chapters 14, 15, 16, and 17 respectively.

19 See chapter 11.

20 See chapter 14.

21 See chapter 8.

22 See chapters 6 and 15 respectively.

23 See chapter 5.

24 See chapters 3 and 18 respectively.

25 See chapter 18.

26 See chapter 18.

27 See chapter 18.

28 See chapter 6.

29 See chapter 5.

30 See chapters 4, 5, 6, and 7.

31 See chapters 12, 19 and 16 respectively.

32 See chapter 5.

33 See chapter 6.

34 See chapter 7.

35 See chapters 3, 6, 7, 10, 11, 12, 13, 14, and 16.

36 See chapters 12 and 1 respectively.

37 Cormode, "The Practice of Lament," 1.

38 See chapter 9.

39 See chapter 14.

40 See chapter 15.

41 See chapter 15.

42 See chapter 9.

43 See chapter 2.

44 See chapters 3, 4, 5, and 18 respectively.

45 See chapter 13.

46 See chapter 19.

47 See chapter 14.

48 See chapter 10.

49 Lo Alaman, *We Sang A Dirge: Poems, Laments, and Other Things that Matter to God* (Franklin, TN: Seedbed, 2020), 9.

50 See chapter 11.

51 See chapter 3.

52 Arthur Frank, *At the Will of the Body: Reflections on Illness* (Boston: Houghton Mifflin, 1991), 2.

53 Frank, *At the Will of the Body*.

54 See chapters 3, 4, and 5.

55 See chapters 8, 13, 15, 16, 17, 18, 19, and 20.

56 See chapters 6,7, 9, and 15.

57 See chapter 15.

58 Cormode, "The Biblical Practice of Lament," 1.

59 Lee Roy Martin, "Lament and Hope in Psalm 130," *Pharos Journal of Theology* 100 (2019), 3.

60 Martin, "Lament and Hope," 5

61 Martin, "Lament and Hope," 7.

62 See chapter 2.

Contributors

Peter Althouse is Professor of Theology and Ph.D. Director of Global Contextual Theology at Oral Roberts University. His publications include *Spirit of the Last Days: Pentecostal Eschatology in Conversation with Jürgen Moltmann* (T & T Clark), *Catch the Fire: Soaking Prayer and Charismatic Renewal* (Northern Illinois University Press), and Pentecostals and the Body (Brill). He is Immediate Past President of Society for Pentecostal Studies and former co-editor of *Pneuma: The Journal of the Society for Pentecostal Studies*.

J. Kwabena Asamoah-Gyadu is currently President and Baëta-Grau Professor of Contemporary African Christianity and Pentecostal Theology at the Trinity Theological Seminary, Legon, Ghana.

Glenn Balfour (Ph.D. Nottingham University) has served in both church leadership roles and theological higher education throughout his adult life. He currently serves in a full-time capacity at Missio Dei, and as Assemblies of God GB Theologian in Residence. His teaching specialisms include New Testament studies, Greek, and Hebrew. He has developed a range of teaching resources in both biblical languages.

Rebekah Bled is a Ph.D. Candidate in Theology at Oral Roberts University. Her publications include chapters in *Proclaiming Christ in the Power of the Holy Spirit* (2020), *Good News to the Poor* (2022), and *The Remaining Task of the Great Commission* (2023). She also served as Associate Editor for these titles.

Kim E. Boyd is Assistant to the Provost for Exceptional Teaching and Innovation and Dean of the College of Education at Oral Roberts University. Previously, she served as the Associate Dean and an instructor of elementary and professional education. Dr. Boyd was recently reappointed as a Commissioner for the Council of Accreditation for Educator Preparation (CAEP). Dr. Boyd sits on several education boards at the national and international levels and has presented at numerous conferences, focusing on performance-based assessment at state, national, and international levels.

Mathew Daniel (DMin Center for Global Leadership Development) is Co-National Training Coordinator together with his wife. Their expertise is in developing resources for NGOs and pioneering new centers. They have spoken at the annual Meeting on World Federation for Mental Health, contributed to "Hands That Heal" curriculum, and speak at meetings and schools, colleges, and network meetings to train staff in India and abroad. Mathew has also written an article on Human Trafficking for the South Asia Bible Commentary.

Suhasini Daniel is Co-National Training Coordinator and together with her husband. They have prepared around thirty-five modules for use in NGOs. Their work has been recognized by the Maharashtra Government (Certificate of Gratitude) as they have partnered with the Government to offer restoration for the victims of trafficking rescued from brothel-based slavery. The U. S. Department of Justice awarded them the Crime Victims' Rights Award, April 2015.

David D. Daniels III is the Henry Winters Luce Professor of World Christianity at McCormick Theological Seminary in Chicago, Illinois, USA, having joined the faculty in 1987, and a trustee of Oral Roberts University, Tulsa, Oklahoma, USA.

Philida Rosalind Ignacio is Assistant Program Director at Youth at Heart, a non-profit organization that works with children and youth from underserved populations in Tulsa, OK. holds a Master of Arts degree in Counseling and a Master of Education in Educational Leadership and is currently pursuing her Ed.D. focused on trauma-informed practices in education.

Daniel D. Isgrigg (PhD, Bangor University) is Associate Professor of History of Spirit-Empowered Christianity at Oral Roberts University, Tulsa, Oklahoma, USA. He also serves is the Managing Editor for *Spiritus: ORU Journal of Theology*. Isgrigg is the author of several books including *Pentecost in Tulsa* (Seymour Press, 2021) and *Imagining the Future: The Origin, Development, and Future of Assemblies of God Eschatology* (ORU Press, 2021). He has also published articles in the areas of early Pentecostalism and Oral Roberts studies.

Ulrik Josefsson is President at ALT School of Leadership and Theology and Director for The Institute of Pentecostal Studies. He holds a PhD in Practical Theology from Lund University. He has written numerous articles on Pentecostalism and Practical Theology. Ulrik is co-editor for

Journal of Leadership and Theology and vice chair for World Alliance for Pentecostal Theological Education (WAPTE).

Jun Kim is a Korean Pentecostal scholar, known for his expertise in historical and theological studies on divine healing and Asian Pentecostalism. He currently serves as the Academic Dean at Asia Pacific Theological Seminary (APTS) in the Philippines and as the Vice-Chair of the Asia Pentecostal Society. In addition to his academic roles, He has been a missionary to the Philippines since 2004. He obtained his Ph.D. from Oxford Centre for Mission Studies, UK.

Hanna Larracas is a PhD student at Oral Roberts University where her research focuses on Pentecostal theologies of grief and suffering. Residing in the San Francisco Bay Area, Hanna serves as a chaplain for hospice patients and bereavement coordinator for families navigating experiences of grief, loss, and making meaning after encounters with death. Hanna earned her BA in Theology at Southeastern University ('17) and her M.Div. at Boston University ('20).

Niclas Lindgren is the Director of PMU, the Swedish Pentecostal Relief and Development Aid Agency. He holds a Master's degree in Political Science and International Relations. He was raised in a missionary family in Tanzania and has for many years been involved in global relief and mission. Niclas is chairing PRDP (Pentecostal Relief and Development Partners), a global network consisting of development and relief practitioners from the Pentecostal World Fellowship. He is also a member of the PWF World Missions Commission.

Wonsuk Ma, A Korean Pentecostal, serves as Executive Director of the Center for Spirit-Empowered Research and Distinguished Professor of Global Christianity at Oral Roberts University, Tulsa, Oklahoma. He previously served as Dean of the College of Theology and Ministry at Oral Roberts University, and Executive Director of the Oxford Centre for Mission Studies, Oxford, UK. He serves as co-chair of The Global Network of Spirit-Empowered Scholars, Empowered21.

Cory J. May is an assistant professor of theological and historical studies at Oral Roberts University, Tulsa, Oklahoma. His research interests include Colonial African American Christianity, the North American Slave Narratives, African American literature, and the sociopolitical theologies of Martin Luther King, Jr., and Reinhold Niebuhr.

Alex Mayfield is Assistant Professor of History at Asbury University. His research and teaching interests include Pentecostal and charismatic movements, mission history in East Asia, and digital methodologies. Dr. Mayfield is a principal investigator for the China Historical Christian Database and serves as a technical advisor to the Chinese Christian Posters projects and the Dictionary of African Christian Biography.

Robert D. McBain is Research Coordinator of the Holy Spirit Resource Center and a Ph.D. in Theology candidate in the College of Theology and Ministry at Oral Roberts University, Tulsa, OK, USA, researching how Pentecostals understand, interpret, and respond to depression. He also serves as the Book Review Editor for *Spiritus: ORU Journal of Theology* and *Salubritas: International Journal of Spirit-Empowered Counseling*.

Audrey McCormick is a PhD in Theology candidate at Oral Roberts University working under the advisory of Daniel Isgrigg. Her doctoral research focuses on divine union and the significance of Song of Solomon in early Pentecostal spirituality. Audrey is the Co-Lead Pastor at her local church in Concord, CA and the Community Educator at Options Health, a non-profit crisis pregnancy center where she authored a sexual risk avoidance program for teens and parents.

S. Ofotsu Ofoe BSc (Medical Sciences, Ghana); BDS (Dental Surgery, Ghana). He is currently studying for an MA (Theology and Mission) at the Akrofi-Christaller Institute of Theology, Mission and Culture, Ghana. He is the director of conversation at the Centre for African Christian Spirituality (CEFACS), Pentecost University, Ghana.

Opoku Onyinah serves as co-chair of the Global Network of Spirit-Empowered Scholars, Empowered21. He is the immediate past president of Ghana Pentecostal and Charismatic Council and the immediate past chairman of the Church of Pentecost, Ghana, with branches in 135 countries. He was also the first international mission direction of the Church of Pentecost and the founding rector of Pentecost University. Currently, he lectures at Pentecostal University, Accra, Ghana, and is the president of the Bible Society of Ghana.

Jean-Daniel Plüss (Ph.D. in Religious Studies from the Catholic University of Leuven, Belgium) chairs the European Pentecostal Charismatic Research Association and is president of the Swiss Global Christian Forum Foundation. He has been involved in various international ecumenical dialogues involving Pentecostals and older church traditions. He has written numerous articles on Pentecostalism and a book on the history of Swiss Pentecostalism.

Polly Tjihenuna is a Namibian Masters of Divinity student at Oral Roberts University, Tulsa, Oklahoma, where she formerly served as the Dean's Fellow. She currently serves as the Women's Chaplain Coordinator at ORU.

Sanna Pauliina Urvas is Professor of Systematic Theology at Theological School of Finland. Urvas' research focuses on patristic and ecumenical sources alongside Pentecostal theology. She is a founding member of *Finnish Pentecostal Theological Symposium* and a member of *Symposium Patristicum Fennicum* among other scholarly research fellowships. She is part of PWF Christian Unity Commission and PWF Creation Care Task Force. Urvas received her theological education at University of Helsinki, Finland, and has served in IK Bible College, Finland, and Wabash College, IN, USA.

Melody J. Wachsmuth is from the United States but has been based in Croatia for the last twelve years. She works as a mission researcher, writer, and teacher throughout Southeastern Europe and published her first book, *Roma Pentecostals Narrating Identity, Trauma, and Renewal in Croatia and Serbia* (Brill) in 2022. She is on the Board for the newly formed traveling Roma Bible School and helped establish the Friends of A Rocha group in Croatia.

Aizaiah G. Yong (Ph.D. Claremont School of Theology) is Assistant Professor of Spirituality at the Claremont School of theology. He is an ordained pentecostal Christian minister, practical theologian, and healing companion who has served in religious and higher education leadership for over a decade devoting his energy to personally and socially transformationally work that centers QTBIPOC communities.

Amos Yong (Ph.D. Boston University) is Professor of Theology & Mission at Fuller Theological Seminary.

Select Bibliography

Atkinson, William P. *Trinity After Pentecost.* Eugene, Oregon: Pickwick Publications, 2013.

Augustine, Daniela C. *The Spirit and the Common Good. Shared Flourishing in the Image of God.* Grand Rapids, Michigan: Eerdmans Publishing Company, 2019.

Blazer, Dan G. *The Age of Melancholy: Major Depression and Its Social Origin.* Florence, UK: Routledge, 2005.

Brown, Candy Gunther. *Testing Prayer: Science and Healing.* Cambridge, MA: Harvard University Press, 2012.

Butler, Geoffrey. "Plague, Pentecostalism, and Pastoral Guidance: Luther's Wisdom for the Contemporary Church." *Pneuma* 43 (2021): 5–24.

Constantineanu, Corneliu. "'Instruments of Justice:' Biblical Contributions to a Public Theology of Engagement in Eastern European Context." *International Journal of Public Theology* 14:3 (2020): 355–71.

Courey, David J. *What Has Wittenberg to Do with Azusa?: Luther's Theology of the Cross and Pentecostal Triumphalism.* London: Bloomsbury, 2015.

Cyprian, Saint, and Phillips Campbell. *The Complete Works of Saint Cyprian of Carthage.* Merchantville: Evolution Publishing, 2013.

El Maarouf, Moulay Driss, Taieb Belghazi, and Farouk El Maarouf, "COVID-19: A Critical Ontology of the Present," *Educational Philosophy and Theory* 53:1 (2021):71–89.

Engelbert, Pamela F. *Who Is Present in Absence? A Pentecostal Theological Praxis of Suffering and Healing.* Eugene, OR: Pickwick, 2019.

Faulkner, John Alfred. *Cyprian the Churchman.* Marrickville: Wentworth Press, 2016.

Firth, David, and Paul Wegner, eds. *Presence, Power and Promise.* Nottingham: Apollos, 2011.

Fitzmyer, Joseph A. *The Acts of the Apostles.* New York: Doubleday, 1998.

Freeman, Dema. *Pentecostalism and Development.* London: Palgrave Macmillan, 2012.

Hall, Douglas John. *God and Human Suffering: An Exercise in the Theology of the Cross.* Minneapolis, MN: Augsburg, 1986.

Hauerwas, Stanley and William H. Willimon. *Resident Aliens: Life in the Christian Colony.* Nashville: Abingdon Press, 1989.

Haykin, Michael. 2011. "The Holy Spirit in Cyprian's To Donatus." *Evangelical Quarterly* 83:4 (October 2011): 321-329.

Herms, Ronald, John. R. Levinson, and Archie T. Wright, eds. *The Spirit Says: Inspiration and Interpretation in Israelite, Jewish, and Early Christian Texts*. Berlin / Boston: De Gruyter, 2021.

Hick, John. *Evil and the God of Love*, rev. ed. New York: Harper and Row, 1978.

Hiebert, Paul G. "The Flaw of the Excluded Middle." *Missiology* 10: 1 (January 1982): 35–47.

Jones, Serena. *Trauma + Grace: Theology in a Ruptured World*, 2nd ed. Louisville, KY: Westminster John Knox, 2019.

Keener, Craig S. *Spirit Hermeneutics: Reading Scripture in Light of Pentecost*. Grand Rapids: Eerdmans, 2016.

Kennedy, Jeff, *Father, Son, and the Other One*. Lake Mary, FL: Passio, 2014.

Koduah, Alfred. *Christianity in Ghana Today*. Accra: Advocate Publishing Ltd., 2004.

Larbi, E. Kingsley. *Pentecostalism: The Eddies of Ghanaian Christianity*. Dansoman, Accra: Centre for Pentecostal and Charismatic Studies, 2001.

Lebacqz, Karen. *Justice in an Unjust World: Foundations for a Christian Approach to Justice*. Minneapolis: Augsburg PubHouse, 1987.

Levinson, John R., *Filled with the Spirit*. Grand Rapids: Eerdmans, 2009.

Lewis, C. S. *The Problem of Pain*. London: The Centenary Press, 1940.

Ma, Boying. *A History of Medicine in Chinese Culture*. Singapore: World Scientific Publishing Company, 2020.

Mandryk, Jason. *Global Transmission, Global Mission: The Impact and Implications of the COVID-19 Pandemic* Kindle Edition. Downers Grove, IL: Operation World, 2020.

Marshall, Chris. *The Little Book of Biblical Justice: A Fresh Approach to the Bible's Teaching on Justice*. Intercourse, PA: Good Books, 2005.

Maunder, Chris. *Oxford Handbook of Mary*, ed. September 2019. DOI: 10.1093/oxfordhb/9780198792550.001.0001

McBain, Robert D. *Depression, Where is Your Sting?* Eugene, OR: Resource Press, 2021.

McCaulley, Esau. *Reading While Black: African American Biblical Interpretation as an Exercise in Hope*. Downer's Grove, Illinois: IVP Academic, 2020.

Menzies, William W. and Robert P. Menzies. *Spirit and Power: Foundations of Pentecostal Experience*. Grand Rapids: Zondervan, 2000.

Miller, Donald and Tetsunao, Yamamori. *Global Pentecostalism: The New Face of Christian Social Engagement*. Berkley: University of California Press, 2007.

Moltmann, Jürgen. *Jesus Christ for Today's World*. Minneapolis, MN: Fortress Press, 1994.

_____. *The Crucified God*. London, UK: SCM Press, 1974.

_____. *Theology of Hope: On the Ground and Implications of a Christian Eschatology*. James W. Leitch, trans. London: SCM Press, 1967.

Piper, John, *Coronavirus and Christ*. Wheaton: Crossway, 2020.

PMU, "Global Pentecostalism and Agenda 2030" https://pmu.se/wp-content/uploads/2019/09/39918001-GLOBAL-PENTEKOSTALISM-AND-AGENDA-2030-ENG-word-FINAL-20190906....pdf.

Rambo, Shelly. *Spirit and Trauma: A Theology of Remaining*. Louisville, KY: Westminster John Knox Press, 2010.

Rorke, Bernard, and Jonathan Lee. "Roma Rights in the Time of COVID," Belgium: European Roma Rights Centre, September 2020. http://www.errc.org/uploads/upload_en/file/5265_file1_roma-rights-in-the-time-of-covid..pdf.

Scrutton, Tasia. *Christianity and Depression*. London, UK: SCM Press, 2020.

Stronstad, Roger. *The Charismatic Theology of St. Luke: Trajectories from the Old Testament to Luke-Acts*, 2nd Edition. Grand Rapids: Baker Academic, 2012.

Swinton, John. *Resurrecting the Person*. Nashville, TN: Abingdon, 2000.

Thompson, Damian. *Waiting for Antichrist: Charisma and Apocalypse in a Pentecostal Church*. New York: Oxford University Press, 2005.

Trevors, J. T. "Total Abuse of the Earth: Human Overpopulation and Climate Change." *Water, Air, Soils Pollution: An International Journal of Environmental Pollution* 205 (2010): 113–114.

Vondey, Wolfgang, ed. *The Routledge Handbook of Pentecostal Theology*. London: Routledge, 2020.

Williams, Joseph W. *Spirit Cure: A History of Pentecostal Healing*. Oxford: Oxford University Press, 2013.

Wright, N. T. *God and the Pandemic: A Christian Reflection on the Coronavirus and Its Aftermath*. Grand Rapids, MI: Zondervan, 2020.

Yang, Fenggang, Joy K. C. Tong, and Allan H. Anderson, eds. *Global Chinese Pentecostal and Charismatic Christianity*. Leiden: Brill, 2017.

Yong, Amos. *In the Days of Caeser: Pentecostalism and Political Theology*. Grand Rapids, MI. Eerdmans, 2010.

_____. *Spirit of Love. A Trinitarian Theology of Grace*. Waco, Texas: Baylor University Press, 2012.

Zizioulas, John D. *Being as a Communion*. Studies in Personhood and the Church. Crestwood, New York: St Vladimir's Seminary Press, 1985.

Name and Subject Index

A
Abraham, 10, 22
abuse, 16–18
activist theory of the church, 343
Acts, empowerment in, 32–37
Adam, 119, 120, 122
advocacy, 201–202, 341–342
Africa
   contemporary Pentecostal responses to COVID-19 pandemic in, 251
   contemporary Pentecostal theology in, 253–260
   COVID-19 pandemic as evil virus in, 250
   COVID-19 pandemic religious responses in, 252–253, 262–263
   divine healing and, 108
   Ebola crisis in, 341
   health-and-wealth theology in, 284–285
   Pentecostal-charismatic Christianity in, 302
   Pentecostalism in, 247, 284
   prayer in, 285
   prophetic prayer movement in, 261
   Spanish influenza in, 261
   trust in religious leaders in, 340–341
African American Pentecostal-charismatic churches, 216–217
African Americans, 211
African Independent Churches (AICs), 302
African Independent Pentecostal communities, 285
Agabus, 15, 36
Agape (Croatia), 195
agitation, 19–20
Akerlund, Truls, 362
Albania, 196
Alexander, Kimberly, 84, 126
ambiguous loss, 282
Amos, Elton, 241
Anderson, Allan H., 181, 301
Anglican Alliance, 322
Anglican Church, 104, 105
Anglican Communion, 322
Anna, 39n12
anti-intellectualism, 215
Antonine Plague, 332n4
anxiety, 123
apostles, 15–16, 23. *See also* disciples
Appleby, Blanch, 89
Arianism, 159
Artificial Intelligence (AI), 24
Asamoah-Gyadu, J. Kwabena, 96, 112, 284, 302, 378–379
Asian American Pentecostal-charismatic churches, 216–218
Assemblies of God, 84, 105, 109, 270–271, 272, 274
Assyria, 12–13
asylum seekers, in Bosnia and Herzegovina, 196–197
Athanasius, 311
Atkinson, William, 155, 160
Augustine, 158
Augustine, Daniela, 155, 156, 165, 166–167
Augustinian perspective, 120, 121–122
Azusa Street revival, 215, 306

B
Bakker, Henk, 54
Bakker, Jim, 261
Balkans, 194–195
baptism

forms of, 48
of the Holy Spirit, 302–303, 304–307, 308–309, 310–312
of Jesus Christ, 28, 31
of suffering, 52, 59
Barnabas, 35
barren fig tree, parable of, 14
Basilica of St. Paul Outside the Walls, 326
Basil of Caesarea, 159
believers, attributes of, 157
Berkhof, Louis, 104
Bernard, David, 94
Berwald, Mrs. Tyred, 91–92
Bethel Church, 267, 275
Bialecki, Jon, 268–269
Biden, Joe, 254
Bihac, Bosnia and Herzegovina, 196–197
Black, Indigenous, People of Color (BIPOC), 211, 215
Black Death, 319
Black Lives Matter, 211–212
Black Pentecostal engagement, 231–232
Blake, Charles Edward, Sr., 94, 235–240, 244, 381
Boddy, A. A., 86
body painting, 17
body piercing, 17
bonds, 45
Bonnke, Reinhard, 108
born-again experience, 262
Bosnia, 195, 196–197
Boubonic Plague, 318–319
Boulton, E. C. W., 305
Bread of Life (Serbia), 195
brothel managers, 178
Browder, A. F., 87
Brusco, Elisabeth, 338
Bundy, David, 340
Bush, Cori, 93

Byrd, Andy, 378
Byzantine Empire, 318–319

C
Caecilius, 50, 51
calamities, divine concept of, 14–16
Cape Town Commitment, 348
Carthage, plague in, 55–56
Catherine of Sienna, 319
Catholicism/Roman Catholic Church, 104, 321, 329
celebrations, during the pandemic, 248
Certificate of Peace (Certificate of Sacrifice), 53
Chan, Simon, 156
Charles IV (King of Spain), 319–320
child abuse, 140
China, 68, 69–71, 72
Chinese medicine, 69–71
Chinese Pentecostals
  disdain for medicine/medical care by, 75–76
  end-time plagues and, 77–78
  healing of, 71–80
  as healing specialists, 74
  introduction to, 67–68
  Latter Rain theology and, 77–78, 79
  missionary tongues and, 72–73
  personal responsibility and, 74–76
  plagues and, 71–78
  pragmatic conversion and, 72–74
  relational sources of sickness and, 76–77
  theology overview of, 78–80
Cho, David Yonggi, 126
Cho, Paul Yonngi, 107–108
Choil, Jashil, 107–108
Christian and Missionary Alliance, 74
Christianity, 104, 378. *See also* Pentecostals/Pentecostalism; specific denominations

Christian nationalism, 213
Christian racialized nationalism, 63–64n2
Christians/Christian community, 158–161, 165–167, 194. *See also* Pentecostals/Pentecostalism; specific denominations
Chrysostom, 311
church. *See also specific denominations*
  activist theory regarding, 343
  adaptations of, 269–270, 321, 324–325, 331
  agitation in, 19–20
  attendance growth of, 324–325
  as catching up to knowledge revolution, 23–24
  confessional theory regarding, 343
  conversionist theory regarding, 343
  as cooperating with God, 20–24
  COVID-19 pandemic effects on, 3, 19, 111, 265–266
  COVID-19 pandemic response of, 19–20, 321–330, 331
  family focus of, 327
  friendship through, 146–147
  Holy Spirit's work in, 329
  as identifying with poor and vulnerable, 340
  as kingdom of God, 21
  as kingdom of God signifier, 156
  mental health help from, 144–147, 327–328
  metaphors regarding, 343
  mission of, 293
  nature of, 328–330
  online services of, 324–325
  outside the walls, 326
  as peace-bearers, 145–146
  prayer in, 20–21
  pruning of, 21
  reconsidering methods of, 21–22
  restriction resistance by, 111, 128
  role and identity of, 342–344
  self-help groups in, 147
  social problem role of, 337
  society and, 345–346
  support for poor and vulnerable by, 22–23
  for those in need, 327–328
  unity in, 62
  widening parameters of, 329
church and community mobilization (CCM) approach, 349
Churchill, Winston, 323
Church of God, 85
Church of God (Cleveland, TN), 95
Church of God in Christ (COGIC), 94, 235–240, 243–244, 269–270
Church of Pentecost (CoP), 302–303, 306–307, 308, 310
City of Faith, 109
civil society, role of, 345
Claudius, 15, 36
color-blindness, 219
compassion, 92–94, 379
confessional theory of the church, 343
confessors, categories of, 53–54
Congar, Yves, 329
conspiracy theories, 1–2
Constantinople, 319
conversionist theory of the church, 343
Copeland, Kenneth, 96–97, 251, 254
Cornelius, 34, 309
Cornelius (Bishop of Rome), 54
COVID-19 pandemic
  biblical plague linking with, 16–19
  communal nature of, 112
  compliance and cooperation regarding, 94–97
  conspiracy theories regarding, 1–2
  discovery of, 1
  effects of, 83, 139–140, 265, 350
  as evil virus, 249–251, 254

as intervention from God, 18
knee-jerk reactions to, 117
our tasks regarding, 126–129
overview of, 9–10
Pentecostal response to, 93–94
politicization of, 57, 93, 139–140, 212–213, 254
protocols regarding, 2
reimagining, 140–141
resistances in, 111, 128
saving lives from, 128–129
shared responsibility regarding, 337
Spanish Influenza as compared to, 293–294
spiritualizing of, 3, 18
statistics regarding, 1, 83, 103, 127, 231, 265
transmission of, 307
cowpox virus, 319–320
Cox, Harvey, 268, 302
Craig, Robert, 88
creation, 119–122, 160
Croatia, 195
Croatian Baptist Aid, 195
Crosby, Robert C., 272, 273
culture, being the church in, 342–344
Cyprian, St. (Thaschus Caecillius Cyprianus)
   conception of shame and, 50–51
   conversion of, 51
   De Mortalitas, 318
   empathetic resonance and, 61–63
   episcopate turmoil of, 52–55
   Holy Spirit and, 57–61
   humility of, 44–48
   introduction to, 43–44
   On Mortality, 58
   persecution and, 51–52
   plague of, 55–56, 60–61
   salvation viewpoint of, 60
   salvific experience of, 46–47
   testimonies of character of, 48–51

On the Unity of the Church, 62
Cyril of Jerusalem, 311

D

Dankwa Akuffo-Addo, H. E. Nana Addo, 306–307
David, 12
Davis, Herbert, 239–240
death, 86–90, 268, 269–271, 272, 273
Decius (Emperor of Rome), 52–53, 54–55
democracy, 349
demonic forces, 76, 254
De Mortalitas (Cyprian), 318
demythologization, 104
dependence, in society, 344
depression, 142–143, 144–147, 150n6
Dillon, Michele, 233
disabilities, healing and, 288–289
disciples, 36, 109, 143–144, 146
disease, 78–80, 111–112, 117–118, 123–125
distance/remote learning, 359–362
Domitian (Emperor of Rome), 51
Dubai consultation, 4–5
Dulles, Avery, 343
Duncan-Williams, Nicholas, 251, 254–256, 261
Dunn, Robert F., 88

E

Eastern Syrian fathers, 164–165
Ebola crisis, 341
ecclesiology, 343
education, COVID-19 pandemic disruptions to, 359–362, 371
Egypt, 10–12
Eli, 125
Elizabeth, 29–30
Elymas, 35
empathetic resonance, 61–63
England, Spanish Influenza in, 86

ergotism, 148
eschatology, 155–157, 267–269, 383
Evangelical Lutheran Church of America, 322
Evangelical Relief Agency (ERA), 200–202
evangelicals, statistics regarding, 195
evangelism, healing role in, 110
Eve, 119, 122, 163
evil, 120, 250–251

F

Fabian, St., 54
faith, 88–89, 341
Faith-Cure Movement, 288
the Fall, 15, 16, 118–119, 122, 123–125, 163–164
family, 370
famine, 10–11, 15, 350
Ferguson, Lula, 89
fiery serpent, plague of, 12
Fiji, Spanish Influenza in, 86
Finished Work Pentecostal Stream, 288
firstborns, death of, 11–12
flood of Noah, 10
flourishing, 157
Floyd, George, 211, 267
forgiveness, 61–63, 146
Foster, Richard, 369
Frank, Arthur, 382
Freeman, Dena, 338
friendship, development of, 146–147
funerals, COVID-19 pandemic effects on, 3–4

G

Gabriel (angel), 30
Galileans, 14
Gani, Irwan, 161
Garr, Alfred G., 72–73
Ge Hong, 70, 75
gender backlash, 350

generosity, 201
Gentiles, 34, 37
Geoffrion, Timothy, 362–363
Germany, 345
"Germany prays together," 321
Ghana
  baptism of the Holy Spirit in, 304–307, 308–309, 310
  church adaptations in, 326
  data analysis in, 307–309
  medical science concerns in the pandemic in, 306–307
  Pentecostal movements in, 302
  tarrying meetings in, 305–306
Giddens, Antony, 344
Gilyard, Anthony, 269
Global Christian Forum, 330
God, 18, 20, 21, 57–58, 108, 151n22, 158–161, 193
goodness, in creation, 119–122
gospel, 220, 338–339
government, abuse in, 16–17
Grant, Beth, 180–181, 272
Gregory Nazianzen, 159
Gregory of Nyssa, 159, 160
Grey, Jacqueline, 328
grief, 90, 269–271, 282, 293–294, 375–376, 377
Grunewald, Matthias, 147–148
Gumbel, Nicky, 325
Gyimah, James Kwaku, 310–311

H

Haarala, Veli-Pekka, 166
Habermas, Jurgen, 234
Hadrian (Emperor of Rome), 51
Hakala, Anna-Riina, 163
Hall, Douglas, 123
Hauerwas, Stanley, 343
healing
  believer's authority regarding, 96
  in China, 69–71

Chinese Pentecostals and, 71–78
disabilities and, 288–289
expectations of, 287–288
extent of, 106–108
forms of, 107
holiness approaches to, 79
as hope, 275
inner/emotional, 275
kingdom of God and, 110
lack of experience of, 290
of the land, 106
medicine and, 240
"not-yet" reality of, 109–111
Pentecostal views on, 78–80, 88, 288
personal responsibility regarding, 70–71, 74–76
storytelling regarding, 274–275
of suffering, 222
theologies of, 86–90, 287–289
through partnership, 222
validity of, in Christian life and mission, 104–106
healing houses, 105
healing imagination, 274
health-and-wealth theology, 260–262, 284
healthcare, 3, 241–243
heart, significance of, 49
herald metaphor of the church, 343
Hermeneutic of Equality, 64n3
Herzegovina, 195, 196–197
Hick, John, 119
Hill, Timothy, 95
Hillsong Church, 267
Hodges, Melvin, 181
Holiness movement, 105, 292
Hollenweger, Walter, 301
Holmes, Barbara, 234
Holy Spirit
    abilities of, 37
    baptism of, 302–303, 304, 309–312
    characteristics of, 363
    church work by, 329
    cooperation with, 37–38
    Cyprian's viewpoint regarding, 47–48, 57–61
    in educators, 369–370
    empowerment in Acts of, 32–37
    empowerment reception of, 28
    expectations of healing through, 287–288
    function of, 363
    as helper in weakness, 161
    indwelling of, 147
    introduction to, 27–28
    in Jesus, 30–32
    John the Baptist and, 29–30
    laying on of hands and, 35, 309–310, 311
    medical science concerns in the pandemic and, 306–307
    in mission of God, 320
    outpouring of, 160
    overview of, 37–38
    as a person, 160
    relationship with, during COVID-19 pandemic, 367–369, 370
    reliance on, during COVID-19 pandemic, 366–367
    salvation role of, 304
    as second blessing, 303–304
    as "S Factor," 233
    speaking in tongues and, 72–73, 216, 303, 305
    tarrying meetings for, 305–306
    transformative power of, 60
    virgin birth narrative and, 29
    visible empowerment of, 28–29
Holy Trinity Brompton (HTB), 325
Hong Hai, 71
Hong Kong, 67–68, 72
Hood, Allen, 270

hope, 267–269, 271–275, 376, 380–381, 382–383
Hosanna! Music, 284
Huffman, John B., 88
human body, abuse of, 17
human trafficking
  brothel managers in, 178
  COVID-19 pandemic impact on, 184–186
  effects of, 175
  overview of, 174–175
  players in, 177–178
  in Pune, 183–184
  response to, 180–183, 186–188
  statistics regarding, 174–175
  traffickers/trafficking agents in, 178
  understanding world of, 177–180
  vulnerability factors regarding, 175–177
Hungary, 327–328
Hunter, Harold, 86–87
Hurricane Michael, 273
hydroxychloroquine, 260

I

illness, extent of, 106–108
India
  COVID-19 pandemic in, 184–186
  human trafficking overview in, 174–175
  human trafficking response in, 180–183, 186–188
  introduction to, 173–174
  plague in, 68
  Pune in, 183–184
  Spanish Influenza in, 85
  vulnerability factors in, 175–177
individualism, 127
Indonesia, 161
Influence (magazine), 272
inner/emotional healing, 275
institution metaphor of the church, 343

International House of Prayer (IHOP), 267, 270
intimate partner violence (IPV), 140
Irenaean perspective, 119
Irenaeus, 160, 163
Isenheim Altarpiece, 147–148
Isgrigg, Daniel, 362
Israelites, 12–13

J

Jamieson, S. A., 90–91
Japan, 282
Javier de Balmis, Francisco, 319–320
Jenkins, Philip, 302
Jesus Christ
  baptism of, 28, 31
  betrayal of, 150n13
  as breathing on disciples, 311–312
  compassion, 380
  death of, 194
  deity of, 159
  eschatological vision of, 293
  expectations of, 20
  forsakeness of, 143, 151n22
  friendship by, 146–147
  healings by, 104, 109–110, 125, 312
  Holy Spirit and, 30–32, 39n10
  as identifying with poor and vulnerable, 339–340
  justice and, 194, 199
  mission of, 31–32, 340
  peace from, 145
  plagues and, 14–15
  resurrection of, 256–257
  sabbatical law and, 128–129
  second coming of, 257–259
  solidarity from, 148
  temptation of, 31
  triumphal entry of, 141
Job, 290
John, the apostle, 33–34
John the Baptist, 29–30

Jones, Bob, 269
Jones, Serene, 271, 273–274
Joseph, 10–11
Joshua, 311
joy, 165
jubilee principle, 13, 22–23
Judah, exile of, 13
Judas, 150n13
judgment, signs of, 317
justice, 192–194, 201–202
Justinian (Emperor of Byzantine Empire), 318–319

K

Kärkkäinen, Veli-Matti, 156, 161, 344
Kashf Foundation, 166
Keller, Timothy, 193
Kenya, 351–352
Kim, Ik-du, 110
Kim, Matthew D., 272
King, J. H., 88
kingdom of God, 21, 110, 155, 156, 161, 380
knowledge revolution, 23–24
Koduah, Alfred, 301–302
Korea, 110

L

lament, 269, 375, 382–383
Land, Steven, 268
Larchet, Jean-Claude, 124
Larracas, Hanna, 377
Latino/a communities, COVID-19 pandemic effects on, 211
Latino/a Pentecostal-charismatic churches, 216–217
Latter Rain theology, 77–78, 79, 283–284
laying on of hands, 35, 309–310, 311
Lazarus, 125
Lee Wu Si, 73
libellatici, 53

The Life and Passion of Cyprian (Pontius), 48–49
limitation, 123
Li Shing Fat, 75
lockdown, 253–260, 285
loneliness, 123
longings and losses, 376–377
loss, making spiritual sense of, 377–382
love, trinitarian, 158–161
Luce, Alice, 85
Luce, Ron, 24
Lukan corpus, empowerment in, 27–32
Luther, Martin, 24
Lutheran World Federation, 348
Lynas, Mark, 1–2

M

Ma, Wonsuk, 377
MacNutt, Francis, 275
Makandiwa, Emmanuel, 251, 259–260, 261
Malleret, Thierry, 248
Marcus Aurelius (Emperor of Rome), 51
marginalized communities, COVID-19 pandemic effects on, 192, 210–211, 212. *See also specific communities*
Marshall, Alfred, 178
Martin, Lee Roy, 382–383
martyrs, 53–54
Mary (mother of Jesus), 29, 30, 162–165
Mason, C. H., 85
materialism, 261–262
Maunder, Chris, 162
Mawangdui texts, 70
Maximinus Thrax (Emperor of Rome), 51
Maxwell, David, 302–303
Mayfield, Alex, 378

McCaulley, Esau, 199, 202
McClennan, Sharon, 274
McPherson, Aimee Semple, 90–92
medical pragmatism, 71
medicine
   Chinese, 69–71
   Church of God in Christ (COGIC) viewpoint regarding, 235–240
   disdain for, by Chinese Pentecostals, 75–76
   healing and, 240
   Pentecostal viewpoint regarding, 87–89
   viewpoint of Pentecostals/ Pentecostalism regarding, 87–89, 93–94
Mensah, John, 310
mental health, 140, 144–147, 282, 327–328
Mephibosheth, 125
migrants, in Bosnia and Herzegovina, 196–197
Miller, Donald, 233, 346
Milligan, Mollie, 88
mind, significance of, 49
missionary tongues, 72–73
Mok Lai Chi, 67, 73
Moldova, 196
Moll, Fran, 86
Moltmann, Jürgen, 139, 143–144, 145, 146–147, 155–156, 165, 271
monasteries, plague effects on, 319
Montenegro, 196
Moses, 160, 311
Mukti Mission, 183
Mundis, Greg, 93
Mung San Ling, 75–76
mutual indwelling, 160
mutual relevance, 233, 381–382
mystical relation metaphor of the church, 343
mysticism, 319

N

Ndifon, Charles, 93
Nero (Emperor of Rome), 51
New Apostolic Reformation, 95
new birth, 152n24
New Medicine (Chinese medicine), 70–71
New Testament, justice and plagues in, 14–16, 193
Niebuhr, Richard, 342, 343
Nigeria, 285
Noah, 10
North Macedonia, 196
Norton, Nellie Andrews, 86
Novatian, 54–55
Novation Schism, 54

O

Oath Keepers, 63–64n2
Ofoe, Stephen Ofotsu, 377
Old Testament, justice and plagues in, 10–14, 193
Olivet Discourse, 14–15
Omenyo, Cephas Narh, 301
On Mortality (Cyprian), 58
On the Unity of the Church (Cyprian), 62
Onyinah, Opoku, 310
Oral Roberts University (ORU), mission of, 361–362
Ositelu, Gabriel, 302
Otabil, Mensa, 251, 253, 256–257, 261
Owiredu, Stephen, 311
Oyakhilome, Chris, 251, 252

P

pain, 117–123
pandemics, 1, 9–10. *See also* COVID-19 pandemic
Pannenberg, Wolfhart, 156, 161
Parable of the Weeds, 21

Parsons, W. J., 85, 87
Passover, 22, 256
pastoral task, 146
patience, pain and, 121–122
Paul, the apostle, 35, 36, 46, 309
peace-bearers, Christians as, 145–146
Pentecost, 160, 309
Pentecostal-charismatic Christianity, 214–222, 268, 302. *See also* Pentecostals/Pentecostalism
Pentecostal disrespectability politics, 96
Pentecostal Evangel, 84
Pentecostal Holiness Advocate, 89
Pentecostal Mariology, 157, 161–165
Pentecostal Relief and Development Partners, 338–340
Pentecostals/Pentecostalism
  characteristics of, 252
  compassion of, 92–94
  compliance and cooperation by, 94–97
  contemporary, 248–249, 251, 253–260
  COVID-19 pandemic responses of, 105–106, 251, 252–253, 283–286, 293–294, 350–353
  dispensational eschatology in, 292–293
  diversity of, 301
  grief response of, 293–294
  growth of, 301, 345–346
  healing of, 92–94
  human trafficking response of, 181
  introduction to, 247–248
  leadership characteristics in, 362
  medicine viewpoint of, 87–89, 93–94
  as multi-faced, 343–344
  partnership with, 346–350
  plagues viewpoint of, 78–80
  pneumatology of, 303–304
  prayer and, 285
  Progressive Pentecostalism, 291–292, 338
  prophetic prayer movement in, 261
  relief and development in, 341
  response to suffering by, 291–294
  salvation as mark of, 304
  social action importance in, 293, 346
  as social movement, 337–338
  Spanish Influenza response of, 293–294, 379
  spirituality of, 283, 377
  statistics regarding, 97, 195
  theodicies of, 289–291
  theology of, 253–260
  triumphalism in, 286–291
  voice and advocacy by, 341–342
  worship in, 283–284
  writings regarding, 346
Pentecostal Truths, 73, 78
Pentecostal World Fellowship, 351
persecution, 51–52
personal responsibility, healing and, 70–71, 74–76
personhood, trinitarian communion and, 158–159
Peter, the apostle, 33–34, 104, 309
Petersen, Douglas, 346
Pharaoh, 10, 11–12
phenomenology, 283
Philip, 34
Phule, Jyotiba, 183
Phule, Savitribai, 183
pimps, 178
Pisgah Home Movement, 292
Plague of Cyprian, 55–56, 317–318, 379
plagues
  Antonine Plague, 332n4
  Black Death, 319
  Boubonic Plague, 318–319

in China, 68, 72
Chinese Pentecostals and, 71–78
of Cyprian, 55–56
defined, 9
end-time, 77–78
in Hong Kong, 67–68
in India, 68
in the New Testament, 14–16
in the Old Testament, 10–14
Pentecostal views on, 78–80
Plague of Cyprian, 55–56, 317–318, 379
sanitarian approaches to, 72
smallpox, 319–320
summary of, in the Bible, 16
PMU (Swedish Pentecostal relief and development organization), 340, 347, 352
Pobee, John S., 302
Pontifical Council for Interreligious Dialogue, 330
Pontius of Carthage, 48–49, 55–56, 57
poor/poverty, 22–23, 166, 175–176, 339–340, 348, 350
populism, 215
pragmatic conversion, 72–74
prayer
  in African Pentecostal communities, 284–285
  in the church, 20–21
  Church of God in Christ (COGIC) and, 237–238
  as COVID-19 pandemic response, 251, 255–256, 293–294
  reconsidering methods of, 21–22
  as Spanish influenza response, 261, 293–294
  in tarrying meetings, 305–306
presence of God, 164–165
Procopius, 318–319
procreation, 119

Progressive Pentecostalism, 291–292, 338. *See also* Pentecostals/Pentecostalism
proof texting, 379
prophecy, regarding COVID-19 pandemic, 259–260
Prosperity and the Coming Apocalypse (Bakker), 261–262
prosperity gospel, 249–251, 254, 261–262, 378–379
protesting, 211–212
Proud Boys, 63–64n2
Punj, Shweta, 175
Putnam, Robert, 344

Q

qualitative research, 364

R

racial disparities, 241–243
racialized nationalism, 63–64n2
"Racial Reconciliation Manifesto," 241–242
Rambo, Shelly, 272
Ramirez, Erica, 96
realism, 45
reconciliation, 61–63
Reformed Pastoral Service (Hungary), 327–328
reincarnation, 152n24
relational cosmology, 69–70
religion, in development and relief, 340–341
repentance, 61–63, 218–222, 380
responsibility, assuming, in justice, 202
restoration, healing and, 108
"Resuming Care-Filled Worship and Sacramental Life During a Pandemic," 322
resurrection, promise of, 218–222
Revivalism, 292

Rhone, Terence, 241
Robeck, Cecil, 292
Roberts, Oral, 103, 109–110
Roma communities
   COVID-19 pandemic and, 195–198
   hope to, 198–201
   introduction to, 191–192
   lockdown resistance of, 285
   obstacles to engagement with, 197–198
   statistics regarding, 196
   suffering of, 286
Roman Catholic Church. *See* Catholicism/Roman Catholic Church
Roma networks, 199–201
Romania, 195, 196
Romani Pentecostals, 285
Rowe, Dorothy, 142
Runion, Hannah, 89

S
Sabbath, 18
sacrament metaphor of the church, 343
sacraments, during COVID-19 pandemic, 322
sacrificati, 53
salvation, 60, 126, 304
Samaritans, 33–34
Samples, W. C., 88
Sanneh, Lamin, 261
Sarai, 10
Schoonmaker, C. H., 85–86
Schwab, Klaus, 248
science
   Church of God in Christ (COGIC) engagement and, 235–240
   racial disparities and, 241–243
   role of, 231–232
   Spirit-empowered engagement and, 232–235

second blessing, baptism in the Holy Spirit as, 303–304
Second Temple, 33
self-help groups, 147
Semple McPherson, Aimee, 90–92
Seppälä, Serafim, 164–165
Septimius Severus (Emperor of Rome), 51
Serbia, 195, 196, 200
sermons, reconsidering methods of, 21–22
servant metaphor of the church, 343
"Serving a Wounded World in Interreligious Solidarity," 330
sex trafficking. *See* human trafficking
Shackleford, Mollie, 89
shame, conception of, 50–51
shared story of future hope, 376, 382–383
Sheard, J. Drew, 244
Sheikh, Fatima, 183
sickness, 69–71, 74–75, 76–77
Simon of Taybutha, 164–165
Simpson, A. B., 74
sin, 45–46, 74–75, 146
slavery, 174–175
smallpox, 319–320
social action, 293
social capital, 344
social distancing, 18, 140
social engagement, 182–183
social injustice, 182–183
social justice, 192
society, being the church in, 342–346
sociological imagination, 344
Solomon's Temple, 33
Southeastern Europe, Pentecostal and Evangelical churches in, 194–195
Spanish Influenza
   Aimee Semple McPherson and, 90–92
   compliance and cooperation

regarding, 94–97
COVID-19 pandemic as compared to, 293–294
overview of, 84–86
Pentecostal responses to, 92–97, 379
physical effects of, 85–86
responses to, 320
statistics regarding, 84, 91
theologizing, 86–90
speaking in tongues, 72–73, 216, 303, 305
Spirit-empowered Christianity, 232–233, 250–251
Spirit-empowered communities, 43–44, 111–112
Spirit-empowered Movement, 233–234
Spirit-filled womanhood, 161–165
spirits, relational cosmology and, 69–70
spiritual ecumenism, 329–330
spiritual gifts, 216
spiritual warfare, 76–77
St. Anthony's Fire (ergotism), 148
St. Anthony's Monastery, 147–148
Stephen, 33
Stetzer, Ed, 269
storytelling, for trauma recovery, 274
Stronstad, Roger, 304
Studebaker, Steven, 157
Stylianopoulos, Theodore, 157
suffering. *See also* pain
  baptism of, 52, 59
  communal nature of, 112
  community importance in, 290
  defined, 289–290
  elements of, 123
  experiences of, 282
  God and, 151n22, 290
  healing of, 222
  historical perspective on Pentecostal responses to, 291–294

as part of creation, 123
prosperity *versus*, 250
theologies of healing *versus*, 287–289
trauma *versus*, 273
sustainable development goals (SDGs), 348
Sweden, 345
Swedish Pentecostal Mission, 340–342
Swedish Pentecostal movement, 347–348

T
Tabernacle of David, 283–284
tabernacle tax, 13
Tang Tong Shen, 73
Tao Hongjing, 70, 75
Taskforce for Relief and Development, 351
Taylor, G. F., 87, 88, 89, 293
Taylor, John, 199
teachers, during the COVID-19 pandemic, 359–362
temptation, 123
ten virgins parable, 258–259
Tertullian, 51–52, 54, 311
Thompson, Damian, 268
Three Percenters, 63–64n2
thurificati, 53
Tillich, Paul, 158
Together Toward Life, 107
Tomlinson, A. J., 85, 86, 293
Tomlinson, Mary Jane, 87
traffickers/trafficking agents, 178
trafficking. See human trafficking
Trägårdh, Lars, 344
Trajan (Emperor of Rome), 51
trauma, 271–275
triumphal entry, of Jesus, 141
triumphalism, 216, 281–282, 286–291
Trump, Donald, 96

trust, in society, 344
Tulsa, Oklahoma, Spanish Influenza in, 90–92
Tung Wah Hospital (Hong Kong), 72
Turner, David, 141
Twain, Mark, 174
2030 Agenda (United Nations), 348–349, 350

U

"The UK Blessing," 321
Ukraine, 196
United Nations, 2030 Agenda of, 348–349, 350
United Pentecostal Church, 94
United States, 210–218, 231
universal equality, 201

V

vaccinations, 93–94, 127, 210–211, 215, 239–240, 285, 319–320
Valerian (Emperor of Rome), 61
Vineyard Church movement, 284
virgin birth, 29
Voices of Lament, Hope, and Courage (World Council of Churches), 323
Vondey, Wolfgang, 142
the vulnerable, 22–23, 339–340

W

Wacker, Grant, 304
Ware, Frederick, 234
watchdog, role of, 349
weapons of mass destruction, 17
well-being, 157, 158–165
Werner, George, 267
Wesleyan-Pentecostal Stream, 288
West Africa, Spanish Influenza in, 86. *See also* Africa
White nationalism, 217
Wigglesworth, Smith, 88–89

Williams, Joseph, 87
Willimon, William, 343
Wilson, William J., 242
women, 157, 161–165, 175–177
Woo Kwai Shan, 76–77
Wooley, C. H., 84–85
Word of Faith movement, 284
workplace, COVID-19 pandemic effects on, 2–3, 210, 211
World Communion of Reformed Churches, 322
World Council of Churches (WCC), 322–323, 330
World Evangelical Alliance, 323, 348
World Food Program, 350
World Health Organization (WHO), 1, 2
worship, 111, 283–284
Wright, N. T., 112, 117, 125, 127

Y

Yamamori, Tetsunao, 233, 346
Yoakum, Finis E., 292
Yong, Amos, 155, 158
Youngblood, C., 87
Yugoslavia, 195, 196

Z

Zeng Kam, 77
Zizioulas, John, 155, 158159

www.ingramcontent.com/pod-product-compliance
Lightning Source LLC
Chambersburg PA
CBHW070044080526
44586CB00013B/903